CORPORATE STRATEGIC PLANNING

Columbia Studies in Business, Government, and Society
Eli M. Noam, General Editor

Corporate
Strategic Planning

NOEL CAPON, JOHN U. FARLEY,

and JAMES M. HULBERT

New York . Columbia University Press . 1987

The Ernest A. Barvoets Foundation,
through a special grant, has assisted in the publication
of this work

Library of Congress Cataloging-in-Publication Data

Capon, Noel.
Corporate strategic planning.

(Columbia studies in business, government, and
society)
Bibliography: p.
Includes index.
1. Strategic Planning. 2. Corporate planning.
I. Farley, John U. II. Hulbert, James M. III. Title.
IV. Series.
HD30.28.C375 1987   658.4'012   87-18239
ISBN 0-231-06380-6

Columbia University Press
New York   Guildford, Surrey
Copyright © 1988 Columbia University Press
All rights reserved

Printed in the United States of America

Hardback editions of Columbia
University Press books are Smyth-sewn
and are printed on permanent and durable acid-free paper
Book design by J.S. Roberts

Columbia Studies in Business, Government, and Society

Eli M. Noam, General Editor

Betty Bock, Harvey J. Goldschmid, Ira M. Millstein, and F. M. Scherer, editors. *The Impact of the Modern Corporation.* 1984

Eli M. Noam, editor. *Video Media Competition: Regulation, Economics, and Technology.* 1985

Harold G. Vatter. *The U.S. Economy in World War II.* 1985

Donna A. Demac, editor. *Tracing new Orbits: Competition and Cooperation in Satellite Development.* 1986

Merrit B. Fox. *Finance and Industrial Performance in a Dynamic Economy: Theory, Practice, and Policy.* 1987

Peter S. Rose. *The Changing Structure of American Banking.* 1987

Noel Capon, John U. Farley, and James M. Hulbert. *Corporate Strategic Planning.* 1988

Contents

Foreword xi

Chapter 1: The Study of Corporate Strategic Planning 1

   1.1   *Introduction* 1
   1.2   *Origins of the Study* 2
   1.3   *Scope of the Study* 5
   1.4   *Sample Design* 6
   1.5   *Data Collection* 8
   1.6   *A Profile of The Sample* 9
   1.7   *Hypotheses* 14
   1.8   *Analysis* 15
   1.9   *Organization of the Book* 16
   1.10 *Summary* 18

I CORPORATE AND STRATEGIC PLANNING . . . 23

Chapter 2: The Nature of Strategic Planning 25

   2.1   *Introduction* 25
   2.2   *The Concept of Strategic Planning* 25
   2.3   *Planning as an Organizational Design Variable* 32
   2.4   *Planning as an Economic Variable* 33
   2.5   *Approaches to Modeling Planning* 36
   2.6   *Planning: A Functional Approach* 36
   2.7   *Planning: A Process Approach* 44
   2.8   *Reconciling the Process and Functional Perspectives*
         of Planning 46
   2.9   *Classification of Planning Practice* 47
   2.10 *Strategic Planning by the Five Planning Categories* . . . 52
   2.11 *Summary* 60

Contents

Chapter 3: A Description of Planning Practices 62

3.1 *Introduction* 62
3.2 *Planning Organization and Personnel* 63
3.3 *Adaptive Dimensions of Planning* 64
3.4 *Integrative Dimensions of Planning* 77
3.5 *Summary* 96

Chapter 4: Planning: Two Methods of Overview 102

4.1 *Introduction* 102
4.2 *Planning Process Synthesis* 103
4.3 *Dimensions of Planning: Adaptive and Integrative* . . . 111
4.4 *A Final Synthesis* 121
4.5 *Summary* 124
     Appendices to Chapter 4 127

II PLANNING AND ENVIRONMENT, STRATEGY, AND ORGANIZATION 141

Chapter 5: Planning and the Environment 143

5.1 *Introduction* 143
5.2 *Conceptualizations of Environment* 144
5.3 *Relationship of Planning to Environment* 147
5.4 *Environment and Performance* 151
5.5 *Issues for This Study* 153
5.6 *Results* 155
5.7 *Summary* 159

Chapter 6: Planning and Strategy 161

6.1 *Introduction* 161
6.2 *What Is Strategy?* 161
6.3 *Corporate Strategy* 163
6.4 *Corporate Strategy and Performance* 170
6.5 *Business-Level Strategy* 173
6.6 *Results* 176
6.7 *Summary* 191

Chapter 7: Planning and Organization 194

7.1 *Introduction* 194
7.2 *Formal Organization Structure* 194
7.3 *Organizational Climate* 201
7.4 *Organization and Performance* 203
7.5 *Results: Formal Organization Structure* 205
7.6 *Results: Organizational Climate* 210
7.7 *Summary* 215

Contents

III "INTERMEDIATE" MODELS RELATING
    PLANNING TO ENVIRONMENT, STRATEGY,
    AND ORGANIZATION 219

Chapter 8: Scale Structures: Planning, Environment,
    Strategy, Organization Structure, and
    Organizational Climate 221

  8.1   *Introduction* 221
  8.2   *Procedures for Construction and Analysis of Scales* ... 221
  8.3   *Organizational Climate* 223
  8.4   *Environment* 231
  8.5   *Strategy* 237
  8.6   *Organization Structure* 242
  8.7   *Summary* 247
       Appendices to Chapter 8 250

Chapter 9: A Gestalt Perspective on Planning 257

  9.1   *Introduction* 257
  9.2   *Developing the Groups by Clustering* 258
  9.3   *Relationships Among the Planning, Environment,*
       Strategy, Organization Structure and Organiza-
       tional Climate Groups 266
  9.4   *Summary* 276

IV INTEGRATION 279

Chapter 10: Planning and Performance 281

  10.1   *Introduction* 281
  10.2   *Previous Studies of the Value of Planning* 282
  10.3   *Measures of Performance* 292
  10.4   *Tests of Planning/Performance Relationships* 294
  10.5   *Presence/Absence of Planning: Self-Reports* 296
  10.6   *Deductively Developed Planning Categories* 298
  10.7   *Inductively Developed Planning Groups* 302
  10.8   *Combination Deductive/Inductive Planning Groups* .. 306
  10.9   *Adjusted Return Performance Measure* 307
  10.10 *Planning Process Summary Measures* 308
  10.11 *Planning Function Elements* 311
  10.12 *Planning Practices of Firms Which Perform Well* 314
  10.13 *Planning/Performance Contingency Relationships* ... 323
  10.14 *Summary* 328

Chapter 11: Summary and Synthesis 331

  11.1   *An Overview of the Study* 331

Contents

11.2 *How Do the Firms Plan?* 332
11.3 *The Context of Planning: Relationships Between Planning and Environment, Strategy, Organization Structure, and Organizational Climate* 336
11.4 *Does Long-Term Strategic Planning "Pay"?* 340
11.5 *Synthesis* 341
11.6 *Implications for Future Research* 351
11.7 *Implications for Managerial Practice* 357
11.8 *"The New Breed of Strategic Planner"* 362
11.9 *Conclusion* 363

Appendix I Research Methodology 365
A.1 *Introduction* 365
A.2 *Instrument Design and Testing* 366
A.3 *Data Collection Procedures* 372
A.4 *Data Preparation* 375
A.5 *Summary* 375

Appendix II. The Questionnaires 377

Appendix III. Tables of Standard Deviations 437

References 441

Author Index 467

Subject Index 473

Foreword

The popularity of strategic planning increased rapidly among large U.S. corporations during the 1970s. In embarking upon this research, our original intent was to try to assess the impact of planning on both financial performance and other aspects of management. Our goals were broad and ambitious, and we are more humble now than we were when we initiated this project. However, we believe that we have succeeded in taking a broad view, and in addition have been able to show how results from many researchers in various fields fit together. We also believe that we have developed a set of measurement instruments that can prove useful to others embarking on broad studies of strategic management. Our instruments on planning, environment, strategy, organization structure, and organizational climate have already been useful for cross-cultural replication, and we hope to see further applications in other settings. Nonetheless, the entire process involved in the planning and execution of this study took much more time than we had ever dreamed possible, even though we thought we were being harshly realistic when we set out.

We are indebted to many people and organizations for their help. Generous support for the work was provided by Booz Allen and Hamilton, and by the Center for Strategy Research at Columbia Business School. Author Capon acknowledges support from the Redward Foundation. Interviewees at the 113 firms in our sample were generous with their time. Dean Boris Yavitz of the Graduate School of Business was most helpful and supportive. Peter Sweeny, Polly Judson, and Larry Ward were skillful interviewers, and Don Pardew supervised the field work with professional skill. Greg Carpenter, Thomas Christian, Scott Hoenig, Elizabeth Martin, Kishore Pasumarty, Srinivas Reddy, Raj Sisodia, Claudia Ulbright, and Sara Wright were hard-working and creative assistants. David Lei's contributions were especially important, and his dedicated application and cheerful enthusiasm were an inspiration to us all.

All shortcomings and errors are, of course, our own.

Chapter 1

The Study of Corporate
Strategic Planning

1.1 Introduction

Throughout the last decade, methods and techniques of corporate and strategic planning became the focus of substantial conceptual and empirical development in both the business and academic worlds (e.g., Rothschild 1976, 1979; Hofer and Schendel 1978; Steiner 1979; Hax and Majluf 1984). The newer approaches to planning have not only had dramatic influences on how some firms are managed but have also resulted in wholesale restructurings of the products and services that firms offer and the markets in which they compete *(New York Times* 1980). Furthermore, ideas about corporate and strategic planning have affected many managers through management development courses, as well as through a flood of books aimed at improving managers' practice of their art (Rothschild 1979, Peters and Waterman 1982, Naisbitt 1982). In addition, whole new areas of specialization and, in some companies, career paths, have arisen around areas such as corporate planning, corporate development, business planning, and the like. Quite clearly, something fundamental has influenced not only American management but also management throughout the world (Capon, Farley, and Hulbert 1980).

Yet these changes have been so recent and so rapid – occurring since the mid-1970s for many firms – that it seems we have scarcely had a chance to catch our breath and take stock. (See, however, Steiner 1983.) Corporate strategies, planning systems, organization structures, and even managers have been changed willynilly, with little opportunity to step back and evaluate the status, direction, and magnitude of the changes. In this book we attempt to:

1. Document the planning practices of major United States manufacturing corporations as of 1980
2. Identify problems with those planning systems
3. Investigate the relationships between companies' planning systems and environment, strategy, organization structure, and organizational climate
4. Investigate the relationship between planning and economic performance

These are, we believe, ambitious goals. However, the excellent cooperation given by more than 100 major U.S. manufacturers and the devoted and conscientious efforts of a team of researchers have combined to give us an opportunity to deal with these issues.

1.2 Origins of the Study

1.2.1 EVOLUTION OF PLANNING CONCEPTS

Formal business planning is largely a post-World War II phenomenon and was adopted by many United States corporations in the 1960s (Steiner 1963; Warren 1966; Vancil, Aguilar, and Howell 1968; Ringbakk 1969, 1971, 1972). (See Hofer 1976 for an early review of the extant research on planning.) Beginning in the mid 1960s however, there was a flowering of interest in the strategic content of companies' planning; the work of Ansoff was an important stimulus to the development of corporate strategy as an area of concern to practitioners, consultants, and academics (Ansoff 1965).

The changing environments of the 1970s stimulated great corporate interest in planning of all kinds as means to deal with environmental uncertainty. A variety of conceptual developments and technological advances gave further impetus to the awakened concern, and many companies began to place high priority on improving the planning of strategy, often reorganizing as part of the process.

The concept of the experience curve was widely popularized early in this period; it suggests that total unit costs may continue to decline with greater experience in making and selling a product, rather than follow the economists' assumed U-shape long-run average cost curve (Boston Consulting Group 1972). Its implications with respect to business strategy and financial planning were further developed in the form of the product portfolio (Day 1977, Hedley 1977, Kiechel 1979, Hax and Majluf 1983a). Some research has suggested that the portfolio approach to strategic planning has become widely accepted and extended (Haspeslagh 1982), though others are critical of its usefulness (Kiechel 1982). In its most basic form the portfolio approach classifies products, services, or businesses into one of four quadrants based on measures of market growth and market share. Different kinds of objectives and strategies are then developed, depending upon the classification. More recently, these ideas have been further developed in the area of competitive strategy (Henderson 1979).

Many experts felt that market growth and market share, while useful measures, were insufficient by themselves to portray satisfactorily the differing strategic circumstances of widely varying products and services. General Electric, for example, in conjunction with McKinsey & Company, developed a richer scheme involving a nine-way rather than a four-way classification of each business (*Business Week* 1975, Hax and Majluf 1983b). A similar system, named the Directional Policy Matrix, was developed by Shell Chemical U.K. (Hussey 1978), and others have subsequently developed or employed similar schemes (Patel and Younger 1978). We have dubbed all such extended portfolio schemes "policy matrices," and they figure significantly in our study of planning.

The policy matrix, with its broader scope, was used by General Electric (GE) at a fairly high level within the company. Instead of being applied to individual products, it was used at the level of the SBU (Strategic Business Unit), an aggregation of products and markets that could, in many ways, be viewed as a stand-alone business within the complex, decentralized GE structure. This example of the interrelationship between planning systems and the partitioning of the company for strategic planning purposes raises the issue of organization structure (Wright 1974). The strategy-structure relationship had already been the subject of much work (e.g., Chandler 1962), and these relationships were advanced both prescriptively and descriptively during the 1970s.

The work of Rumelt (1974), which was descriptive although certainly not without prescriptive implications, focused on relationships among strategy, structure, and performance in major U.S. manufacturing firms. His findings are important to any student of strategy, a key contribution being the way in which this work drew attention to the possibility of developing empirical generalizations at the corporate level. His results, which build upon Wrigley's (1970) earlier study, also suggest a fresh view of diversification strategy. Prescriptively, consultants have pursued the close alignment of strategy and organization structure, the best known exposition being the Strategy Center concept (Wright 1974), which suggests that market maturity should be reflected not only in structure but also in systems, procedures, and even management style.

Empirical analysis of relationships between strategic variables and performance also advanced during the 1970s. The Profit Impact of Market Strategy (PIMS) project, originally established at at General Electric and now lodged at the Strategic Planning Institute, became the home of a growing data bank on business strategy and performance (Schoeffler, Buzzell, and Heany 1974; Buzzell, Gale, and Sultan 1975). The PIMS project focuses on the individual business unit level rather than the corporation as a whole. Its strategic generalizations have been widely disseminated, and hundreds of corporations have contributed information on their strategies, organization processes, and performance to the data base. There have been other studies that focused on strategy-performance relationships (e.g., Schendel and Patton 1978) and several that have attempted to relate planning practice to performance. (See Armstrong 1982 for a review.)

1.2.2 THE PLANNING LITERATURE

By the mid to late 1970s a number of authors were reporting widespread adoption of formal planning by large corporations: United States (Kudla 1976, Ang and Chua 1979), United Kingdom (Higgins and Finn 1977), and Holland (Eppink, Keuning, and De Jong 1976). Further, the breadth of interest in planning is evident from a review of the post-1980 literature in the field. (In this section we do not attempt a comprehensive review, but rather we highlight the major foci of interest.)

There is rather extensive industry-specific literature on strategic planning, though it tends to take the form of challenges posed to, rather than applications in, particular industries. Industries addressed include advertising (Kover 1982), aquaculture (Chaston 1982), airlines (Bouamreme and Flavell 1980), banking (Wood and La Forge 1979, Holmberg and Baker 1982, Kudla 1982, McRorie 1982, Austin and Scampini 1984, Hart 1984), chemicals (Unger 1983), insurance companies (Malecki 1983, Hampton 1984) and agents (Jones 1981), municipal governments (So 1984), retailing (Mulligan 1981, Russell 1983), savings and loan associations (Metzger 1981), shale oil (Engi 1984), telecommunications (Probert 1981), utilities (Jaedicke 1981, Sekiguchi and Storey 1984), and even nonprofit and community organizations (Barber and Kelly 1981).

A number of functional specialties have shown an interest in planning. Not surprisingly, management information system experts seem to have shown the most interest (Shuman 1982, Mills 1984, Wallace 1984), but others include accountants (Parker 1980, Holland

1983, Raimond 1983), consultants (Henry 1982), controllers (Weele 1980), human resource experts (Devanna et al. 1982, Ward 1982), market researchers (Halpern 1984), purchasers (Adamson 1980) and R&D specialists (Kimmerly 1983).

Finally, though the vast majority of the literature focuses on U.S. corporate and strategic planning, we have pointed out elsewhere (Capon, Farley, and Hulbert 1980) that international diffusion of basic notions of corporate and strategic planning has been rapid, especially in Canada (Rose 1982, Von Lanzenaur and Sprung 1982, Frederick 1983) and the United Kingdom (Al-Bazzaz and Grinyer 1980, Bhatty 1981, Dyson and Foster 1983). A wide variety of other countries is also represented in the literature including Australia (Galer and Kasper 1982), France (Schollhammer 1970, Montebello and Bulgues 1982), Hungary (Csath 1983), India (Das and Mohanty 1981), Japan (Kono 1984), New Zealand (Wright 1982), Singapore (Ghosh and Nee 1983a, b), South Africa (Woodburn 1984), Sweden (Jonsson and Petzaell 1982), and West Germany (Strigel 1970; Keppler, Bamberger, and Gabele 1979; Kriekebaum and Grimm 1982; Scholz 1984).

In all this work, however, there has been no comprehensive attempt to assess overall relationships among planning activity, strategy, and performance while controlling for such obvious potential sources of variance as environment and organization. (The studies of Grinyer and his co-workers, in the United Kingdom [Grinyer and Norburn 1974, 1975; Grinyer, Yasai-Ardekani, and Al-Bazzaz 1980; Grinyer and Yasai-Ardekani 1981; Al-Bazzaz and Grinyer 1980; Grinyer, Al-Bazzaz, and Yasai-Ardekani 1986] come closest to achieving this goal.) This work approaches the study of planning more nearly comprehensively than most of its precursors.

1.3 Scope of the Study

The central focus of this study is on the planning practices of major manufacturing corporations. Whereas many studies have investigated individual elements of firms' planning systems, our aim in this study was to be comprehensive; indeed more than 500 different measures on planning systems, practices, and processes are used. We sought to identify what were likely to be the "best" planning practices and therefore used as our sample frame major U.S. manufacturing corporations drawn from the *Fortune* 500 at a particular point in time. We found that some companies engage in very limited planning or none at all, others do little corporate planning but plan extensively at lower levels, while others have planning systems that are fully integrated from lower levels to corporate.

While these data are valuable in their own right, they also serve as benchmarks for future studies. Our study is essentially cross-sectional and, though some longitudinal measures are incorporated in the data base, it is difficult to draw many conclusions about the dynamics of systems. However, the comprehensiveness of this study should make it possible to extend the work longitudinally in the future.

Although the planning system is an important organizational design variable and the focus of this study, it must be seen in context. The firm, viewed as an organism interacting with an environment, can use a planning system to aid in negotiating its environment by developing strategy. Furthermore, the planning system should be linked to other organization design variables, both structural characteristics and organizational climate or culture. A comprehensive study of planning should not, therefore, just investigate planning practice but should also attempt to identify the interrelationships among the firm's planning system and its environment, strategy, organization structure, and organizational climate. We collected more than 300 additional measurements in these areas.

As noted earlier, the aims of the study are ambitious. To achieve them demands both novel measures and analyses. We believe that through our careful choice of sample, the extensiveness of the data collected, and our multipronged analytic attack we would have a reasonable chance of accomplishing our aims. The reader must judge to what extent we have succeeded.

1.4 Sample Design

Since a major goal of strategic planning is reconfiguration of the firm's assets into more productive use, a natural population for such study was the *Fortune* 500 list of leading U.S. manufacturers. This group consists largely of multiproduct, multimarket firms that constantly face the resource reallocation problems for which planning should be helpful. Whereas many of the studies noted in section 1.2.2 used a mail questionnaire methodology, and other students of planning and strategy have employed scenarios (Fredrickson 1984,

Fredrickson and Mitchell 1984), and data coded from published case studies (Paine and Anderson 1977, Miller and Friesen 1977), for a comprehensive study of the type we contemplated, it was clear that personal interviews were required. Financial and time budgets limited our sampling frame to the 258 *Fortune* 500 manufacturing companies headquartered East of the Mississippi River (in 1979). This half of the *Fortune* 500 was fairly representative of the total, though weighted somewhat toward larger companies. From these firms, 155 companies were randomly selected. This was a deliberate over-sampling for our minimum acceptable sample size of 100 companies, for we expected both rejections and untoward delays in scheduling interviews. One hundred and thirteen companies were eventually included in the sample. Of the remaining 42, only 9 refused to be interviewed, while the remaining 33, whose responses ranged from very enthusiastic to lukewarm, could not be scheduled during the interviewing period. The list of participating companies follows.

American Chain & Cable Company
  Incorporated
Aluminum Company of America
American Can Company
American Home Products
  Corporation
American Motors Corporation
American Standard Incorporated
Amstar Corporation
Armstrong Cork Company
Avon Products Incorporated
Bangor Punta Corporation
Bausch & Lomb Incorporated
Becton, Dickinson & Company
Belco Petroleum Corporation
Bethlehem Steel Corporation
Black & Decker Manufacturing
  Company
Bristol Myers Company
Brockway Glass Company
Celanese Corporation
Cincinnati Milacron Incorporated
Cluett, Peabody & Company
  Incorporated
Colgate-Palmolive Company
Continental Corporation
Continental Oil Company

Corning Glass Works
CPC International
Crown Central Petroleum
  Corporation
Dana Corporation
Diamond International Corporation
Digital Equipment Corporation
E.I. Du Pont de Nemours
  & Company
Eastman Kodak Company
Eaton Corporation
Exxon Corporation
Fairchild Industries Incorporated
Firestone Tire & Rubber Company
Ford Motor Company
Foxboro Company
Fruehauf Corporation
GAF Corporation
General Electric Company
General Foods Corporation
General Host Corporation
General Tire & Rubber Company
The Gillette Company
GK Technologies Incorporated
B.F. Goodrich Company
Goodyear Tire & Rubber Company
W.R. Grace & Company

Great Northern-Nekoosa
  Corporation
Gulf Oil Corporation
Hammermill Paper Company
Harsco Corporation
Hershey Foods Corporation
Hobart Corporation
Ingersoll-Rand Company
International Business Machines
International Paper Company
Johnson & Johnson
Kennecott Copper Corporation
Koppers Company Incorporated
Libbey-Owens-Ford Company
Lone Star Industries Incorporated
M. Lowenstein & Sons Incorporated
Martin Marietta Corporation
McGraw-Hill Incorporated
McLouth Steel Corporation
Mead Corporation
Merck & Company Incorporated
Mobil Corporation
Nashua Corporation
NCR Corporation
New York Times Company
NL Industries Incorporated
Ogden Corporation
Olin Corporation
Owens-Illinois Incorporated
Pennwalt Corporation
Pfizer Incorporated
Philip Morris Incorporated
PPG Industries Incorporated
Questor Corporation
Republic Steel Corporation

Revere Copper & Brass
  Incorporated
Revlon Incorporated
Rohm & Haas Company
Saxon Industries Incorporated
Schering-Plough Corporation
SCM Corporation
Scott Paper Company
Joseph E. Seagram
  & Sons Incorporated
The Sperry & Hutchinson Company
Sperry Rand Corporation
Squibb Corporation
Standard Brands Incorporated
Standard Oil Company of Ohio
Stanley Works
Stauffer Chemical Company
Sterling Drug Incorporated
J.P. Stevens & Company
  Incorporated
St. Joe Minerals Corporation
St. Regis Paper Company
Sun Chemical Corporation
Sybron Corporation
Texaco Incorporated
TRW Incorporated
Uniroyal Incorporated
U.S. Steel Corporation
Warner Communications
  Incorporated
Warner Lambert Company
Washington Post Company
Westinghouse Electric Corporation
Wheelabrator-Frye Incorporated
Xerox Corporation

SOURCE: Standard & Poors Corporation Records 1980

1.5 Data Collection

Data were collected by full-time interviewers in the respondents' offices during early 1980. Two questionnaires were used; each required from one to two hours for completion. The process of questionnaire development is described in appendix I. Interviews were conducted in two parts, one with the chief planning officer or, in absence of such a position, with the executive whose responsibilities were judged closest to that role. All firms in our sample engaged in some form of planning or budgeting at several levels, so such a person was always identifiable. The questionnaire (questionnaire I in appendix II) used in this part of the interview included sections on company goals, corporate strategy, the planning system, making resource allocation decisions, organization structure, and organizational climate. Many items were sensitive and required insight into the realities of corporate management that could be provided only by such a senior person.

Respondents for the other questionnaire (questionnaire II in appendix II) were knowledgeable assistants designated by the executive who responded to questionnaire I. Items in questionnaire II were mainly descriptive, involving operating structures, organization of the planning effort, the corporate environment, and corporate operations and strategy. Interviews with the assistant were typically held first to familiarize the interviewers with the company.

All items on both questionnaires were metric when at all feasible, and open-ended items were avoided whenever possible. All scaled items were five-point semantic differential or Likert scales. In addition, five years of financial performance data were gathered from *Value Line* (1977-1981) (Bernhard 1959).

Some researchers have argued against the use of single informants in studies such as this (Phillips 1981), though others have argued the opposite position with considerable vigor (Brown et al. 1985). Our position is that the informants we chose were the most appropriate, with the possible exception of the CEO, for the domains that our questionnaires were designed to investigate. Furthermore, given limited resources in a tradeoff between more observations per firm and more firms, more firms seemed the expeditious course to follow.

1.6 A Profile of The Sample

1.6.1 FINANCIAL

Of the 113 firms in the sample, 30 percent fell into the top *Fortune* 100 and 58 percent in the top *Fortune* 200. While the upward skew in company size made our sample less representative of the *For-*

tune 500 than we had aimed for, it was more likely that we would identify state-of-the-art planning practices since large companies are more likely to have sophisticated planning systems.

Our companies are large (table 1.1), averaging $4.9 billion in sales revenues and slightly more than $2.0 billion in total capital in 1979.[1]

Table 1.1
Key Financial Characteristics of the 113 Sampled Companies

	Mean			Standard Deviation		
	1977	1979	1981	1977	1979	1981
Sales ($B)	3.8	4.9	6.6	7.6	9.9	13.8
Profits[1] ($M)	186.0	266.6	337.4	408.0	523.1	723.2
Total Capital ($B)	2.0	2.2	3.0	3.3	3.7	4.7
Return-on-Capital (%)	10.4	12.3	10.7	2.3	4.4	2.5
Return-on-Equity (%)	12.4	14.9	12.4	2.5	4.9	2.9
Return-on-Sales (%)	5.0	5.6	5.2	1.8	3.0	2.1

[1]All profit related characteristics are after-tax.

Revenues and capital increased significantly between 1977 and 1981. Generally, the sample was achieving respectable levels of profitability, though there was considerable variability. The firms are generally manufacturers, but they are diverse in terms of businesses, product life cycle profiles, extent of international operations, and interrelationships among businesses.

1.6.2 TYPE OF BUSINESS

Multiproduct businesses are most likely to be able to make effective use of strategic planning, and such diversity characterizes our sample.

Using PIMS business classifications (table 1.2), products manufactured for industrial markets accounted for 56.6 percent of sales, divided about evenly among capital goods, raw or semifinished materials, components and supplies. Service revenues accounted for 8 percent of the total, indicating the extent to which these manufacturers had thus far succeeded in an economy-wide tendency to diversify into services. The remaining 35.4 percent of revenues was accounted for by consumer products, chiefly nondurables.

In total, the 113 companies operated in 387 two-digit Standard Industrial Classification (SIC) manufacturing codes and in 181 single-digit nonmanufacturing categories, again reflecting con-

Table 1.2

Sample Company Revenues by Type of Business

Type of Business	Percent of Revenues	
	Mean	Standard Deviation
Industrial/Commercial/Governmental Products Manufacturing		
Capital Goods	13.0	(25.8)
Raw or Semi-finished Materials	14.5	(27.5)
Components for Incorporation into Finished Products	18.4	(27.4)
Supplies or Other Consumable Products	10.7	(19.3)
	56.6	(38.5)
Consumer Products Manufacturing		
Durable Products	8.6	(21.0)
Non-durable Products	26.7	(37.2)
	35.4	(38.2)
Services		
Retail and Wholesale Distribution	4.2	(11.5)
Other Services	3.8	(10.4)
	8.0	(14.7)

siderable diversity in revenue sources. The most frequently cited manufacturing categories were chemicals and allied products (43%), fabricated metal products (34%), and nonelectrical machinery (26%). The most popular nonmanufacturing codes were mining (29%), transportation and public utilities (23%), wholesale trade (21%), retail trade (19%), and services (19%). The 113 firms on average competed in 5.9 two-digit manufacturing and nonmanufacturing businesses, a remarkably large number given the breadth of SIC definitions at the two-digit level.

1.6.3 PRODUCT LIFE CYCLE

A key tenet of strategic planning involves careful management of businesses at various points in their life cycles, and attention to developing new products and identifying new market segments is central. Various definitions of life cycle stages exist; we selected a fourfold classification, for it provides sufficient richness while permitting respondents to answer without undue difficulty.

The stages of the cycle are defined as:

Introductory Stage: Primary demand for product class just beginning to grow; products or services still unfamiliar to many potential users.

Growth Stage: Demand growing at 10 percent or more annually in real terms; technology and/or competitive structure still changing.

Maturity Stage: Product or services familiar to vast majority of prospective users; technology and competitive structure reasonably stable.

Decline Stage: Weaker competition exiting; real sales volume declining.

Table 1.3 shows that by far the largest percentage of revenues (65%)

Table 1.3
Sample Company Revenues by Product Life Cycle Stage

Stage of Product Life Cycle	Percent of Revenues
Introductory	4.7
Growth	21.2
Maturity	65.0
Decline	8.9

is generated by mature products, reflecting the large percentage of American industry that operates in mature markets. Nevertheless, a healthy 21.2 percent of revenues came from products in the growth stage. While only 4.7 percent of sales represented products in the introductory stage, this low percentage no doubt understates their anticipated importance in the relatively near run. As a comparison, data from Australian companies suggest that United States manufacturers have a vigorous bias toward new products, reflected in the relatively large fraction of sales in introductory and growth stages of their revenue mixes (Capon, Christodolou et al. 1987).

1.6.4 INTERNATIONAL OPERATIONS

International operations add considerable complexity to the planning task, with many large organizations operating in upward of 100 countries. Reflecting the increasingly global economy in which U.S. firms participate, our sample averaged 25.4 percent of revenues from sources outside the United States, with an average of 20 owned overseas manufacturing subsidiaries. In fact, 69 percent of our firms earned more than 15 percent of their revenues from overseas, and just 16 percent earned less than 5 percent.

Table 1.4 shows how sales and production are distributed

Table 1.4
Sample Company Distribution of International Operations:
Sales and Production

Geographic Area	Percent of Sample in Each Area with More than One Percent of:	
	Sales	Production
North America	100	100
Western Europe	85	72
Central and South America	68	56
Far East	60	41
Africa	27	12
Australasia	53	35
Middle and Near East	27	6
Eastern Europe	16	2
Indian Subcontinent	11	9

globally. In addition, for the average firm, 4.5 regions account for more than 1 percent of sales, while 3.3 regions account for at least 1 percent of production. As might be expected, owing to scale economies, investment risk, and other factors, companies tended to be less diverse in manufacturing than in sales. Also, there is a generally low involvement in Africa, the Middle and Near East, Eastern Europe, and the Indian Subcontinent.

1.6.5 INTERBUSINESS RELATIONSHIPS

Analysis of SIC code structure sheds some light upon diversity; however, it by no means tells the whole story since strategic planning is also concerned with how businesses fit together. A useful scheme for this purpose was developed by Rumelt in his study of diversification strategy (1974). The major breaks in his scheme are: Single Business (more than 95% of revenues from one business), Dominant Business (more than 70% of revenues from one business), Related Business (more than 70% of revenues from a group of businesses related in technology, marketing, or manufacturing), and Unrelated Business (less than 70% of revenues from either one or a set of related businesses).

Rumelt's system applied to our sample (table 1.5) shows

Table 1.5
Sample Company Inter-Business Relationships

Rumelt Classification	Percent of Sample Companies	Percent of Rumelt Sample
Single Business	12	15
Dominant Business	27	25
Related Business	44	41
Unrelated Business	17	19
	100	100

that, like his sample, the greatest percentage of companies fall into the related category. Although the overall distribution for our sample closely resembles Rumelt's 1969 sample, the "extremes" of Single Business and Unrelated Business appear to be slightly less popular.

1.7 Hypotheses

Our approach to this study was not exploratory. The items on the questionnaires were painstakingly assembled from existing literature, both empirical and theoretical, and from a wide variety of fields discussed in literature reviews on planning (chapter 2), environment (chapter 5), strategy (chapter 6), organization (chapter 7), and planning and performance (chapter 10).

On the other hand, there are many areas where explicit, detailed theory and constructs are loosely or even poorly defined, or where prior research simply does not exist—particularly with regard to strategic planning. In fact, the further we delved into the substantive knowledge base in the many areas involved in this study, the more we realized that a significant amount of received wisdom—often presented as apparently tested hypotheses—is based on hunches or on value judgments. Examples include what "good" environments in which to do business are, what "good" strategies are, how firms "should" organize, what a "productive" organizational culture is, which strategies should be matched with which organization structures, and so forth.

A little reflection should lead to the conclusion that it is unlikely that there is a single "best" answer to these questions, for too many workable solutions exist in parallel. While the literature contains a variety of specific results and even more propositions and conjecture about what should be the case, nowhere are all of these pulled together into a coherent theory. Furthermore, there are important gaps in knowledge and theory. Nonetheless, as we point out in most chapters, the majority of our tests involve explicit hypotheses concerning the directions of effects for firms with sophisticated planning systems.

Most of our hypotheses depend in one way or another upon some classification system for planning. We expect that firms with "good" planning systems will be different from those with "poor" planning systems or with no planning at all. However, well-tested, comprehensive category systems for planning just do not exist in the literature, and an initial task in this research was to develop such a system as a key analytic tool. Much of our analysis is based on the resulting deductively developed category scheme (see chapter 2), and the hypotheses, discussed in the relevant chapters, flow from the scheme in a straightforward manner.

1.8 Analysis

Analysis is dominated by the fact that the number of raw variables measured far exceeds the number of observations (companies). In all, there were more than 500 different items describing planning and an additional 350 plus items measuring environment, strategy, organization structure, and organizational climate. Each of these sets of measurements, not surprisingly, was shown to be highly multidimensional in factor analyses.

With such a volume of data, the analytic problems are formidable – in part because the options are many. We have chosen to operate at two extremes, as well as in the middle. At one pole we provide a series of detailed item-by-item descriptions; at the other we build "informationally efficient" models and seek interrelationships through multivariate techniques. In the middle range, the data are reduced to scales developed from subsets of individual items on the basis of theory, earlier literature, and data structure.

Besides these various interrelationships involving planning, the question remains whether planning – either alone or in particular combinations with environment, strategy, and organization – affects financial performance. This is a complex problem, for there are so many ways of looking at planning and its interrelationships with environment, strategy, and organization. We attack this issue from various directions.

As noted, for the majority of the measurements, there are anticipated (hypothesized) patterns, based on either specific literature or on general precepts governing accepted wisdom about managing large multimarket, multiproduct firms. Generally, we contrast a group of 24 companies with the best developed planning systems (identified in chapter 2 as Corporate Strategic Planners) with the other firms in the sample.

While the basic building blocks of our analyses are standard statistical tests (chi-squares, correlations, analyses of variance, t-tests, etc.), the analytical approach stresses general patterns rather than focusing on specific significant results.[2] Order statistics are used frequently, particularly to position the most sophisticated planners (Corporate Strategic Planners) relative to other firms in the sample. Besides the standard caveats about various types of measurement and statistical error, caution must be exercised in interpreting some specific results because ordinal measurements (chiefly scales) are treated as metric, although effort is made to limit across-item comparisons to items measured similarly.

In addition to the univariate analyses, various multivariate procedures are used to attempt intermediate and overall summaries of results, since the individual measurements are correlated with one another to a greater or lesser extent. Included are the development of scales to summarize information in substantively related areas: planning, environment, strategy, organization structure, and organizational climate. In some instances, factor analysis is used to help with scale construction. In addition, firms with similar characteristics in terms of these areas are identified with cluster analysis.

1.9 Organization of the Book

The book is organized into four parts. Part I consists of three chapters that focus on the nature of planning. Chapter 2 develops two approaches for examining planning systems – a process framework and a functional framework; a set of criteria for classifying planning practice and for identifying the 24 firms we name Corporate Strategic Planners is also developed here. Chapter 3 presents a detailed, item-by-item description of planning using the functional framework developed in chapter 2 as an organizing principle. Chapter 4 takes a more holistic perspective of analysis in two ways: by testing a model of planning based on the process framework and by examining a series of planning scales developed using the functional framework summarizing the content of chapter 3.

The three chapters in part II present a detailed item-by-item view of planning as it relates to environment, strategy, organization structure, and organizational climate. Chapter 5 deals with the relationships between planning and the firm's environment, and in chapter 6, we turn to the content of strategy. Despite our focus on planning in this study, it is clear that the selection of an effective strategy should be one of planning's primary goals. At the same time, we recognize that strategy may in fact emerge by routes other than planning. The chapter focuses on major dimensions of corporate strategy, such as goals and mission, market and entry strategy, international posture, acquisition and divestiture, and company size. Chapter 7 deals with planning and two aspects of organization, specifically organization structure and organizational climate.

In part III, two chapters attempt to develop more aggregate linkages of planning with environment, strategy, organization structure, and organizational climate. Chapter 8 develops sets of scales on environment, strategy, organization structure, and organizational climate; these are then related to planning. Chapter 9 groups the firms into clusters (gestalts) on the basis of similarities in the environments they face, their strategies, their organization structures and their organizational climates. Relationships are then explored between similarly developed planning groupings and these various gestalts.

Part IV attempts integration in two ways. Chapter 10 will be for many readers one of the most crucial and interesting. It attempts to link planning to performance in terms of direct planning-performance relationships measured in several different ways, in terms of planning profiles of particularly successful firms and in terms of possible contingent relationships. Chapter 11 attempts to integrate the results and concludes with conventional admonitions to subsequent researchers. While our results excite and intrigue us, we feel they are no more than prologue, and this chapter is largely addressed to those researchers who will follow.

Two appendices describe the processes of questionnaire design and data collection and present the questionnaires in full. We recognize that these materials will be of more interest to some of our readers than to others. However, we believe it important to pass along the experiences we gained as a way of facilitating future research on a subject we believe merits further exploration. In addition, an appreciation of the methodology employed gives readers a firmer foundation with which to assess our findings.

We have attempted to develop a parallel suborganization in the book that allows readers to follow an analytical stream consistent with their preferences; this is summarized in table 1.6. The sections indicated in column A of the table provide a complete sequence of univariate analyses. The sections in column B provide a coherent multivariate analytical treatment of the results. Of course, we hope that many readers will choose a menu from both column A and column B. Major literature reviews are indicated by (*) in table 1.6.

1.10 Summary

Despite the burgeoning interest in planning, both as an element of business practice and a subject for academic study, a comprehensive investigation of planning practice that captures the vast changes of the 1970s is needed. This study attempts to fill what we perceive to be a gap in knowledge, not only as regards planning practice but also as regards the interrelationships among planning and environment, strategy, and organization. We also contribute to the literature that relates planning and financial performance.

Our study is based on extensive data collected in personal interviews with corporate planning personnel from more than 100 major U.S. manufacturing organizations; our analysis plan was multifacted, involving a variety of approaches from simple univariate to complex multivariate analyses. In part II, we develop an overview of planning.

NOTES

    1. Means were used throughout for companies in the sample that were lost due to merger or acquisition during the period under study.

    2. In general we display p-levels associated with rejection of the null hypothesis. On occasion, we use formal hypothesis testing using strict significance levels as indicated in the text or table.

Table 1.6
Analysis Plan

	Analytic Focus	Analytic Procedures	
		A Univariate analysis	B Multivariate analysis
I CORPORATE AND STRATEGIC PLANNING			
Chapter 2. The Nature of Strategic Planning*	Identification of five Planning Categories	Five Classifications based on 3 sets of criteria	None
	"Strategicness" of planning analyzed across firms in the five Planning Categories	Planning Categories compared on 53 "Strategicness" items	Six statistical scales produced by factor analysis of 98 items. Discriminant functions used as reliability checks. Planning Categories compared on factor scores.
Chapter 3. A Description of Planning Practices	Planning description	Corporate Strategic Planners contrasted on 501 items describing planning	None
Chapter 4. Planning: Two Methods of Overview	Data reduction of detailed planning items	None	Principal components used to build a "soft model" of the planning process. Planning Categories are compared.
			Ten adaptive scales and 33 integrative scales developed from individual planning items. Each scale compared among Planning Categories.

Table 1.6 (Continued)

II PLANNING, AND ENVIRONMENT, STRATEGY, AND ORGANIZATION

| | Analytic Focus | Analytic Procedures | |
		A Univariate analysis	B Multivariate analysis
Chapter 5. Planning and the Environment*	Relationships of Planning to environment	Corporate Strategic Planners contrasted on items involving historic and anticipated-future environment	None
Chapter 6. Planning and Strategy*	Relationships of planning to strategy	Corporate Strategic Planners contrasted on items involving strategy	None
Chapter 7. Planning and Organization*	Relationships of planning to organization	Corporate Strategic Planners contrasted on items involving organization structure and organizational climate	None

III "INTERMEDIATE" MODELS RELATING PLANNING TO ENVIRONMENT, STRATEGY, AND ORGANIZATION

	Analytic Focus	A Univariate analysis	B Multivariate analysis
Chapter 8. Scale Structures: Planning, Environment, Strategy, Organization Structure, and Organizational Climate	Data reduction of detailed environment, strategy, organization structure and organizational climate items related to planning scales and Planning Categories	None	Scales developed to summarize environment, strategy, organization structure and organizational climate; scales correlated with 43 planning scales developed in Ch. 4. Factor analytic procedures used as illustration of scale development.

| | Analytic Focus | Analytic Procedures | |
		A Univariate analysis	B Multivariate analysis
Chapter 9. A Gestalt Perspective on Planning	Firms grouped on bases of similarities in planning, environment, strategy, organization structure, and organizational climate	None	Sets of groups of similar firms formed by cluster analyses; mean scale values compared; planning groups related to other groups; all sets of groups compared to Planning Category membership.
IV INTEGRATION			
Chapter 10. Planning and Performance*	Impact of Planning on Performance	Performance by self-reported planners and the five Planning Categories compared	Performance related to planning scales (Ch. 4), "soft model" summary measures (Ch. 4), planning groups (Ch. 9).
		Planning practices of "good performing" firms highlighted	Performance contingency relationships of planning with environment, strategy, organization structure and organizational climate.
Chapter 11. Summary and Synthesis	Results pulled together and interpreted. Directions for Future Research	Summary of univariate results	Summary of multivariate results.

*Contains major literature review

PART I
CORPORATE AND STRATEGIC PLANNING

The focus of the three chapters in this section is on corporate planning systems. Frameworks are developed for viewing planning, the planning practice of our sample firms is analyzed in detail, and planning is also examined holistically.

Chapter 2 is the major conceptual chapter of the book. The nature of planning in general and strategic planning in particular is discussed, and two alternative perspectives with which to view planning are developed – a process perspective and a functional perspective. The functional perspective, which comprises two key dimensions – adaptive and integrative – is used to develop a category system of planning sophistication which is then validated.

Chapter 3 presents a detailed description of planning practice and describes how the 24 firms which have the most sophisticated planning systems (the Corporate Strategic Planners) differ from the other firms in the sample.

Chapter 4 is the first of a series of steps aimed at treating planning in a more holistic fashion by developing integrative models. First, a comprehensive planning process model is tested. Second, a series of planning scales is developed and tested against the Planning Category system.

Chapter 2

The Nature
of Strategic Planning

2.1 Introduction

Planning in general and formal planning in particular have
been an important part of the culture in many business organizations
for some time. Sometimes at the corporate level, and often at other
levels, companies require the development of formal written plans in
accordance with prescribed methods and formats. These may be
business plans but more often are operating plans for manufacturing,
marketing, or cash management. Many firms have decades of experience with such operational plans.

In this chapter, however, we focus on strategic planning.
We review various attempts to characterize it and present our own
definition. We discuss planning in terms of both organizational design
and economic contribution and then introduce two perspectives from
which planning may be viewed. This discussion is a prelude to the
development of a category scheme with which to view planning practice in general. This scheme, the major analytic device employed in
the study, is then validated.

2.2 The Concept of Strategic Planning

2.2.1 REVIEW

Compared with various types of operational planning,
whose purpose is to specify short-term objectives and actions for
marketing, production, finance, etc., the concept of strategic planning is less clearly defined. For some students of the subject, the

terms *corporate planning, long-range planning, strategic planning, formal planning,* and just plain *planning* seem interchangeable, while for others, distinctions and definitions differ. Lorange and Vancil (1976), for example, suggest that:

> conceptually the (strategic planning) process is simple: managers at every level of a hierarchy must ultimately agree on a detailed, integrated plan of action for the coming year...starting with the delineation of corporate objectives and concluding with the preparation of a one- or two-year profit plan.

Naylor (1979) defines strategic planning as "long range planning with a time horizon of three to five years," whereas Saunders and Tuggle (1977) use "long-term" and "strategic" synonymously with corporate planning to describe:

> organization-wide planning which covers all major functions, which is inclusive of goals as well as means, and which is long range in nature, but effectively integrated into the management system utilized by senior management.

Note that each of these authors presents a different viewpoint of strategic planning; here Lorange and Vancil take a fairly short-term perspective, whereas Naylor sees a three to five year period as a necessary condition. The Saunders and Tuggle definition is typical of a broad and all-encompassing view, perhaps most succinctly expressed by Hofer (1976), who suggests that:

> strategic planning is concerned with the development of a viable match between an organization's capabilities and the risks present in its environment.

Several authors argue that strategic planning should also deal with certain important issues in addition to having the characteristics discussed earlier. Litschert and Nicholson (1974), for example, suggest that:

> Strategic planning...is the highest level of decision-making concerning a company's basic direction and purpose in order to assure long-term health and vitality to the organization. Such decisions tend to be enduring – i.e., not easily reversible – broad in scope, and concerned with goals and means of attainment.

In their view, strategic and long-term planning are distinguishable:

> ...strategic planning is actually a component of the long-range planning process. It is generally agreed that long-range planning is a process which involves making a sequence of interrelated decisions aimed at achieving a desirable future environment for the enterprise.

Fox (1975) takes a similar view, stating that the label "strategic planning" connotes "identification and action on important matters, matters that are important in the longer term." Holloway and King (1979) emphasize the importance of other characteristics, stating that:

> Strategic planning is, simply put, the process of positioning an organization so that it can prosper in the future. There are several implications that flow from this definition. First, it is about decision making...Next, there are long range connotations. Next, it has to do with the inevitable obsolescence of existing products or processes and the provision for new ones to take their places. Finally, it deals with choices related to the organization itself as opposed to personal choices.

Hall (1974) also feels that "strategic" implies importance and defines "strategic" planning as "long-range anticipatory decision making which is undertaken to affect the direction of the entire organization." Carlson (1978), however, makes explicit an emphasis on environmental change in defining long-range strategic planning as "a process which allows organizational members to assess the future and make provision for it."

Other authors seem less directly concerned with the nature of strategic planning. For example, although one of the best known articles on planning practice uses the term *strategic planning,* it is mainly concerned with organizing the planning process in a divisionalized company. Vancil and Lorange (1975) write:

> The widely accepted theory of corporate strategic planning is simple: using a time horizon of several years, top management reassesses its current strategy by looking for opportunities and threats in the environment and by analyzing the company's resources to identify its strengths and weaknesses. Management may draw up several alternative strategic scenarios and appraise them against the long-term objectives of the organization. To begin implementing the selected strategy (or continue a revalidated one), management fleshes it out in terms of the actions to be taken in the near future.

In our view, the theory may not be simple, and certainly the practice is not. A consideration of some of the elements in Vancil and Lorange's definition does, however, suggest clues to what may make planning "strategic"—for example, a fairly long-term planning horizon, a process involving an environmental analysis and internal assessment, and the development of alternative scenarios. Similarly, Joaquim (1979) stresses environmental analysis and the development of options as integral to strategic planning.

As indicated earlier, many authors do not seem to

distinguish the concept of "strategic" planning from long-range or corporate planning. Examples include De Noya (1979), Steiner (1974) (although he emphasizes the key role of strategies), Roney (1977), Carlson (1978), Saunders and Tuggle (1977), Higgins and Finn (1977), and Gotcher (1977). In a similar fashion, Kudla's (1976) earlier work equated strategic and long-range planning and combined some elements of corporate and divisional planning as follows:

> Corporate planning is defined as a formalized, structured process which includes the establishment of corporate goals and objectives and the development of divisional plans as a means to achieve them.

His study of 14 companies suggests the importance of changes in top management, changing environments, and increased firm size and complexity as stimulants to corporate planning. It also outlines the roles of participants in decentralized planning processes and highlights conditions for more effective planning. More recently, however, Kudla (1978) was more explicit about strategic planning, defining it as:

> the systematic process of determining the firm's goals and objectives for at least three years ahead and developing strategies for the acquisition and use of resources to achieve these objectives.

His survey of 323 companies sought information on five "key areas of strategic planning." In Kudla's view, these key areas include quantified objectives, environmental surveillance, types of plans (he suggests that strategic planning "requires the development of a system of plans which cover all functional areas"), pro-forma financial statements, and planning control.

Hussey (1972) expressed a skeptical view when he pointed out that:

> All strategic planning systems should be designed to encourage flair, an acceptance of the challenge of change and to nurture that all too scarce commodity, management talent. All too often, the strategic planning systems of multi-national companies are a series of forms which worship conformity. Where management skill is inadequate, vision is narrowed...

Clearly, in Hussey's view, formal planning systems are not an unmitigated good, and systems that encourage creativity and deal with change are important elements of better planning.

One theme does, however, seem to unify many of the articles dealing with this general subject area: the concern with an uncertain environment and its implications for planning. Gotcher (1977), for example, suggests that "firms must adapt to...changing environmental conditions or ultimately perish." In the same study, he notes that "the terms *corporate planning, strategic planning* and *long range planning* were not clearly differentiated in the minds of the majority of planners." No clear patterns of response to change emerged in Gotcher's study, which concludes pessimistically by noting (among other points) that "forecasting seems to be an undeveloped art." Robinson, Hichens, and Wade (1978) imply that the impetus to use newer approaches to planning and resource allocation results in large part from environmental change, pointing out that:

> In a reasonably stable economic environment the normal method of comparing the prospects of one business sector with another, and for measuring a company's strengths and weaknesses in different sectors, is to use historical and forecast rates of return on capital employed in each sector to provide a measure of the sector's prospects or the company's strength.

In their view, such approaches are no longer sufficient, for a variety of reasons, including the fact that:

> world-wide inflation has severely weakened the validity and credibility of financial forecasts, particularly in the case of businesses which are in any way affected by oil prices.

Dealing with uncertainty was one of Hall's (1974) major concerns, and he points out that both reduction and quantification of uncertainty have been employed in strategic planning efforts – although he is skeptical about the results. Eppink (1978) is similarly concerned, suggesting that the development of strategic flexibility is a way of making the organization less vulnerable to unforeseen change. Carlson (1978), feeling that few organizations are not faced with complex and turbulent environments, suggests that strategic planning is the key to dealing with the resulting problems. Lorange (1976), too, makes a similar point in suggesting that "to identify the most relevant strategic options, the corporation needs to adapt continuously to the environment."

2.2.2 OUR PERSPECTIVE ON STRATEGIC PLANNING

Our perspective on strategic planning uses many of the elements discussed by the scholars noted in this section. We believe that strategic planning is a conceptual endeavor aimed at securing competitive advantage for the firm. The search for competitive advantage implies a goal of obtaining some degree of monopoly power for some period of time and a consequent ability of the firm to consistently make profits over and above the rate it would earn under perfect competition. Since such advantages in a given product/market tend to be eroded over time by competitive pressures, obtaining high returns over the long run is a key operational objective that requires continual shifts of resources across technologies and markets.

This perspective implies that the firm should choose which environments to address, as well as identify and choose from a variety of ways in which they may be addressed. It implies that decisions, comprehensively thought out in a formal manner, must be made about both securing and allocating resources over the long run. Since we are concerned with the firm as an entity, the corporate focus seems the most appropriate, though we accept that strategic planning may also be performed at lower levels in the organization – within the division or SBU, for example. In succeeding sections we lay out the elements of Corporate Strategic Planning in more depth; the key elements are "environmental," "long-run," "formal," "corporate," and "resource allocation."

2.2.3 STRATEGIC PLANNING AND ALTERNATIVE APPROACHES

Our work is predicated on the value of a formalized strategic planning approach (synoptic formalism) to strategy development, though alternative methods do exist for developing effective strategies. In a pioneering work, Mintzberg (1973) identified three strategy formulation modes: entrepreneurial, adaptive, and planning. More recently, Wheelwright (1984) has noted that strategic planning (as we have discussed it) is predominantly considered to be an objective, analytic, data-based activity; he suggests that a reasonable alternative method is what he calls the value-based incremental approach (logical incrementalism), in which a set of beliefs and convictions about how the firm will conduct its business and how it will treat others overrides its concerns for product/market positions. Drawing on earlier work on logical incrementalism (Quinn 1980), and the science of muddling through (Lindbloom 1959, 1979), Wheelwright identifies key elements of the two approaches (table 2.1a) and contrasts two companies that he believes exemplify the two polar approaches – Texas Instruments and Hewlett-Packard, respectively. He also highlights pitfalls of the two approaches (table 2.1b). See also Fredrickson (1983), who has elaborated six dimensions of difference – motive for initiation, concepts of goals, relationship between means and ends, concept of choice, and analytic and integrative comprehensiveness – between the two approaches in a strategic decision-

Table 2.1
Two Contrasting Approaches to Strategy Formulation[1]

Table 2.1a   Elements of the Two Approaches

Strategic Planning Approach	Value-Based Incremental Approach
Rational and analytical	Logical and incremental
Portfolio positioning is key	Management beliefs are key
CEO is the strategist	CEO sets the values
Strategy is by the few	Strategy is by the masses
Trade-offs guided by each business strategy	Trade-offs guided by values and beliefs
Unique business strategies	Generic business strategies
Unique functional strategies	Primarily generic functional strategies
Competitor and opportunity driven	Practical and acceptable to the organization
Staff analysis for evaluation	Management commitment for evaluation
Major strategic decisions articulated and decided at the top	Major strategic decisions evolved and confirmed by the organization
Strategic change based on promise of projected results	Past performance used as best indicator of future results
Comprehensive and explicit	Prioritized and implicit
Structure of the environment is key determinant of success	Collective management behavior is key determinant of success

Table 2.1b   Pitfalls to Guard Against in the Two Approaches

Strategic Planning Approach	Value-Based Incremental Approach
Too much attention to financial analysis	Too much attention to product research and development
Insufficient emphasis and attention given to marketing and sales	Insufficient attention given to manufacturing operations
With only a few big bets, committing resources too soon or too late	With many small bets needed, not enough good new ideas
Costly mistake of wrong big bet	Staying too long with yesterday's winner
Too much power to central staffs and financial analysts	Too much power to line managers with past track record (insufficient analysis)
Failure to identify high-value, stabilizing markets	Failure to identify new, high-technology markets
Failure to focus on a few major businesses	Failure to control many small businesses
Overcontrol and over-reaction (too many and too frequent changes in strategy)	Inability to redirect effort and reallocate resources (not enough control)
Lack of commitment to follow-through and implementation	Lack of attention to competitors and long-term positioning moves

[1]Reproduced from Wheelwright (1984)

making context. Finally, Camillus (1982) has attempted an integration of the two approaches in which relative emphasis on the "analytic" (synoptic formalism) and "interactive" (logical incrementalism) components of strategic planning is linked along a temporal dimension.

2.3 Planning as an Organizational Design Variable

A planning system, "strategic" or other, is per se an important element of organizational design. Organizational design encompasses areas such as the formal-institutional macrostructure (e.g., departmentalization, authority, responsibility), reward systems (e.g., compensation, promotion), people (recruiting, selecting, training), leadership styles, and degrees of centralization, specialization and independence of subunits (Galbraith and Nathanson 1978, 1979). Since organizational design encompasses all the permanent features and internal relationships within a firm, it has a critical influence on the outputs and effectiveness of the organization as a whole. Organizational design provides the overall technology for turning the decisions of strategic choice into action so that desired performance is attained. According to some theorists (Hall and Saias 1980), organizational design also establishes the foundation and context for future strategy formulation, since the nature of the firm's structure and processes orients the organization's outlook and perceptions of the environment.

The planning system is the key organizational design variable examined in this book. When such a system is working well, it plays important roles in both strategy formulation (as discussed in section 2.2) and strategy implementation. The planning system is a midrange organizational design variable that links the formal macrostructure (the least flexible design variable) to the day-to-day patterns of behavior within the firm by providing the context within which many microorganizational decisions are made. More importantly, the planning system encompasses other aspects of organizational design: decentralization of decision-making, communication patterns and performance evaluation. Furthermore, planning system design can be tailored to a firm's individual needs (Henry 1981).

Whereas researchers from many disciplines – from formal organization theory to production management – have emphasized the need to plan, the perspectives adopted by each area represent indirectly the multidimensionality of planning. Operations management theorists base the need to plan on effective sequencing and balancing of system inputs and outputs to prevent disruptions and inefficiency. Organizational theorists describe the importance of planning in more holistic terms, pointing out that it provides for achieving unity of effort (integration) among the organization's subunits. Others consider the main purpose of planning to be assisting strategy formulation by providing an external or environmental orientation.

The essential common idea underlying these various formal viewpoints and paradigms is that planning provides direct and immediate practical benefits, and also meets a variety of other important organizational needs that are less tangible. These varying views indicate the richness and depth of planning as an attribute of organizational design.

An analogy is provided by the biological organism. The organism's skeletal structure can be regarded as an analogy for the fixed macrostructure. Planning is an element of the nervous system. The nervous system serves both an external adaptive function by sensing out the environment and an internal coordination function by guiding both involuntary and voluntary functions so that the organism's actions are effective.

In subsequent chapters we examine the externally-oriented relationships of planning to both environment (chapter 5) and strategy (chapter 6), and the internally-oriented relationships to other organizational design variables – organization structure and organizational climate (chapter 7).

2.4 Planning as an Economic Variable

Most of the interest in planning has come from fields in which research concentrates on the internal functioning of organizations, rather than on the market environments in which the firm functions. Microeconomists who are interested in market environments tend to have an aversion to the word *planning*, based primarily on their distaste for replacement of market mechanisms by bureaucracy, especially in centrally planned economies. Strategic planning, a management tool internal to the firm, is largely ignored by economists; it is typically treated as just another factor of production used in appropriate quantity and quality in profit maximization calculations. The general view seems to be that large, complex organizations are difficult to manage and that they tend not to perform exceptionally well over the long run unless bolstered by significant and permanent market power.

However, the general goals of strategic planning fit comfortably into the context of the profit maximizing firm. "Good" planning involves shifting of resources (human and financial) from uses where competitive forces have eroded returns to new uses in which higher than average returns may be realized, at least for a time. Planning's emphasis on innovation and market development is also consistent with the important work of Schumpeter (1942).

More recently, in his work on markets and hierarchies, Williamson (1975) has developed (or rediscovered) a number of concepts and has incorporated them into a microeconomic framework. Several relate to the goals of effective planning, since Williamson's work is based on the idea that internal organization (hierarchy) often has attractive properties over market transactions. For example, hierarchies may permit parties to deal with uncertainty and complexity in an adaptive, sequential fashion.

Corporate Strategic Planning is one of a number of available ways to replace market transactions by decision processes within the firm—that is, by bringing important resource allocation decisions into a hierarchical organization structure. Williamson also talks of "elite staff(s)," which bring special forms of expertise to multiproduct, multimarket firms; corporate planners clearly constitute one type of such elite staff.

Williamson lists six advantages of hierarchy when market mechanisms have basic imperfections. Each has some relationship to planning.

1. *"Bounded rationality.* Hierarchy extends the bound on rationality by permitting the specialization of decision-making and economizing on communication expense."

Planning is a highly information intensive activity. When planning works well, it serves an integrative purpose that can help avoid the loss of resources through bureaucratic inertia and inefficiency.

2. *"Uncertainty.* Hierarchy permits interdependent units to adapt to unforeseen contingencies in a coordinated way and furthermore serves to 'absorb' uncertainty."

At the core of strategic planning is the development of contingent forecasts and plans for dealing with uncertainty about the future. Furthermore, the portfolio approach to planning – with different roles assigned to different products or services at different points in their histories – allows various businesses to share uncertainty in an organized way.

3. *"Information impactedness.* Hierarchy extends the constitutional powers to perform an audit, thereby narrowing (prospectively at least) the information gap that obtains between autonomous agents."

Again, a key tenet of corporate planning is the free flow of information within the organization – even among units that compete with each other.

4. *"Opportunism.* Hierarchy permits additional incentive and control techniques to be brought to bear in a more selective manner, thereby serving to curb small-numbers opportunism."

It is well known that indeterminacy results in situations where both buyer and seller can exert powerful influence over a market. Of all the principles in the Williamson analysis, this is probably the one least remedied by planning, although the problem itself may be exacerbated by the strategic search for high profit investments in developing markets.

5. *"Atmosphere.* As compared with market modes of exchange, hierarchy provides, for some purposes at least, a less calculative exchange atmosphere."

It is not clear that Williamson's heart is really in this notion, but it seems to come close to the idea of organizational climate.

6. *"Small numbers.* Hierarchy permits small-numbers bargaining indeterminacies to be resolved by fiat."

Small numbers of producers and/or buyers in a market can often exercise significant market power. Strategic planning, with its emphasis on the development of new products and new markets or segments, may frequently help the firm avoid classic monopsony-monopoly bargaining, particularly in vertical customer-supplier situations.

Williamson further points out that multidivision structures (M-form), which generally grow from successful unitary form (U-form) functional organizations, require specialized staffs to assist the general office with strategic decision-making – "involving planning, appraisal and control, including the allocation of resources among the (competing) operating divisions... The resulting structure displays both rationality and synergy: the whole is greater than the sum of the parts (p. 137)." Finally, Williamson sees significant transaction costs involved with traditional external capital market processes that allocate resources among several U-form firms and suggests that the internal M-form organization may have advantages for such capital allocation functions.

2.5 Approaches to Modeling Planning

We have developed two interrelated ways to analyze the elements of planning; we term these the process approach (how planning is done) and the functional approach (why it is done). For some purposes a process view seems to have greater expository and analytic value while for others a functional perspective seems to be more appropriate. The functional approach is used throughout chapter 3 as the framework for a detailed description of planning. The process approach is used in chapter 4 to analyze how the elements of planning fit together.

2.6 Planning: A Functional Approach

The functional perspective on planning is concerned with the "why" planning is done – what is the purpose, what problems does it solve, and what are the benefits? From a review of the literature in section 2.2, we have identified two key functions of a "good" planning system: adaptation and integration.

The *adaptive* dimension, associated with the discussion in section 2.2, is concerned with the coalignment of the organization and the environment. It is outwardly focused, concerned with factors such as positioning the firm for the future through the selection of environments in which to operate and the determination of strategies with which to compete.

The *integrative* dimension is, by contrast, internally focused. Regardless of the environmental and strategic decisions that may flow out of a planning process, an equivalent set of managerial processes is required to hold the organization together. To the extent that integration is performed as part and parcel of the planning system, we term this the integrative dimension of planning.

2.6.1 THE ADAPTIVE DIMENSION

Perhaps the major distinction between the "old" planning and "new" planning is the degree of emphasis placed on the adaptive dimension – the series of decisions that determine the future alignment of the firm and its environment. Whereas earlier planning systems often focused on the integrative dimension and were largely budgeting, adaptive planning is both externally oriented and long range in perspective. In this section we selectively review the recent empirical research on the adaptive dimension of planning. Later in the book (chapters 3 and 4), we use the ideas developed by previous researchers to elaborate on important adaptive elements of "good" planning systems.

2.6.1.1 Environmental Analysis

Given the pace of change faced by many large corporations, planning should focus on anticipating changes in the environment, developing the consequences of those changes, and making the decisions necessary to equip the firm to deal with those consequences. Early recognition of trends is crucial (Reinhardt 1984), and a firm stressing adaptive planning would devote considerable effort to gathering information from the environment (Rhyne 1985), since accurate and objectively assessed environmental information is a necessary precondition for developing anticipatory responses (Aguilar 1967).

Godiwalla, Meinhart, and Warde (1979) noted that scanning, searching, and investigating the external environment are uncertain and slow processes whose results are needed primarily at top corporate levels. Studies of individual companies have demonstrated commitment to environmental scanning. For example, Ciba-Geigy uses scanning to identify major opportunities and set meaningful objectives (Jones 1981); General Electric identifies four categories of the environment – social, political, economic, and technological – which provide the framework for environmental search and planning (Wilson, George, and Solomon 1978); and Royal Dutch Shell develops scenarios (Wack 1985).

Management systems are often not up to the demands placed on them by sophisticated planning systems (Darden and Sinkula 1982, Naylor 1983, Cymbala 1984). However, Jain (1984) sets out levels of organizational responsibilities to handle environmental scanning in a series of four separate but progressive phases and argues that such scanning should be an evolving activity that is custom-designed for each company.

A number of studies have highlighted marketing information as a critical input, especially in declining markets (e.g., Schofield 1983). However, other environmental analyses are also vital (Diffenbach 1983), including political and regulatory analysis (Jonsson and Petzaell 1982; Katz, Zavodnik, and Markezin 1983; Windsor and Greanius 1983), especially in relatively unfamiliar environments (Wright, Townsend, Kinard, and Iverstine 1982). There are, nonetheless, indications that environmental analysis is done only sporadically and then as a reaction to events (Thomas 1980).

One particular aspect of external information gathering and analysis concerns competitors. The importance of developing competitive strategies has been highlighted in recent years (Porter 1980, Merrill and Schweppe 1984), and a number of writers have discussed methodologies for obtaining information on competition (e.g., Montgomery and Weinberg 1979).

2.6.1.2 Time Horizons

Emphasis on the adaptive aspect of planning generally means using fairly long time horizons in the planning process, though the appropriate one varies from business to business. Normative literature suggests that longer time horizons reinforce the adaptive features of planning, though empirical evidence along these lines is scarce. Miller and Friesen (1983) found a significant positive relationship between innovation and planning time horizons, and Mintzberg (1973) noted that adaptive strategy formulation resulted in longer time horizons for planning.

2.6.1.3 Generation of Alternatives

Given the uncertainty that generally surrounds forecasts of future business environments, adaptive planning should cause alternatives and options to surface as part of the planning process. The notion of selection of environments in which to compete is also related to ideas of flexibility, scenarios, and contingency planning (Michael 1980, Windsor and Greanias 1983). Contingency planning is claimed to be increasingly important in a world of apparently growing uncertainty (Ghosh and Nee 1983a, b; Sloan 1984), and one recent study reported that multiple planning scenarios were used by half of a sample of *Fortune* 1000 firms. In general, however, they were not part of the formal strategic planning process (Linneman and Klein 1983).

2.6.1.4 Globalness

Since we are concerned with large corporations, many of which are both multinational in scope and facing increasing worldwide competition from multinational competitors, we believe there should be a significant global dimension to planning. We do not, however, underestimate the difficulty of global planning, requiring as it does integration across widely differing environmental conditions. Research suggests that firms often fall into dangerous pitfalls when engaging in multinational global planning, especially in terms of headquarter-subsidiary relationships (Brandt, Hulbert, and Richers 1980; Hulbert and Brandt 1980).

2.6.1.5 Portfolio Perspective

Another characteristic of adaptive planning is based on the idea that, at a point in time, the various businesses comprising the corporation may be assigned different strategic objectives. Growth objectives may dominate for some businesses, while cash generation or profits are more important for others (e.g., Day 1977). In such a framework, the products and/or businesses are viewed as comprising elements in a portfolio, and the overall performance of the portfolio (corporation) is optimized over time as the roles of the elements shift. Despite the attention that various tools of adaptive planning (policy matrices, product life cycles, capital asset pricing models, etc.) have received in the business press, they have received very little attention outside of basic description and example in the planning literature (Gelb, Christensen, Cooper, and DeKluyver 1982; Naylor 1982; Naylor and Tapon 1982; Hax and Majluf 1983a, b; Neidell 1983). In fact, the attention they do get is often negative in terms of their usefulness (Miesing 1983, Randall 1984), though Haspeslagh (1982) reported fairly widespread use. (See also Wind and Mahajan 1981.) One class of models that does appear to have had some degree of practical application as a result of work by consulting firms (Marakon Associates 1980, Strategic Planning Associates 1981) and academic scholars (Fruhan 1979, Rappaport 1981) is *value-based* planning models, so termed since they focus on the impact of managerial decisions on shareholder value (Woo 1984). Sophisticated computer models are mentioned infrequently (Larreche and Srinivasan 1981, Holloway and Pearce 1982, Holmes 1983, Rector 1983, Tomlinson and Dyson 1983, Jain 1984), and again often negatively.

2.6.1.6 Resource Allocation

A related issue is concerned with the extent to which allocation of various scarce resources is made as part of the planning process. Whereas adaptive planning generally focuses on rationing and allocating capital, other resources may also be allocated strategically. Most of the thinking in this area seems to involve people (Lopez 1981; Devanna, Fombrun, Tichy, and Warren 1982; Metz 1984), but raw materials are also mentioned (Fenniza 1980).

2.6.1.7 Investment Criteria

Finally, firms planning adaptively are likely to use different criteria to evaluate investment opportunities and to make long-term/short-term trade-offs explicit (Banks and Wheelwright 1979). The more adaptive the planning system, the more likely that externally driven criteria such as market share, market growth, and so forth are employed, rather than more internally oriented criteria such as forecast net profit, cash flow, and return on investment.

2.6.1.8 Summary on Adaptive Planning

In this section we have focused on the adaptive aspect of planning. The adaptive dimension is externally oriented, focusing on the environments in which the firm is, and may in the future, be functioning. We have suggested seven major characteristics that we expect to be manifest in adaptive planning – environmental analysis, longer time horizons, generation of alternatives, globalness, portfolio perspective, link to resource allocation, and choice of investment criteria.

It is the adaptive dimension of planning that we believe best captures the concept of strategic planning. The reorientation of planning systems that gave rise to the idea of "new" planning, and to the use of the modifier "strategic," was associated with an attempt to shift the focus of attention of firms' planning efforts from one that was internally oriented to one more externally focused. Firms that practice strategic planning are more likely to incorporate the seven major characteristics described above in their planning practices. In our lexicon, strategic planning is planning that places its emphasis on the adaptive function of planning.

However, a firm may plan extensively yet incorporate few, if any, of the adaptive elements discussed in this section. Such planning is internally, rather than externally, focused and is frequently concerned with financial issues. We term such planning financial planning.

2.6.2 THE INTEGRATIVE DIMENSION

The *integrative* planning dimension must be balanced with the adaptive dimension of planning. With inadequate integrative systems, an organization continuously seeking to adapt to its current environment while simultaneously searching out new and promising environments to enter is likely to run out of control. In addition to the outwardly focused managerial processes that seek to identify opportunities, to diminish threats, and to manage the firm's many environmental relationships, an equivalent set of managerial processes is needed to hold the organization together. However, too much control, rigidity, and an inability to confront the environment actively is likely to lead to the organization's becoming increasingly out of touch with its surroundings.

The notion of balance between environmental adaptation and organizational control is closely linked to Lawrence and Lorsch's (1967) ideas of differentiation and integration. In their view, differentiation deals with the extent to which the organization develops a series of unique and independent subunits to adapt to its task-environment; integration involves the achievement of unity of effort among the various subsystems so that the organization as a whole may achieve its objectives.

2.6.2.1 Methods for Achieving Integration

A number of methods have been suggested for obtaining integration: communication flows (Allen 1978), high influence of linking functions (Allen 1978), integrative teams and committees (Galbraith 1973), participation in decision-making (Dickson 1981), conflict resolution mechanisms (Walker and Lorsch 1970, Lorsch and Allen 1976), and evaluation and reward systems (Allen 1978).

Athreya's (1970) important early study highlighted the role of planning in achieving integration, but Woodburn (1984) has noted that the integrative function has generally been ignored in the planning literature, even though the requirement for integration increases with organizational complexity (see also Hulbert and Brandt 1980: 122-27). Notwithstanding other methods of achieving organizational integration, the corporate planning system is a potent unifying device. At lower levels within the firm, planning can help ensure that individual subunits have an agreed-upon focus; at the corporate level, the planning system can help in ensuring that the total organization and its individual subunits are heading in the chosen direction. A number of elements in the planning system can combine to provide overall integration, in part by supporting or encompassing some of the mechanisms noted above. In this section we selectively review research on the integrative dimension of planning. Later in the book (chapters 3 and 4), we use the ideas developed by previous researchers to elaborate on important integrative elements of "good" planning systems.

2.6.2.2 Over-Time

Shant, Niblack, and Sandalls (1973) have advocated achieving both integration and environmental adaptation by planning for multiple time horizons and by varying the extent to which long-range planning and short-term planning are tightly matched.

2.6.2.3 Organizational Depth

Lorange (1980) proposed that communications from corporate that reach deep into the organization strengthen the company's control and integration, and Steiner (1983) has emphasized the importance of managing information flows to link strategy formulation and implementation.

2.6.2.4 Top-Down Versus Bottom-Up Planning

Many researchers have argued that whereas top-down planning practices should be dominant in relatively undiversified firms, a more bottom-up style should emerge as the company diversifies because of decreasing CEO intimacy with the firm's various businesses (e.g., Ackerman 1970). Empirical findings, however, generally support top-down approaches. Horovitz and Thietart (1982) found that profitable firms, both diversified and nondiversified, employed a top-down planning approach, whereas Woodburn (1984), in his study on South African companies, noted that the top-down planning format was found in most of his sample, regardless of industry, diversification, or other factors. Only when the environment was perceived to be complex did a more bottom-up approach emerge.

2.6.2.5 CEO Involvement

Planning is a prime task of top management (Taylor 1984), and involvement by the CEO is not only a critical integrating factor but is also said to be absolutely vital to the success of planning (Higgins 1981; Eadle, Ellison, and Brown 1982; Holmberg and Baker 1982; Gattis 1983; Hart 1984). (We suspect that the same can be said about CEO involvement in other innovations in the management of complex organizations.)

2.6.2.6 Role of Line Management

That line management must play a critical role in planning has been documented extensively (e.g., Katz 1978, Ball 1982, Dyson and Foster 1982, Nielsen 1983b, Oliver and Garber 1983, Leff 1984). Involvement of middle managers may also be important (Link 1983), but there is uncertainty in the literature about how far down in the organization active participation should reach for effective planning. In any event, organizations can reduce uncertainty resulting from high task complexity by allowing members to participate in the goal- and policy-making processes (Tannenbaum 1968). Lorange (1980) asserts that there should be little or no ambiguity in terms of the role that line general managers are expected to play in the planning process, and Al-Bazzaz and Grinyer (1980) note that one of the main potential weaknesses inherent in all planning processes is the lack of support from either top and/or line management. A lack of sympathy or understanding of planning concepts militates against effective contribution from line managers.

2.6.2.7 Role of Planners

Athreya (1970) notes the integrative roles played by both the planning office and the planners in facilitating communication flows between staff and line, and line and line, and Khandwalla (1973) and Mintzberg (1978) argue that formalization of the planning process is a very powerful integrator. Planners can either stimulate internal company creativity (innovation) by playing roles of "instigator" and "decision-maker" or coordinate internal management by more passive roles such as "analyst" or "coordinator" (Camillus 1980). (See also Sayles n.d.)

2.6.2.8 Status of Planners

Lorange and Vancil (1976) suggest that success of planning depends not only on its formality for the company as a whole but also on the status of the chief planner (see also Steiner 1970 and Steiner and Schollhammer 1975), the presence of well-trained planners (Nielsen 1983a), and the creation of a suitable organization for planning (Nielsen 1983b, Nauert 1983, Bandeen 1984) that is tailored to fit the firm's needs (Michael 1980, Jaedicke 1981).

2.6.2.9 Control

Camillus (1975) believes that the control aspect of formal planning can serve as an important integrative device, but some authors have argued that implementation is often more difficult than anticipated, often because the reward structures remain based on short-term performance and run counter to long-term strategic management (Horovitz 1979, Ford 1981, Lenz and Lyles 1981, Meadows 1981, Brown 1983, Metz 1984).

2.6.2.10 Financial Integration

Despite the positive attributes of planning, some authors argue that it often becomes too complex to be effective (Schaffir and Lobe 1984), sometimes culminating in a burdensome budgeting exercise (Taylor 1984). Other authors argue that the minority of firms that plan succeed in doing so effectively (Ford 1981). Furthermore, planning may be adopted as a response to a firm's business environments becoming more complex and unstable (Lindsay and Rue 1980), leading to inevitable disappointment.

2.6.2.11 Summary on Integrative Planning

As discussed earlier, there are many integrating elements within the planning system and many types of integration that the organization requires for effective functioning. We shall examine many of these, but since the thrust of this book is the examination of corporate planning, our major focus is on corporate-wide integration. This is represented by the extent to which individual second-level* units tend to act autonomously versus the extent to which they are held together in serving some overarching corporate purpose. Given that the organizational device with which we are primarily concerned is the planning system, we employ as a key distinguishing characteristic the extent to which the firm truly develops corporate plans. We call firms that do *corporate planners*. In contrast, *division planners* rely solely, or at least primarily, on sets of plans developed at some lower level. While we do not mean to suggest that lower level

*Second level is a generic term for the level immediately below corporate. Depending on the organization, it may be identical to, e.g., a division, sector, or SBU.

plans are not valuable, they are not corporate plans and cannot therefore serve the key function of integration of the total organization. To the extent that the planning process is designed to integrate the organization vertically, from corporate to lower levels, we expect that it will also display many of these other elements of integration.

2.7 Planning: A Process Approach

2.7.1 OVERVIEW

Planning can also be viewed as an input ▶ process ▶ output system. *Inputs* are the prerequisites, without which planning cannot take place; *process* involves the activities that constitute "what gets done" in planning, as well as the internal organizational environment in which planning activities take place; and *outputs* concern the end products of the planning activities, including the plans themselves and their uses (Kennedy and Mahapatra 1975).

In figure 2.1 we have expanded this simple model to encompass seven building blocks. Although the classifications are imperfect and to some extent arbitrary, they provide a helpful framework for organizing this rather complex system.

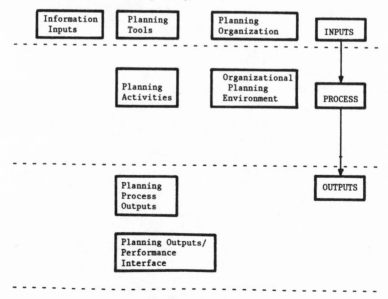

Figure 2.1
Planning Process Constructs

2.7.2 PLANNING INPUTS

Planning inputs, the basic building blocks of planning, are *information inputs, planning tools,* and *planning organization.* Information inputs are data collected externally and internally for planning purposes. Planning tools are the models and conceptual frameworks employed to organize and analyze the information inputs. Planning organization is concerned with the people and organizational positions that are involved in planning and their degree of involvement and influence in the process. Data (information inputs) are processed by people (planning organization) using models and frameworks as aids to planning (planning tools).

2.7.3 PLANNING PROCESS

The planning process consists of two elements–*planning activities* and *organizational planning environment.* Planning activities are the what and how of planning. Included are the degree to which resource allocation decisions are made as part of the planning process, the criteria employed, planning effort on acquisitions and divestitures, and so forth. A second element of the process is organizational planning environment, covering the internal environment in which planning takes place. This includes the relationships between planning and line management.

2.7.4 PLANNING OUTPUTS

As a result of planning activities, planning outputs are generated. We identify two output elements–*planning process outputs* and *planning outputs/performance interface.*

Planning process outputs comprise the plans themselves–their existence, their contents, and so forth. Planning outputs/performance interface is concerned with what happens after the plans are produced. It deals with the evaluation processes of organizational performance versus planned goals and represents the key feedback component of the planning system.

2.7.5 SUMMARY ON THE PROCESS APPROACH TO PLANNING

The process approach to analyzing planning has important advantages. First, it focuses on key elements of the system by identifying the crucial pieces that must be in place for a planning system to exist. Second, it captures a time dimension of planning that is lacking in the functional (adaptive/integrative) approach. Planning inputs must be in place before the process itself can operate; planning process outputs are produced only after the process is completed. Furthermore, the notion of a planning cycle is captured in the planning outputs/performance interface construct, which focuses on evaluation of performance against plan. For the moment, we avoid the temptation to draw lines and arrows between the boxes in figure 2.1. In chapter 4, however, we move toward identifying a model linking the process elements.

2.8 Reconciling the Process and Functional Perspectives of Planning

Individual elements of planning can be viewed from both a process and a functional perspective. For example, effort spent in collecting competitive information is an *information input* from a process perspective, yet it fulfills an *adaptive* function from a functional perspective. Similarly, review meetings to evaluate performance against plan are an element of *planning outputs/performance interface* from a process perspective but are *integrative* from a functional perspective.

How a particular planning element is viewed depends on the particular perspective being taken. As noted earlier, as we proceed through the book, we employ one or the other perspective as appropriate. At one time we did consider using just one organizing perspective to focus our analysis and presentation of results. Using both approaches makes the book somewhat more complex, but we believe that there are also resultant gains in richness.

In chapter 3 we present a detailed item-by-item analysis of the planning behavior of our sample companies. This description is organized by planning function, though membership of items in one of the seven major building blocks of the planning process is also indicated. In chapter 4 we use the process perspective as we group planning items into the seven process building blocks to develop an information-efficient "soft-model" analysis of planning via principal components. Later in chapter 4 we return to a functional perspective and develop sets of planning scales that are organized as adaptive and integrative. This view is also used in chapter 8, where we employ the two sets of scales in intermediate model analysis, and in chapter 9, where we empirically develop groupings of similar firms based on their planning characteristics. In chapter 10, which deals with planning and performance, both the functional and process perspectives are employed.

2.9 Classification of Planning Practice

In chapter 1 we noted that there is no accepted, well-tested, and comprehensive system for classifying planning practices. In this book we use both deductive and inductive approaches to developing such classification systems. A deductively based system, based on a few planning variables, is developed from theory in this chapter. It is used in later chapters to examine the many facets of planning, environment, strategy, and organization. An inductively based system, developed by taking many measures of planning and empirically grouping "similar" firms, is presented in chapter 9. We shall see that the inductive and deductive approaches produce rather similar results.

2.9.1 DEVELOPMENT OF THE DEDUCTIVE PLANNING CATEGORY SYSTEM

As we noted earlier, much of the previous research on planning does not make qualitative distinctions about planning; companies either plan or they do not. (This dichotomy is particularly true in studies of the impact of planning on performance, which we discuss in detail in chapter 10.) We indicated that such distinctions are needed to really understand the planning process, and our deductive classification scheme is developed with this need for richness squarely in mind.

Classification proceeds in the steps shown in figure 2.2. The first question involves the presence or absence of longer term plans at either the corporate or division (SBU) level. For a firm to be classified as one that planned at all, a physical document had to be prepared. Thus, a slide presentation, however detailed, would not qualify as a plan even if other criteria were satisfied. On this basis, seven firms were classified as Non-Planners.

For the 106 firms classified as Planners, two qualitative aspects were considered. The first classification is based on the integrative dimension of planning and focuses on whether or not the firm had a corporate-level plan. Seventy firms responded affirmatively that they prepared a corporate plan. However, for a number of these, the corporate plan consisted of little more than an assemblage of documents produced at a lower level, "stapled together," and summarized. Such corporate plans do not satisfy the spirit of integration, and those companies are classified as division-level planners. Surprisingly, a handful of firms that said they did not develop a corporate

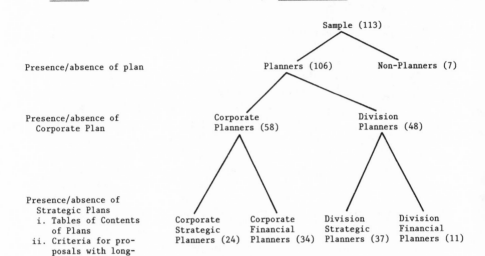

Criteria   Classification

Presence/absence of plan

Presence/absence of
   Corporate Plan

Presence/absence of
   Strategic Plans
   i. Tables of Contents
      of Plans
   ii. Criteria for pro-
       posals with long-
       run benefits

Figure 2.2
Firm Classification Procedure

plan ultimately produced this document. As a result of these classificatory decisions, the 70 self-reported corporate planners were reduced to 58; 48 firms were division-level planners.

The second qualitative aspect of companies' planning, involving the adaptive dimension, is the extent to which firms practice strategic planning as opposed to a more budgetarily oriented financial approach to planning. Two criteria were employed in this classification. The first uses the tables of contents of corporate and lower level plans to establish whether or not the plans have significant strategic content. The types of headings we noted as strategic included strategic issues, sector strategy, strategic thrust, competitive analysis, and so forth. A heavy emphasis on sales projections, forecasts, capacity utilization, and pro forma profit and loss statements, to the exclusion of most of the strategic items, was taken as indication of financial planning.

The second basis for making the strategic versus financial distinction was based on the nature of the criteria used in evaluating proposals that might yield long-run benefits. Ten criteria were analyzed—five of which are strategic and five of which are financial. The strategic criteria are: impact on company resource needs, product/market share position, forecast market share growth, growth of market for which expenditure is requested, and forecast sales growth. The financial criteria are: impact on earnings per share, forecast net operating profits, short-term cash flow benefits, forecast return on investment, and discounted cash flow analysis. Respondents rated the importance of each of these criteria on a five-point scale. Totals of ratings for the five strategic criteria and the five financial criteria were compared. Each firm was assigned to the category for which it had the largest sum. In total, 61 firms are classified as strategic planners (24 corporate, 37 division-level) and 45 as financial planners (34 corporate, 11 division-level).

The criteria are summarized in table 2.2; application to the 113 companies was surprisingly straightforward. The companies were assigned to categories by two coders; difficulties, which involved less than 10 percent of companies, were resolved by discussion since they generally involved information missed by one coder. The five categories are used as a key tool of analysis throughout the book:

Category 1: Corporate Strategic Planners. These 24 companies exhibit the most sophisticated form of planning. There is a significant strategic dimension to their planning at both corporate and lower levels. The corporate plan is a document that takes a corporate perspective and is not just an agglomeration of lower level plans.

Category 2: Division Strategic Planners. These 37 companies do not develop a formal written plan that takes a corporate perspective. However, strategic planning is done at lower levels in the organization. Thus, the planning system focuses on the development of a series of lower level strategic plans with little or no corporate perspective.

Category 3: Corporate Financial Planners. These 34 companies do develop a formal written corporate plan. However, neither it, nor lower level plans are strategic; rather they focus very clearly on financial planning, the development of pro forma budgets, and so forth, based on a series of assumptions about the future environment.

Category 4: Division Financial Planners. These 11 companies do not develop formal corporate plans, and none of their planning is strategic. They do, however, develop a series of financial plans for lower level units. There is, however, no evidence that these lower level financial plans are agglomerated into a corporate financial plan in any way more complex than adding together the budgets.

Category 5: Non-Planners. These 7 companies show no evidence of any corporate or division-level planning system, be it either strategic or financial.

Since this classification scheme plays a critical role throughout the remainder of the book, it is important that we develop

Table 2.2
Responses Required to Meet Classification Standards

Planning Category	Prepare Corporate Plan?	Prepare Division Plan?	Table of Contents	Capital Expenditure Criteria	Rationale
Corporate Strategic	Yes	Yes	Strategic	Strategic $\geq$ Financial	Content, commitment and process in place to do strategic corporate-wide planning.
Division Strategic	No(Yes[1])	Yes	Strategic	Strategic $\geq$ Financial	Content, commitment and process for strategic planning at group/division level. May or may not have formalized/financial corporate-wide planning.
Corporate Financial	Yes	Yes	Financial	Financial $\geq$ Strategic	Content and process reflect financial planning, corporate-wide.
Division Financial	No	Yes	Financial	Financial $\geq$ Strategic	Content and process reflect financial planning without integration at the corporate level.
Non-Planners	No	No	--	Financial $\geq$ Strategic	No evidence of any formalized planning process or system.

[1]Firms which produced corporate plans consisting of "stapled-together" lower level plans were classified as "No!"

some feel for how the scheme works with regard to both substance and content. We do so with two kinds of analysis:

   1) analysis of correspondence between our classification scheme and self-assessment of planning, which we discuss in the remainder of this section, and
   2) analysis of differences in the extent of strategic planning as practiced by the five groups, which we discuss in section 2.10.

2.9.2 CORRESPONDENCE WITH SELF-REPORT

Each respondent was asked the question,
"Does your company develop a formal Corporate Plan (or plans) on a regular basis?"
The self-classifications and assignment of firms to our five Planning Categories compare as follows:

	Self-Report on Corporate Planning		
Classification Based on Our Assessment	Corporate Planners	Noncorporate Planners	Total
Corporate Strategic Planners	24	0	24
Division Strategic Planners	19	18	37
Corporate Financial Planners	27	7	34
Division Financial Planners	0	11	11
Non-Planners	0	7	7
	70	43	113

These results have substantive implications, as well as meaning, for our subsequent analyses. In terms of the latter, throughout most of the book we focus on the two dozen firms we classify as Corporate Strategic Planners. All 24 firms so classified under our scheme agree that they are corporate planners, so danger of misclassification here is minimal. Similarly, all 18 firms we classify as Division Financial Planners and Non-Planners declare that they do not do such planning. The basic disagreements involve the firms classified as Corporate Financial Planners and Division Strategic Planners—particularly the latter. Of the 37 firms that we classify as Division Strategic Planners, half consider themselves corporate planners. We believe that the differences between our scheme and self-report reflect a substantive confusion about corporate planning, since these firms generally have sophisticated planning systems but fail to pass our "value added to the plan" test at the corporate level. Preliminary analyses indicated that the Division Strategic Planners in fact exhibit patterns quite different from those of the Corporate Strategic Planners.

Substantively, our inference is that many companies that prepare corporate plans with substantial strategic content do not bridge the difficult gap from division (or SBU) to the corporate level. We suspect, also, that many others that think they do strategic planning in fact do complex financial planning. Except for the Division Strategic Planners, there is general agreement between self-reported planning and our definitions (69 of 76 firms corresponding to the self-assessment and only seven Corporate Financial Planners differing).

2.10 Strategic Planning by the Five Planning Categories

2.10.1 A FACTOR ANALYTIC ASSESSMENT OF STRATEGICNESS IN PLANNING

The five-group categorization scheme depends heavily on process and procedure but is relatively light on "strategic" content. To investigate strategic content, we developed an analysis of strategic planning using a set of the items from the questionnaires that describe strategic aspects of planning. This analysis adds texture to the Planning Category Scheme and is a sort of validity check as well. In assessing the situation, we looked for the key characteristics of adaptive planning described earlier, for it is the adaptive dimension that most clearly differentiates "strategic" planning from other forms of planning.

We focused on five elements discussed in section 2.6.1:

1. Environmental analysis
2. Long time horizons
3. Generation of alternatives
4. Globalness
5. Portfolio perspective, including issues of differential strategic objectives, resource allocation, and investment criteria, plus a sixth:
6. Stage of development of the company's planning process

The sixth characteristic is consistent with the stages of planning notion advanced by Glueck and his co-workers (1980). Corporations are unlikely to catapult themselves into the full-fledged process of strategic planning from a state of no planning. The stage of development of planning is likely to be associated with factors such as the presence of formal written plans, the degree of integration evidenced by the planning system, and the degree to which plans are taken seriously and actually affect decisions.

With these six elements in mind a priori, those variables in the questionnaires that might relate to one or more of these elements were identified and the data factor analyzed. A total of 98 variables were selected; 53 of these had varimax rotated loadings of more than 0.5 on one (and only one) of six extracted factors (table 2.3). The resulting six significant factors together accounted for about 40 percent of the communal variance, and the factor structure generally tends to confirm our expectations regarding groupings of planning characteristics. In fact, among the six factors expected a priori, only the generation of alternatives fails to show up in a consistent pattern.

The first common factor – effort expended in gathering information about the environment – primarily involves forecasting. Closely related to our concept of openness to the environment, all variables loading together measure effort devoted to environmental forecasting, internally generated or purchased externally. This factor indicates that commitment to environmental scanning typically involves seeking a broad range of information; indeed, it seems that the decision to scan for environmental information is a rather basic one that may have a fundamental impact on the orientation of the whole company.

The second factor – use of strategic planning tools – is also easy to interpret and is heavily loaded by variables involving the application of portfolio analysis concepts, one measure of our notion of the setting of differential strategic objectives. This factor also addresses integration in that commitment to use of policy or portfolio matrices is not isolated but seems to be associated with fairly widespread use at both corporate and lower levels and in a wide variety of applications. Multilevel and multiuse applications of portfolio or policy matrices suggest a developed planning process, but whether this diffusion is due to a rapid and enthusiastic voluntary adoption, the missionary zeal of consultants and some corporate planners, or some other cause must await further analysis. Capon, Farley, and Hulbert (1980) have noted that there are indications that international diffusion of planning is affected by all of these influences.

The third factor – extent of corporate planning – is loaded heavily by variables that denote the development of a formal plan at the corporate level, and not positively by variables describing activity at lower levels, such as division or SBU. This factor relates to "corporateness" in the planning effort. A high score on factor three would imply a fairly substantial level of development of the planning effort

Table 2.3
Profiles of Strategic Planners and Strategic Variables

Factor Name and Variables Contained:	Factor Loadings (Varimax Rotation) Greater Than .50	Analysis of Variance of Individual Items Across Planning Groups		
		Significant?	End-Points Correct?	Order Correct?
Effort Expended in Gathering Information About the Environment (All Load on Factor 1)				
Extent of effort or resources expended by corporate planning in forecasting domestic economy over last 5 years.	.70	Yes	Yes	Yes
Extent of effort or resources expended by corporate planning in forecasting foreign economy over last 5 years.	.68	Yes	Yes	Yes
Extent of effort or resources expended by corporate planning in forecasting technological areas over last 5 years.	.59	Yes	Yes	No
Extent of effort or resources expended by corporate planning in forecasting governmental areas over last 5 years.	.69	No	Yes	No
Extent of effort or resources expended by corporate planning in forecasting social/cultural factors over last 5 years.	.56	Yes	Yes	No
Extent of effort or resources expended by corporate planning in forecasting for purchased materials or components over last 5 years.	.76†	No	No	No
Extent of effort or resources expended by corporate planning in forecasting financial markets over last 5 years.	.74†	No	Yes	No
Extent of effort or resources expended by corporate planning in forecasting industry-level demand over last 5 years.	.71	Yes	No	No
Extent of effort or resources expended by corporate planning in forecasting competitive areas over last 5 years.	.61	No	Yes	No
Use of Strategic Planning Tools (All Load on Factor 2)				
Development of policy or portfolio matrices at the corporate level.	.73	Yes	Yes	Yes
Portfolio analysis used at lower levels in the organization.	.78	Yes	Yes	Yes
Extent that product portfolio approach developed by the Boston Consulting Group influenced content of corporate strategies.	.50	Yes	Yes	No
Extent that policy matrices such as those developed by Shell Chemical, General Electric, and McKinsey influenced the content of corporate strategy.	.54	Yes	Yes	No
Policy matrices and/or portfolio analyses are used for setting resource allocation priorities.	.87†	Yes	Yes	No
Policy matrices and/or portfolio analyses are used to analyze competitors.	.87†	Yes	Yes	No
Policy matrices and/or portfolio analyses are used to analyze customers.	.81	No	Yes	Yes
Policy matrices and/or portfolio analyses are used to analyze suppliers.	.77	No	Yes	Yes

Policy matrices and/or portfolio analyses are used as a cash flow management tool.	.82	No	Yes	Yes

Ex. ?nt of Corporate Planning
(All Load on Factor 3)

Is there a corporate plan?	.68	Yes	Yes	Yes
Are there corporate goals/objectives?	.54	No	Yes	Yes
Is there corporate market analysis?	.66	No	Yes	Yes
Is there corporate customer analysis?	.53	No	No	No
Is there corporate competitive analysis?	.64	No	Yes	No
Is there corporate company analysis?	.71	Yes	Yes	Yes
Number of headings in the corporate plan?	.88†	Yes	Yes	Yes
Is there other environmental analysis at the corporate level?	.56	Yes	Yes	Yes
Are there key issues/problems/opportunities at the corporate level?	.55	Yes	Yes	Yes
Is there a corporate strategy?	.64	Yes	Yes	Yes
Are there second level strategies in the corporate plan?	.65	Yes	Yes	Yes
Are there third level strategies in the corporate plan?	.52	Yes	Yes	Yes
Does company develop a normal corporate plan (or plans) on a regular basis?	.71†	Yes	Yes	Yes
Does company develop a series of formal lower level plans on a regular basis?	-.71	Yes	Yes	Yes

Depth of Planning
(All Load on Factor 4)

Is there a second level plan?	.64	Yes	Yes	No
Is there a second level mission?	.52	Yes	Yes	Yes
Are there second level goals/objectives?	.62	Yes	Yes	Yes
Is there second level market analysis?	.78	Yes	Yes	Yes
Is there second level customer analysis?	.71	No	No	No
Is there second level competitive analysis?	.78†	Yes	No	No
Is there second level company analysis?	.70	Yes	Yes	Yes
Number of headings in second level plans?	.86†	Yes	Yes	Yes
Is there other environmental analysis at the second level?	.68	Yes	Yes	Yes
Is there issues/problems/opportunities analysis at the second level?	.50	Yes	Yes	Yes
Is there second level business strategy?	.74	Yes	Yes	Yes
Are there third level strategies?	.50	Yes	Yes	Yes

Time Horizon of Planning
(All Load on Factor 5)

Time horizon of longest plan which is guiding for the corporation.	.78	Yes	Yes	No
Time horizon of 2nd longest plan which is guiding for the corporation.	.80†	Yes	Yes	No
Time horizon of 3rd longest plan which is guiding for the corporation.	.82†	No	No	No
Number of time horizons of formal plan types.	.72	Yes	No	No

Globalness of Planning
(All Load on Factor 6)

Production strategies are developed on a worldwide basis.	.77†	Yes	Yes	Yes
Marketing strategies are developed on a worldwide basis.	.78†	Yes	No	No

Table 2.3 (continued)

All corporate planning done on a worldwide basis.	.67	Yes	Yes	Yes
All second level planning is conducted on a worldwide basis.	.65	No	Yes	Yes
Procurement strategies are developed on a worldwide basis.	.59	No	Yes	Yes

†Variables used later in discriminant analyses.

at the corporate level; it is a key integrative component of the planning system and the one on which we focus in this study.

In contrast, factor four – depth of planning – comprises variables describing the complexity and stage of development of planning efforts at what we call the "second level" – the division or SBU level in most companies. Extraction of the third and fourth factors supports our informal observations that elaborate planning may be practiced at both the corporate level and the level below corporate but that the two are not necessarily related. Companies scoring high on both factors three and four, however, would be those with the most highly integrated planning systems.

The fifth factor – time horizon of planning – is the expected long-range factor. However, the inclusion of the number of time horizons variable suggests that this factor also bears on the planning integration issue.

The sixth factor – globalness of planning – consists mainly of variables dealing with a global approach to planning and strategy formulation. The loadings here suggest that, as with portfolio and policy matrices, companies either plan and strategize globally across functions and levels or they do not. This factor is consistent with our earlier conception of an open, opportunity-driven perspective on planning and indicates a commitment to planning and strategy development on a worldwide basis.

In summary, the relationship between our a priori set of strategic planning characteristics and the factor analytic solution of related variables is an encouraging one. Of the six factors we postulated, *environmental analysis* (factor 1), *long time horizons* (factor 5), *portfolio perspective* (factor 2), and *globalness of planning* (factor 6) come through clearly as single factors. *Generation of alternatives* does not emerge, but advanced *integration* of the planning system is present in the solution, though not as a single factor.

In the next section, we present the results of three analyses of patterns in the six empirically derived strategic planning factors for the five Planning Categories developed in section 2.9. The first involves item-by-item analysis of the 53 individual measurements that load heavily in the factor analysis. The second analysis involves comparison of mean factor scores of the six strategic planning factors for the Planning Categories. Third, we examine the ability of a selected handful of variables, identified from the factor analysis, to classify companies into the five Planning Categories.

2.10.2 PLANNING CATEGORIES AND INDIVIDUAL MEASUREMENTS

The 53 variables with heavy loadings in table 2.3 were each subjected to one-way analysis of variance for the five Planning Categories. The results are presented in three different ways on the right side of table 2.3:

1. Significant differences of within-group means among the five Planning Categories
2. Correct positioning of within-group means for the two extreme cases (Corporate Strategic Planners and Non-Planners generally being at the end points of the distribution of means, with the Corporate Strategic Planners at the "better" end.)
3. Correct ordering of the within-group means (Corporate Strategic Planners, Division Strategic Planners, Corporate Financial Planners, Division Financial Planners, and Non-Planners). This ordering is based on judgment that the defect of division strategic planning (lack of corporate integration) is less severe than that of corporate-level financial planning (lack of strategic outlook.)

Corporate Strategic Planners would, for example, be expected to devote more corporate effort to information gathering, use more formal planning techniques, and take a more global view than corporations that comprise the other groupings; the Non-Planners would, in each case, be expected to be at the opposite extreme. Overall, the results are:

Number of significant differences over Planning
    Categories   38(72%)
Number of items for which the means of the end-points
    are "correct"   45(85%)
Number of items for which all the means are
    "correctly" ordered   32(60%)

All of these patterns are far more consistent than would be expected by chance. Reproduction of expected order (test 3), the most demanding test, occurs in more than half the cases, and the end-point means (test 2) are correct 85 percent of the time. Finally, more than two thirds of the individual ANOVAs (test 1) are significant. However, results from the factor analysis indicate that the measurements themselves are far from independent; factor scores computed from the analysis thus provide an overview of these results.

2.10.3 PLANNING CATEGORIES AND FACTOR SCORES

Mean factor scores for each of the six factors for each Planning Category are presented in table 2.4. Since virtually all the factor loadings in table 2.3 are positive, the factor scores relate positively to the values of the individual variables. One-way analyses of variance of mean factor scores across Planning Categories show significant differences in factor scores for five of the six individual factors and for an overall score. Furthermore, the order of the means follows a general pattern of relative sophistication of planning. The Corporate Strategic Planners are first in terms of the use of strategic planning tools, extent of corporate planning, and depth, and globalness of planning. Only for time horizon of planning are they not first or second. The Non-Planners score lowest on all but one individual factor, and the Division Financial Planners also tend to be low except for effort expended on gathering environmental information. The Division Strategic Planners tend to be second, although there was trading in positions of Division Strategic and Corporate Financial Planners – a pattern that persists throughout the book.

2.10.4 CLASSIFICATION AND PREDICTION
FOR PLANNING CATEGORIES

Further validation of the classification scheme is given by use of a five-group discriminant function to classify firms according to this scheme. Since the 53 variables in table 2.3 are far more than can be reasonably used in a discriminant function, a subset of 12 explanatory variables was chosen. The two variables with the largest factor loadings on each of the six factors were selected, all of which (table 2.3) had loadings of at least 0.7. These variables can be viewed as "representative" of the six factors, and their selection is objective in that the firm classification scheme itself is not related to their choice.

Overall, 74 of the 113 firms are classified correctly on the basis of these 12 variables (table 2.5) – a result far better than would be expected by chance. However, this result is unsurprising given the factor analysis results, for the discriminant function uses a subset of the measurements that define the factors, More importantly, since the classification scheme is roughly ordinal, it is useful to note that

Table 2.4
Mean Strategic Planning Factor Scores by Planning Category

Planning Category	Strategic Planning Factors						Overall Strategic Planning Score (Mean of Factor Score Means)
	Factor 1 Effort Expended in Gathering Environmental Information	Factor 2 Use of Strategic Planning Tools	Factor 3 Extent of Corporate Planning	Factor 4 Depth of Planning	Factor 5 Time Horizon of Planning	Factor 6 Globalness of Planning	
Corporate Strategic (n = 24)	.18(2)	.38(1)	.63(1)	.36(1)	.00(3)	.39(1)	.32(1)
Division Strategic (n = 37)	-.03(4)	.00(2)	-.26(3)	.35(2)	.03(2)	.23(2)	.06(2)
Corporate Financial (n = 34)	.05(3)	-.01(3)	.20(2)	-.30(3)	.29(1)	-.32(4)	-.02(3)
Division Financial (n = 11)	.30(1)	-.35(4)	-.93(5)	-.45(4)	-.09(4)	-.16(3)	-.28(4)
Non-Planners (n = 7)	-1.18(5)	-.69(5)	-.26(4)	-.98(5)	-1.42(5)	-.76(5)	-.88(5)
Significant† Differences Across Groups	Yes	No	Yes	Yes	Yes	Yes	

†α = .01

Corporate and Strategic Planning

Table 2.5
Classification of Firms in Planning Category
by Discriminant Function

Firm's Planning Category (Table 2.1)	Corporate Strategic Planners	Division Strategic Planners	Corporate Financial Planners	Division Financial Planners	Non-Planners	Total
	Firms Classified By Discriminant Function As:					
Corporate Strategic Planners	20	1	3	0	0	24
Division Strategic Planners	7	19	5	4	2	37
Corporate Financial Planners	5	5	23	1	0	34
Division Financial Planners	0	1	1	6	3	11
Non-Planners	0 / 32	1 / 27	0 / 32	0 / 11	6 / 11	7 / 113

only 16 firms are not classified in either the correct category or in an immediately neighboring one. The major off-diagonal result is a tendency to overclassify firms as Corporate Strategic Planners, in large part because of some use of formal planning tools by firms that have not yet arrived at an overall level of planning sophistication that would allow them to be considered "strategic" by our classification system. We stress that these results on classification are a verification of how our category system of five Planning Categories works rather than a justification of it.

2.11 Summary

In this chapter we examined the nature of strategic planning as discussed in the literature and presented our own perspective. We discussed the role of planning both as an organizational design variable and as an economic variable and suggested that there were at least two approaches from which planning can be viewed, a process approach and a functional approach. Both approaches are used in this book.

Two dimensions underlie the functional approach: adaptive and integrative. *Adaptation* is externally driven and is concerned with the choice of environments and matching the organization to environments; *integration* is internally focused and is concerned with harnessing the organization's resources so that the various parts of the firm pull together rather than head off in various directions.

The underlying principle of the process approach is an input►process►output system that embraces three input elements (information inputs, planning tools, planning organization), two process elements (planning activities, organizational planning environment) and two output elements (planning process outputs, planning outputs/ performance interface).

Subsequently, a category system of four planning types (Corporate Strategic Planners, Division Strategic Planners, Corporate Financial Planners, Division Financial Planners) and a group of Non-Planners was identified; a set of criteria was developed for assigning firms to groups and the 113 sample firms classified according to the criteria.

We then examined responses about planning from the sample, discovering that the Corporate Strategic, Corporate Financial, Division Financial, and Non-Planners perceive their planning to be more or less consistent with our classification as regards the corporateness and strategicness of their planning; there is, however, more confusion about the firms we classify as Division Strategic Planners, many of which see themselves as Corporate Planners.

Next, a factor analysis showed that strategic planning involves an emphasis on gathering information from the environment, the use of strategic planning tools, the development of longer term plans, and a global approach to planning and strategy development. We also postulated the generation of alternatives and stage of development of the company's planning process as key factors. These could not be confirmed, but the notion of planning integration emerged quite strongly, especially in the separate corporate and depth of planning factors. When the empirically developed strategic planning factors were compared to the Planning Category system, there was good overall correspondence. Finally, a subset of variables that loaded on the factors performed well in classifying the companies into the Planning Categories.

On the basis of these analyses of the sample firms' own evaluation of their planning and of differences in strategic planning over the five Planning Categories, we concluded that the category system is a useful and valid tool for analysis.

In the next chapter we examine the nature of planning in detail according to *adaptive* and *integrative* functions. For each element examined we compare results for the sample as a whole with the most sophisticated planners, the Corporate Strategic Planners.

Chapter 3

A Description
of Planning Practices

3.1 Introduction

This chapter provides a detailed description of planning
practices in our sample of 113 firms. We begin with a section on planning organization and personnel. The remainder of the chapter is
divided into two parts. The first presents results concerning the adaptive dimension of planning – efforts of the firm to coalign with its environment. This section deals with matters such as obtaining information from the environment, the strategic orientation of planning, use
of strategic planning tools, resource allocation criteria, and the comprehensiveness of the final plans. The second part deals with the integrative dimension of planning. It is concerned with issues such as
formal integration of plans; internal information flows; the focus of
influence and participation in, and the nature of, the goal and
strategy formulation process; the roles of line management and planners; the integrative value of planners; status and authority of planners; key planning activities; the extent to which the planning process
is established and formalized; the planning and performance review
process; and the role of goals.

Many of the measurements are on 5-point ordinal scales and
are reduced to summary statistics such as means. Since this approach
treats summary statistics computed from ordinal data as metric, caution in interpretation must be exercised. We seek consistent patterns
and try to avoid overinterpretation of marginal results. The basic
analysis involves contrasts of the Corporate Strategic Planners with
the rest of the sample. Throughout the chapter, which is organized
around the adaptive-integrative planning model, we also indicate

which of the seven elements of the planning process model contains the item in question.

3.2 Planning Organization and Personnel

Although the planning organization is not necessarily isomorphic with the operating organization, we found that, at the second level more than 90 percent of our sample is organized in the same way for both activities. Of the 10 percent that are organized differently, roughly half the planning units are profit centers and the personnel in charge of plan preparation also have operating responsibility.

The commitment of money and manpower to planning is substantial but not overwhelming. The average corporate planning department contains 7.4 professionals and has an annual budget of $604,000. However, in a later comparative study, we found that major Australian manufacturing companies spend almost ten times as much per sales dollar on corporate planning as our sample (Capon, Farley, and Hulbert 1985). The corporate planning departments of the Corporate Strategic Planners are on average half again as large and have significantly larger budgets than those of the other Planning Categories.

Planning is very labor intensive, and human inputs are generally acknowledged to be critical to both effective creation and implementation of plans. Planning specialists, economists, and financial specialists constitute the three leading backgrounds in corporate planning departments. Functional skills (in order: marketing, finance, engineering, and manufacturing) are the most prevalent skills among second-level planners. Rotation of line personnel through planning is minimal, even though such rotation is a recognized way of both familiarizing line personnel with planning and securing their commitment and cooperation. Firms classified as Corporate Strategic Planners have approximately twice as many second-level planners, and they show more commitment to rotation of line managers through planning than the other firms do.

Chief corporate planners average about four years on the job (significantly more than second-level planning managers) and have spent almost 15 years with the company. Their most likely backgrounds are in marketing or market development, finance (especially the firms classified as Corporate and Division Financial Planners), and operations. More than four fifths have graduate training, about half of them MBAs, but only 28 percent have special training in planning. Chief planners are thus experienced and well trained, with long-term organizational service, but they are not planning "specialists" and do not fit the frequently conjured up "whiz kid" image. They are generally satisfied with their jobs, those in the Corporate Strategic Planning firms significantly more so, and are also optimistic about advancement. Few see planning as an important career path; rather, most chief planners apparently view their planning assignments as a temporary stage in the experience-building process.

3.3 Adaptive Dimensions of Planning

Adaptive dimensions of planning include gathering environmental information, strategic orientation of planning, use of strategic planning tools, planning efforts in resource allocation and dealing with uncertainty, the making of key resource allocation decisions, and contents of the final plans. "Adaptation" runs unambiguously from low to high for almost all measurements, and Corporate Strategic Planners are expected to be in the polar high position.[1]

3.3.1 ENVIRONMENTAL INFORMATION

Since planning is essentially a forward-looking activity, forecasts are a critical input. Obtaining information from the external environment represents an adaptive element of planning, in contrast to the flow of internal information, which is integrative. We examine environmental information from two perspectives – the degree of effort expended in obtaining relevant forecasts and the anticipated impact on the planning process if externally obtained forecasts were to become unavailable. We also place special emphasis on competitive analysis. We expect that the Corporate Strategic Planners would commit greater effort to forecasting, would suffer more from loss of external forecasts, and would put more effort into competitive analysis.

3.3.1.1 Forecasting Effort

Analysis of ten types of forecasts (table 3.1) shows that our sample spends relatively little effort on forecasting.[2] Most effort is devoted to forecasts of the domestic economy and industry-level demand, with competitive forecasts being the only other area for which the effort expended is greater than the scale midpoint. At the more strategic end of the spectrum, sociocultural, human resources,

Table 3.1†

Effort Spent on Obtaining Environmental Information[1,2]

Type of Forecast	Sample Mean	Corporate Strategic Planners Mean	Rank
Domestic Economy	3.44	3.88	1***
Industry-level Demand	3.44	3.50	3**
Competitive	3.21	3.38	1*
Financial Markets	2.92	3.17	1
Governmental (legis- lative, regulatory)	2.86	3.17	1
Purchased Materials or Components	2.78	2.83	2
Technological	2.64	3.04	1**
Foreign Economies	2.58	3.13	1**
Human Resources	2.50	2.92	1**
Socio-Cultural	2.36	3.00	1***

[1] Means on 5-point scale: 1 = no effort, 5 = a great deal of effort

[2] Significant differences among types of forecast*** and Planning Categories***

†All items classified as Information Inputs from a process perspective.

***p < .01, **p < .05, *p < .10

foreign economies, technological, and purchased materials and components are the areas where least forecasting effort is spent.

That the major forecasting effort is on the demand side is not surprising, but we had expected somewhat more concern in areas such as sociocultural and technological, given the turbulence that many firms are experiencing. It is intriguing to speculate whether the relative dearth of this kind of forecasting effort is due to proven inability to forecast or to lack of concern. We suspect the latter, since most companies are not set up to deal with the kind of forecasting problems that result from external structural change (Capon and Hulbert 1986).

Except for rather conventional industry demand forecasts, Corporate Strategic Planners put significantly more effort into forecasting than the other Planning Categories do. They expend the most effort for eight of the ten forecast areas, especially the areas involving longer term environmental matters.

3.3.1.2 Unavailability of Forecasts

Overall, respondents believe that the impact of being unable to purchase externally supplied forecasts would be relatively small (mean of 2.46 on a 5 point scale: 1 = no impact, 5 = severe impact); there are no differences among Planning Categories.

3.3.1.3 Competitive Analysis

Competitive analysis should be a major determinant of strategy development (Porter 1980) and hence an important element of adaptive planning. However, the focus of most competitive analysis is at the second level of management or in marketing (table 3.2). In both cases a somewhat shorter term view of competitors and competition as more or less fixed is more likely to be taken than if the analysis were a major corporate planning activity.

Table 3.2†

Competitive Analysis[1]

Locus[2]	Sample Mean	Corporate Strategic Planners Mean	Rank
Second-Level Planning Activity	3.81	4.2	1
Sales and Marketing	3.52	3.71	1
Major Corporate Planning Activity	3.23	3.13	4
Focus[3]			
Analyze Products	3.30	3.33	2
Identify Cost Structures	2.81	3.16	1

[1]Means on 5-point scale: 1 = disagree, 5 = agree on locus/focus of competitive analysis

[2]Significant differences among planning loci***

[3]Significant differences among planning foci*** and Planning Categories**

†All items classified as Planning Activities from a process perspective.

***p < .01

As regards the focus of competitive analysis, the major efforts are in analyzing competitors' products, with less effort placed on equally important strategic issues such as identifying competitors' cost structures.

3.3.2 STRATEGIC ORIENTATION

Both the effort placed on different types of planning and the extent to which planning is global in scope reflect the strategic orientation of planning.

3.3.2.1 Types of Planning

All firms put significantly more effort into plans (table 3.3) with "strategic" orientation (long-range, acquisition, and divestiture planning) than into operational planning. Modest effort is placed into

Table 3.3†

Strategic Orientation of Planning[1,2,3]

"Strategic" Planning	Sample Mean	Corporate Strategic Planners Mean	Rank
Long Range (5-10 years)	3.67	4.21	1***
Acquisition	3.51	3.80	1***
Divestiture	3.21	3.25	2**
Long Run Mission	2.86	3.46	1***
Contingency	2.21	2.29	2***
"Non-Strategic" Planning			
Action or Operational (1-3 years)	2.99	2.79	4***
Short-term Emergency	2.35	2.04	4***

[1] Means on 5-point scale: 1 = no effort, 5 = a great deal of effort expended

[2] Significant differences among types of planning*** and Planning Categories***

[3] Results are from a 7 × 5 (plan type × Planning Category) two factor ANOVA. Item-by-item significance is based on univariate analysis. Results throughout the chapter refer to analogous ANOVAs.

†All items classified as Planning Activities from a process perspective.

***p < .01

long-run mission planning, but little into contingency or emergency planning. As expected, the Corporate Strategic Planners make greater corporate commitments to "strategic" planning types overall, though they are less clearly dominant for divestiture and contingency planning; they also place less emphasis on shorter term planning.

The most popular time horizon for the firm's guiding long-range plan, chosen by 60 percent of firms, is five years, followed by three years (23%) and ten years (12%). The remaining firms use a time horizon of two years or less; Corporate Strategic Planners use the longest time horizons.

One modest surprise is that relatively little effort goes into contingency planning; only 40 percent of the firms develop formal contingency plans as part of their long-range planning effort. Of these, more than half develop such plans at both the corporate and second level: 14 percent at corporate alone, and 33 percent only at the second level. Seventy percent include both uncontrollable environmental factors and controllable strategic actions as contingent variables.[3]

3.3.2.2 Global Orientation of Planning

Despite considerable emphasis on the globalization of U.S. business over the last decade, planning in general is only modestly global. Corporate planning is slightly more global than second-level planning, but there is little difference among the various types of planning for functional strategies (table 3.4). Corporate Strategic

Table 3.4†
Global Orientation of Planning[1,2]

Global Orientation of:	Sample Mean	Corporate Strategic Planners Mean	Rank
Overall Planning			
Corporate Planning	3.25	4.07	1***
Second-level Planning	2.84	3.42	1
Functional Planning			
Procurement Strategies	3.04	3.58	1*
Production Strategies	2.95	3.50	1***
Marketing Strategies	2.88	3.29	2**

[1] Means on 5-point scale: 1 = disagree, 5 = agree that planning is global

[2] Significant differences among Planning Categories***

†All items classified as Planning Activities from a process perspective.

***p < .01, **p < .05, *p < .10

Planners have succeeded in making their planning more global, particularly at the corporate level. This finding is consistent with our assessment of the strategic content of planning presented in chapter 2.

3.3.3 STRATEGIC PLANNING TOOLS

Information obtained from the environment and from within the organization is rarely used in raw form; rather it is typically subject to analysis and summary. The choice of method for summary can be very important. In this section we examine the extent to which our sample firms use certain analytic frameworks, models, and computer systems to process raw data in their planning processes.

3.3.3.1 Analytic Devices

As noted in chapters 1 and 2, the 1970s saw the development of a number of analytic devices to aid in the resource allocation process, and these play a prominent role in most discussions of strategic planning. Among the better publicized are product portfolio analysis developed by the Boston Consulting Group (Day 1977, Hax and Majluf 1983a), policy matrices of the types associated with Shell Chemical Company (Hussey 1978), and with General Electric and McKinsey & Company (*Business Week* 1975, Hax and Majluf 1983b), the strategy center concept developed by the Arthur D. Little Consulting Company (Patel and Younger 1978), a pragmatic approach to portfolio and strategy analysis advocated by Booz Allen and Hamilton, product/market fit analysis associated with Igor Ansoff (Ansoff 1965), and results of the Profit Impact of Market Strategy studies (PIMS) (e.g., Schoeffler, Buzzell, and Heany 1974).

Given the high visibility of most of these devices, their general influence is less than we expected (table 3.5). Of the six approaches examined, the portfolio analysis approach of the Boston Consulting Group (BCG) was reported as having influenced corporate strategy significantly more than any other, but even the sample mean for this item does not exceed the scale midpoint. The Corporate Strategic Planners report greater use of these devices overall, an effect most marked for the techniques we identified as most influential.

Anticipated future influence of these various tools shows a similar pattern, and there are no significant differences between past and expected future uses. Contrary to the unexpectedly low degree of influence of the tools themselves, however, was a high level of agreement with the statement that, in the company's experience, "it was generally most profitable to have the largest share of a served market"—an opinion that is at the foundation of many strategic planning tools and a major empirical finding from PIMS (Buzzell, Gale, and Sultan 1975).

More detailed analysis of responses to portfolio model questions reveals that about two thirds of the sample use one or more of these tools, and almost 50 percent report using them at both corporate and second levels. Not surprisingly, Corporate Strategic Planners are the most extensive users, and three quarters of this group use one or more of these planning aids at both corporate and second levels.

Corporate and Strategic Planning

Table 3.5†
Past and Expected Impact of
Analytic Devices on Content of Corporate Strategy[1]

Portfolio Models	PAST[2] Mean	Corporate Strategic Planners Mean	Corporate Strategic Planners Rank	ANTICIPATED[3] Mean	Corporate Strategic Planners Mean	Corporate Strategic Planners Rank
Product Port-folio (Boston Consulting Group)	2.95	3.30	1*	3.00	3.17	2***
Policy Matrices (Shell Chemi-cal, GE/ McKinsey)	2.18	2.65	1**	2.37	2.63	1
Strategy Center Concept (A.D. Little)	2.04	2.51	1	2.02	2.42	1
Portfolio & Strategy Analyses (Booz Allen)	1.81	1.79	3	1.90	1.83	4
Other Models						
Product/Market Fit Analysis (Ansoff)	1.84	1.88	3	2.06	1.92	3
PIMS (Strategic Planning Institute)	2.19	2.51	1	2.35	2.75	1

[1]Means on 5-point scale: 1 = no influence, 5 = very great influence

[2]Significant differences among models*** and Planning Categories***

[3]Significant differences among models*** and Planning Categories***

†All items classified as Planning Tools from a process perspective.

***p < .01, **p < .05

Applications of portfolio models (table 3.6) have been more or less limited to longer term resource allocation and cash flow, in contrast to more extensive uses, such as competitor, customer, and supplier analysis suggested by Porter (1980). Corporate Strategic Planners consistently make more extensive use of the portfolio models than the other Planning Categories.

3.3.3.2 Models and Computer Systems

Corporate-level models are used moderately, and only 27 percent of respondents indicate no use whatsoever.[4] Most widely used

Table 3.6†

Specific Use of Portfolio Models[1,2]

Type of Use	Sample Mean	Corporate Strategic Planners Mean	Rank
Cash Flow Management Tool	2.47	2.75	1
Guide to Setting Resource Allocation Priorities	2.41	3.33	1**
Analyze Competitors	2.05	2.75	1**
Analyze Customers	1.60	2.17	1*
Analyze Suppliers	1.24	1.67	1

[1]Means on 5-point scale: 1 = never used, 5 = extensively used

[2]Significant differences among types of use*** and Planning Categories***

†All items classified as Planning Tools from a process perspective.

**p < .05, *p < .10

are forecasting, planning, and budgeting models (by 58% of the companies), followed by econometric models (31%). Only 19 percent of the companies claim use of decision models, and just 7 percent are using models based on PIMS. Virtually without exception, companies using models report that they are being used regularly and are perceived as having a relatively high degree of usefulness (mean of 3.87 on a 5-point scale: 1 = not at all useful, 5 = very useful). Corporate Strategic Planners use models more than the other Categories.

Second-level planners employ models less than corporate planners do. Forecasting models are indicated in use by 31 percent of the companies, financial and decision models by 23 percent, and planning models by 19 percent. Overall, 61 percent of companies report use of at least one type of model at the second level. Corporate Strategic Planners and Division Strategic Planners make significantly more use of models at this level than the other firms do.

Five types of computer systems dedicated to planning were identified: company-wide planning data systems, systems to compare actual performance with goals, systems to analyze performance, systems to perform financial analyses, and stored data bases. Overall, 53 percent of the sample reported the use of at least one such system. The highest usage rate (only 19%) is for company-wide planning data systems; 14 percent have systems comparing actual performance with goals; the same proportion have systems for performing financial analyses.

Thirty-four percent of companies reported use of at least

one type of system that links a corporate planning system with
second-level units. Four types of such linking systems were identified:
strategy-linking models, data entry and retrieval, data management,
and input/output systems. Overall, the use of computer systems for
purposes other than relatively straightforward financial analysis is
limited.

3.3.4 PLANNING EFFORTS

The extent of planning efforts in two key adaptive areas is
addressed in terms of the focus of effort on resource allocation and on
dealing with uncertainty.

3.3.4.1 Resource Allocation

Influence upon resource allocation is the key to effective
planning (table 3.7). There is good agreement across companies that
the planning process has improved the company's long-range resource
allocation decisions, that it is a key device for allocating corporate
resources throughout the company, that long-range allocations are
made as an integral part of the corporate planning process, and that it
assures allocation of scarce resources to high-yield uses. In each case

Table 3.7†
Resource Allocation Emphasis in Planning[1,2]

The Planning Process:	Sample Mean	Corporate Strategic Planners	
		Mean	Rank
has improved the company's long range resource allocation decisions	3.90	4.24	1**
is a key device for allocating corporate resources throughout the company	3.87	4.38	1**
assures that scarce resources are allocated to high yield use	3.45	3.88	1
Long range resource allocation decisions are made as an integral part of the corporate planning process	3.82	4.13	1*

[1]Means on 5-point scale: 1 = disagree, 5 = agree

[2]Significant differences among Planning Categories***

†All items classified as Planning Activities from a process perspective.

***p < .01, **p < .05, *p < .10

the Corporate Strategic Planners are in the expected first position and are significantly different overall.

3.3.4.2 Uncertainty and Risk Reduction

Dealing with uncertainty about the future is an important element of longer term decisions about resource allocation today (table 3.8). Overall, there is general agreement that planning has not

Table 3.8†
Role of Planning in Dealing with Uncertainty[1]

Planning:	Sample Mean	Corporate Strategic Planners Mean	Rank
†† has not constrained the strategic risk taking behavior of lower level managers[2]	3.52	3.62	1
is a means for systematically dealing with uncertainty	3.36	3.88	1*
enables the company to avoid unacceptably high levels of risk	3.25	3.46	1

[1]Means on 5-point scale: 1 = disagree, 5 = agree

[2]Significant differences among Planning Categories**

†All items classified as Planning Activities from a process perspective.

††Scale reversed for easier exposition.

**p < .05, *p < .10

constrained the strategic risk-taking behavior of lower level managers, is rather a means of systematically dealing with uncertainty, and has enabled companies to avoid unacceptably high levels of risk. Corporate Strategic Planners are in the expected extreme positions and significantly different overall.

3.3.5 RESOURCE ALLOCATION DECISIONS

A key characteristic of strategic planning involves budgetary distinctions between expenditures designed to bring long-run versus short-run benefits and the criteria employed for evaluating expenditure proposals designed to bring long-run benefits. This is a key difference between strategic planning (which should make such distinctions explicitly) and financial planning (which often does not make such distinctions).

3.3.5.1 Long-Run/Short-Run Distinctions
An essential ingredient of strategy development is acknowledgment that various investments yield different patterns of return in the near run versus the longer run. Our sample indicates that a clear distinction is made between long-run and short-run benefits for investments both in market development and in research and development (table 3.9), and this is certainly a positive result. How-

Table 3.9†
Budgetary Distinction Between Long-Run and Short-Run Benefits[1,2]

Budget Type	Sample Mean	Corporate Strategic Planners Mean	Rank
Market Development	4.06	4.33	1*
Research & Development	3.66	4.08	2**

[1]Means on 5-point scale: 1 = no distinction; 5 = very clear distinction

[2]Significant differences among budget types*** and Planning Categories***

†All items classified as Planning Activities from a process perspective.

***p < .01, **p < .05, *p < .10

ever, the distinction is made more clearly for market development than for research and development, a somewhat worrisome situation given the generally longer and more uncertain yields associated with R&D. Corporate Strategic Planners are more inclined to make long-run/short-run distinctions than others, as expected.

3.3.5.2 Resource Allocation Criteria for Long-Run Benefits
The criteria used for evaluation of expenditure proposals for long-range benefits are of critical importance. Of 12 different criteria, all except short-term cash flow benefits are evaluated as more important than the scale midpoint (table 3.10). The most important criterion is forecast return on investment; it and track record of the unit requesting funds are the only criteria to average more than 4.0 on the 5-point scales. Other highly rated criteria are: forecast sales growth, growth of market for which expenditures requested, impact on company resource needs, forecast net operating profit, and discounted cash flow analysis. Since this set of criteria was used in chapter 2 to characterize the Corporate Strategic Planners, the importance of the individual criteria are of course significantly different among Planning Categories.

Table 3.10 also shows that Corporate Strategic Planners are the polar group for four of the five "strategic" criteria and for both

Table 3.10†
Criteria for Evaluation
of Expenditure Proposals for Long-Range Benefits[1,2]

"Strategic" Criteria	Sample Mean	Corporate Strategic Planners Mean	Rank
Forecast sales growth	3.91	4.29	1**
Growth of market for expenditure requested	3.90	4.29	1***
Impact on company resource needs	3.80	3.96	2
Forecast market share growth	3.67	4.24	1*
Present market share position	3.48	4.15	1***
"Non-Strategic" Criteria			
Forecast return on investment	4.35	4.21	5
Discounted cash flow analysis	3.92	3.75	4
Forecast net operating profit	3.90	4.04	2
Impact on earnings per share	3.57	3.50	4
Short term cash flow benefits	2.96	2.50	5*
Historical Criteria			
Track record of unit requesting funds	4.07	4.33	1*
Track record of manager of unit requesting funds	3.66	4.04	1**

[1]Means on a 5-point scale: 1 = totally unimportant, 5 = very important

[2]Significant differences among evaluation criteria*** and Planning Categories***

†All items classified as Planning Activities from a process perspective.

***p < .01, **p < .05, *p < .10

"historical" criteria (which reflect success of past decisions) but are at the opposite polar group or next to polar positions for four of the "nonstrategic" criteria. The Corporate Strategic Planners place great emphasis on strategic criteria such as growth in sales, market share and market growth, and present market share position; they weigh forecast ROI, discounted cash flow analysis, impact on EPS, and short-term cash flow benefits less heavily than the other Planning Categories.

Respondents were asked how these criteria would differ (if at all) under different market growth conditions. In cases where market growth is less than or equal to real GNP growth, 54 percent reported that it would make no difference, 10 percent indicated that they would not be likely to enter such a market, and 31 percent said that more emphasis would be placed on short-term considerations. When market growth is significantly higher than real GNP growth, about the same percentage (53%) indicated no difference on all criteria. Twenty-five percent reported a greater emphasis on financial measures, but a surprisingly small percentage (20%) indicated more emphasis on market share or differential advantage. No significant differences are found across Planning Categories, indicating that a key criterion in many planning paradigms (market growth) may actually play a relatively minor role in making distinctions when evaluating proposals for resources.

3.3.6 CONTENT OF PLANS

An important strategic issue is the extent to which the contents of the final plans focus on strategic matters.

3.3.6.1 Corporate Plan

Respondents whose firms develop corporate plans were asked to provide either a copy of the table of contents of the most recent corporate plan or to indicate the major headings of the plan. The responses to this question were employed to develop a 12-category coding scheme.

The Corporate Strategic Planners use several headings significantly more often: goals and objectives, company analyses, other environmental analyses, key issues/problems/opportunities, and corporate, second-level, and third-level strategies. They also use mission and market analyses more frequently. The Corporate Financial Planners use headings of forecasts and budgets and customer analysis more frequently. The total number of nonbudgetary headings for the Corporate Strategic Planners is significantly greater than for the Corporate Financial Planners, indicating a more strategic approach to planning.

3.3.6.2 Second-Level Business Plans

A similar analysis for second-level business plans revealed that the Corporate Strategic Planners have plans with more headings than the other Planning Categories (the Division Strategic Planners were a close second). As with corporate plans, these headings deal with strategic elements of planning to a greater extent than those of the Financial Planners (Corporate and Division).

3.4 Integrative Dimensions of Planning

Integrative dimensions of planning comprise those elements that tend to provide organizational integration and coordination. Planning is not, of course, the only means for integration, though it may be particularly important for companies with diverse product/market businesses. Included under integrative elements are: formal integration of plans; information flows and exchanges; patterns of influence and participation in, and the nature of, the goal and strategy formulation processes; the roles of line management and planners; the integrative value of planners; the status and authority of planners; key planning activities; formalization of planning; planning and performance review; and the role of goals. For most measurements, the degree of integration implied by a particular item runs clearly in one direction; we expect the Corporate Strategic Planners to be in the polar position in that direction.

3.4.1 FORMAL INTEGRATION OF PLANS
        Two key elements of plan integration are across function and over time.

3.4.1.1 Corporate/Functional Plans
        Functional plans are integrated with corporate planning to only a moderate extent (table 3.11). Financial plans, as expected, are more integrated, but plans involving marketing, manufacturing, and human resources are less so. There are significant differences

Table 3.11†
Integration of Functional Plans with Corporate Planning[1,2]

Functional Area	Sample Mean	Corporate Strategic Planners Mean	Rank
Financial	4.05	4.38	1*
Marketing	3.15	3.29	1
Manufacturing	3.06	3.33	1***
Human Resources	2.72	3.38	1*

[1]Means on 5-point scale: 1 = disagree, 5 = agree on a high degree of coordination

[2]Significant differences among functional areas*** and Planning Categories***

†All items classified as Planning Activities from a process perspective.

***p < .01, * < .10

among Planning Categories, and for each functional area the Corporate Strategic Planners have the highest degree of integration.

3.4.1.2 Time Horizons

A second element of organizational integration involves the relationship between preparation of the firms' long-run and short-run plans. The received wisdom of planning is not only that coordination between longer run strategic plans and shorter run operational plans is desirable but also that longer run plans should be prepared first and short-run plans made to fit within the parameters defined by the long-run plan.

The systems of preparation used by our sample firms surprised us (table 3.12). About 80 percent of firms produce plans with

Table 3.12†

Development of Long-Range and Short-Range Plans[1]

Plan Development Method	Percent of Sample	Corporate Strategic Planners Percent	Rank
Prepared independently and not coordinated	32	42	1
Long-range plan prepared first, short-range plan fitted into long-range plan	32	42	1
Short- and long-range plans prepared simultaneously	15	13	3
Short-range plan prepared first, longer-range plan then extended	17	0	5
Short-range plan prepared first, long-range plan modified from previous year	3	0	5

[1]Significant differences among Planning Categories*

†All items classified as Planning Activities from a process perspective.

*p < .10

more than one time horizon – generally two; a third of both Corporate Strategic Planners and Corporate Financial Planners plan with three time horizons. However, only 32 percent prepare long-range plans first and then fit the short-range plans into them. The Corporate Strategic Planners, as expected, use this approach most frequently. Surprisingly, they are also the leading group for independent preparation and lack of coordination in the development of short-run and long-run plans, the category that accounts for another 32 percent of the total sample. Perhaps, however, they have recognized the potential dangers of too close coordination, where strategic planning deteriorates into a long-term budgeting exercise, and have therefore chosen to keep the short-term and long-term activities completely separate. Finally, a minority of firms prepare short- and long-run plans simultaneously.

It appears that, despite the pervasiveness of planning, much remains to be done in integrating plan development across different time horizons, though the Corporate Strategic Planners seem to be the most sophisticated in this regard.

3.4.2 INFORMATION FLOW

One way in which planning can help achieve integration is through the flow of information through the organization. While the creation of too much information clearly has negative consequences, the free flow of information is a sine qua non for effective planning.

3.4.2.1 Forecast Transmission from Corporate

Earlier in this chapter, the degree of effort devoted to forecasting a variety of environments was discussed. Superior integration can be achieved to the extent that this information is made available to lower levels in the organization and can be used for planning.

In general, there is only limited transmission of forecasts to lower levels in the organization. Transmission is highest in areas that receive the greatest forecast effort – the domestic economy and industry level demand (table 3.13).

The Corporate Strategic Planners are the most committed to forecast transmission and lead in nine of ten forecast areas. Canonical analysis between effort expended in different forecast areas and extent of transmission confirmed the pattern that higher within-firm effort on forecasting is related to greater transmission.

3.4.2.2 Internal Information Transmission

Quality internal information is, of course, needed to augment environmental forecasts. Companies are in general satisfied with the quality of planning information that is obtained from accounting, finance, manufacturing, and sales and marketing – more so for finance and less so for manufacturing (table 3.14). There are no differences among Planning Categories.

3.4.2.3 Information Exchange at the Corporate Level

Across all firms, there is a relatively high level of information exchange between the planning group and corporate officers (table 3.15). It is especially high at the most senior levels, but the relatively low degree of exchange with senior line officers (especially

Table 3.13[†]

Forecast Transmission from the Corporate Level[1,2]

Forecast Type	Sample Mean	Corporate Strategic Planners Mean	Rank
Domestic Economy	3.68	3.88	1***
Industry-level Demand	2.96	3.88	1***
Purchased Materials and Components	2.74	3.08	1***
Competitive	2.74	3.17	1***
Governmental (legislative, regulatory)	2.58	2.96	1**
Foreign Economies	2.57	3.42	1***
Technological	2.38	2.67	1**
Social/Cultural	2.30	2.58	1**
Human Resources	2.27	2.54	1
Financial Markets	2.15	2.17	3**

[1]Means on 5-point scale: 1 = no transmission, 5 = extensive transmission

[2]Significant differences among type of forecast*** and Planning Categories***

†All items classified as Information Inputs from a process perspective.

***$p < .01$, **$p < .05$

Table 3.14[†]

High Quality Information for Planning
Obtained from Functional Areas[1,2]

Functional Area	Sample Mean	Corporate Strategic Planners Mean	Rank
Finance	3.88	3.92	2
Accounting	3.78	3.83	2
Marketing and Sales	3.51	3.67	2
Manufacturing	3.26	3.33	2

[1]Means on 5-point scale: 1 = disagree, 5 = agree that high quality information is received

[2]Significant differences among functional areas***

†All items classified as Information Inputs from a process perspective.

***$p < .01$

Table 3.15†

Information Exchange Frequency at Corporate Level[1,2]

Organizational Position	Sample Mean	Corporate Strategic Planners Mean	Rank
CEO/COO/Executive Committee	4.1	4.21	2
Executive V.P.	4.14	4.30	1
Chairman/Vice Chairman	4.10	4.00	3
Planning and Staff	4.02	4.10	1
Treasurer/Controller/Financial V.P.	3.93	3.43	3**
Senior Line Executives	3.45	3.15	5

[1]Means on 5-point scale: 1 = no exchange, 5 = extensive exchange

[2]Significant differences among organizational positions***

†All items classified as Planning Organization from a process perspective.

***p < .01, **p < .05

for the Corporate Strategic Planners) is probably a bad sign for implementation.[5]

3.4.3 INFLUENCE AND PARTICIPATION
3.4.3.1 Internal Influence Sources

Patterns of influence on eight aspects of planning by the board of directors, the CEO, top second-level line management, and the planning department are shown in table 3.16. Not only are there significant differences in influence among the four management groups overall, but also for each management group there are significantly different patterns among elements of the process. The most apparent pattern is the relative lack of influence of the board of directors – even in matters such as final approval of the plan. The high level of influence of the CEO overall is especially evident in final approval and in developing corporate objectives, goals, and strategies; the major patterns of influence of top second-level line managers, however, are in mission definition and goal setting at the second level. The corporate planning department is dominant in terms of format but also, somewhat surprisingly, in terms of assumptions used in the final plan. This latter finding may provide the planners with considerable leverage on the entire process. (In interpreting the results on influence of the corporate planning department, it is important to remember the identities of our respondents.)

Table 3.16†

Patterns of Internal Influence on the Planning Process[1,2]

Planning Process Element	Board of Directors[3]			CEO[4]			Top Second Level Line Management[4]			Planning Department[4]		
	Sample Mean	Corporate Strategic Planners Mean	Rank	Sample Mean	Corporate Strategic Planners Mean	Rank	Sample Mean	Corporate Strategic Planners Mean	Rank	Sample Mean	Corporate Strategic Planners Mean	Rank
Approval of Final Corporate Plan	2.90	3.25	1	4.50	4.92	1***	2.25	2.58	1	3.04	2.92	3*
Assumptions Used in Final Plan	1.42	1.42	3	3.39	3.42	3	2.78	3.04	1	4.03	4.21	2***
Objectives Embodied in Final Plan	2.33	2.63	1	4.33	4.54	2***	3.06	3.25	1	3.64	4.04	1***
Strategies Embodied in Final Plan	2.06	2.17	2	4.13	4.25	2***	3.35	3.50	2*	3.52	3.92	1***
Development of Missions for Second Level Units	1.39	1.42	3	3.67	3.67	3	4.40	4.46	4***	3.04	3.21	1*
Setting Corporate Goals	2.13	2.08	3	4.68	4.75	3	2.40	2.46	3	3.46	4.03	1***
Setting Second Level Goals	1.40	1.54	1	3.96	4.00	2	4.04	4.42	1**	3.14	3.58	1*
Format of Plan	1.12	1.17	3	2.70	2.63	3	1.94	1.96	3*	4.45	4.83	1***

[1] Means on 5-point scale: 1 = not at all influential, 5 = very influential

[2] Significant differences among the four management groups***

[3] Significant differences among items***

[4] Significant differences among items*** and among Planning Categories***

†All items classified as Planning Organization from a process perspective.

***p < .01, **p < .05, *p < .10

Except for the responses concerning boards of directors, there are significant differences among Planning Categories. As a result, CEO influence on approval of the final corporate plan is especially high for Corporate Strategic Planners, though many other aspects of planning seem to be delegated to the planning department. By contrast, top second-level line management has the highest degree of influence overall in the Corporate Strategic Planners – generally a good sign for implementation. Key influence in the setting of second-level goals is most frequently provided by second-level management, though the CEO and the planning department are also important.

The results from the perspective of the Corporate Strategic Planners are mixed. The highest degree of line influence is clearly a positive factor, but this is offset to some extent by the degree of planning department influence over the plan. Finally, Corporate Strategic Planners are not consistently the leading Category in terms of CEO influence.

Notwithstanding the influence of the various positions in the planning process, influence on the content of the final corporate plan is highest for the CEO, followed by the executive V.P. (table 3.17). Only the influence for senior line executives is below the scale midpoint, which, as noted earlier, may have unfortunate consequences in implementation.[6] The Corporate Strategic Planners report

Table 3.17†
Influence on Final Content of the Corporate Plan[1,2]

Organizational Position	Sample Mean	Corporate Strategic Planners Mean	Rank
CEO/COO/Executive Committee	4.54	4.86	1**
Executive V.P.	4.06	4.20	2
Chairman/Vice Chairman	3.90	5.00	1
Treasurer/Controller/Financial V.P.	3.59	3.75	1
Planning and Staff	3.40	3.83	1
Senior Line Executives	2.58	2.72	1

[1]Means on 5-point scale: 1 = not-at-all influential, 5 = extensive influence

[2]Significant differences among organizational positions*** and Planning Categories***

†All items classified as Planning Organization from a process perspective.

*** p < .01, ** p < .05

the greatest degree of influence overall, a factor that may indicate a more participative planning process in these firms.

3.4.3.2 Internal and External Influences

Outsiders may play an important role in strategic planning, especially in the early phases of adoption of planning, when considerable external expertise may be sought. Examples are academic consultants, consulting firms, and senior executives hired from consulting companies, close competitors, or other industries. The influence of outsiders was compared to a benchmark of senior executives promoted from within the organization (table 3.18). The

Table 3.18†

Internal and External Influences on Key Strategic Decisions[1,2]

Source of Influence	Sample Mean	Corporate Strategic Planners	
		Mean	Rank
Senior executives promoted from within the organization	4.59	4.75	2
Senior executives hired from different industries	2.16	2.21	2
Consulting firms	2.10	2.17	2*
Senior executives hired from close competition	1.84	1.29	5***
Senior executives hired from consulting companies	1.48	1.33	4
Academic consultants	1.37	1.46	1
Senior executives hired from academic institutions	1.13	1.17	2

[1]Means on 5-point scale: 1 = no influence, 5 = a great deal of influence

[2]Significant differences among sources of influence***

†All items classified as Planning Organization from a process perspective.

***p < .01, *p < .10

results are very clear; strategy and planning are largely home grown. All of the external influences average less than 2.2 on the 5-point scale compared to 4.59 for managers promoted from within. There are no significant overall differences among Planning Categories, though the Corporate Strategic Planners (surprisingly) rank lowest overall on external influence.

      Similar patterns of little influence by outside consultants were found for both acquisition and divestiture decisions. The exception is for after-the-fact validation of both types of decision where outsiders' degree of influence is moderate.

3.4.4 GOAL AND STRATEGY FORMULATION PROCESS

An important integrative issue is the manner in which goals and strategy are developed.

The CEO was reported to set corporate goals in slightly more than 60 percent of the firms and corporate strategy in slightly less than 30 percent; by contrast, the Corporate Strategic Planners reported significantly lower fractions of goal and strategy setting by CEOs (33% for goals and 15% for strategy), while six of the seven Non-Planners reported that corporate strategy was set by the CEO. CEOs rarely set second-level goals. Consistent with the findings on influence in the planning process, boards of directors did not play a leading role in setting either corporate goals or corporate strategy.

Processes more frequently involve negotiation than pure top-down approaches. Negotiations between the CEO and second-level line management were reported by slightly more than 30 percent of firms for both corporate goals and corporate strategy and by about 20 percent for second-level goals. Negotiation between a corporate management group and second-level management was reported at 20 percent for corporate goals, 30 percent for corporate strategy, and 60 percent for second-level goals. The Corporate Strategic Planners reported greater overall levels of participation than the other Planning Categories.

3.4.5 PLANNING AND LINE MANAGEMENT

For effective planning, senior line management is particularly important. Planning is of course not costless, and the implicit cost represented by the commitment of valuable management time probably exceeds the planning budget itself in many cases. Indeed, senior operating managers reported an average of four hours per week working on long-term planning (significantly more for the Corporate Strategic Planners who reported spending almost seven hours). Line managers apparently view planning (table 3.19) as a means to help develop long-range policies and strategies, although there is a worrisome tendency to see a heavy focus on developing shorter term plans and budgets as well.

Senior managers of the Corporate Strategic Planners are viewed as embracing both long- and short-term purposes to a greater extent than the other Categories and conversely tending not to view planning as arbitrarily imposed from the top. Although their strong

Corporate and Strategic Planning

Table 3.19†

Senior Line Managers' Views of Planning[1,2]

The Purpose of Planning is:	Sample Mean	Corporate Strategic Planners	
		Mean	Rank
to develop corporate strategy and long range planning policies	4.15	4.38	1*
to develop a set of action programs and operating plans	3.98	4.13	1
to provide a frame of reference for the operating budget	3.89	3.92	2
to identify external opportunities and threats	3.62	3.88	1
†† not "to satisfy corporate and get them off my back"	3.42	3.75	1
a mind stretching creative exercise	3.05	3.25	1***

[1]Means on a 5-point scale: 1 = very few senior executives feel this way, 5 = most senior executives feel this way

[2]Significant differences among items*** and Planning Categories***

†All items classified as Organization Planning Environment from a process perspective.

††Scale reversed for easier exposition.

***p < .01, *p < .10

agreement with the short-term purposes of planning is worrisome, it may result from the overall greater commitment to planning per se by the Corporate Strategic Planners.

3.4.6 INTEGRATIVE VALUE OF PLANNERS

The planners themselves can also fulfill important integrative functions. We examine three areas: the value added by corporate planning, the degree of integration within the planning group, and various other integrative functions that the planners fulfill.

3.4.6.1 Value Added by Corporate Planning

The planning systems of most companies involve some aggregation or review of second-level plans, and the involvement of a corporate group is a means by which value can be added to plans developed at a lower level. Table 3.20 indicates that such additional

Table 3.20†

Added Value of Corporate Planning

Over Completed Second-Level Plans[1,2]

Areas	Sample Mean	Corporate Strategic Planners Mean	Rank
Financial	3.38	3.90	1***
Markets	2.90	2.88	3***
Competitive Analysis	2.86	2.79	3***
Organizational Structures	2.26	2.08	4*
Research and Development	2.23	2.46	2**
Raw Materials Requirements	2.09	2.04	3**
Human Resources	2.04	1.92	3*

[1]Means on 5-point scale: 1 = no added value, 5 = major added value

[2]Significant differences among areas*** and Planning Categories***

†All items classified as Planning Activities from a process perspective.

***p < .01, **p < .05, *p < .10

value is generally viewed as modest. Except for financial elements, Corporate Strategic Planners fall in the middle of the distributions.

3.4.6.2 Planning Group Integration

Generally, corporate planning departments are seen as having a high degree of overall integration; there is both a feeling of teamwork and a well-defined "chain of command" within planning (table 3.21). Management is in general viewed as taking an interest in the output of the corporate planning department, but a disturbing finding is the lack of agreement that the goals and objectives of the corporate planning department are clear to everyone. Overall, the Corporate Strategic Planners have higher levels of integration than the other groups.

3.4.6.3 Corporate Planning Activities

The various functions that the corporate planning group fulfills can be classified into five areas: specific planning tasks, overall planning responsibility, assistance at the corporate level, assistance at the second level, and improving planning performance. Corporate Strategic Planners should devote more effort to each of these.

Effort devoted to specific activities under each heading is assessed in table 3.22. The overall picture is one of balanced effort in most spheres of planning, with less effort devoted to ancillary activities such as improving data quality or identifying financing needs.

Corporate and Strategic Planning

Table 3.21†

Planning Group Integration[1,2]

Integrative Elements	Sample Mean	Corporate Strategic Planners	
		Mean	Rank
There is a feeling of teamwork in the Corporate Planning Department[a]	4.19	4.21	3**
Management takes an active interest in the output and recommendations of the planning department[a]			
a) Senior[a]	3.96	4.25	1**
b) Second-level[a]	3.67	3.88	1
The "chain of command" for planning is well defined[3,a]	3.92	4.42	1***
People in the company are familiar with planning models[b]	3.18	3.58	1***
Goals and objectives of the corporate planning department are clear to Everyone[a]	2.93	3.04	2**

[1]Means on 5-point scales

  [a]1 = not at all characteristic, 5 = very characteristic
  [b]1 = not at all familiar with, 5 = very familiar with and using

[2]Significant differences among items*** and Planning Categories***

[3]Question asked as "poorly defined"; scale reversed for exposition

†All items classified as Organization Planning Environment from a process perspective.

***p < .01, **p < .05

It is interesting that, despite relatively little direct involvement with second-level planning, a fair amount of the corporate planning groups' effort goes into consulting activities for second-level management. The most effort is expended on helping with goals and objectives, strategies, and planning formats.

    The Corporate Strategic Planners expend the most effort in 60 percent of the activities, particularly in those for which all groups devote a great deal of effort. Not surprisingly, Corporate Strategic Planners are much more concerned with improving planning performance, but they are less concerned with assistance at the second level.

3.4.7 STATUS AND AUTHORITY OF PLANNERS

    Despite the fact that planning is in essence a staff function, planners need a certain measure of authority in order to fulfill their integrative roles. Indications of power and authority include reporting relationships of the planners and authority of corporate planning in dealing with second-level plans.

3.4.7.1 Reporting Relationships

As indicated by their reporting relationships, the status of planners is relatively high. Forty-four percent of chief corporate planners report to the chairman or president (more than any other position), while another 28 percent report to an executive vice president. Only 5 percent report to a financial officer (treasurer or controller), and 27 percent report elsewhere in the organization. There are minor differences for Corporate Strategic Planners, whose chief corporate planner is slightly more likely to report to the executive V.P. and slightly less likely to report to the chairman or president.

At the second level, 60 percent of the firms have formal planning positions. In two thirds of these cases, second-level planners report to the senior second-level line officer, while 22 percent report to a subordinate line officer. A small minority report to the second-level controller. The Corporate Strategic Planners are not different from the others in this respect.

3.4.7.2 Corporate Planning Authority

In general, corporate planners do not have the authority to accept or reject second-level plans or even to obtain substantive revisions (table 3.23). They do have some ability to obtain procedural revisions, but their major role is in review and criticism, where they are perhaps able to bring their broad company perspective to bear on individual plans. The Corporate Strategic Planners are no different from the other firm Categories – somewhat surprising given that they no doubt have more planning expertise.

3.4.8 PLANNING ACTIVITIES

In addition to serving as the vehicle by which plans are written, the planning process encompasses a number of different integrative activities. These are encompassed in conflict resolution, nature of the planning process, and various roles of planning (table 3.24). The Corporate Strategic Planners are most in agreement for two thirds of the 20 items.

3.4.8.1 Conflict Resolution

While planning may involve some bargaining, it is – somewhat surprisingly – not seen primarily as a device to resolve conflicts. However, for each of the three items, the Corporate Strategic Plan-

Table 3.22†

Effort Expended in Various Corporate Planning Activities[1,2]

Specific Planning Tasks	Sample Mean	Corporate Strategic Planners Mean	Rank
Define guidelines, formats and time tables for planning activity	4.08	4.33	1***
Prepare specific studies	3.77	4.08	2
Develop macro forecast of the economy, financial markets, political environment, etc.	3.17	3.63	1**
Develop better accounting and financial data for strategic planning	2.78	2.79	3*
Overall Planning Responsibility			
Identify areas of new business opportunity	3.46	3.75	1
Develop and write corporate plan	3.39	4.04	1**
Monitor and control progress versus plan	3.04	3.04	2
Assistance at Corporate Level			
Help corporate management formulate goals and objectives	4.05	4.38	1**
Help corporate management formulate strategy	3.69	4.50	1***
Help management with acquisition plans	3.69	3.88	2
Help management with divestiture plans	3.12	3.21	1
Help management with identification of financing needs	2.63	2.29	5
Assistance at Second Level			
Review and evaluate second level plans	3.93	4.00	3**
Integrate second level plans with corporate plan	3.77	4.08	1***
Help second level management formulate goals and objectives	3.46	3.54	2**
Help second level management formulate strategy	3.32	3.29	4**

Table 3.22 (continued)

Improving Planning Performance	Sample Mean	Corporate Strategic Planners Mean	Rank
Improve quality of strategic thinking of corporate management	4.02	4.21	1***
Access overall effectiveness of the planning process	3.75	3.92	1*
Improve quality of strategic thinking by second level management	3.64	4.04	1***
Reorganize company around better defined business units	2.52	3.08	1***

[1]Means on 5-point scale: 1 = no effort, 5 = high degree of effort

[2]Significant differences among planning activities*** and Planning Categories***

†All items classified as Planning Activities from a process perspective.

***p < .01, **p < .05, *p < .01

Table 3.23†

Authority of Corporate Planning Over Second-Level Plans[1,2]

Specific Planning Tasks	Sample Mean	Corporate Strategic Planners Mean	Rank
Review and Criticize	4.10	4.21	2***
Obtain Procedural Revisions	3.31	3.33	3***
Obtain Substantive Revisions	2.61	2.67	3
Accept and Reject	2.08	2.04	4

[1]Means on 5-point scale: 1 = no authority, 5 = complete authority

[2]Significant differences among tasks*** and Planning Categories***

†All items classified as Planning Activities from a process perspective.

***p < .01

Table 3.24†

Activities Encompassed in the Planning Process[1,2]

Conflict Resolution[2]	Sample Mean	Corporate Strategic Planners Mean	Rank
Planning:			
is a device to assure that conflicting expectations are resolved	3.06	4.21	1***
is a means of organizational conflict resolution	2.38	3.08	1
involves a great deal of bargaining	2.72	3.04	1
Planning Process[2]			
Our planning effort is an adaptive, evolving, learning activity	4.42	4.75	1***
††In this company, daily routine does not drive out planning effort"	3.58	3.90	1
††Our planning effort is not a routinized activity"	3.44	3.50	2
In the planning process in this company, all key personnel contributed their fair share of effort	3.52	3.83	1
Planning is often characterized by distortion of data	1.99	2.08	1
Role[2]			
Planning:			
††does not act simply as an agency for assembling financial reports	4.10	4.25	2
is necessary to sequence future activities	3.73	4.21	1*
plays a central role in the organization's communication network	3.70	4.13	1***
has had a measurable positive effect on sales and profits	3.26	3.33	2
is a means of ensuring that specialized knowledge is stored and available to the whole organization	3.12	3.54	1

Table 3.24 (continued)

Role (continued)	Sample Mean	Corporate Strategic Planners Mean	Rank
plays an important role in auditing ongoing activities	2.93	3.04	2
encourages development of new businesses by combining expertise and resources from lower level units	2.54	3.00	1

[1]Means on 5-point scale: 1 = disagree, 5 = agree

[2]Significant differences among planning items*** and Planning Categories***

†All items classified as Planning Activities from a process perspective.

††Scale reversed for expositional purposes.

***p < .01, *p < .10

ners have the highest mean score, particularly for viewing planning as a device to ensure the resolution of conflicting expectations.

3.4.8.2 Planning Process

There was general agreement (significantly greater for the Corporate Strategic Planners) that the planning effort is an adaptive, evolving, learning activity rather than a routinized one. Respondents did not believe that planning efforts were subordinate to daily routine and felt overall that key personnel contribute their fair share of effort to planning. Planning was not believed to be characterized by distortion of data.

3.4.8.3 Role of Planning

There was broad agreement about the central role played by planning in the organization's communications network, and planning was viewed as necessary to sequence future activities; the Corporate Strategic Planners were significantly higher in both cases. There was less agreement that planning encourages development of new businesses or that it encourages more effective use of information. Respondents did not think that a major function of planning is to act as an agency for assembling financial reports. Respondents were neutral on whether planning had a measurable positive effect on sales and profits – a harbinger of things to come in our assessment of the impact of planning on performance. The pattern for Corporate Strategic Planners is the expected one of viewing planning as more important.

3.4.9 FORMALIZATION OF PLANNING

Overall, the degree of formalization of the planning system was high. For example, there is a high degree of regularity in updating of corporate plans. Five sixths of the firms indicated annual updating, with just 14 percent reporting a less frequent updating or updating as needed. Only two firms indicated more frequent updating.

Integration through broad distribution of the corporate plan is low. Only a quarter of the firms give access to operating managers at the second or third level; the Corporate Strategic Planners' distribution is only slightly deeper.

At the second level, 19 different types of plans were identified from open-end responses. These ranged from integrated business plans, prepared by 92 percent of the companies, to plans for a given function or market area. More than 50 percent of the firms each prepare 20 or more different integrated business plans. Overall, about a quarter of these plans are reviewed at the corporate level, and four fifths of the firms indicated that standard formats have been developed and that the vast majority of individual businesses conform to those formats. Less conformity was reported for the Corporate Strategic Planners, perhaps indicating somewhat more flexibility in their planning processes.

3.4.10 PLANNING AND PERFORMANCE REVIEW

Equally critical for organizational integration as the development of the plans themselves are the review processes. In this section we examine the frequency and depth of performance review, the review criteria, the atmosphere in the planning and performance review processes, and the use of goals and incentives.

3.4.10.1 Performance Review: Frequency

Three quarters of firms that plan at the corporate level indicated that regular reviews of performance against plan are held; two thirds reported annual review, 16 percent indicated a biannual review, and 16 percent reviewed performance against corporate plan on a monthly basis. The highest frequency of review was reported by the Corporate Financial Planners, which clearly placed an emphasis on short-term results. The majority of the Corporate Strategic Planners indicated annual review, while 30 percent reported biannual review – a pattern that is generally consistent with the received wisdom that performance should be reviewed against long-term plan relatively infrequently in order to allow the process to keep a long-term perspective. Almost all of the Corporate Strategic Planners (more than any other Planning Category) indicated that review is performed regularly, and only a small fraction indicated review "as needed."

However, specific performance goals for planning departments are not clearly established. Numerical or quantified procedures are not used extensively for review, and only 20 percent of the companies indicated any specific reports that detail the performance of the corporate planning group.

At the second level, three quarters of the firms indicated that performance is reviewed against plan on a regular basis. More than 90 percent of both the Corporate and Division Strategic Planners indicated regular review of second-level performance against plan, significantly higher than the other firms. Mean effort expended in monitoring and controlling performance versus plans is moderate (3.0 on a 5-point scale: 1 = no effort, 5 = high degree of effort), with no significant differences among Planning Categories.

3.4.10.2 Plan and Performance Review Process

Formal analysis of variances between plan and actual performance is required by 76 percent of companies, the rest having no such structured review procedures. In such reviews, half of these companies indicated that written narrative explanation of differences is required, 30 percent that quantitative analysis of causes of differences is required, and 20 percent that both written narrative and quantitative explanations are required. The atmosphere existing at review varies from "relaxed" to "tense and confrontational," slightly more skewed toward the latter, with no differences among Planning Categories.

3.4.10.3 Performance Review: Goals, Criteria, and Compensation

Virtually all of the respondents indicated that performance goals vary over second-level units. Most also report an incentive compensation scheme for second-level line managers, but only 40 percent indicated that the incentive compensation is based on progress in meeting long-range goals. Surprisingly, this does not differ according to Planning Category.

Open-ended responses about criteria for such incentive compensation grouped into three categories: short-term performance, longer term performance, and subjective or qualitative factors. Short-term performance is by far the most common criterion, cited by 86 percent of respondents. Longer term performance was cited by only 30 percent, and subjective or qualitative factors by 20 percent. More detailed analysis of performance criteria for second-level managers (table 3.25) confirms that the major criterion is short-term profit. While longer run criteria are more important for the Corporate Strategic Planners, they stress short-term performance more than any other Planning Category. It seems reasonable to assume that those companies involved in strategic planning would be more

Table 3.25†
Performance Criteria Used for Second-Level Managers[1,2]

Criteria	Sample Mean	Corporate Strategic Planners Mean	Rank
Achievement of Short-Term Profits	4.32	4.58	1*
Implementation of Planned Strategy	3.69	4.00	1***
Achievement of Strategic Objectives	3.64	3.83	1
Quality of Planning Effort	3.16	3.70	1***

[1]Means on 5-point scale: 1 = not at all important, 5 = very important

[2]Significant differences among criteria*** and Planning Categories***

†All items classified as Planning Outputs/Performance Interface from a process perspective.

***p < .01, *p < .10

likely to base incentive compensation on long-run considerations. Our findings suggest, however, that the strategic perspective has not yet penetrated to these key motivating influences. This is reinforced by the fact, which does not differ over Planning Categories, that only moderate effort is expended in monitoring and controlling progress versus plans.[7]

Corporate goals play a more important role in monitoring performance and motivation than for outside appearances (table 3.26). For Corporate Strategic Planners, goals are a significantly more important integrative mechanism than for the other Planning Categories. The most important use of second-level goals is as standards to evaluate business unit performance, significantly more so than as a basis for formally determining an incentive. Again, we see that factors other than short-term performance play a minor role in determining incentives.

3.5 Summary

This chapter provides a detailed description of the planning practices of our 113 sample firms. The chapter is organized along the lines of a functional perspective – that is, in terms of adaptive and integrative elements of planning (chapter 2). On the basis of the Plan-

Table 3.26†
Role of Goals[1]

Corporate:[1,2]	Sample Mean	Corporate Strategic Planners	
		Mean	Rank
Provide challenge and motivation	3.79	4.21	1**
Monitor current performance	3.73	4.17	1**
Evaluation of past performance	3.46	3.96	1**
Communication to external publics	3.02	3.21	4
Used to activate contingencies	2.60	3.08	1**
Second Level:[3,4]			
Standards to Evaluate Business Unit Performance	4.04	4.42	1*
Basis for formally determining incentive	3.60	4.04	1

[1]Means on 5-point scale: 1 = do not serve important role, 5 = serve important role

[2]Significant differences among roles*** and Planning Categories***

[3]Means on 5-point scale: 1 = not important use, 5 = very important use

[4]Significant differences among roles*** and Planning Categories**

†All items classified as Planning Outputs/Peformance Interface from a process perspective.

***p < .01, **p < .05, *p < .10

ning Category system developed in chapter 2, we compared the most sophisticated Planning Category – the Corporate Strategic Planners – with the others. Because so many results are reported in this chapter, this summary refers back to key tables.

The firms that plan commit significant human and financial resources to planning, though proportionately less than similar firms based elsewhere – in Australia, for example (Capon, Christodoulou, Farley, and Hulbert 1984). Most are organized the same way for planning as they are for operations – that is, divisionally. Chief corporate planners have limited experience with planning but have long-term service with their firms. There is minimal rotation of line personnel through planning, though this is greatest for the Corporate Strategic Planners.

Adaptation. Adaptive elements of planning focus on matters related to strategic change. As expected, Corporate Strategic Planners are more adaptive in their planning than the other firms, though there are a number of surprises.

Corporate Strategic Planners devote more effort to forecasting, though investment in forecasts is modest in general and all firms focus the most effort on forecasting near-term industry demand (table 3.1). Competitive analysis is also important but is not a major corporate planning activity. We had expected to find more emphasis on the less traditional and longer term areas of forecasting (sociocultural, technological, human resources) and more attention to analysis of competitive cost structures.

All firms claim to put more effort into long-range planning, and planning for acquisition and divestiture, than into operational planning. The Corporate Strategic Planners have the longest time horizons (greater than the median of five years). Despite the increasing emphasis on globalization of business, planning is only modestly global overall, though the Corporate Strategic Planners have succeeded in globalizing their planning systems to a greater degree (table 3.4). Surprisingly, contingency planning is rare for all firms.

The much-discussed conceptual frameworks for developing strategic content (the various portfolio models, for example) are viewed as having relatively little influence on the content of corporate strategy (table 3.5) – certainly less than we had expected but nonetheless more or less consistent with some existing empirical research and the general state of the planning literature reviewed in chapter 2. Forecasting models, planning and budgeting models, and computer systems dedicated to planning are used by more than half of the firms, with somewhat greater use at corporate than at the second level. The Corporate Strategic Planners are the most intensive users of all analytic devices, especially portfolio models, where their depth of usage is greatest; although they expect such use to continue, the overall historical and anticipated influence even on them is modest.

Firms believe that planning has improved resource allocation (table 3.7), and resource allocation is especially well integrated into the planning process for the Corporate Strategic Planners. Planning has assisted to some extent in dealing with uncertainty and risk – benefits that are especially apparent to the Corporate Strategic Planners. The sample as a whole makes budgetary distinctions between expenditures that have short-run and long-run benefits. While "strategic" criteria are most used by the Corporate Strategic Planners for expenditures that bring long-run benefits (table 3.10), the sample as a whole uses both "nonstrategic" (particularly financial) and "strategic" criteria extensively. Market growth, measured relative to GNP growth, has no effect on investment criteria for more than half the firms.

The content of the final plans differs among Planning Categories. Both the corporate and second-level plans of Corporate Strategic Planners are more extensive and emphasize both internal and environmental analyses, problems and opportunities, and strategy development.

Integration. Integrative elements of planning tend to hold the corporation together in the sense of causing the various parts to pull in the same direction. Planning by the Corporate Strategic Planners also tends to be more integrative than by the other firms.

Across the sample as a whole there is a surprisingly limited degree of integration of plans. There is only limited coordination of functional plans, other than financial, with corporate plans, though the Corporate Strategic Planners do more coordination. Most firms plan with more than one time horizon, but coordination of long-range and short-range plans is also very modest. Only a third of the firms prepare a long-range plan first and then fit the short-range plan into it.

There is more inter-unit transmission of internal information than there is of information about the environment. Planners generally feel that good quality information is available from the functional areas (table 3.14). There is also extensive exchange of information between the corporate planning group and both top corporate management and senior line executives. Transmission of forecasts from corporate to lower levels is modest; exchange of forecasts is greatest for areas that receive the most forecasting effort (industry-level demand and domestic economy) and more extensive for the Corporate Strategic Planners than the others.

The major single influence on planning is the CEO, particularly in terms of setting goals and objectives, developing strategies and approval of the final plan (table 3.16). Top second-level line managers also have considerable influence, especially for developing second-level missions and setting second-level goals, but boards of directors have surprisingly little influence. Influence on key strategic decisions is greatest from executives promoted from within as opposed to consultants or executives hired from outside. Planning personnel have considerable influence over the planning process, including the format and schedule, though they also influence the content of plans through their control over planning assumptions. Line management and planning group influence is greatest in the Corporate Strategic Planners, though they are not the leading Category for CEO influence. Corporate goal and strategy formulation frequently involves negotiation, a feature that distinguishes Corporate Strategic Planners from the other firms; they appear to be less top-down driven and have processes that are more participative.

Line management is generally positive about planning, though both short and long-range plans are seen as equally important overall (table 3.19). Senior managers in the Corporate Strategic Planners are the most positive and also spend the most time on long-range plans.

The "chain of command" for planning is well defined, and management takes an active interest in the output and recommendations of the corporate planning group, especially in the Corporate Strategic Planners. The planning group puts significant effort into a wide range of different activities (table 3.22), including securing information and setting guidelines for planning, assisting corporate- and second-level management with goal and strategy formulation, and improving planning performance. In general, the Corporate Strategic Planners put more effort into these activities than the other firms do. The goals and objectives of planning are, however, only moderately clear, and the degree of value added by the corporate planning group over completed second-level plans is seen as modest.

Chief corporate planners tend to report to a high level in the organization but in general do not have the authority to accept and reject second-level plans. Their influence is exerted primarily through review and criticism.

Planning plays a central role in the firm's communication network and serves as a means of sequencing future activities (table 3.24). Planning is not, however, seen as a conflict resolution mechanism, though it is seen by the Corporate Strategic Planners as a device to resolve conflicting expectations.

Corporate plans are generally updated annually, but plans are not distributed widely throughout the organization. Review of performance against plan is regular – most often annual – more frequent for the firms that basically do financial planning and less so for Corporate Strategic Planners. Many different types of second-level plans (primarily functional) are developed, mostly conforming to standard formats. Again, performance review is regular, especially for the Corporate Strategic Planners. Most firms require formal analysis of variances between plan and actual performance, most often requiring written explanation of differences. Atmosphere at review ranges from "relaxed" to "tense and confrontational."

Incentive compensation schemes are present for most second-level line managers. Performance criteria in general are more heavily emphasized by the Corporate Strategic Planners, but short-term profits dominate longer term measures for all firms. In fact, the most important substantive result of this chapter may be that short-run performance measures remain the dominant single criterion for judging the performance of line managers, a practice almost certain to limit their strategic thinking, as well as the usefulness of long-term planning.

NOTES

1. Frequently in this chapter we refer to corporate planning activities. For those companies that develop bona fide corporate plans, the focus of responses is typically on these plans; for those firms that do not develop corporate plans, the focus is on the highest level plans developed. In some cases, responses of Non-Planners fall definitionally at the scale end points.

2. The particular test reported in this volume is a two-way ANOVA. One factor is always Planning Category; the topic of interest constitutes the second factor. Significance is reported across each of the two factors and for individual items across the Planning Categories.

3. Acquisition and Divestiture planning are subsumed under corporate planning to a limited degree (5-point scale: sample means 3.35, 3.19 respectively). There are no differences among Planning Categories, though Corporate Strategic Planners are the least likely group to subsume acquisition planning under corporate planning.

4. The results presented in this section are largely based on open-end responses; they are not, therefore, directly comparable with responses from the previous section.

5. The results reported in this paragraph are based on respondents' identification of the five persons outside of their group with whom they have the most contact.

6. See footnote 5.

7. The performance criteria discussed in this paragraph are perhaps better considered as adaptive elements. They are, however, discussed here so that all plan/performance review items can be presented together.

Chapter 4

Planning:
Two Methods of Overview

4.1 Introduction

Chapter 3 contains a detailed, item-by-item analysis of the
501 measurements on the planning systems of our sample companies.
The description also highlights the behavior of the most sophisticated
planners – the Corporate Strategic Planners. While this approach provides considerable detail about the process of planning, it lacks overview of the planning process. From the detailed view, it is difficult to
make general statements about the underlying dimensions of planning, which generally depend on relationships among items that are
not at all independent. The problem of evaluating interrelationships
between different aspects of the planning process is increased by the
large number of measurements relative to the 113 available observations. In addition, because of the extensive detail, we were unable to
make more than a passing reference to the other four Planning
Categories – Division Strategic, Corporate Financial, Division Financial, and Non-Planners.

In this chapter we attempt to remedy these deficiencies. In
section 4.2, we employ the process view of planning introduced in
chapter 2 and develop a "soft" model of the entire planning process as
a means of investigating the extent to which different elements of the
process form a coherent structure. In section 4.3, we reduce the 501
planning items to a set of 43 planning scales and investigate the planning behavior of the five Planning Categories on those scales.
Whereas the two sets of analyses are in one sense two different ways
of looking at the same phenomenon, each produces output useful for
different purposes.

4.2 Planning Process Synthesis

In chapter 2 we developed a process model of planning, inputs ▶ process ▶ outputs, which consists of seven building blocks-three involving inputs, two involving process, and two involving outputs. These are identified in figure 4.1, which is reproduced from chapter 2. From this perspective, we wish to investigate whether or not our results show patterns of consistency or whether they are disjointed and unrelated. This assessment involves the development of a coordinating model. Unfortunately, a major analytical problem faced throughout the study is the fact that there are far more measurements than there are observations – 501 planning measurements on the 113 firms. This renders direct application of conventional multivariate methods unworkable as a means of attempting to establish patterns in the entire set of measurements. However, Wold (1975a, b, 1977, 1978, 1980) has suggested an approach called "soft modeling" that proved useful in overall synthesis of the planning findings. Soft modeling usually involves the extraction of variables summarizing information on blocks of related measurements and examination of the relationships among these summary variables. The goal is to develop

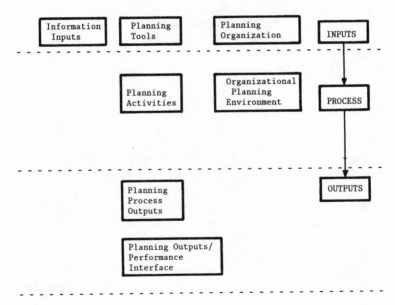

Figure 4.1
Planning Process Constructs

an overall picture of structure, the interrelationships of individual variables within each block being secondary.

Our basic approach involves two steps:

1. The original measurements are summarized in terms of principal components for each variable group in figure 4.1.

2. A path-like structure involving partial correlations of principal components is developed to relate the seven variable blocks. In general, we hypothesize that the patterns of positive intrablock relationships should carry over to generally positive interblock relationships.

4.2.1 DATA REDUCTION AND PRINCIPAL COMPONENTS

Principal components analysis of each block of measurements in figure 4.1 provides an objective approach to data reduction while keeping the entire data base intact. It is particularly useful in this case because of the excess of raw measurements over observations. Principal components analysis has the additional desirable feature of providing a much smaller set of summary measurements, which are weighted combinations of intrablock measurements, and which retain maximum within-group information in the sense of explanation of the within-group communal variability. Furthermore, since the components within each block are themselves orthogonal, collinearity among them as summary measures is not a problem. Finally, the approach does not require judgment about which of the individual measurements to use.

4.2.2 HOW MANY COMPONENTS?

Choice of the number of principal components used to summarize each block of measurements is an important decision. Unfortunately, some conventional approaches to this problem are not very useful in this case. For example, a total of 130 principal components have eigenvalues greater than unity (table 4.1), so the correlation matrix of even these 130 components is still singular. On the other hand, by using a random splitting procedure (Lehmann and Morrison 1979), an average of three (never more than five) eigenvalues in any of the seven groups are significantly different from one. Scree procedures produced approximately the same results. We chose to identify three principal components from each of the seven groups; that is 21 measurements in all.

Preliminary analysis of these principal components indicated sharp and systematic differences in correlations among them

Table 4.1

Patterns in Principal Components of Planning Variable Groups

Planning Inputs	Number of measurements in group	Number of eigenvalues greater than 1
Information Inputs	27	9
Planning Tools	54	17
Planning Organization	106	34
Planning Process		
Planning Activities	146	21
Organizational Planning Environment	58	17
Planning Outputs		
Planning Process Outputs	69	18
Planning Outputs/ Performance Interface	41	14
	501	130

(table 4.2). While the first principal components are highly correlated, the second and third principal components show patterns of correlation closer to those that would be expected by chance. These numbers indicate that we should focus on relationships among the first principal components, since the others appear more idiosyncratic to the particular groups. It is important to recognize that this is an extremely severe data reduction procedure and that the results that follow should be considered tentative and exploratory.

4.2.3 THE FIRST PRINCIPAL COMPONENTS

The basic composition of the seven first principal components is summarized in table 4.3, which also indicates the number of items loading heavily (element of orthonormal eigenvector × square root of eigenvalue = 0.5 or greater), and in table A4.1 in the appendix to this chapter, which lists the items that load heavily on each component. (Although each principal component in fact "contains" information from all variables, the measurements most heavily weighted are those that contribute most to the informational content of that component.) As the tables indicate, there is a large amount of specific variability associated with each of the components, but there is also a pattern of consistency in terms of signs of loadings and types of measurements that group together. (These patterns of consistency are also used later in assessing planning-performance relationships.)

Corporate and Strategic Planning

Table 4.2
Patterns in Correlations of Three Principal Components
Summarizing Each of Seven Planning Variable Groups

| | Number of Significant Correlations | | |
	Between pairs of first principal components	Between pairs of components in which one is a first principal component†	Between pairs of components in which neither is a first principal component†
Number of distinct correlations	21	84	84
Number of correlations significant at α = .05	21	6	7

†Excludes within-group components which are definitionally orthogonal.

The patterns for each group seem to provide an overall picture of "good" planning practice:

  • Significant effort goes into *Information Inputs*, including preparation and distribution of various long- and short-term forecasts of environmental domains.
  • *Planning Tools* are regularly and broadly used and permeate into lower levels of the organization. Included are various portfolio models, together with econometric and other formal models.
  • In *Planning Organization*, the CEO, senior line managers, and the planning department are all involved in the setting of goals and the development of strategies.
  • *Planning Activities* involve resource allocation, integration of functional plans, communication, and cooperation. However, the planning department also has some substantive clout in revision of lower level plans.
  • The *Organizational Planning Environment* is positive, from top to bottom of the organization, with experienced planners, clear goals, and cooperative senior management.
  • *Planning Process Outputs* are comprehensive; strategies are well defined and the plans are regularly and frequently reviewed and updated.

Table 4.3
Composition of First Principal Components of Planning Variable Groups

	Number of measurements in group	Number of measurements loading on first principal component†	Proportion of variance explained by first principal component	First component loads heavily on:
Planning Inputs				
Information Inputs	27	15	28.4%	Effort devoted to developing and disseminating forecasts
Planning Tools	54	21	14.2%	Use of contemporary strategic planning tools
Planning Organization	106	12	13.8%	Influence of CEO, line managers and planning department on forming goals and strategies in the planning process
Planning Process				
Planning Activities	146	13	10.7%	Effort devoted to planning, coordination and implementation of plans
Organizational Planning Environment	58	15	19.8%	Involvement in, and acceptance of, the planning process by line managers
Planning Outputs				
Planning Process Outputs	69	20	21.2%	The breadth and variety of plans prepared at various levels
Planning Outputs/ Performance Interface	41	5	23.4%	How plans are used to monitor performance
	501	101		

†See appendix/table A4.1 for list of specific items loading on each component.

• In terms of *Planning Outputs/Performance Interface*, planned strategies play an important role in establishing goals and evaluating operating managers.

4.2.4 RELATIONSHIPS AMONG FIRST PRINCIPAL COMPONENTS

The simple correlations among the first principal components are significant for all 21 pairs (table 4.4). All signs in table 4.4 are positive, and this result, combined with the positive loadings of the individual variables on each principal component shown in table A4.1, indicates a fabric of positive relationships among the individual measurements constituting the planning groups.

There is, however, reason to suppose that precedence relationships exist among the variable groups, meaning that some of these components may play the role of mediating variables. For example, as presented in figure 4.1, the development of a planning organization, the selection of information requirements and the identification of planning tools in all likelihood precede both the growth of organized activities within the planning operation and the development of organizational linkages required to make planning effective. These dimensions may govern the planning process outputs, which in turn may then affect implementation of planning in the operating units and the control functions of planning – planning outputs/performance interface. The network of partial correlations (figure 4.2) indicates that the ordered paths implied by such a structure are significant; however, experiments with rearrangement of some of the components produced much the same patterns. It is important to recognize that these results are highly tentative owing to both the measurement problems discussed earlier and the lack of a basis with which to identify unambiguous structures like those in figure 4.2.

These results are even more tentative when viewed in the light of results of an analysis of the estimated mean values of the seven first principal components computed for each of the five Planning Categories. Given the consistent "good" planning characteristics of the Corporate Strategic Planners in chapter 3, and assuming that weights in each of the principal components imply that higher values indicate "better" planning, we expected significant differences among Planning Categories for each of the seven principal components. In fact, not only were there no such significant differences, but also there was not even a consistent pattern in the means. Thus, despite the reasonable relationships found among the planning variables using the process-model framework, it appears that the level of aggre-

Table 4.4

Simple Correlations Between First Principal
Components from Planning Variable Groups†

	Planning Tools	Planning Organization	Planning Activities	Organizational Planning Environment	Planning Process Outputs	Planning Outputs/ Performance Interface
Information Inputs	.38	.27	.35	.42	.35	.20
Planning Tools		.48	.54	.57	.45	.40
Planning Organization			.73	.65	.46	.47
Planning Activities				.69	.45	.44
Organizational Planning Environment					.53	.65
Planning Process Outputs						.49

†All correlations significant at α = .05

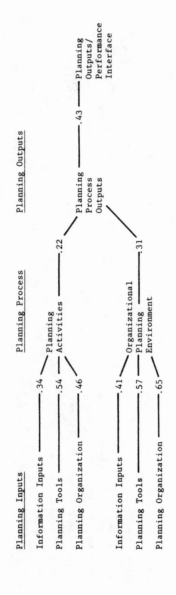

Figure 4.2

Partial Correlations Between First Principal Components
in "Soft Model" of Planning Network[†]

†Partial correlations computed conditional on all variables to the left in the diagram.
All significant at α = .05.

gation implied by use of a single principal component for each block of the process model is too high to allow reasonable inter-Category analysis.

4.2.5 SUMMARY

The "process" view of planning demonstrates that elements of planning hold together in a "soft" model, and the results generally paint a systematic picture of how the elements of planning relate. Planning appears to be a coherent, if complex, logically interrelated set of activities that sequence in a reasonable pattern. The next section develops an in-depth analysis of the purposes that planning serves.

4.3 Dimensions of Planning: Adaptive and Integrative

We have now developed two summaries of the information contained in the 501 measurements of our study of planning practice. The first, in chapter 3, involved detailed analysis of the individual planning items. This produced a rich description of planning in general and a profile of the Corporate Strategic Planners in particular. However, the analysis does not allow for exploration of the relationships between elements of the process. The second summary, described earlier in this chapter, aggregates the items into just seven principal components. This produces a picture of overall coherence of the elements of planning but very muddy profiles of the Planning Categories. On the basis of the results of these two rather polar approaches to summary, it seems that an intermediate approach might be useful – one that does not attempt such extreme aggregation as the principal components but that produces a more reasonable conceptual summary than that available from chapter 3.

One approach is to summarize the planning measurements by developing a set of scales based on subsets of key items. These are developed here on the basis of the two functional dimensions within which the planning literature was discussed in chapter 2 – adaptation, leading to coalignment of the organization and the environment, and internal organizational integration.

These scales serve a double purpose in this book. The first is to provide a summary overview to examine differences in adaptive and integrative emphasis for the Planning Categories; these results are presented in this chapter. The second use of the scales is as a rich multidimensional set of measurements for study of the relationships between planning on the one hand and environment, strategy, organization structure, and organizational climate on the other; these results are presented in subsequent chapters.

4.3.1 CONSTRUCTION OF SCALES

From the items discussed in chapter 3, 43 planning scales were constructed – 13 adaptive scales and 30 integrative scales. The process of scale construction involved a combination of factor analytic results and conceptual development. In the latter, two independent judges grouped items that appeared to represent a particular underlying construct and that were then tested for consistency. Scales were constructed by averaging the items composing the scale. Descriptions of the scales in terms of their meaning, the constituent items and the Chronbach αs are found in table A.4.2 in the appendix to this chapter.

The scales are labeled so that a high value on a scale corresponds to "more" of the planning element indicated by the scale label. For example, a high value on *Environmental Information* means that the firm expends a large amount of effort in seeking information from the environment; a low value means that, relatively speaking, the firm expends little effort. In general, a high scale value implies that the firm is exhibiting "good" planning practice, according to received wisdom (chapter 2). However, in some cases, notably among the integrative scales, there is some ambiguity regarding "good" planning practice.

The scales constitute an intermediate summary in our analysis of planning. There are fewer of them (43 scales versus 501 measurements), so analysis is more manageable. Nonetheless, there is some loss of information through aggregation and because all of the items are not used in scale construction. Furthermore, it must be remembered that the scale values are standardized, meaning that individual scores represent relative and not absolute values.

4.3.2 DEVELOPMENT OF ADAPTIVE SCALES

The adaptive scales are patterned along the lines of our analysis of strategic planning in chapter 2. Included are scales that measure environmental orientation, strategic orientation, use of planning tools, resource allocation, and plan comprehensiveness.

4.3.2.1 Environmental Orientation

Two scales measure the *environmental orientation* of the firm and the extent to which it obtains external information.

Environmental Information measures the overall effort that the firm expends in forecasting ten different aspects of the external environment.

Competitive Analysis is composed of five items designed to tap the overall effort placed by the firm on competitive analysis.

4.3.2.2 Strategic Orientation

Five scales were developed to measure the *strategic orientation* of planning:

"Strategic" Planning uses five items to capture the extent to which the planning effort is strategically oriented and concerned with developing long-range plans, long-run mission, contingency plans, and planning for acquisitions and divestitures.

Time Horizon is the time horizon of the firm's guiding long-range plan.

Globalness is composed of five items and measures the extent to which planning effort and the development of marketing strategy, procurement strategy, and production strategy is performed on a worldwide basis.

Portfolio Change uses two measures designed to capture the explicit emphasis that the planning group puts into acquisition and divestiture.

Resource Allocation uses three items to measure the extent to which resource allocation decisions are made as part of the planning process.

4.3.2.3 Planning Tools

Two scales capture the extent to which the firm uses *planning tools* as part of its planning process:

Portfolio Models consists of eight items that measure the extent to which portfolio and policy matrices are used as part of the planning process, both in general and for specific uses such as resource allocation and supplier, competitor, and customer analysis.

Model Use is developed from a count of models (not portfolio or policy) and computer systems for planning that are operational in the firm.

4.3.2.4 Resource Allocation Decisions

Two scales were developed to capture the long-run nature of the criteria used to make *resource allocation decisions:*

Long-Run Expense Distinction comprises two items and measures the extent to which the firm makes a distinction between short-run and long-run benefits in its expenditures for marketing and R&D.

Strategic Criteria consists of ten items that measure the relative use of strategic (market growth, market share, forecast sales growth, forecast market share growth, impact on company resource needs) versus financial (short-term cash flow, earnings per share, forecast net operating profit, forecast ROI, discounted cash flow) criteria for investments to yield long-run benefits.

4.3.2.5 Plan Comprehensiveness

The final two scales measure the *plan comprehensiveness* of final long-range plans at both the corporate and second levels:

Corporate is based upon the number of headings in the corporate plan.

Second Level is based upon the number of headings in the long-run second-level plan.

4.3.3 ADAPTIVE SCALES AND THE FIVE PLANNING CATEGORIES

The adaptive scales (table 4.5) show strong and consistent patterns of difference among Planning Categories. Overall, there is a clear pattern of significance; twelve scales are significant at $\alpha = .05$ and nine at $\alpha = .01$.

Overall, the group order has the expected monotonic relationship: Corporate Strategic Planners > Division Strategic Planners > Corporate Financial Planners > Division Financial Planners > Non-Planners. For eight of the scales, the ordering of firm Categories is perfectly monotonic.

The Corporate Strategic Planners are in the expected polar position for 10 of the 13 scales and are clearly the most "adaptive" firms. Only for portfolio change (where they are third), and time horizon and long-run expense distinction (where they are second), are they not the most "adaptive." For 12 of the 13 scales, the Non-Planners are, as expected, in the least "adaptive" position.

The Division Strategic Planners are in the expected second position for 8 of the 13 scales. They score ahead of the Corporate Strategic Planners for only portfolio change, a scale that appears to be characteristic of planning systems other than those of the Corporate Strategic type.

The Corporate Financial Planners are in the expected third position for 9 of the 13 scales; again they score ahead of the Corporate Strategic Planners on just the portfolio change scale.

Table 4.5
Planning Category Scale Means
For Adaptive Planning Scales

	Planning Categories					Significant
	Corporate Division		Corporate Division			Differences
daptive	Strategic Strategic		Financial Financial		Non-	Among
lanning Scales	Planners Planners		Planners Planners		Planners	Categories
Environmental Orientation						
Environmental	.35(1)[1]	.02(3)	-.01(4)	.07(2)	-1.34(5)	**
Information						
Competitive Analysis	.34(1)	.21(2)	-.10(3)	-.34(4)	-1.27(5)	**
Strategic Orientation						
"Strategic" Planning	.34(1)	.33(2)	.02(3)	-.44(4)	-2.30(5)	**
Time Horizon	.18(2)	.07(3)	.06(4)	.37(1)	-1.88(5)	**
Globalness	.49(1)	.21(2)	-.31(3)	-.36(4)	-.74(5)	**
Portfolio Change	.03(3)	.20(1)	.07(2)	-.17(4)	-1.21(5)	NS
Resource Allocation	.45(1)	.02(2)	-.06(3)	-.12(4)	-1.13(5)	*
Planning Tools						
Portfolio Models	.46(1)	-.01(2)	-.04(3)	-.23(4)	-.94(5)	*
Model Use	.35(1)	.21(2)	-.10(3)	-.33(4)	-1.28(5)	**
Resource Allocation Decisions						
Long Run Expense	.36(2)	-.30(4)	.02(3)	.52(1)	-.59(5)	*
Distinction						
Strategic Criteria	.44(1)	.03(2)	-.07(3)	-.30(4)	-.89(5)	**
Plan Comprehensiveness						
Corporate	.72(1)	-.13(3)	.04(2)	-.78(5)	-.75(4)	**
Second-Level	.58(1)	.24(2)	-.20(3)	-.69(4)	-1.77(5)	**

Figures in parentheses denote ordinal position of the means for each Planning Category.

**α = .01, *α = .05

The Division Financial Planners are in the expected fourth position for 9 of the 13 scales. Somewhat surprisingly, they score ahead of all firms for both time horizon and long-run expense distinction; they are second for environmental information.

Notwithstanding the fact that parts of three of the scales played a role in defining the Planning Category system, the strong consistency of results provides confirmation that the Planning Category system does indeed capture the fundamental nature of strategic planning, the "adaptive" dimension; high scale values in general imply good planning practice.

4.3.4 DEVELOPMENT OF INTEGRATIVE SCALES

The concept of integration in planning, which is probably less well developed and clear than adaptation, involves 30 scales in 10 areas. The areas include formal integration of plans; information flow; influence and participation in, and the process of, goal and strategy formulation; planning and line management; integrative value of planners; status and authority of planners; formalization of planning; planning and performance review and goals. The individual items that make up the scales and the Chronbach α s are shown in table A4.2 in the appendix to this chapter.

4.3.4.1 Formal Integration of Plans

Two scales measure the extent of *formal integration* in the planning process:

Corporate/Functional consists of four items which measure the extent to which functional planning (financial, marketing, human resource and manufacturing) is coordinated with corporate planning.

Over-time measures the number of time horizons for which the firm develops comprehensive plans.

4.3.4.2 Information Flow

Three scales measure the extent of corporate planning related *information flows* within the organization:

Top Down measures the extent to which forecasts of ten environmental areas are transmitted from corporate planning to the second level.

Internal measures the quality of information for planning obtained from four functional areas in the firm.

Corporate Planning Exchange measures the overall extent to which corporate planning exchanges information with five senior management areas within the firm.

4.3.4.3 Influence and Participation

Five scales measure the extent of *influence and participation* of various roles on key decisions within the firm.

One scale measures the influence of the *Board of Directors*, and three scales measure the influence of different internal management groups – *CEO, Top Second Level Line Management,* and *Corporate Planning* – in eight aspects of the planning and strategy formulation process.

The *Internal* scale measures the relative influence of persons inside the firm over six groups of external influencers on key firm decisions.

4.3.4.4 Goal and Strategy Formulation Process

Two scales capture the nature of the *goal and strategy formulation* process:

Bottom-Up Formulation is based on five items and portrays the extent to which goals and strategy are developed in a bottom-up process, rather than set at the most senior levels in the company and communicated downward.

CEO Negotiation comprises three items that capture the degree of negotiation between the CEO and second-level management in goal and strategy formulation.

4.3.4.5 Planning and Line Management

Two scales capture the relationship between *planning and line management:*

Relative Staff/Line Nature of Planning is made up of five items and measures the relative extent to which staff and line management have responsibility for planning.

Line View of Planning comprises five items that capture the extent to which line management has a positive view of the planning process.

4.3.4.6 Integrative Value of Planners

Two scales measure directly the *integrative value of planners* in the planning department:

Added Value consists of seven items that measure the value that the corporate planning department adds over and above completed second-level plans.

Planning Group Integration comprises six items that capture the extent to which the planning department is integrated into the firm.

4.3.4.7 Status and Authority of Planners

Two scales measure the nature of the *status and authority of planners* within the corporation:

Reporting Importance identifies the level in the organization to which the planners report.

Planning Authority is based on four items and captures the extent of the corporate planning group's authority in examining second-level plans.

4.3.4.8 Formalization of Planning

Five scales measure the extent to which the firm has an established process and there is *formalization of planning:*

Corporate is based on three items and measures the extent to which corporate planning is established.

Second-level is based on six items and measures the extent to which second-level planning is established.

Plan Density Preparation is a count of the number of integrated business plans prepared in the corporation.

Plan Density Review is a count of the number of second-level plans reviewed at the corporate level.

Plan Distribution Depth is based on four items and

measures the degree of access that managers in the firm have to the corporate plan.

4.3.4.9 Planning and Performance Review

Five scales focus on the *planning and performance review* process:

The first two scales are each based on three items and measure the degree to which the *Plan Review Atmosphere* and the *Performance Review Atmosphere* are tense and confronting, rather than relaxed.

Performance Review Frequency measures the frequency of long-run performance review at corporate and the second level.

Performance Review Criteria consists of four items that measure the degree to which second-level management is measured by long-run rather than by short-run criteria.

Performance Review Depth is based on four items and measures the degree to which explanation of performance is required of second-level managers in the review process.

4.3.4.10 Goals

Finally, two scales focus on company *goals*:

Use of Goals comprises seven items that measure the extent to which corporate and second-level goals are actively used in the corporation.

Goals for Planning is based on two items and measures the extent to which the performance of the corporate planning group is evaluated.

4.3.5 INTEGRATIVE SCALES AND THE FIVE PLANNING CATEGORIES

Table 4.6 contains means of each of the integrative scales for the five Planning Categories. Not surprisingly, because of the relatively underdeveloped nature of the integration concept in planning and its less clear role in distinguishing "strategic" planning, the results are overall less strong than for the adaptive dimension, though they are certainly far from random. Eighteen of the 30 scales are significant at $\alpha = .05$, 17 at $\alpha = .01$.

The expected order of relationships for integration is different than for adaptation. Corporate-level planning is expected to be more integrative than second-level or divisional planning; also, strategic planning is expected to be more integrative than financial planning. However, the degree of corporate–wide integration is expected to be greater for any type of corporate planning than for lower

Table 4.6

Planning Category Scale Means for Integrative Planning Scales

Integrative Planning Scales	Corporate Strategic Planners	Division Strategic Planners	Corporate Financial Planners	Division Financial Planners	Non-Planners	Significant Differences Among Categories
Formal Integration of Plans						
Corporate/Functional	.40(1)[1]	-.03(3)	.10(2)	-.44(4)	-.99(5)	**
Over-time	.22(2)	.05(3)	.29(1)	-.10(4)	-2.28(5)	**
Information Flow						
Top Down	.32(1)	.08(3)	.11(2)	-.34(4)	-1.50(5)	**
Internal	.09(1)	.02(2)	.01(3)	-.07(4)	-.34(5)	NS
Corporate Planning Exchange	.13(2)	-.08(4)	.10(3)	.20(1)	-.83(5)	NS
Influence and Participation						
Board of Directors	.20(1)	-.14(4)	.19(2)	-.12(3)	-.64(5)	NS
CEO	.19(2)	.01(3)	.20(1)	-.06(4)	-1.57(5)	**
Top Second Level Line Management	.26(1)	.01(4)	.05(3)	.12(2)	-1.36(5)	**
Corporate Planning	.31(1)	.15(2)	.02(3)	-.20(4)	-1.64(5)	**
Internal	.15(1)	.07(3)	-.02(4)	-.58(5)	.12(2)	NS
Goal and Strategy Formulation Process						
Bottom Up	.16(1)	.02(3)	.05(2)	-.16(4)	-.68(5)	NS
CEO Negotiation	.36(1)	-.06(3)	-.03(2)	-.10(4)	-.59(5)	NS
Planning and Line Management						
Relative Staff/Line Nature of Planning	-.10(2)	.03(3)	-.15(1)	.33(4)	.37(5)	NS
Line View of Planning	.36(1)	-.03(3)	.06(2)	-.04(4)	-1.30(5)	**
Integrative Value of Planners						
Added Value	-.01(3)	.39(1)	.08(2)	-.49(4)	-1.65(5)	**
Planning Group Integration	.34(1)	.19(2)	-.03(3)	-.51(4)	-1.21(5)	**
Status and Authority of Planners						
Reporting Importance	.36(1)	0(4)	.03(3)	.15(2)	-1.59(5)	**
Planning Authority	-.01(3)	.24(1)	.17(2)	-.42(4)	-1.40(5)	**
Formalization of Planning						
Corporate	.79(1)	-.13(3)	.20(2)	-1.12(4)	-1.24(5)	**
Second level	.20(2)	.25(1)	.15(3)	-.20(4)	-2.45(5)	**
Plan Density Preparation	.46(1)	-.08(4)	-.03(3)	.17(2)	-2.10(5)	**
Plan Density Review	.28(2)	-.06(3)	.31(1)	-.19(4)	-1.80(5)	**
Plan Distribution Depth	.52(1)	-.18(4)	-.06(3)	-.03(2)	-.50(5)	*
Planning and Performance Review						
Plan Review Atmosphere	.13(1)	.02(3)	-.04(4)	.12(2)	-.57(5)	NS
Performance Review:						
Atmosphere	.16(1)	.05(3)	-.14(4)	-.19(5)	.15(2)	NS
Frequency	.27(2)	.35(1)	-.11(3)	-.62(4)	-1.27(5)	**
Criteria	.28(1)	.03(2)	-.03(3)	-.12(4)	-.77(5)	NS
Depth	.01(2)	-.12(4)	.19(1)	-.15(5)	-.09(3)	NS
Goals						
Use of Goals	.58(1)	-.28(3)	.10(2)	-.24(4)	-.62(5)	**
Goals for Planning	.12(2)	.05(3)	.16(1)	-.53(4)	-.61(5)	NS

[1]Figures in parentheses denote ordinal position of the means for each Planning Category.

$*\alpha = .05$, $**\alpha = .01$

level strategic planning – that is, Corporate Strategic Planners >
Corporate Financial Planners > Division Strategic Planners > Division Financial Planners > Non-Planners.

Only seven of the scales have the predicted monotonic relationship, but another 10 would produce the predicted order with just
one switch of neighboring Categories. As regards the individual Planning Categories, for 19 of the 30 scales of the Corporate Strategic Planners are in the expected polar integrative position; they are in the second position for nine additional scales. The Non-Planners are in the
opposite nonintegrative polar position for all but three of the scales.

The Corporate Financial Planners, expected to be second in
terms of integration, are in the most integrative polar position for six
of the scales and in second place for another ten scales. Although corporate financial planning seems nonadaptive, it does, as expected, appear relatively integrative.

The Division Strategic Planners are in the polar integrative
position for 4 scales, second place for 4 scales, and in the expected
third position for 15 scales. Finally, the Division Financial Planners
are in their expected fourth position for 20 scales.

Overall then, it appears that the integrative dimension also
captures a fundamental aspect of the planning process; high scale
values in general imply "good" planning practice.

4.3.6 SUMMARY

The foregoing analysis reduced the 501 planning items to a
set of 43 scales that capture the essence of the planning process. In
moving away from actual measurements on well-defined items, we
have lost the individual responses and developed dimensionless
numbers (relative, not absolute) as measures. On the positive side, we
have been able to gain a more holistic sense of the planning process,
particularly as it is practiced by firms other than the Corporate
Strategic Planners, and in doing so have been able to validate the
Planning Category system.

Despite the fact that the Category system was developed
from a handful of items, it has proved to be a powerful tool at this
level of analysis of planning, intermediate between the detail of individual measurements in chapter 3 and the aggregation represented
by the "soft model" discussed earlier in this chapter. The expected
order of categories was, however, different for each of the two functional dimensions of planning; strategic planning (corporate then division) dominated adaptation, and corporate planning (strategic then
financial) dominated integration. Overall, the results support the ex-

pected orderings of Planning Categories, though results are somewhat stronger for the adaptive than for the integrative dimension. For 15 of the scales the ordering is monotonic, while for another 10 integrative scales, a single switch of neighboring Categories produces the expected order. Finally, the responses from the Corporate Strategic Planners show a strong tendency to load in the top polar positions representing both adaptive and integrative planning.

4.4 A Final Synthesis

In section 4.2 we used principal components as a means of summarizing planning from the process perspective. In this section we use factor analysis similarly to focus on the adaptive and integrative dimensions of planning. The two sets of scales (13 adaptive scales and 30 integrative scales) were factor analyzed separately.

4.4.1 FACTOR ANALYTIC SOLUTIONS OF ADAPTIVE AND INTEGRATIVE SCALES

The two factor analyses constitute yet another step in aggregation, producing five aggregate summary measures.

4.4.1.1. Adaptive Scales

The 13 adaptive scales produced a two–factor solution on the basis of a scree test; varimax rotated loadings are presented in table 4.7. Although it is somewhat difficult to glean the underlying dimensionality, factor 1 seems to be related to *comprehensiveness* of strategic planning; it contains the two planning comprehensiveness scales and both environmental information and model use, each of which suggests high commitment. The second factor seems to be related to *depth* of strategic planning; it contains strategic criteria, portfolio models, competitive analysis, and portfolio change and suggests the extent to which strategic planning is integrated into the firm's ongoing activities.

4.4.1.2 Integrative Scales

Factor analysis of the 30 integrative scales produced a three-factor solution; varimax rotated loadings are presented in table 4.8. Once again the underlying structure is difficult to discern. The first factor is focused on *influence and integration*; it contains many of the influence scales, corporate/functional integration and two information flow scales. Factor 2 includes scales on the formalization of planning, over-time integration, and reporting importance of plan-

Table 4.7

Factor Loadings of Adaptive Planning Scales

Adaptive Planning Scales	Factor 1 Comprehensiveness	Factor 2 Depth
Environmental Orientation		
Environmental Information	.65	-
Competitive Analysis	-	.86
Strategic Orientation		
"Strategic" Planning	.62	-
Time Horizon	.74	-
Globalness	-	.32
Portfolio Change	-	.40
Resource Allocation	.50	-
Planning Tools		
Portfolio Models	-	.72
Model Use	.61	-
Resource Allocation Decisions		
Long Run Expense Distinction	-	-
Strategic Criteria	-	.70
Plan Comprehensiveness		
Corporate	.57	-
Second-Level	.56	-
Percent of Communal Variance Explained	22%	19%

ners and is labeled *formalization*. The final factor, which captures the notion of tense and confronting plan and performance review atmospheres, as well as top-down goal and strategy formulation is termed *authoritarianism*.

4.4.2 PLANNING CATEGORIES AND FACTOR SCORES

Mean factor scores of the five factors produced four significant results and almost perfect ordering of cell means among Planning Categories (table 4.9). Both the two adaptive factors, *comprehensiveness* and *depth*, produced the expected order for the adaptive function: Corporate Strategic Planners > Division Strategic Planners > Corporate Financial Planners > Division Financial Planners > Non-Planners; this is consistent with the individual scale ANOVA's reported earlier. Score means are significantly different among Categories for both factors.

Score means are also significantly different among Planning Categories for the first two integrative factors. For *influence and integration* the Planning Categories ordered as expected for the integrative function: Corporate Strategic Planners > Corporate Financial Planners > Division Strategic Planners > Division Financial Planners > Non-Planners. For *formalization,* the expected order would be obtained with a single switch of neighboring categories, Corporate Financial Planners and Division Strategic Planners.

Table 4.8
Factor Loadings of Integrative Planning Scales

Integrative Planning Scales	Factor 1 Influence and Inte- gration	Factor 2 Formal- ization	Factor 3 Auth- oritar- ianism
Formal Integration of Plans			
Corporate/Functional	.75	-	-
Over-Time	-	.62	-
Information Flow			
Top Down	-	.62	-
Internal	.47	-	-
Corporate Planning Exchange	.44	-	-
Influence and Participation			
Board of Directors	.74	-	-
CEO	.72	-	-
Top Second Level Line Management	.54	-	-
Corporate Planning	.70	-	-
Internal	-	-	-
Goal and Strategy Formulation Process			
Bottom Up	-	-	-.52
CEO Negotiation	-	.38	-
Planning and Line Management			
Relative Staff/Line Nature of Planning	.42	-	-
Line View of Planning	.47	-	-
Integrative Value of Planners			
Added Value	-	.56	-
Planning Group Integration	-	-	-
Status and Authority of Planners			
Reporting Importance	-	.68	-
Planning Authority	.45	-	-
Formalization of Planning			
Corporate	-	.44	-
Second-Level	-	.70	-
Plan Density Preparation	-	-	-
Plan Density Review	-	-	-
Plan Distribution Depth	-	-	-
Planning and Performance Review			
Plan Review Atmosphere	-	-	.71
Performance Review:			
Atmosphere	-	-	.80
Frequency	-	-.46	-
Criteria	.44	-	-
Depth	.41	-	-
Goals			
Use of Goals	.50	-	-
Goals for Planning	-	-	-.32
Percent of Communal Variance Explained	12%	11%	8%

Corporate and Strategic Planning

Table 4.9

Factor Scores Means of Planning Categories

Adaptive	Corporate Strategic Planners	Division Strategic Planners	Corporate Financial Planners	Division Financial Planners	Non-Planners	Significant Differences Among Categories
Factor 1 - Comprehensiveness	.54(1)	.12(2)	-.02(3)	-.24(4)	-1.97(5)	**
Factor 2 - Depth	.47(1)	.15(2)	-.11(3)	-.39(4)	-1.22(5)	**
Integrative						
Factor 1 - Influence and Integration	.37(1)	-.05(3)	.12(2)	-.28(4)	-1.13(5)	**
Factor 2 - Formalization	.42(1)	.23(2)	.12(3)	-.46(4)	-2.52(5)	**
Factor 3 - Authoritarianism	-.04(5)	-.04(4)	.02(3)	.23(1)	.08(2)	NS

**α = .01

4.5 Summary

In this chapter we took two quite distinct approaches in obtaining more holistic views of the planning process by reducing the set of 501 individual planning items to smaller numbers of underlying dimensions.

The planning process perspective enabled us to show that the planning system holds together when subject to "soft" model analysis. The functional perspective allowed us to develop sets of adaptive and integrative scales and to test them individually and collectively (via factor analysis) against the Planning Category system. Not only are the Corporate Strategic Planners generally both adaptive and integrative, and the Non-Planners neither, but also the ordering of the other Categories is in general as expected.

Of course, as we discussed in chapter 2, the same measures of planning are constituent items of both approaches. Table 4.10 summarizes the manner in which the items form a part of each analytic treatment. All 501 items were used in the planning process analysis; a subset of these was employed to develop scales in the functional approach. Four building-blocks of the planning process are composed of items that are either adaptive or integrative but not both; planning tools are adaptive, whereas planning organization, organizational planning environment, and planning outputs/perfor-

Table 4.10
Summary of Planning Items Used
in Process and Functional Perspectives of Planning

Process Perspective	Functional Perspective		Not Used	Total
	Adaptive	Integrative		
Planning Inputs				
Information Inputs	10	14	3	27
Planning Tools	32	0	22	54
Planning Organization	0	53	53	106
Planning Process				
Planning Activities	29	27	90	146
Organizational Planning Environment	0	41	17	58
Planning Outputs				
Planning Process Outputs	31	25	13	69
Planning Outputs/Performance Interface	0	23	18	41
Totals	102	183	216	501

mance interface are integrative. The other three building blocks contain both adaptive and integrative items. The 216 items that comprise the planning process model, but are not used to develop scales, consist of three types: a miscellaneous group of planning activity items that do not readily lend themselves to any form of grouping (face valid or empirical); items that are closely correlated with other items that are used in the scales and add little additional value; and a series of nominal scale variables that are severely unbalanced and hence probably unstable.

This concludes our detailed analyses of planning; we now turn to investigation of the relationships between planning and environment (chapter 5), strategy (chapter 6), and organization (chapter 7).

Appendices to Chapter 4

Table A4.1†

Variables Loading Heavily on First Principal Components
for "Soft" Model of Planning
(All Variables in All Groups Load Positively)

Planning Inputs

Information Inputs

Corporate planning department prepares and distributes forecasts for the
    domestic economy
Corporate planning department prepares and distributes forecasts for
    industry demand
Corporate planning department prepares and distributes forecasts for
    foreign economy
Corporate planning department prepares and distributes forecasts for
    government behavior
Corporate planning department prepares forecasts on technology
Corporate planning department prepares forecasts for competitive behavior
Corporate planning department prepares forecasts on materials
Significant effort goes into long term social forecasts
Significant effort goes into material availability forecasts
Significant effort goes into financial forecasts
Significant effort goes into forecasting industry level demand
Significant effort goes into forecasting competitive behavior

Planning Tools

Policy or portfolio matrices are developed at the corporate level
Portfolio analysis is used at lower levels
Models are used for corporate planning
Econometric models are used regularly
Forecasting, planning and budgeting models are used regularly
Models are judged to be useful
Models are used for planning at the second level
Computer systems are linked to planning
Policy or portfolio matrices are used to allocate resources
Policy or portfolio matrices are used to evaluate competitors
Policy or portfolio matrices are used to evaluate customs
Policy or portfolio matrices are used to evaluate suppliers
Policy or portfolio matrices are used as a cash management tool
The Boston Consulting Group approach is used
Strategic thinking has been influenced by BCG
Strategic thinking has been influenced by PIMS

Planning Organization

The CEO is influential in setting the assumptions for planning
The CEO is influential in setting objectives embodied in the plan

Table A4.1 (continued)

Planning Organization (continued)

The CEO is influential in setting strategies
The CEO is personally involved in evaluation and approval of the
   corporate plan
The CEO is influential in approval of the final plan
The corporate planning department influences the planning forecast
The corporate planning department influences the assumptions used in the plan
The corporate planning department is influential in setting corporate
   goals
The corporate planning department influences the objectives introduced in the plan
The corporate planning department influences the strategies embodied in the plan
Second level line managers are involved in forming objectives for the plan
Second level line managers are involved in setting strategies

Planning Process

Planning Activities

Extensive corporate planning effort goes into long term planning
Long range resource allocation is an integral part of the corporate
   planning process
Corporate planning has improved the company's long range resource
   allocation
Corporate planning puts significant effort into helping corporate
   management formulate strategy
Corporate planning puts significant effort into helping corporate
   management formulate goals and objectives
Corporate planning puts significant effort into helping corporate
   management improve the quality of strategic thinking of management
Corporate planning puts significant effort into helping corporate
   management integrate second level plans with corporate plans
Corporate planning puts significant effort into helping corporate
   management assess the overall effectiveness of the planning process
The corporate planning department has the authority to obtain substan-
   tive revision on second level plans
The planning process plays a central role in the organization's
   communication network
Human resource planning is coordinated with corporate planning
Marketing planning is coordinated with corporate planning
Manufacturing planning is coordinated with corporate planning

Organizational Planning Environment

Number of years experience at second level with current corporate
   planning systems
Number of years of experience at second level with current second level
   planning system
Number of years of experience in developing long term plans

Table A4.1 (continued)

Organization Planning Environment (continued)

Senior managers spend time working on longer term planning problems
Second level managers are involved in developing corporate strategy
Senior managers believe that the purpose of planning is to develop
    corporate strategy and long range planning policies
Senior managers believe that the purpose of planning is a mind
    stretching, creative exercise
Line personnel are rotated through the corporate planning department
Other people in the company who are actively involved in planning are
    familiar with planning concepts
The board is supportive of planning
The chain of command for planning is well defined
Management takes an active interest in the output and recommendations of
    the planning department
Second level managers take an active interest in the output and
    recommendations of the planning department
There is a feeling of team work in the corporate planning department
Goals and objectives are clear to the planning department

Planning Outputs

Planning Process Outputs

The company prepares a formal corporate plan
The corporate plan contains company analysis
Corporate level strategy is defined
The corporate plan is updated annually and not less frequently
The corporate plan is updated regularly
Number of identifiable headings in the corporate plan
Second level long range plans are prepared
Second level plans exist
Second level plans are integrated
Second level plans have market analysis
Second level plans have competitive analysis
Second level plans have company analysis
Number of identifiable headings in the second level plan
The plan has a standard annual budget format for the second level units that
    are integrated with the long-term plans of those units
Business level strategy is defined
Third level strategy is defined
Second level plans are updated annually or more frequently
Contingency plans are developed and frequently updated
The long range plan is the key guiding plan for the corporation

Planning Outputs/Performance Interface

Second level goals are used as standards to evaluate the business and
    performance
Second level goals are used as a basis for formally determining an
    incentive
Specific performance goals have been established for the planning group
The quality of planning effort is important in evaluation of second
    level managers
Implementation of planned strategy is important in evaluation of second
    level managers

†Within each block, all items load in the same direction. Some actual
questionnaire items have been restated for better understanding; some
individual items have been combined in one statement for expositional
purposes.

Table A4.2
Elements of Planning Scales

Adaptive Scales

Category	Name	Variables	Notes	α^1
Environ-mental Orientation	Environ-mental Informa-tion	Degree of effort devoted to forecasting: a) Domestic economy b) Foreign economics c) Government d) Socio-cultural e) Technology f) Raw materials g) Human resources h) Financial markets i) Industry-level demand j) Competitors	Higher value means more cor-porate fore-casting effort	.89
	Competi-tive Analysis	Intensity of Competitive Analysis: a) As major planning activity b) As a major second-level activity c) Added value of corporate over second-level d) Use of policy/ portfolio matrices e) Effort on cost structure analysis	Higher value means greater intensity of effort	.45
Strategic Orientation	"Strategic" Planning	Degree of effort to: a) Long-range planning b) Long-run mission planning c) Formal contingency planning d) Acquisition planning e) Divestiture planning	Greater effort means greater strategicness	.76
	Time Horizon	Time horizon of guiding long-range plan	Longer time horizon is more strategic	†

Table A4.2 (continued)

Adaptive Scales

Category	Name	Variables	Notes	α
Strategic Orientation (continued)	Global- ness	Worldwide Orientation to: a) Corporate planning b) Second-level planning c) Marketing strategy d) Procurement strategy e) Production strategy	Greater world- wide orienta- tion means more globalness	.85
	Portfolio Change	Intensity of acquis- ition and divestiture focus: a) Subsumed under corporate planning b) Degree of effort	Higher value means more em- phasis on port- folio changes	.78
	Resource Allocation	Planning focus on re- source allocation: a) Key resources allo- cated b) Resource allocation integral to plan c) Scarce resources al- located to best use	Higher value means resource allocation more integrated into planning pro- cess	.77
Planning Tools	Portfolio Models	Matrices used: a) BCG portfolio tool b) General Electric policy matrix c) Strategy center concept Matrices used for: d) Resource allocation e) Competitor analysis f) Customer analysis g) Supplier analysis h) Cash flow management tool	Higher value means greater use	.88

Corporate and Strategic Planning

Table A4.2 (continued)

Adaptive Scales

Category	Name	Variables	Notes	α
Planning Tools (continued)	Model Use	Numbers of models/ computer systems used: a) Models at corporate b) Models at second-level c) Computer systems d) Computer systems linking corporate planning with second level planning	Higher value means greater model/computer system use	.52
Resource Allocation Decisions	Long-Run Expense Distinc-tion	Long-run distinction made for expenses for: a) Market development b) R&D	Higher value means more long-run dis-tinction	.72
	Strategic Criteria	Relative use of criteria: Strategic vs. Financial a) market growth f) short-term cash flow b) market share g) earnings per share c) fore-cast sales growth h) forecast net op-erating profit d) fore-cast market share growth i) fore-casted ROI e) impact on com-pany re-source needs j) discounted cash flow	Strategic > Financial: relatively more stra-tegic	.78
Plan Com-prehensive-ness	Corporate	Number of headings in corporate plan	More headings means more comprehensive	††
	Second-level	Number of headings in the long run second-level plan	More headings means more comprehensive	††

Table A4.2 (continued)

Integrative Scales

Category	Name	Variables	Notes	α
Formal Integration of Plans	Corporate/ Functional	Degree of coordination with corporate planning: a) Financial b) Marketing c) Human resources d) Manufacturing	Higher value means tighter coordination	.77
	Over-time	Number of time horizons for comprehensive plans	More time horizons means greater integration	††
Information Flow	Top Down	Degree of transmission of forecasts from corporate: a) Domestic economy b) Foreign economies c) Government d) Socio-cultural e) Technology f) Raw materials g) Human resources h) Financial markets i) Industry-level demand j) Competitors	Higher value means greater transmission	.91
	Internal	Quality of information from: a) Finance b) Marketing c) Accounting d) Manufacturing	Higher value means better overall quality	.85
	Corporate Planning Exchange	Frequency of corporate planning exchange with: a) CEO/Executive committee b) Finance/Treasurer c) Senior line management d) Executive VP e) Planning staff	Higher value means greater information exchange	.80

Table A4.2 (continued)

Integrative Scales

Category	Name	Variables	Notes	α
Influence and Parti-cipation	Board of Directors	Influence in: a) Assumptions in cor-porate plan b) Objectives in cor-porate plan c) Strategies in cor-porate plan d) Approval of cor-porate plan e) Missions for second-level units f) Present corporate goals g) Second-level goals h) Format of corporate plan	Higher value means greater overall influ-ence	.75
	CEO	Influence in: a) Assumptions in cor-porate plan b) Objectives in cor-porate plan c) Strategies in cor-porate plan d) Approval of cor-porate plan e) Missions for second-level units f) Present corporate goals g) Second-level goals h) Format of corporate plan	Higher value means greater overall influ-ence	.79
	Top Sec-ond-level Line Man-agement	Influence in: a) Assumptions in cor-porate plan b) Objectives in cor-porate plan c) Strategies in cor-porate plan d) Approval of cor-porate plan e) Missions for second-level units f) Present corporate goals g) Second-level goals h) Format of corporate plan	Higher value means greater overall influ-ence	.75

Table A4.2 (continued)

Integrative Scales

Category	Name	Variables	Notes	α
Influence and Partici- pation (con- tinued)	Corporate Planning	Influence in: a) Assumptions in cor- porate plan b) Objectives in cor- porate plan c) Strategies in cor- porate plan d) Approval of cor- porate plan e) Missions for second- level units f) Present corporate goals g) Second-level goals h) Format of corporate plan	Higher value means greater overall influ- ence	.88
	Internal	Relative Influence by Insiders-executives promoted from within over: a) Academic consultants b) Consulting firms c) Executives from aca- demics d) Executives from compe- titors e) Executives from con- sulting companies f) Executives from differ- ent industries	Higher value means higher relative influ- ence from in- siders	.52
Goal and Strategy Formulation Process	Bottom Up	[reverse scale of] In- tensity of goal and strategy development by BOD and CEO: a) BOD sets goals b) BOD sets strategy c) CEO sets goals d) CEO sets strategy e) CEO/Top management sets second-level goals	Higher value means greater bottom up em- phasis	††

Table A4.2 (continued)

Integrative Scales

Category	Name	Variables	Notes	α
Goal and Strategy Formulation Process (continued)	CEO Negotiation	Degree to which CEO negotiates with second level management: a) Corporate goals b) Corporate strategy c) Second level goals	Higher value means more negotiation effort	.40
Planning and Line Management	Relative Staff/ Line Nature of Planning	Degree to which planning and line operations overlap. Second Level: a) Operating people have planning responsibility b) Planning profit centers c) Organization for planning same as operations Third Level: d) Operating people have planning responsibility e) Planning profit centers	Higher value means greater line emphasis	.89
	Line View of Planning	Attitude of line toward planning: a) Creative exercise b) Identifies opportunities and threats c) Develops long-range goals and corporate strategy d) Develops action programs and operating plans e) [reverse of] "Try to satisfy corporate and get them off my back."	Higher value means positive attitude	.58
Integrative Value of Planners	Added Value	Corporate Planning adds value over completed second-level plans: a) Finance b) Human Resources c) R&D d) Marketing e) Organization Structure f) Materials g) Competitor analysis	Higher value means greater added value from corporate planners	.85

Table A4.2 (continued)

Integrative Scales

Category	Name	Variables	Notes	α
Integrative Value of Planners (continued)	Planning Group Integration	People in planning feel that: a) Goals and objectives are clear to everyone b) Management takes active interest in planning department c) Second-level management takes active interest in planning department d) Feeling of teamwork in planning department e) Chain of command for planning defined f) People in planning familiar with content of strategies	Higher value means greater perceived planning group integration	.77
Status and Authority of Planners	Reporting Importance	Chief Corporate Planner's Supervisor is: a) Chairman/President b) Treasurer/Controller c) Executive VP Second-level Planner's Supervisor is: d) Senior second-level operating oficer e) Subordinate second-level operating officer f) Second-level officer	Higher value means higher reporting importance	††
	Planning Authority	Corporate planning has authority to: a) Accept and reject second-level plans b) Obtain substantive revisions in second-level plans c) Obtain procedural revisions in second-level plans d) Review and criticize second-level plans	Higher value means greater corporate authority	.72

Corporate and Strategic Planning

Table A4.2 (continued)

Integrative Scales

Category	Name	Variables	Notes	α
Formalization of Planning	Corporate	Corporate plan: a) Prepared regularly b) Updated every year c) Updated regularly	Higher value means greater formalization	.86
	Second-level	Second-level plan: a) Prepared regularly b) Updated every year c) Updated regularly d) Has standardized format e) Adherence to format (%) f) Integrated with budgets	Higher value means greater formalization	.88
	Plan Density Preparation	Total number of integrated plans prepared	Greater number means greater formalization	††
	Plan Density Review	Total number of plans reviewed at corporate	Higher value means higher formalization	††
	Plan Distribution Depth	Access to corporate plan given to: a) Operating managers b) Third-level managers and above c) Second-level managers d) Senior managers	Higher value means greater distribution depth	††
Planning and Performance Review	Plan Review Atmosphere	Degree to which plan review atmosphere is: a) tense b) confrontational c) non-relaxed	Higher value means more tense and confrontational	.72
	Performance Review Atmosphere	Degree to which performance review atmosphere is: a) tense b) confrontational c) non-relaxed	Higher value means more tense and confrontational	.75

Table A4.2 (continued)

Integrative Scales

Category	Name	Variables	Notes	α
Planning and Performance Review (continued)	Performance Review Frequency	Frequency of Review for: a) Corporate plan b) Second-level plan	Higher value means less frequent	††
	Performance Review/Criteria	Second-level managers achieve: a) Strategic objectives b) Implementation of planned strategy c) High quality planning d) [reverse of] Short-term profits	Higher value means greater long-run focus	.57
	Performance Review Depth	Second-level managers held responsible for variances by: a) Written narrative explanation of differences required b) Explanation of significant differences but no formal procedure c) Quantitative analysis of differences required d) No attempt to analyze	Higher value means more rigorous monitoring	††
Goals	Use of Goals	Corporate goals used to: a) Activate contingencies b) Provide challenge and motivation c) Monitor performance d) Evaluate second-level objectives e) Evaluate past performance Second-level goals used to: f) Evaluate business unit performance g) Determine incentives	Higher value means greater use of goals	.79
	Goals for Planning	Corporate planning has: a) Specific performance goals b) Receives detailed reports on its performance	Higher value means greater emphasis on performance of corporate planning	.65

[1]Chronbach α

†Single Item, α not meaningful

††Scale developed from counts, α not meaningful

PART II

PLANNING AND ENVIRONMENT, STRATEGY, AND ORGANIZATION

Planning is, of course, not an end in its own right but is rather a means by which the firm may decide upon actions to improve its performance. Choice of environment, development of strategy, and building of organization (both structure and climate) are general management problems that planning should help resolve. These areas are the subject of the three chapters in this part of the book.

Chapter 5 deals with general corporate environments (historic and future-anticipated) as they relate to planning. Chapter 6 deals with strategy – particularly with choice of business environments – and planning. Chapter 7 deals with how planning relates to organization structure and organizational climate. In each chapter of this part, we concentrate on univariate comparison of Corporate Strategic Planners with the other firms in the sample. In part III, we use multivariate methods to investigate relationships between planning and environment, strategy, and organization in a more holistic fashion.

Chapter 5

Planning and
the Environment

5.1 Introduction

A major feature of strategic planning is its orientation toward
environmental analysis. However, notwithstanding the importance of
environment and environmental change to an individual business, corporate (as opposed to business) environments pose special problems
for our study of corporate-level planning. First, most multiproduct,
multimarket firms operate in a whole range of business environments. (Recall, for example, that our firms participate, on
average, in nearly six two-digit SIC code industries.) Second, the
received wisdom of strategic planning prescribes that firms managed
strategically at the corporate level should consciously attempt to build
businesses with a mix of environments in terms of market growth and
competitive conditions. The "corporate" environment is, however,
more than the sum of these business environments, though certain
important features of the aggregate of business environments are important in describing the corporate environment.

In this chapter we explore the relationship between the
broad environment and planning systems for the firms in our sample.
We first discuss different conceptualizations of environment and present a number of perspectives from which to view the relationship between planning and the environment. Specific issues facing this study
are highlighted before we present our findings, again focusing most of
our attention on the Corporate Strategic Planners.

5.2 Conceptualizations of Environment

5.2.1 ELEMENTS OF ENVIRONMENT

Early research on firm environments distinguished between task and general environments as key constituent elements. The task environment comprises customers, suppliers, competitors, and regulatory groups that surround the individual business and affect it in the short run. Our sample of firms usually face a multiplicity of such task environments. The general environment, by contrast, includes technological, demographic, economic, and cultural factors that affect all businesses and organizations in both the short and long run. (See, for example, Dill 1958, Emery and Trist 1965, Terreberry 1968.)

More recent conceptualizations of environment have maintained the distinction between general and task environments but have elaborated on the task environment. Ackoff (1981, p. 90), in a scheme that closely resembles that of Glueck (1976), retains the general (contextual) environment but distinguishes between two segments of the task environment (market and transactional). His three elements are:

> *market* environment: those entities that the firm meets in the market place: customers and competitors.
> *transactional* environment: other entities with which the firm acts directly; for example, suppliers, investors, creditors, debtors, and regulators.
> *contextual* environment: everything other than the transactional environment that affects or is affected by the firm and over which it has very little influence, for example, general economic conditions, government expenditures, the weather.

Thompson (1967) contributed the notion of potential task environments (p. 88), recognizing that current activities determine in part future strategic directions. We suggest that the notion of potential environment should also be applied to the contextual environment, for the set of these environments may also change over time when, for example, the firm expands internationally to do business in a new nation-state – a particularly important issue for our sample, which includes many large multinational firms.

Capon and Hulbert (1985) developed an alternative system for environmental categorization based on the *impact* of environmental dimensions on the firm rather than on the environmental dimensions per se. Their marketing-oriented approach focuses on overall demand, competition, and the firm's factor inputs. Its three categories are:

demand impact: that which affects the level of aggregate demand for the firm's product category

competitive impact: that which affects the competitive equilibrium and the proportion of overall demand that is secured by the firm

factor input impact: that which affects the firm's factor inputs

5.2.2 ATTRIBUTES OF ENVIRONMENT

A second approach to the study of environment has been to identify important environmental attributes. An early attempt, based on the notion of interdependence between the firm and its surroundings, identified four types of environments (Emery and Trist 1965):

placid-randomized–resources needed from the environment are randomly distributed, and regardless of the firm's actions, its probability of securing these resources remains constant.

placid-clustered–the pattern of resource availability is sequentially predictable.

disturbed-reactive–the probability of securing resources is determined by the actions of the companies themselves.

turbulent–the probability of securing resources is not even predictable. A turbulent situation exists when the interconnectedness of the firms becomes greater and greater, resulting in an even reduced ability to predict the behavior of other actors.

Building on this conceptualization, and on work by Thompson (1967) and Terreberry (1968), Duncan (1972), whose work has guided much environmental research, identified two key environmental dimensions–simple/complex and static/dynamic. The static/ dynamic dimension captures the degree of change in the firm's environment, whereas the simple/complex dimension addresses the number and diversity of the firm's environmental relationships.

Another important dimension of environment involves uncertainty. Whereas degree of change or turbulence and complexity are generally assumed to represent the "objective" environment (even though they are typically measured as managers' perceptions), uncertainty has been viewed as perceived environment, based in large part on Weick's (1969) argument that the environment is known to the organization only through managerial perceptions. Indeed, Huber, O'Connell, and Cummings (1975) state that firms often influence their own perceptions of environmental uncertainty. (See also Downey and Slocum 1975.)

Duncan (1972) investigated the relationship between four categories of environment (combinations of his two key environmental dimensions, simple/complex and static/dynamic) and perceived uncertainty. For each environmental type he hypothesized different levels of perceived uncertainty (simple/static – low perceived uncertainty; complex/static – moderately low perceived uncertainty; simple/dynamic – moderately high perceived uncertainty; complex/ dynamic – high perceived uncertainty). He found that decision-units with dynamic environments always experience more uncertainty regardless of whether their environments are simple or complex; only if the environment is dynamic are complex environments perceived as more uncertain than simple environments.

Boulton, Franklin, Lindsay, and Rue (1982b) continued Duncan's approach of separating perceived uncertainty from other key environmental characteristics. They view the strategic planner as occupying a boundary role (Aldrich 1979) as gatekeeper for environmental information entering the organization. In the process, planners "absorb uncertainty" (March and Simon 1958: 165) when passing on information. A factor analytic solution of their environmental scales resulted in a conceptually clean four-factor solution of the task environment (customer, supplier, sociopolitcal, technological), whereas a similar analysis that also included uncertainty measures produced an unclear structure; the authors concluded that uncertainty should be treated as distinct from the environmental dimensions themselves. They also found that uncertainty is a strong moderator of the relationship between ernvironmental characteristics and industry groupings but that it has only a limited impact on the relationship between planning systems and environmental characteristics.

Agreement on the distinction between objective and perceived environment is not universal, however, for in research on environment and strategy formulation, Miller and Friesen (1983) treat the three constructs of environmental uncertainty, hostility, and heterogeneity in a parallel manner.

An alternative approach to describing firm environments has been attempted by Hambrick (1983a). Building on Hofer's (1975) list of environmental variables, developed both from the literature and personal observation, Hambrick identified 10 environmental dimensions for which business-level variables existed in the PIMS data base. He then developed eight clusters or settings that, he believed, are recurring environmental types for mature industrial product markets (roller-coaster commodities, disciplined capital goods makers, aggressive makers of complex capital goods, closeted combatants, unruly mob, passive crowd of provisioners, aggressive makers of stable feedstocks and supplies, and orderly producers of mundane supplies). While he regretted the absence of some important environmental variables, Hambrick was nevertheless able to relate his results to Lawrence's (1981) nine-cell, strategic uncertainty × resource tension matrix for viewing environment and organizations. This study is important, both substantively and because the methodology results in the development of clusters of firms defined by their environments (see chapter 9).

5.3 Relationship of Planning to Environment

There are at least three competing perspectives from which to view the relationship between planning and environment: *contingency, managerial choice, and universalistic.*

5.3.1 ENVIRONMENT–TO–PLANNING: THE CONTINGENCY PERSPECTIVE

The contingency theorist would expect the nature of the firm's planning system to be a function of the environmental contingencies it faces. Since the planning system is an important managerial device through which the firm can manage its environmental relationships, the types of planning systems employed across firms should differ according to the mix of business environments they face. To the extent that the planning system and environment are improperly coaligned, firm performance should suffer.

There is extensive research on environment-organization contingency relationships. March and Simon (1958) noted that greater environmental complexity leads to increasing use of feedback mechanisms, more organizational slack, less internal consensus, and lower task specialization. Burns and Stalker (1961) showed that firms in uncertain and changing environments tend to have organic structures and processes, while those in stable environments tend to have mechanistic structures and processes. Other studies have found that uncertain environments are related to extensive environmental surveillance, greater lateral communication, and self-contained tasks (Thompson 1967, Galbraith 1973); rapid program innovation, less formalized job design, and extensive participation in organizational decision-making (Hage and Aiken 1967). Finally, Lawrence and Lorsch (1967) found that the best performing organization units achieve a balance between differentiation and integration, based on their external environments (see also Khandwalla 1973). The fundamental perspective in this research is that environmental forces of various types result in specific structural and design configurations that govern the organization's behavior. In this research stream, strategy is by and large ignored as an explanatory variable.

Direct evidence of specific environment-planning contingency relationships is limited, but some can be adduced from the literature. Early work by Henry (1967) and Litchert (1968, 1971) indicates that emphasis on planning varies across industry. In a more complete study, Lindsay and Rue (1980) selected the two environmental dimensions, complexity and stability, after Duncan (1972) and Harvey (1968). They tested a series of hypotheses developed by classifying firms into the four categories of environment (high and low levels on each dimension) and relating these categories to different elements of planning. They concluded that large firms are attempting to "fit" their long-range planning processes to perceived environmental conditions. Thus, they found that environmental complexity and instability are associated with more complete planning systems, greater use of models and outside consultants as uncertainty reduction devices, greater flows of information in the planning process, older planning systems, and more immediate and tangible goals; they found no relationship to the planning time horizon or to the planning review period.[1]

Miller and Friesen (1983) investigated relationships among three environmental dimensions (uncertainty, hostility, and heterogeneity) and two dimensions of strategy development (analysis and innovation). "Analysis," which is related to the process of planning, is concerned with taking a large number of factors into account in decision-making. Analysis ensures complementarity and synergy of different decisions, planning for future contingencies, and developing industry expertise at high levels in the organization. "Innovation" includes the introduction of new products and technologies, the search for novel solutions to marketing and production problems, attempts to lead rather than follow competitors, and risk taking. The authors found that increased environmental uncertainty (called dynamism) and increased environmental hostility are both related to more analysis; more innovation was found in uncertain and heterogeneous environments. Furthermore, these relationships are stronger in successful than in unsuccessful firms, leading to the conclusion that firms must revise their strategy development processes to cope with changing environments.

Anderson and Paine (1975) developed a model that relates

high and low levels on each of two dimensions (perceived environmental uncertainty and perceived need for internal change) to characteristics of planning systems that would be expected in each of the four conditions. Using data from case studies, they obtained support for a number of hypotheses that relate planning elements to environmental contingencies (Paine and Anderson 1977).

Finally, a few studies have attempted to link environmental contingencies to strategic actions, with mixed results. Smart and Vertinsky (1984) investigated the likely strategic actions of key executives of major manufacturing firms in the face of crisis in their current environments. Environments were conceptualized in terms of turbulence and complexity, and 14 possible strategic actions were identified. Results showed relationships between the firm's environment and the executive's propensity to adopt a particular strategic posture; this was believed related to the executive's perceived ability to control the environment and to the economic implications of change.

On the other hand, Jauch, Osborn, and Glueck (1980) examined relationships of environmental changes and strategic action variables for 358 firms whose case histories were reported in *Fortune* magazine over a 45-year period. Nine environmental challenges (socioeconomic, consumer, technological, governmental, competitor, supplier, ownership, union, distributor) were related to eight strategic categories (financial, mission, market development, market penetration, product extensification, production efficiency, goal emphasis, mergers). There was little indication that common environmental challenges elicit common strategic responses.

In sum, an extensive body of research supports the environmental contingency perspective, especially to organizational processes; a narrower body of work has identified direct environment-to-planning contingencies.

5.3.2 PLANNING–TO–ENVIRONMENT: THE MANAGERIAL CHOICE PERSPECTIVE

The *managerial choice* perspective holds that, instead of the environment determining the nature of the firm's systems and processes, the firm chooses those environments with which it wishes to interact. The managerial choice theorist would expect that the type of planning system used by a firm would cause it to select different environments in which to compete. For example, a planning system that involves extensive environmental scanning and search for new markets and technologies to add to the firm's portfolio may lead the firm into dealing with very different environments than the firm whose planning system is more narrowly based.

Because it is advanced mainly from a theoretical perspective, little empirical work on the managerial choice perspective is available. Theorists such as Weick (1969) and Pfeffer and Salancik (1978) identify strategy as an organization's attempts to control its environment by actions designed to manage interdependencies. A key concept is the enacted environment to which the firm reacts and tries to change. They note that firms may also make the environment work for them through a series of negotiated actions (joint ventures, mergers, acquisitions, etc.).

This perspective has also been used by Bourgeois (1980) in drawing a distinction between corporate and business strategy (see chapter 6). He argues that at the level of the business strategy, much of the firm's environment is fixed and strategic decisions are concerned with how best to compete in the given environment (domain navigation). However, at the level of corporate strategy, much of the firm's environment may be considered variable and a particular set of environmental contingencies are within the firm's power to accept or reject (domain definition).

To the extent that the firm's planning results in actions that modify its environment, a planning-to-environment link might exist.

5.3.3 THE UNIVERSALISTIC PERSPECTIVE

The universalistic perspective implies that there is no necessary relationship between the firm's environment and its planning system, either from the direction of environment-to-planning system, or from planning system-to-environment. To the extent that the conventional wisdom holds a particular type of planning system to be superior to other types (or to no planning at all), firms will tend to adopt that superior system over time, regardless of the task environments they face. In this view, firms employ different types of planning systems at a particular point in time because of their greater or lesser propensity to adopt managerial process innovations.

Universalistic principles of management were sought by many early management theorists. Writers such as Taylor (1911), Urwick (1944), Brown (1945), Weber (1947), Mooney (1947), and Fayol (1949), each focusing on specific domains of interest, ranging from job performance at the worker level to characteristics of bureaucracies, attempted to develop sets of recommendations for all organizations regardless of environment.

In recent years such universalistic approaches to management have fallen out of favor, largely as a result of emphasis on contingency theory, but they have not disappeared completely. In their popular book, Peters and Waterman (1982) articulate a series of principles that characterize their "excellent" corporations: bias for action, staying close to the customer, autonomy and entrepreneurship, productivity through people, hands-on value driven, stick to the knitting, simple form/lean staff, simultaneous loose-tight properties. In his major study of diversification of United States manufacturing firms, Rumelt (1974:77) concludes that, though in the 1949-1959 period the adoption of product-division structures by corporations was strongly contingent upon the administrative pressures created by diversification (including the increased complexity of firm environments), in the 1960s "...divisionalization has become accepted as the norm and managements have sought reorganization along product-division lines in response to normative theory rather than actual administrative pressure."

Our study starts with a universalistic perspective that is later modified with tests of contingency.

5.3.4 OTHER PERSPECTIVES

Two other perspectives imply that a direct relationship between planning and environment does not exist; rather they highlight financial performance as the key variable mediating the planning process. These perspectives, one involving slack resources and the other competitive pressure, are contradictory. The slack resource perspective assumes that good performing firms have the resources to engage in the development of comprehensive planning systems whereas poor performers do not (Cyert and March 1963, Litschert and Bonham 1978). Conversely, the competitive pressure perspective assumes that poor performance increases pressure for change and that one way to identify appropriate new directions for the firm is through the development of a comprehensive planning system (Cyert and March 1963). Similar opposing perspectives resemble arguments about explanations for R&D spending (Capon, Farley, Hulbert, and Lehmann 1986), advertising budgets, and so forth. In either case, the link between environment and planning process would only be indirect through performance, so that direct planning-environment relationships would not be expected.

5.4 Environment and Performance

Although we do not investigate the relationship between environment and performance in this study, we include a brief review for two reasons. First, in chapter 10, we seek direct relationships between planning and performance, and these results should be seen in the context of extant research on direct relationships between environment (this chapter), strategy (chapter 6), organization (chapter 7), and performance. Second, in chapters 10 and 11, we investigate performance contingencies of planning with other organizational components; therefore in this chapter we review performance contingencies involving environment.

In a review of research relating environment to economic performance, Lenz (1981) identified research on both direct and contingent environment to performance relationships.

Much research on direct performance relationships falls in the industrial organization literature and is concerned with the linkage between market structure and performance (see Weiss 1971 and Vernon 1972 for reviews), historically an important issue in setting public policy. This relationship is, however, relatively weak (e.g., Vernon 1972, Phillips 1976), in part because of the heterogeneity of market structures and firm competitive positions, and in part because of the assumption of causality between market structure and performance.

The effects of certain aspects of market structure are not uniform among industries. For example, Cattin and Wittink (1976) found that the relationship between advertising-to-sales ratio and profitability differs markedly among industries, a result confirmed by Bass, Cattin, and Wittink (1978). Within industries, Porter (1979) has postulated the existence of "strategic groups" and suggested that a firm's performance and strategic choices are influenced by strategic group membership. Hatten and Schendel (1977) also detected the existence of strategic groups – in the U.S. beer industry – and found that explanation of performance is aided by measuring a firm's actions in the context of group membership; Hayes, Spence, and Marks (1983) identified strategic groups in the investment banking industry.

In heavily regulated industries, environmental factors seem to have a much greater influence on a firm's profitability than variables controlled by management. Thus, Fruhan (1972) found profitability of domestic trunk air carriers to be heavily influenced by CAB decisions on route and fare structures, and Lenz (1980) found area socioeconomic development and number of competitors to be influential in the profitability of savings and loan associations.

It has also been argued that the relationship between environment and performance is neither direct nor unidirectional (e.g., Gabel 1979). Thus, Hirsch's (1975) studies of the phonographic record and ethical pharmaceutical industries show that organizational action can influence the environment, which in future periods affects performance.

In section 5.3.1 we reviewed some of the literature on environment to organization contingencies. Despite some support for the simultaneous occurrence of certain environmental and organizational characteristics, the leap to performance is rather tenuous. Thus, the supportive Lawrence and Lorsch (1967) study was conducted with a rather small sample. Furthermore, neither Pennings' (1975) test of a "structural-contingency" hypothesis in the brokerage industry nor Child's (1974, 1975) study of the effects of multiple contingencies on organization structure could confirm contingent performance relationships between organization and environment. Although the contingency notion has intuitive appeal, the current state of research in this area is not strongly supportive. Indeed, those who argue for contingency theory frequently believe that contingencies other than environment and organization are the crucial ones (e.g., Miner 1979, Argyris 1973).

5.5 Issues For This Study

Most theoretical work on the environment, taking the perspective of a single business in one nation-state, has assumed that the firm has one set of task and general environments and has aggregated these (often only implicitly) to the level of the firm. We have a different situation, however, as the focus of this study is on the largest manufacturing firms in the United States. These are broadly diversified in regard to type of business (implying a variety of market and transactional environments) and in regard to the degree of international activity (implying different contextual environments; see chapter 1).

Consideration of our sample, and the literature review on conceptualizations of environment and on relationships between planning and the environment, points out a number of issues that must be addressed in any study of the relationship between the firm's environment and its planning system. First, should the focus of measurement be on traditional descriptive elements of environment (e.g., demand and competitive situation) or on environmental attributes (e.g., change, predictability)? Second, which environment should be measured – the firm's historic environment or its anticipated-future environment. Third, should environmental uncertainty be treated as an indicator of objective reality or should it be viewed as a perceptual matter derived from some set of more fundamental environmental dimensions? Fourth, and probably most important, how should the firm's environment be measured?

To deal with the last issue, we decided to study the firm's environment as a whole rather than as a set of subenvironments. Since we are interested in the firm's overall planning system, it seems reasonable to take such a perspective. This approach also avoids the necessity of identifying all of the different subcomponents of the firm's various market, transactional, and contextual environments – a complex task beyond the resources available for our planning study. Even if we had pursued such a complex investigation, we would still have had to aggregate the results up to the firm level. Instead, we asked our respondents to do the aggregation themselves, placing aggregation problems in the heads of the firm's corporate planners where, it could be argued, they belong.

Environmental elements and attributes were both measured. The measurements, both historic and anticipated-future environments, are based on perceptions of environmental characteristics (e.g., change, predictability) across environmental elements (e.g., demand, competition). Examples are the extent of change overall in the market environment faced by the firm and the degree of uncertainty regarding major competitors' actions. In opposition to Duncan's perspective, but consistent with Miller and Friesen (1983), we treat uncertainty as a characteristic of environment. The basis for this decision is that the distinction between "objective" and "subjective" environment seems to us to be a false one. Any measure of environment obtained by asking managers their perceptions is by definition subjective. Thus, perceptions of environmental change or environmental hostility seemed to us to be little different in type from perceptions of environmental uncertainty (or its complement – confidence in predictive ability).

A final issue with which we struggled was environmental complexity. The central role played by environmental complexity in earlier research disposed us to treat it as part of environment. However, we ran into conceptual problems as we reviewed potential measures at the corporate level, the primary focus of the study. Candidate measures for environmental complexity include, for example, the degree of industry diversity (as measured by SIC codes) and degree of international diversity. However, decisions on scope of international operations and product and industry mix represent key strategic decisions. To consider them as environmental rather than strategic measures seemed inappropriate.

Of course, the way environment should be treated is related to the level of analysis. Whereas our focus is at the corporate level, the bulk of empirical research on environment has been conducted at an organizational subunit level, usually the individual business. This is an important distinction. Whereas it is common to view the subunit environment as exogenous (Bourgeois 1980), the notion of active management of the environment at the corporate level renders it endogenous over the longer term (Weick 1969, Pfeffer and Salancik 1978, Ackoff 1981, Capon and Hulbert 1986). Even those who reject the notion of active management of environment must surely recognize that at the corporate level, acquisition and divestiture decisions represent de facto selection of environments.

In summary, it may be appropriate, as Bourgeois suggests, to view the environment at the business level as fixed – at least in the short term. Organizational processes at the business level must be developed to deal with that particular environment, including dealing with its complexity. At the corporate level, however, the environment is very much a variable, and by its strategic decisions the firm modifies environmental imperatives. An extreme exposition of this viewpoint would lead to the conclusion that environment should be viewed as part of strategy at the corporate level. We elected, however, to take an intermediate position, dropping the concept of complexity from our consideration of the environment and treating the related concept of firm diversity as strategic.

5.6 Results

We first describe the historic and anticipated-future environments faced by our sample in terms of market, factor input, technological, and governmental elements. We then report results on perceived uncertainty regarding ten anticipated-future environmental areas. In all cases, we compare the Corporate Strategic Planners with other Planning Categories.

5.6.1 HISTORIC AND ANTICIPATED-FUTURE ENVIRONMENT

Thirteen environmental measures in five categories of environment (table 5.1) were used – 12 for historic (last five years) and 9 for the future (next five years). Four measures involve general external conditions – dealing with market growth, market structure,

Table 5.1
Historic and Anticipated-Future Environment

	Historic (Last 5 Years)			Anticipated-Future (Next 5 Years)			Correlation of Historic and Future Measurement
	Sample Mean	Corporate Strategic Planners Mean	Rank	Sample Mean	Corporate Strategic Planners Mean	Rank	
Market Conditions							
Growth[1]	19.7%	26.0%	2	20.2%	25.5%	1	.79***
Structure[2]	65.8%	69.6%	2*	----	----		NA
Lack of Dominance[3]	53.2%	41.5%	5**	----	----		NA
External Shock[4]	19.5%	16.7%	4	----	----		NA
Market Predictability							
Demand[5]	20.3%	19.1%	4	22.9%	19.1%	5	.67***
Major Competitors' Actions[5]	16.6%	12.1%	5	19.7%	17.4%	4	.85***
Factor Input Problems							
Raw Materials & Supplies[6]	14.8%	19.6%	2***	18.5%	29.8%	2*	.84***
Human Resources[7]	2.6	2.2	4	2.8	2.7	4	.73***
Financing[7]	1.8	1.8	3	2.2	2.3	3*	.59***
Technological Change							
Product[8]	17.8%	21.8%	1	22.4%	28.8%	1**	.77***
Process[9]	3.0	3.0	4**	3.2	3.3	3	.55***
Government Regulation							
Extent[10]	40.8%	29.5%	5**	----	47.9%	1**	NA
Change (increase)[11]	----	----		37.3%	----		NA

1 % of Sales from markets growing in excess of 10% p.a.
2 % of Sales in markets with less than seven major competitors
3 % of Sales in markets where company is not the market leader
4 Stockholder suit or takeover attempt
5 % of Sales unpredictable or worse
6 Significant Availability problems or worse (%)
7 Means on 5-point scale: 1 = no problems, 5 = severe problems
8 % of Sales generated by technology not commercially available;
   1980/1970 - historic, 1990/1980 - future
9 Means on 5-point scale: 1 = no change, 5 = substantial changes in next 10 years
10 % of Sales highly government regulated
11 % of Sales for which government regulation will increase

***p < .01, **p < .05, *p < .10

market dominance, and occurrence of an external shock due to attempted takeover or stockholder suit. Two measures focus on predictability of market demand and of competitive actions. Three measures involve factor input problems in the areas of raw materials and supplies, human resources, and financing. Two items measure changes in product and process technology. Finally, there are two measures of government regulation – one dealing with extent and the other with the expected changes. Eight measures are common to both the historic and anticipated-future environment.

Historically, the business mix of our sample involves about a fifth of revenues from markets growing more than 10 percent per year. Generally competing in oligopolistic market structures (two thirds of sales in markets with limited competition), our firms consider themselves dominant in those markets representing nearly half of their revenues. Given our sample frame, this pattern is unsurprising. The companies have also experienced considerable environmental turbulence. A fifth of sales are in markets subject to unpredictable demand conditions, while almost as great a proportion is viewed as hostage to unpredictable competitive action. Similarly, a fifth of sales are in markets subject to significant technological change. The impact of resource constraints is apparently limited, and a very substantial part of company sales (more than 40 percent) take place in markets perceived to be highly regulated by the government. (There is, of course, double counting in these categorizations.)

Perhaps the most interesting finding is the high correlations between corresponding measures for historic and anticipated-future environment. The turbulence of the mid-to-late 1970s had no doubt affected responses, and the patterns of unpredictability reported were expected to pertain in the future. To the extent that there are differences between the historic and anticipated-future responses, however, the perception is clearly that the environment will become more difficult in the future.

5.6.2 ENVIRONMENT AND THE CORPORATE STRATEGIC PLANNERS

Table 5.1 also compares the historic and anticipated-future environments for Corporate Strategic Planners with the other firms in the sample. In general, no clear profile emerges, though a number of significant differences are indicated. For the historic environment, 5 of 12 items are significant at $p < .10$; 4 of 9 are significant at the same level for the anticipated-future environment. Some of the differences coincide with outcomes that might be expected to result from better quality planning. For example, Corporate Strategic Planners reported significantly more sales from markets where they are dominant and significantly less sales from highly regulated markets over the last five years. Similarly, in the future, they anticipate more sales in markets subject to technological change.

5.6.3 PREDICTING THE FUTURE

We also asked about confidence in ability to assess the contextual environment. Table 5.2 indicates that the sample as a whole is only moderately certain about its ability to make predictions about environments overall. For foreign economies, human resources, and the sociocultural environment, the average score is slightly above the scale midpoint, indicating particular uncertainty. Most confidence (the least uncertainty) is expressed about forecasts of industry-level demand, which is the forecast with the most immediate bearing on planning. Chapter 3 also indicates that the most effort is put into these forecasts.

Table 5.2

Uncertainty Regarding Anticipated-Future Environment[1,2]

	Sample Mean	Corporate Strategic Planners	
		Mean	Rank
Foreign Economies	3.24	3.34	2
Human Resources	3.10	3.09	3
Socio-Cultural	3.03	2.75	5
Governmental	2.74	2.78	2
Domestic Economy	2.66	2.52	5
Purchased Materials & Components	2.61	2.69	1
Competitive Behavior	2.56	2.37	5
Technology	2.55	2.60	2
Financial Markets	2.38	2.31	5
Industry-level Demand	2.24	2.05	5

[1] All measured on 5-point scales on confidence of having an adequate appraisal of the situation regarding each area: 1 = very confident; 5 = not at all confident. Sense of scale reversed for exposition.

[2] Significant difference among environmental areas**

**$p < .05$

Table 5.2 also indicates no significant differences between Corporate Strategic Planners and the other firms. This is surprising, since a priori we expected that more sophisticated planning might lead to less perceived uncertainty. It is interesting to note, however, that Corporate Strategic Planners are in the polar position for a number of key environmental elements. They are most confident in their ability to predict the course of industry-level demand, financial markets, competitive behavior, the domestic economy, and sociocultural trends. Each of these elements is directly or indirectly market-related, and consistent with the adaptive orientation of strategic planning discussed earlier.

5.7 Summary

The "corporate" environment is composed of an aggregate of business environments plus a general environment facing all firms. Much published work on the environment has implicitly focused on fixed strategies and hence on business environments that remain structurally static, at least in the short run, whereas, by contrast, corporate-level planning deals with situations where strategies and hence environments are not static. Given that the firm can choose its business environments and to some extent shape them, there is a very real question of whether environment should be treated as exogenous or endogenous to strategy development. The boundary between the general environment and the business environment is also muddied by the movement toward greater complexity of the product and market mixes of firms like those in our sample.

In this study we took a middle road, dealing with environmental complexity as one element of strategy but leaving general issues of change, predictability, and uncertainty as environmental. While there is no perfect solution available to this dilemma, we view our approach as a judicious way of dealing with what we believe to be a relatively new research problem. We may offend some by our treatment of perceptions of uncertainty as just an attribute of environment, similar to perceptions of change and predictability; our rationale is that we believe all to be perceptual constructs.

Substantively, across a number of environmental dimensions, we find little overall difference between perceptions of the historic and anticipated-future environments. Overall, though, the firms apparently perceive that the environment is becoming more difficult. When we examined environmental differences among the Planning Categories, we found some differences but a lack of pattern. Corporate Strategic Planners seem to operate in more high-change environments (market and product/technological), to have overall more dominant positions in their markets, and to face less govenment regulation, through they anticipate increasingly more. None of the Planning Categories appear particularly confident in their ability to predict future environments, though there is some suggestion that the Corporate Strategic Planners were somewhat more confident than the other firms.

Results on planning-environment relationships based on multivariate analysis are reported in chapters 8 and 9.

NOTES:

1. A recent study by Grinyer and his co-workers (Grinyer, Al-Bazzaz, and Yasai-Ardekani 1986) found only weak evidence of environment-planning system contingencies.

Chapter 6

Planning and Strategy

6.1 Introduction

The most important rationale for developing a strategic planning system is that it should enable the firm to develop more effective strategies. More effective strategies should in turn enable the firm to achieve superior economic performance.

In this chapter we explore the relationship between planning and strategy. We commence by selectively reviewing previous research on strategy. We first identify two different ways in which the term *strategy* is employed – one normative, the other descriptive. We show that strategy is set at different levels within the firm. We then focus on corporate strategy, discussing key elements of corporate strategy and their relationships to economic performance. We conclude with a brief discussion of recent work on business strategy.

This review sets the stage for presentation of the empirical results on the relationships between planning and strategy, comparing the Corporate Strategic Planners with the rest of the sample as we did in previous chapters.

6.2 What Is Strategy?

6.2.1 STRATEGY AS A NORMATIVE CONSTRUCT

Many authors have attempted to define normatively the term *strategy*, derived from the Greek word *strategos*, "the art of the general." For instance, early definitions of corporate strategy from the Business Policy group at the Harvard Business School had this normative bias: "the pattern of major objectives, purposes, or goals and essential policies and plans for achieving those goals stated in such a way as to define what business the company is in or is to be in and the kind of company it is or is to be" (Andrews 1971:25). Hofer and Schendel (1978) discussed strategy in the context of the strategy formulation process, which involves deciding the company's mission, its objectives, and the major policies governing the use of the firm's resources to achieve its objectives. Galbraith and Nathanson (1978, 1979), summarizing Hofer and Schendel, conclude that: "strategy . . . means a specific action . . . to achieve an objective decided upon in strategic planning." Finally, Capon and Hulbert (1986) present a competitively oriented statement suggesting that strategy involves a set of decisions involving the allocation of resources, designed ultimately to sustain or improve competitive position.

6.2.2 STRATEGY AS A DESCRIPTIVE CONSTRUCT

Mintzberg (1978) developed a second approach to strategy. He distinguished between two different meanings of strategy, *intended strategy* and *realized strategy*. Intended strategy is future oriented and refers to the organization's goals and its anticipated resource allocations to reach those goals; "a deliberate, conscious set of guidelines or plans for decisions in the future" (Mintzberg 1978: 935). It is clearly related to the normative definitions of Hofer and Schendel, and the Harvard group, but does not exist for those companies that do not explicitly lay out their objectives and resource allocation priorities. On the other hand, realized strategy is historically oriented and refers to actions actually taken, regardless of whether they in fact arose from a deliberate, conscious set of guidelines or plans; "a pattern in a stream of decisions" (Mintzberg 1978: 935). Realized strategy exists for all firms and can be readily observed and described in the pattern of actions taken by the firm – a kind of revealed preference at the firm level. For any particular firm, its ex post realized strategy may, of course, be quite different from its ex ante intended strategy.

6.2.3 LEVELS OF STRATEGY

Strategy exists at several levels within the firm. Normative definitions that emphasize mission and objectives (e.g., Andrews 1971, Hofer and Schendel 1978) are clearly focused at the highest level of management and are designated as *corporate strategy*.[1] Like Thompson (1967), we view domain (environment) selection as a key element of corporate strategic decisions and reject the more limited notion that strategy involves matching the organization to its environment (Khandwalla 1976), a view that implies a fixed environment. As our discussion of environment in chapter 5 indicates, corporate strategy decisions can have significant implications for the nature of the organization as a whole.

Corporate strategy involves the broad pattern of resource allocation decisions across the firm for achieving its corporate objectives. One aspect of corporate strategy is the choice of product-market domains in which to compete. *Business-level strategy* is that set of decisions, concerned with the firm's resource allocation priorities within a given (i.e., fixed) product-market domain, for achieving its objectives within that domain (Bourgeois 1980). Any firm that is at least marginally diversified (as all of ours are) may have a number of business-level strategies, an idea closely related to the concept of "firm conduct" in the industrial organizational literature. Business-level strategies typically subsume a set of *functional strategies* – marketing, production, research and development, and so forth (Vancil 1979).

One of the first to conceptualize different levels of organizational decision making was Ansoff (1965). He saw three levels: *strategic decisions* – "the selection of the product mix and markets . . . an impedance match between the firm and the environment"; *administrative decisions* – "structuring a firm's resources to maximize profit potential"; and *operating decisions* – "maximize the efficiency of the firm's resource conversion process" (1965: 56). The first two types arguably correspond roughly to corporate strategy and business-level strategy.

Hofer and Schendel (1978) distinguish between tasks associated with corporate- and business-level strategy. At the corporate level the major task is assembling the firm's portfolio of businesses; at the business level the principal task is assessing the stage of the product life cycle and the firm's competitive position (see also Beard and Dess 1981). In the context of this study we are concerned mostly with corporate strategy, though we also discuss business-level and selected functional strategy elements from time to time.

6.3 Corporate Strategy

Research on corporate strategy has its intellectual origins in Chandler's major descriptive study of the growth of General Motors, Sears, Roebuck, Standard Oil, and Du Pont (Chandler 1962). In that study Chandler was mainly concerned with the relationship between the firm's corporate strategy and its form of organizational structure. He isolated four types of strategy, implementation of each of which enables the firm to grow: *expansion of volume* (increased sales in existing markets), *geographic diversification* (entry into new markets defined geographically), *vertical integration* (absorption of the activities of suppliers upstream or customers downstream), and *product diversification* (entry of the firm into new product/markets). He found that these shifts in strategy led to considerable administrative strains, which, over a period of years, resulted in the evolution of the multidivisional structure. The relationship between strategy and structure has been supported in a number of studies. For an extensive review and conceptual synthesis of research on strategy and structure, see Galbraith and Nathanson (1978, 1979) but note Rumelt's (1974) results described in chapter 5.

Ansoff (1965) identified product/market scope, growth vector, competitive advantage, and synergy as his four elements of corporate strategy, whereas Hofer (1976), combining elements from both earlier writers, included present and planned geographic scope, present and planned product/market scope, present and planned distinctive competencies and competitive advantages, present and planned synergies, a corporate purpose, and an overall growth policy that includes both opportunistic and complementary acquisitions and a financial policy.

It is perhaps fair to say that in the descriptive literature of the past 10 years, product diversification strategy has for many authors become synonymous with corporate strategy (see Khandwalla 1976 for a broader view). We argue that in addition to this key element there are at least four other major elements of corporate strategy that typically involve resource allocation decisions made at the highest levels in the corporation: corporate direction, market and entry strategies, international posture, and acquisition and divestiture decisions. Finally, and especially in light of the recent downsizing of some large firms, we treat size as a strategic element (*Business Week* 1985).

6.3.1 CORPORATE DIRECTION: GOALS AND MISSION

In his important early work on corporate strategy, Ansoff (1965) paid a good deal of attention to the notions of objectives, goals, and missions. Whereas some authors have seen intended strategy as a step subsequent to the identification of goals and objectives, many writers view the goal formulation process as part and parcel of strategy itself. The concept of "goal" relates to the use of some standard, yardstick, or criterion at which to aim and by which to measure the firm's performance. Goals may be quantitative (e.g., ROI, EPS, cash flow) or qualitative (e.g., technical or service leadership). According to Glueck and Jauch (1984), goals help the organization to:

- define the relationship to its environment
- coordinate decisions and decision makers
- provide standards to assess performance
- provide more tangible targets than mission statements

Most work on goals has appeared in the normative policy literature. Among other research, Abou-Zeid (1974) investigated organizational goal identification, and Keown and Taylor (1978) constructed a model based on integer programming techniques for dealing with multiple criteria.

If goals are a statement of what the firm is shooting for, mission is a very broad statement of how the firm intends to get there; it is directional and is a statement of how the firm defines itself. There are many ways in which the firm can define itself, some of which were suggested by Ansoff (1965):

1. Resource-based definition: "We are in the coal business."
2. Product-based definition: "We are in the automobile business."
3. Function or need-based definition: "We are in the energy business."
4. Market-based definition: "We make products for middle-income housewives."
5. Technology-based definition: "We are an electronics company."

The mission statement both defines what the firm will do and what it will not do. For instance, a firm with the product-based mission above will make automobiles, but not bicycles, motorcycles, tractors, and so forth. However, it will sell its automobiles to any customers for which it is profitable so to do and use any product and process technology that is appropriate. Conversely, the firm with the market-based definition noted above will make and sell any product, made with any technology, that middle-income housewives would purchase.

6.3.2 MARKET AND ENTRY STRATEGY

Mission represents one approach to identifying a "common thread" for the firm; the notion of a "growth vector" is a second. Ansoff (1965) noted that *market penetration* (growth through increased share of current product markets), *market development* (growth through sales of current products to new markets), and *product development* (growth through sales of new products to current markets) each implies a strong common thread, whereas for *diversification* (growth through sales of new products to new markets), the common thread is less apparent and almost certainly weaker.

A firm may also be viewed as having a general tendency to enter a product market at one stage in the market's development rather than another (Ansoff and Stewart 1967). Among the possible perspectives that a firm may take are:

1. *Pioneer:* the firm commits major R&D resources and tends to pioneer new markets.
2. *Follow-the-leader:* the firm tends to enter markets in the early growth stage.
3. *Segmenter:* the firm tends to enter markets in the late growth stage, when the possibilities for market segmentation are generally most attractive.
4. *Me-too:* the firm tends to enter markets in maturity, often by adopting a low price strategy.

A major resource allocation decision that distinguishes the pioneer and follow-the-leader firms from others is the commitment to research and development. We believe that decisions about the extent of commitment to R&D are typically made at the corporate level and hence are a key element of corporate strategy.

6.3.3 DIVERSIFICATION STRATEGY

As noted above, this area has generated the most empirical work. Wrigley (1970) identified four different types of diversification strategy ranging from no diversification to extensive diversification.

1. *Single product business:* the firm remains in its original business and does not venture into new areas.
2. *Dominant business:* the firm has diversified away from its original business, but the original business remains dominant, accounting for between 70 percent and 95 percent of sales.
3. *Related business:* less than 70 percent of the firm's sales come from a single business, but the firm has diversified by adding activities that are tangibly related to its activities.

4. *Unrelated business:* the firm has diversified into areas that are not related to the original skills and strengths of the firm.

Wrigley's analysis of the *Fortune* 500 manufacturing firms for 1967 identified the modal category as related business (60%), far ahead of unrelated business (20%), dominant business (14%), and single business (6%). A number of Harvard doctoral students replicated Wrigley's empirical work in Europe: United Kingdom (Channon 1973), France (Pooley-Dyas 1972), Germany (Thanheiser 1972), Italy (Pavan 1972) and found in general that, though the proportion of single and dominant businesses was substantial, it was declining as the proportion of related businesses was growing (see Scott 1973 for a review of this work).

Wrigley's product diversification framework formed the basis for Rumelt's (1974) work, perhaps the most influential in the corporate strategy area. Building upon Wrigley's basic structure, Rumelt's major contribution was his elaboration of the relatedness concept, an idea similar to Ansoff's (1965) notion of "synergy," which he considered to have major potential for increasing earnings. Rumelt distinguished between two types of relatedness – constrained and linked. Constrained-relatedness occurs when the group of related businesses all share a common skill or resource; linked-relatedness describes the situation in which the group of businesses emerge by incremental steps from a core, each business linked to the previous one, but without the entire group's drawing upon the common resource. Application of this distinction to the dominant business category results in the formation of three sub-categories: dominant-constrained, dominant-linked, and dominant-unrelated. Firms in which more than 70 percent of sales come from a group of related businesses are identified as either related-constrained or related-linked, depending upon the form of diversification; for unrelated firms a special category was created for conglomerates, and firms were therefore classified as either acquisitive-conglomerate or as unrelated-passive. Finally, and drawing upon the strategic distinction made by Chandler, firms in the dominant category that have grown by vertical integration are identified as dominant-vertical. Despite the qualitative nature of the classification procedure, Montgomery (1982) reclassified Rumelt's (1974) companies with a high degree of reliability.

In his most recent work, Rumelt has reduced the nine-category scheme to seven categories by combining the two unrelated groups into a single unrelated business category, and the dominant-linked and dominant-unrelated categories into a dominant linked-unrelated category (Rumelt 1982). In addition, the distinction between constrained and linked diversification has been quantified by the introduction of a related-core ratio. A tree diagram development of Rumelt's scheme is displayed in figure 6.1.

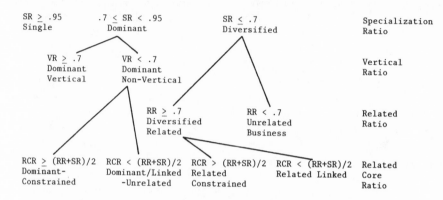

Specialization Ratio (SR): The fraction of the firm's revenues attributed to its largest discrete product-market activity (Rumelt 1974, 1982).

Vertical Ratio (VR): The fraction of the firm's revenues that arise from all by-products, joint-products and end-products of a vertically integrated sequence of processing activities (Rumelt 1974, 1982).

Related Ratio (RR): The fraction of the firm's revenues attributable to its largest group of related businesses (Rumelt 1974, 1982).

Related Core Ratio (RCR): The fraction of the firm's revenues attributable to its largest group of businesses which share or draw on the same common core skill, strength or resource (Rumelt 1982).

Figure 6.1
Rumelt's (1982) Diversification Typology

Rumelt's application of his scheme to the *Fortune* 500 firms over a 25-year period from 1949 to 1974 revealed that the largest individual group in 1949, the single business, had decreased from 42 percent to 14 percent by 1974. Diversification was clearly the major growth strategy of this period, for by 1974 unrelated business (21%), related-linked (23%), and related-constrained (20%) were the three largest groups. See Capon, Farley, Hulbert, and Martin (1987) for development of a Rumelt-like scheme in which the key dimension of "relatedness" is identified as markets served.

6.3.4 INTERNATIONAL POSTURE

Like Chandler, who considered geographic diversification a key strategic element, we consider international diversification to be a major element of corporate strategy. The commitment of resources to foreign countries, in which the set of risks are very different from expansion within the home country, is typically a corporate decision. Associated decisions include form of entry into foreign markets, degree of market development effort in various parts of the world, and extent of foreign manufacturing. The relationship of international diversification to organization structure has attracted a good deal of attention by researchers (Stopford 1968, Stopford and Wells 1972, Hulbert and Brandt 1980, Egelhoff 1982) and is discussed further in chapter 7.

6.3.5 ACQUISITION AND DIVESTITURE

The acquisitive-conglomerate category of Rumelt's (1974) scheme does not fully capture the importance of acquisitions to corporate strategy, for the categorization involves only acquisitions unrelated to the firm's core activity. Firms also make acquisitions of related businesses, and it seems worthwhile therefore to include the firm's disposition (and behavior) to add to its portfolio of activities by acquisition as an element of corporate strategy, regardless of whether an acquired business is unrelated or related to current activities (Salter and Weinhold 1979). Similarly, alteration of the firm's business mix by divestiture is also included as an important element of corporate strategy.

6.3.6 CORPORATE SIZE

Size has been viewed in many different ways: as an exogenous structural characteristic, as a component of organizational context, as an inhibitor of social integration, and as a consequence of organizational goals and strategy. (See Kimberly 1976 for a review.) Notwithstanding these different viewpoints, we take the position that size is a strategic element subject to managerial discretion and that firms are able both to increase and decrease their sizes by taking appropriate action.

As regards increases in size, it has been argued that there are limits to the abilities of firms to grow by internal development (Penrose 1955). Regardless of the validity of such arguments, internal growth is only one method by which the firm can increase in size; growth by merger and acquisition represent both important, and complementary, means by which size increases can be achieved. Furthermore, the firm makes explicit trade-offs between devoting resources to growth, to dividend payments and to stock repurchases.

Although growth in size characterizes the behavior of most corporations, many firms also decide to reduce their size. Thus, the decision to be acquired is, in one sense, a decision to reduce the firm size to zero. Furthermore, decisions to reduce firm size while retaining the corporate identity have become increasingly common (*Business Week* 1985).

Size per se is frequently viewed as a determinant of the structural characteristics of organizations (Kimberly 1976). Furthermore, many authors have argued that increases in size are associated with problems of communication and coordination; we might expect, therefore, that relationships would exist between corporate size and planning practice. There seems to be considerable confusion in the discussions about size in regard to whether it involves sheer economic volume (based primarily on the scale of the markets in which the firm chooses to compete) or complexity (based on the combination of various different markets in which the firm participates). We consider both perspectives.

6.4 Corporate Strategy and Performance

The relationship between corporate strategy and financial performance of the firm has attracted many researchers. The major efforts concern diversification strategy, and two broad approaches can be identified: the business count approach rooted in industrial organization, and the strategic management approach upon which much of our earlier discussion of corporate strategy is based.

6.4.1 BUSINESS COUNT METHODS
The business count approach to studying diversification identifies individual businesses, typically by means of SIC code or other census bureau information, and then essentially counts the number of businesses (Pitts and Hopkins 1982). Various methods have been employed, including simple counts (Carter 1977), share of the largest business (Rhoades 1974), and comprehensive indices such as the Hirschman (1964) index, which gives more weight to larger busi-

nesses, and the entropy index (Jacquemin and Berry 1979), which gives less weight to larger businesses. Despite many attempts, there is little evidence of any relationship between business count diversity measures and corporate financial performance (Gort 1962; Bass 1973; Rhoades 1973, 1974; Carter 1977; Bass, Cattin, and Wittink 1978; Beattie 1980).

The absence of identifiable relationships may result from a lack of validity in these diversity measures; the basic problem with the business count method is that it lacks a theory about how diversification decisions should affect the corporation. For example, a firm with considerable potential for synergy in three mining businesses (gold, bituminous coal, and anthracite coal) appears as diverse at a four-digit SIC code level (U.S. Office of Management and Budget 1972) as a firm with three businesses in life insurance, elevator manufacturing, and doll manufacturing. There is no explicit appreciation in the business count measures that skills, resources, knowledge, assets, and so forth may be transferred across like businesses to improve performance.

An associated body of work involves studies that focus on the method by which diversity is obtained, e.g., external acquisition versus internal development. Although evidence suggests that acquisitive conglomerates have faster rates of growth of assets, sales, and employment than nonconglomerates have (Reid 1968, Weston and Mansinghka 1971), they earn no greater returns on assets or on equity (Weston and Mansinghka 1971, Melicher and Rush 1973, Holzmann, Copeland, and Hayya 1975).

6.4.2 STRATEGIC MANAGEMENT APPROACH

In contrast to the paucity of findings from the business count approach, the strategic management approach to diversification associated with Wrigley and Rumelt has produced significant performance relationships. Based on his nine-category scheme, Rumelt, using five-year averages of return-on-invested capital and return-on-equity, showed that dominant-constrained and related-constrained corporations are the best performers, and that dominant-vertical and unrelated-passive firms are the poorest.

Associated research has demonstrated a link between diversity and performance, providing at least partial support for Rumelt's results (Caves, Porter, and Spence 1980; Bettis 1981; Christensen and Montgomery 1981).[2] In his latest work, Rumelt (1982) again demonstrated a diversity-performance relationship; related-constrained firms are the best performers on a five-year average return-on-invested-capital measure whereas dominant-vertical and unrelated-business firms perform least well. (See Dundas and Richardson 1982 for a discussion of implementing successful unrelated-business strategies.)

The basis for this relationship is not, however, clear. Christensen and Montgomery (1981) suggested that related-constrained firms tend to operate in industries whose market structure leads to above-average profitability, and Rumelt (1982) found that the significant effect for related-constrained firms disappears if the industry effect is factored out.

Other work suggests that industry effects are important predictors of performance. Lieberson and O'Connor (1972) studied a sample of stock exchange-listed firms over the period from 1946 to 1965; they found that the firm's primary industry explains 20 to 30 percent of the variation in profitability and growth. In a similar fashion, Beard and Dess (1979) showed that industry return-on-assets and industry return-on-equity proved to be significant predictors of corresponding measures of firm profitability; intraindustry variables were also significant.

In associated work Bettis (1981) found evidence that related firms are able to achieve higher returns to R&D than unrelated firms, and Capon, Farley, Hulbert, and Martin (1987) demonstrated that firms specialized by market outperform those that are not as specialized.[3]

The overall conclusion from this stream of work seems to be that controlled diversification leads to above-average performance; however, those returns, at least in part, seem to result from operating in industries favored with high profitability. What is not clear from the research is whether related diversification leads to the selection of attractive industries or whether firms in attractive industries diversify in a related manner.

6.4.3 CORPORATE SIZE

The relationship between firm size and profitability has long been a subject of interest to economists working in the industrial organization tradition. Some have used economy of scale arguments to hypothesize a positive relationship, whereas others have suggested that large size leads to inefficiencies, poor communications, delayed decision-making, and so forth. Recent actions of some large U.S. companies to buy back stock and divest large segments of their operations (*Business Week* 1985) suggest that present corporate management believes that downsizing of companies can lead to increased stockholder returns. Reflecting these different perspectives, the empirical research on corporate size and performance has produced conflicting results (Hall and Weiss 1967, Shepherd 1972, Dalton and Penn 1976, Bass, Cattin, and Wittink 1978).

6.5 Business-Level Strategy

Diversified firms are, of course, a collection of businesses. In this selective review of the extensive literature on business strategy, we highlight three aspects: performance-related strategic elements, performance-related business portfolio characteristics, and performance of firms sharing common strategic profiles.[4]

6.5.1 STRATEGIC ELEMENTS

Many studies have identified a positive relationship between market share and profitability. Gale (1972), Shepherd (1972), and Winn (1975) based their findings on publicly available data, whereas Schoeffler, Buzzell, and Heany (1974), and Buzzell, Gale, and Sultan (1975) based their results on business-level data collected under the auspices of the PIMS program. (See Schoeffler 1977 for a description of the PIMS program.) Theoretical support for this finding is provided in part by the notion of the experience curve (an extension of economy of scale ideas) under which firms experienced in developing, producing, distributing, and promoting a product (or group of products) can expect to have lower costs than their less experienced competitors and hence be more profitable (Boston Consulting Group 1972, Abernathy and Wayne 1974, Abell and Hammond 1979). Some authors, however, remain skeptical (Jacobson and Aaker 1985).

Studies that relate capital intensity to firm profitability typically find a negative relationship (Schoeffler, Buzzell, and Heany 1974; Winn 1975; Hatten and Schendel 1977). Winn anticipated a positive relationship on two grounds: first, high capital intensity should provide a barrier to entry and, second, capital intensity is related to firm size, and since size, with an economy of scale argument, should be related to profitability, so too should capital intensity be related to profitability. The basis for the negative relationship is explained in terms of higher levels of fixed costs for the highly capital-intensive firms and consequent profit penalization in times of economic downturn. At the corporate level, Rumelt's (1974) finding that vertically integrated firms have the highest capital intensities and are among the least profitable is also supportive of the capital intensity result.

In associated work, Beard and Dess (1981) investigated the relative importance of corporate-level and business-level strategic decisions in their impact on firm profitability. Corporate-level strategy is operationalized as industry participation, while three elements of business strategy are considered; capital intensity, debt-leverage (unexplainably considered a business-level and not a corporate-level decision), and relative firm size. They found that both industry participation (corporate) and capital intensity and debt-leverage (business) explain variation in firm profitability (ROI and ROE), but they were unable to make unambiguous statements in regard to whether the corporate or business level provides greater explanatory power. They did find, however, that the relative explanatory power of these three variables varies over time, a result they attributed in part to the pattern of the general business cycle. (They did not find a positive relationship of firm's relative sales size to profitability.)

6.5.2 PORTFOLIO CHARACTERISTICS

In chapter 2, we discuss the variety of portfolio and policy matricies that have been developed as strategic decision-making aids. Despite the fact that these matrices are widely cited, little empirical work has been conducted on them. In a rare study, Hambrick, Mac-Millan, and Day (1982) tested prescriptions from the BCG matrix regarding the profitability and cash flow characteristics of 1,000 industrial products businesses occupying the four cells (stars, cash cows, dogs, problem children) using PIMS data. By and large they confirmed expectations for businesses in the four cells, but found that the performance of "dogs" is better than had been expected. They also characterized businesses in the four cells on a series of strategic attributes.

In a companion paper, MacMillan, Hambrick, and Day (1982) examined the association between strategic attributes and profitability of businesses in each of the four cells of the BCG matrix. The strategic variables that contribute the most to explained variance in profitability (ROI and CFOI) are capital intensity ($-$), value added ($+$), and manufacturing costs ($-$). Mature businesses benefit most from resource utilization and product quality, but few generalizations can be made for growth businesses; low-share businesses benefit from concentration of resources on limited segments and liberal credit terms, whereas high-share businesses benefit from premium prices.[5]

6.5.3 STRATEGIC PROFILES

Overarching general frameworks of business-level strategy are few, but one that has attracted some attention recently was developed by Miles and Snow (1978). On the basis of field studies in the college textbook, electronics, food processing, and health-care industries, they identified four recurring strategies, and associated distinctive competences, three of which are viable and one that is not. The three viable strategy types are *defenders* – organizations that engage in little or no product/market development and that often control secure niches in their industries, competing primarily on the basis of price, quality, delivery, or service; *prospectors* – firms that attempt to pioneer product/market development, offer a frequently changing product line, and compete by serving new market opportunities; and *analyzers* – intermediate firms that are less committed to stability than defenders but that make fewer and slower product/market changes than prospectors do.

Firms that make opportunistic deviations from their strategies or that never develop a strategy and the accompanying consistencies are fated to low performance and are labeled *reactors*. Related to each strategic type are functional strategies, organizational structures, and processes that are internally consistent and that tend to perpetuate over time.

Snow and Hrebiniak (1980) tested managerial perceptions of their firm's distinctive competences against the Miles and Snow (1978) category scheme and also tested the proposition that the three viable strategies would perform equally well in any industry, provided that the strategy is well implemented. In general, these propositions are supported, though *reactors* perform no less well than the other categories in heavily regulated industries.

Hambrick (1983b) noted that the Miles and Snow (1978) typology of business strategies is perhaps too generic; it ignores industry and other environmental effects, whereas most strategy literature proceeds from the premise that the firm should align its strategy with environmental imperatives. He also raised questions about Snow and Hrebiniak's impressionistic measures of strategy. Hambrick examined the performance tendencies of the polar successful firms (prospectors and defenders) in different environments, and explored the functional attributes of the two types. He found that defenders and prospectors differ in their performance tendencies across two environmental variables – product life-cycle stage and industry product innovation. In each type of environment examined, defenders outperform prospectors in current profitability and cash flow, whereas prospectors outperform defenders for market share gains, but only in innovative environments. Prospectors have the entrepreneurial attributes of high-product R&D expenses and high marketing expenses; defenders have the efficiency orientation of high capital intensity, high employee productivity, and low direct costs.

It should be noted that the elements upon which the Miles and Snow strategy types are built are at the business level. To the extent that firms make common sets of strategic decisions across many businesses, the strategy types may be raised to the level of corporate strategy.

Miller and Friesen (1977) broaden the scope of enquiry into contingency issues by arguing against the study of simple bi-variate relationships. They suggest that there may be a limited number of relationship sets between environmental, organizational and strategy variables which occur repeatedly. Using raw data for a set of 81 firms obtained from case studies they identify 31 variables categorized as environmental (past and current), organizational, strategy making and financial performance. From a Q-type factor analysis they classify the successful firms into six archetypes (adaptive firm under moderate dynamism, adaptive firm under extreme dynamism, dominant firm, giant under fire, entrepreneurial firm and innovator), and the unsuccessful firms into four archetypes (impulsive firm, stagnant bureaucracy, headless giant, swimming upstream). They view the archetypes as a set of relationships in a temporary state of balance, administrative situations which seem to form a number of *gestalts*. [See Snow and Hambrick (1980) for a discussion of theoretical and methodological issues involved in conducting research on strategy, and Ginsberg and Venkatraman (1984) for a recent review of research on strategy set in a contingency framework].

6.6 Results

In this section we present a detailed set of results on the relationships between planning and strategy, both for the sample as a whole and for the Corporate Strategic Planners. The results are presented according to the six elements of corporate strategy: corporate direction, market and entry strategy, diversification, international posture, acquisition and divestiture and corporate size. The hypotheses involving the Corporate Strategic Planners are in general drawn from the strategy literature just discussed. Overall, we expect the Corporate

Strategic Planners, because of their high-level commitment to strategic planning, to embrace elements of the received wisdom regarding strategy to a greater extent than the other firms do. There is, however, considerable controversy about specific points—e.g., whether it is generally profitable to seek market share.

6.6.1 CORPORATE DIRECTION: GOALS AND MISSION

In general, the hypotheses related to corporate direction are based on the presumption that a clear statement of direction is helpful and that planning, as a purposeful activity, should encourage the development of explicit direction. We first present our results on goals, followed by those on mission.

6.6.1.1 Quantitative Goals

The vast majority of firms (88%) report explicit quantitative long-term goals that serve guiding roles in strategic decisions for the company as a whole. Six types of goals were identified: return goals (e.g., on investment, equity, assets, capital), sales goals (growth, return of sales), stock market goals (EPS, P/E ratio), profits or cash flow goals, financial ratio controls, and dividend maintenance.

The most frequently mentioned goals (table 6.1), noted by

Table 6.1

Quantitative Goals Guiding Strategic Decisions[1,2]

	Sample		Corporate Strategic Planners		
	Goal Present Percent	Goal Dominant Percent	Goal Present Percent	Rank	Goal Dominant Percent
Return Goals (ROI, ROE, ROA, etc.)	63	36	63	2	33
Sales Goals (growth, ROS)	38	7	46	1	9
Stock Market Goals (EPS, P/E ratio)	32	13	46	1*	23
Profits/Cash Flow	25	6	29	2	5
Financial Ratio Controls	12	1	25	2*	1
Dividend Maintenance	7	12	17	1*	14
Others	12	--	9	5	--

[1]Percentages sum to over 100 as a result of multiple responses

[2]Significant differences among types of goals** (for present and dominant) and Planning Categories*

**p < .05, *p < .10

well over half of the sample with goals and also considered dominant by most firms, are of the return type (ROI, ROE, ROA, and so forth). Intermediate in mention are sales goals, stock market goals, and profits/ cash flow goals. Financial ratio controls and dividend maintenance were mentioned by few respondents. Multiple nonconflicting goals are relatively common. Corporate Strategic Planners have more goals than the others, and are also more likely to have goals expressed in terms of earnings per share, price/earnings ratio and dividend maintenance.

About half the sample reported that quantitative goals were adjusted for inflation; there were significant differences across Planning Categories, and two thirds of the Corporate Strategic Planners made such adjustments.

6.6.1.2 Qualitative Goals

Seventy-three percent of respondents indicated that their companies had formed qualitative goals, although these appear less important than quantitative goals. Open-end descriptions of these are grouped into five categories: leadership in quality, service or image, focus/concentrate on segment, technological leadership and advantage, maintain acceptable financial posture and societal goals.

In terms of these goals, those most frequently mentioned are leadership in quality, service or image (table 6.2). A quarter of the firms indicate a goal of focus or concentration; others are noted less

Table 6.2
Presence of Qualitative Goals[1,2]

	Percent of Sample	Corporate Strategic Planners	
		Percent	Rank
Leadership in quality service or image	35	33	3
Focus/concentrate on segment	25	17	4
Technological leadership and advantage	21	38**	1
Maintain acceptable financial posture	19	33**	1
Societal goals	16	25	1

[1]Percentages sum to over 100 as a result of multiple responses

[2]Significant differences among types of goal*** and Planning Categories**

***p < .01, **p < .05

frequently. The major qualitative goals are thus more an extension of the quantitative goals than they are conflicting with them. Corporate Strategic Planners have a significantly higher mention of technological leadership and advantage and maintaining acceptable financial posture. The former probably indicates particular concern with new products and new markets.

6.6.1.3 Change in Corporate Goals

Goals should be relatively unchanging if they are to be of strategic importance. In response to questions about the last time that a significant change of type or level of goals had been made, the overall response was on average 7.2 years previously. There are, however, significant differences among Planning Categories; goal changes of three years on average for the Corporate Strategic Planners compared to more than 14 years for the Non-Planners. Among six categories of goal change (table 6.3), financial factors and upgrade/update are the most frequently mentioned.

Table 6.3
Changes in Corporate Goals[1]

	Percent of Sample	Corporate Strategic Planners Percent	Rank
Financial Factors Change	58	83***	1
Upgrade or Update	42	50	1
Formalization or Explicitness	21	21	3
Instituted New Goals	16	25	1
General Qualitative Additions	12	8	3
Focus or Philosophy	12	4	5

[1]Significant differences among types of goal change*** and Planning Categories***

***p < .01

6.6.1.4 Second-Level Goals

All but one company reported that different types of performance goals are set for different second-level operating units. Under reasons for using different goals, differing competitive environments are mentioned by 40 percent of firms; 26 percent indicate that there are different financial demands or different levels of capital intensity, and about 20 percent indicate different business conditions. There are no differences among Planning Categories. It seems that all firms are attempting to implement strategies involving different approaches to investment at different stages in product life cycles, planning being only one of a number of ways to develop such strategies.

6.6.1.5 Mission

Mission is a statement – usually based on types of products, markets, or technologies – that specifies a broad direction the firm will take to secure its quantitative goals. We have taken a restrictive view of mission. For example, a vague statement that focuses on unspecified growth or service to stockholders, employees, or society at large is of little strategic value and is not considered to fall within the scope of our construct. From open-end responses on mission, five categories were developed: product based, product/market combinations, natural resource, technology, and function or need. Responses that could not be classified according to this scheme were deemed not to be mission statements. Although 60 percent of the companies provided a formal mission statement, only 27 percent of the sample could be classified as having a mission statement by our criteria. Of these, about half had product-based missions; technology missions and missions based on function/need each contributed 20 percent, with product/market combination missions and natural resource-based missions making up the remainder. There are no significant differences in mission types among Planning Categories. Although our criterion for acceptance of a mission statement is an exacting one, nonetheless, the relatively small number that we found was unexpected.

Mission statements should be expected to change fairly infrequently. Surprisingly, however, of the companies with a classifiable mission statement, 83 percent had changed that statement in the previous five years – more frequently than corporate goals. From open-end responses to the question of what changes had been made, 35 percent of firms indicated that this was their first mission statement, 27 percent indicated that the statement had been made more specific, and 38 percent that it had been expanded. The four most cited reasons for change are a new CEO (29%), newly developed capabilities (21%), recommendations from line management (14%), and unsatisfactory past performance (32%). One company noted political or regulatory action as a reason. There are no differences among Planning Categories.

6.6.2 MARKET AND ENTRY STRATEGY

Decisions related to market participation and entry are among the most important elements of modern strategic management. A series of 12 questions examines many of the basic tenets associated with effective strategy – e.g., enter high growth markets, seek large market shares, attempt to create protection from competitive entry through patents. Corporate strategic planning should be instrumental in pushing firms in these directions. The results (table 6.4) generally follow what has been the pattern of results in this chapter – some indication of differences in the expected direction but generally a mixed pattern.

Overall, the sample seeks classic strategic position – high growth, large share, and the possibility of differentiation. Exit seems to attract less attention than entry. Vertical integration is generally unimportant, as is capital intensity.

Table 6.4
Explicit Nature of Corporate Strategy[1,2]

	Item Loads Heavily on This Factor in a Factor Analysis	Sample Mean	Corporate Strategic Planners Mean	Rank
We seek to enter high growth markets	1	4.18	4.38	1
We seek situations where we can attain a large share of served markets	1	4.17	4.54	1***
We seek situations where product differentiation is important	1	4.07	4.46	1*
We seek situations where economies of scale are significant	1	3.45	3.92	1***
We seek to enter markets with small numbers of competitors	3	2.92	2.82	4
We seek situations requiring low capital intensity	-	2.91	2.92	3
We seek situations where patents are important	1	2.83	3.50	1*
We seek to vertically integrate forward to final markets	2	2.69	2.58	4
We seek to enter or develop service businesses	2	2.43	2.71	2
We seek to vertically integrate backward toward source of supply	2	2.04	2.38	3
We seek situations where scarce resources are important	2	2.04	2.13	3
We attempt to exit from markets with large numbers of competitors	3	1.84	1.71	5

[1]Means on 5-point scale: 1 = disagree, 5 = agree

[2]Significant differences among items*** and Planning Categories***

***p < .01, *p < .10

Individual strategic elements show some interesting patterns among Planning Categories. The Corporate Strategic Planners have the highest ratings for seeking high growth markets, large shares of served markets, product differentiation, scale economies, and patent protection, significantly so in the latter four cases. These are important elements of the received wisdom regarding strategy making.

Some further insight into these patterns is gained from a factor analysis of the 12 items. Factors on which the items load (all greater than 0.50) are also shown in table 6.4. The first factor contains the items accepted as effective strategy, which differentiate the strategic planners on the high side; the second factor focuses on vertical integration moves; and the third involves competitive structure. Factor scores confirm the significant difference of the Corporate Strategic Planners on the items loaded on the first factor.

6.6.2.1 Product/Market Strategies

Historic and anticipated emphases on various product/market combinations (table 6.5) indicate a generally consistent pattern of Corporate Strategic Planners assigning significantly greater importance to various combinations of new markets and new products. In the past, there was clearly less emphasis on diversification than is anticipated in the future for all firms, though historic and future dependence on existing products for new markets and new

Table 6.5
Product/Market Growth Strategies[1,2]

	Past Five Years			In The Future		
	Sample Mean	Corporate Strategic Planners		Sample Mean	Corporate Strategic Planners	
		Mean	Rank		Mean	Rank
Existing Products/ Existing Markets	4.31	4.13	4	3.73	3.29	5
New Products/ Existing Markets	3.22	3.88	1*	3.72	4.04	1
Existing Products/ New Markets	3.03	3.42	1*	3.23	3.38	2
New Products/ New Markets	2.38	3.0	1*	3.24	3.63	1*

[1] Means on 5-point scale : 1 = not at all important, 5 = very important

[2] Significant differences among growth strategies***, Planning Categories*** and Past and Future**

***p < .01, **p < .05, *p < .10

products for existing markets are viewed as roughly the same. Growth from existing products in existing markets (market penetration) is most important for the sample as a whole but less so for the Corporate Strategic Planners; these firms tend to be more oriented toward new ventures, and in the future toward options involving new products. Growth via market penetration is anticipated to be less important overall in the future, resulting in a major requirement for orderly development of new venture strategy.

A similar pattern is shown in responses about general approaches to introduction of new products and services (table 6.6). All firms attempt to avoid entry late in the life cycle, but early following of successful innovation is favored slightly over pioneering or late entry into established markets. No overall pattern of significant differences occurs among Planning Categories, though Corporate Strategic Planners appear to favor an innovative posture. There is, of course, considerable controversy about which entry strategy is most effective (Robinson and Fornell 1985).

Table 6.6
New Product and Service Introductions[1]

We attempt to be:	Sample Mean	Corporate Strategic Planners Mean	Rank
Early followers of initial entrants in established and fast growing new markets	2.99	2.59	5
First to market with new products & services	2.93	3.04	1
Later entrants in established but still growing markets	2.75	2.63	4
At the cutting edge of technology	2.48	2.71	1
Entrants into mature stable markets	2.27	1.96	4**
Entrants in declining markets	1.28	1.08	5*

[1]Means on 5-point scale: 1 = never, 5 = always

**p < .05, *p < .10

6.6.2.2 Research and Development

On average, 2.3 percent of corporate revenues are spent on R&D activities; 15 companies report spending 5 percent or more. There are no significant differences among Planning Categories, though the mean for the Non-Planners is lowest at 1.6 percent. Overall, a higher percentage of expenditures goes to new product research (1.27%) compared to new process research (0.93%). This dominance of new product expenditures holds true for all Planning Categories.

Elements of research and development (table 6.7) show a highly applied emphasis and overall a preference to grow internally rather than via acquisition. Again, there are no overall significant differences among Planning Categories, though the Corporate Strategic Planners display a greater tendency than the other firms to high-risk, innovative, internal R&D.

Table 6.7
Research and Development Emphasis[1,2]

	Sample Mean	Corporate Strategic Planners	
		Mean	Rank
The emphasis of R&D expenditures is highly applied	3.95	4.00	2
R&D effort tends to avoid high risk activity	3.37	3.08	5
This company considers itself to be highly technically innovative	3.08	3.38	1
This company prefers to seek growth via acquisitions rather than internal R&D	2.59	2.50	4

[1]Means on 5-point scale: 1 = disagree, 5 = agree

[2]Significant difference among emphases**

**p < .05

6.6.3 DIVERSIFICATION

We take a multifaceted approach to studying diversification. Measures include those based on the Rumelt framework and a simple index constructed from Standard Industrial Classification (SIC) data. All things equal, the more diverse the firm's operations, the more useful planning should be in a coordinating role, regardless of the nature of the diversification. However, one of the major contributions of strategic planning is careful choice of where to compete, both in terms of industry and in terms of stages of the product life cycle from which revenues are derived; these elements of diversification are also examined.

6.6.3.1 Corporate Diversification

Because of small samples, Rumelt's system is collapsed into four broad categories – firms that are single businesses, firms that are dominant businesses, firms in related businesses, and firms composed of unrelated businesses (table 6.8).[6] Even so, small sample sizes for single business (n = 13) and unrelated business (n = 19) preclude further statistical analyses for these strategy types, though it is interesting how few conglomerates show up in the sample. The fraction of dominant businesses does not vary among Planning Categories; this is not surprising, because strategic planning has, perhaps, a potentially smaller role here than in more diverse businesses. Significantly more Corporate Strategic Planners are in the related business category, diversification that implies an organic form of growth where relationships to existing businesses are carefully managed as new businesses are added.

A diversity index was calculated by summing the number of two-digit SIC codes in which the companies operated. The lowest level is for the Non-Planners (mean of 4.29) and the highest level for the Division Financial Planners (mean of 7.18); the differences are not significant among Planning Categories.

Table 6.8
Diversity of Operations[1]

Rumelt Category	Percent of Sample	Corporate Strategic Planners	
		Percent	Rank
Single Business	12	4	5
Dominant Business	27	25	4
Related Business	44	63	1*
Unrelated Business	17	8	5

[1]Significant differences among Rumelt Categories* and Planning Categories*

6.6.3.2 Specialization and Vertical Integration

Our sample firms as a whole view themselves as more specialized than their competitors, more so for marketing systems and production processes than for capital equipment owned. The Strategic Planners, Division and Corporate, are significantly more specialized than the other groups. Overall, the companies view themselves about as vertically integrated as their major competitors, with no significant differences among Planning Categories.

6.6.3.3 Product Categories

On the basis of the PIMS product categories used earlier (chapter 1), no significant differences are found among Planning

Categories (table 6.9). The Corporate Strategic Planners tend not to be raw materials producers (which tend to be organized around operations), but they are relatively more likely to produce capital goods and manufactured components. Given the recent attempts by many manufacturing companies to move into low-capital-intensity service businesses, the low percentages are surprising, particularly for the Corporate Strategic Planners, which might be expected to be able to reconfigure assets more quickly. The lack of significant differences among Planning Categories indicates that companies use a variety of management approaches to achieve the same strategic ends.

Table 6.9
Sources of Revenues: PIMS Product Categories

Type of Business	Percent of Sample	Corporate Strategic Planners Percent	Rank
Industrial/Commercial/Governmental Products Manufacturing			
Capital Goods	13.0	17.2	2
Raw or Semi-finished	14.5	5.9	5
Components for Incorporation into Finished Products	18.4	21.7	1
Supplies or Other Consumable Products	10.7	12.0	3
	56.6	56.8	
Consumer Products Manufacturing			
Durable Products	8.6	8.2	4
Non-durable Products	26.7	27.4	2
	35.4	35.6	
Services			
Retail and Wholesale Distribution	4.2	3.4	4
Other Services	3.8	4.2	3
	8.0	7.6	

6.6.3.4 Stage of Product Life Cycle

Somewhat more surprisingly, no significant differences in sources of revenue by life cycle stage are found among Planning Categories (table 6.10). The Corporate Strategic Planners have, however, succeeded in reducing sales in later stages slightly more, a result later replicated in our discussion of divestiture. Again, it appears that various management approaches have been used to manage the

product life cycle mix, and planning has not been particularly successful in this regard.

Table 6.10
Source of Revenues: Stage of Product Life Cycle

	Percent of Sample	Corporate Strategic Planners Percent	Rank
Introductory	4.7	5.0	1
Growth	21.2	23.3	2
Maturity	65.0	64.6	5
Decline	8.9	7.1	5

6.6.4 INTERNATIONAL POSTURE

Global market strategies are becoming increasingly important, and strategic planning should be helpful in their development.
All Planning Categories averaged more than 20 percent of revenues
from abroad, highest for the Corporate and Division Strategic Planners (28%) but not significantly greater than the others. Corporate
Strategic Planners are more diversified internationally than the other
Planning Categories in terms of both sales and production (table
6.11), though for all firms (not surprisingly) sales are significantly
more international than manufacturing.

Table 6.11
Companies with More Than One Percent of
Sales or Production in Nine Geographic Regions

	Sales[1]		Production	
	Percent of Sample	Corporate Strategic Planners Percent	Percent of Sample	Corporate Strategic Planners Percent
North America	100	100	100	100
Western Europe	85	92	72	88
Central & South America	68	71	56	58
Far East	60	83	41	50
Australasia	53	67	35	46
Africa	27	42	12	13
Middle & Near East	27	38	6	4
Indian Subcontinent	11	17	9	17
Eastern Europe	16	29	2	4

[1]Corporate Strategic Planners significantly higher at $\alpha = .01$

6.6.4.1 Sales

Of nine regions, the mean number of areas of the world accounting for more than 1 percent of sales volume is 4.5. More than half the companies are represented in Western Europe, Central and South America, the Far East, and Australasia. Corporate Strategic Planners have higher representation in all regions outside North America.

However, the mean percentage of sales outside the United States (exports and overseas manufacture – 25.4%) is not significantly different among Planning Categories, though the Corporate Strategic Planners have the highest – 27.8 percent.

6.6.4.2 Production

The mean number of regions of the world accounting for more than 1 percent of production volume is 3.32. The Corporate Strategic Planners are represented more heavily in seven of the eight regions outside North America, but the differences are not significant.

These results do not flow through to the extent of production activity in total outside of the United States. The mean number of manufacturing subsidiaries outside of the United States – 19.3 – is not significantly different among Planning Categories. The percent of wholly-owned subsidiaries similarly does not differ among Planning Categories, though the Corporate Strategic Planners have the highest percentage.

6.6.4.3 International Marketing Strategy

Most companies seek foreign markets in which existing products and technologies can be marketed, the Corporate Strategic Planners significantly more so. There is less agreement that new products are introduced in overseas markets after the United States, indicating either that many products developed in the United States are not sold overseas or that new products are introduced in approximately the same time frame in different countries. Companies do not tend to make major modifications of products and programs to penetrate foreign markets, though they report a tendency to shift from exporting to overseas manufacture.

What emerges is a tendency toward a pattern of exporting strategies and products developed in the United States, attempts to change the foreign customer environment rather than adapt offerings to foreign environments. If true, this does not augur well for the future competitiveness of large U.S. firms in international markets.

6.6.5 ACQUISITION AND DIVESTITURE

Whereas acquisition and divestiture can be viewed as simply strategic means to broaden and shape product offerings, they pose special management problems that deserve attention.

6.6.5.1 General Patterns

Our sample had been active in acquisition and divestiture; 66 percent of the companies report significant acquisitions during the preceding five years, and 61 percent report divesting, liquidating, or otherwise eliminating important operations in the same time frame. Only 12 percent of the sample indicate that they were not involved in either significant acquisition or divestiture activity.

The mean number of acquisitions in the previous five-year period is 4.8 (7.8 when just those companies that had made acquisitions are considered), and 1979 realized sales volume from an individual acquisition averaged $56M. The modal number of acquisitions is 2, but 16 companies reported 10 or more acquisitions.

The mean number of divestitures is 3.8 (6.2 when just those companies that had divested operations were considered). The sales volume that those divested operations would have been expected to generate in 1979, if they had been retained, averages $105M per divested operation. The modal number of divested operations is 1, but 12 companies report 10 or more divestitures.

There are no significant differences in the extent of acquisition and divestiture activity by Planning Category, though there are some interesting patterns. The Corporate Strategic Planners average more acquisitions (10), with the Division Strategic Planners second. The average 1979 sales revenues of acquisitions of the Corporate Strategic Planners ($416M) are the largest, followed by the Corporate Financial Planners ($326M) and Division Strategic Planners ($303M).

The Division Financial Planners reported the most divestitures, followed by the Division Strategic and Corporate Strategic Planners.

6.6.5.2 Life Cycle

Estimates of the percentages of 1979 revenues attributable to the four product life cycle stages from acquisitions (when acquired) and from divestitures (when divested) are shown in table 6.12. The modal life cycle stage of maturity for both acquisitions and divestitures simply reflects that category's dominance economy wide. For acquisitions, a substantial percentage of sales revenues is attributable to the growth stage. As expected, the most revenues of divested operations (more than 85%) are in maturity and decline stages. There are no significant differences among Planning Categories.

These results in general conform to the conventional wisdom regarding acquisitions in early stages and divestitures in later stages of the life cycle, though the extent of acquisition and divestiture in maturity is somewhat higher than might have been expected. The lack of significant differences among Planning Categories indicates once again, that much the same sort of strategic results may come from a variety of management processes.

Respondents anticipate a much more important role to be played by both acquisitions and divestitures in their corporate strategy over the next five years than the last five years, with no significant differences among Planning Categories.

Table 6.12
Acquisitions and Divestitures:
Sales Revenue by Product Life Cycle[1]

	Acquisitions			Divestitures		
		Corporate			Corporate	
	Percent	Strategic Planners		Percent	Strategic Planners	
	of Sample	Percent	Rank	of Sample	Percent	Rank
Introductory	3.9	1.0	4	2.5	5.3	2
Growth	43.7	37.2	4	12.0	13.3	3
Maturity	50.5	60.7	2	65.1	56.7	3
Decline	1.0	1.1	2	20.4	24.7	2*

[1]Significant differences among life cycle stages**, and between acquisitions and divestitures***

***p < .01, **p < .05, *p < .10

6.6.6 COMPANY SIZE

There is no clear presumption about how sheer company size should be related to planning, and neither is size typically recognized per se as an important strategic variable. In fact, Corporate Strategic Planners have the largest average revenues in 1977, 1979 and 1981 (table 6.13), though revenue growth was highest for the Non-Planners and Corporate Financial Planners. Since the Corporate Strategic Planners are no more diverse than the other firms, since they have about the same business mix, and since they tend to have growth goals, the relatively slow growth rate of the Corporate Strategic Planners (almost certainly *not* a strategically planned result) may indicate performance problems.

Table 6.13
Company Revenues ($ B) by Planning Category[1]

	1977	1979	1981	Percent Increase (1977-1981)
Corporate Strategic Planners	5.50	6.93	9.78	78%
Division Strategic Planners	4.52	5.86	7.24	60%
Corporate Financial Planners	2.48	3.41	4.76	92%
Division Financial Planners	2.78	3.60	3.95	42%
Non Planners	1.46	1.37	3.41	134%

[1]Significant differences over time** and among Planning Categories**

**p < .05

6.7 Summary

In this chapter we distinguished between corporate- and business-level strategy, and between strategy as a normative construct (intended strategy) and as a descriptive construct (realized strategy). Our focus was generally at the corporate level and we isolated six distinct facets of corporate strategy – corporate direction, market and entry strategy, diversification, international posture, acquisition and divestiture, and corporate size. We dealt with both intended and realized strategy. As in the previous chapters we presented results for the sample as a whole and for the Corporate Strategic Planners.

In general, our firms had multiple but nonconflicting quantitative goals (mostly of a return type) and qualitative goals at the corporate level. Second-level performance goals differed across business units. Rigorous mission statements were found less frequently than we expected but, somewhat surprisingly, were changed more frequently than the goals. The Corporate Strategic Planners differed little overall in terms of goals or mission, though they tended to have more quantitative goals than the other firms, to be more likely to adjust them for inflation, and to change goals in general more frequently.

All firms rated the elements of effective market and entry strategy more heavily than others, the Corporate Strategic Planners more so. Although market penetration had been the dominant growth strategy overall in the past, the firms expected investments in new product R&D to make new product strategies more important in the future; this pattern was especially noticeable for the Corporate

Strategic Planners, which also showed a greater tendency to high-risk internal innovation.

In line with previous work on diversification, Rumelt's related category contained the modal number of firms, noticeably so for the Corporate Strategic Planners, very few of which were in the polar categories of single or unrelated business. Modest differences among Planning Categories were found for the PIMS product categories. Businesses in the mature stage of the product life cycle generated the majority of revenues, and, surprisingly, the distribution for Corporate Strategic Planners was practically identical to the sample as a whole.

Our sample firms were diversified internationally for both sales and production, but the Corporate Strategic Planners tended to be more international than the sample as a whole.

Significant acquisition and divestiture activity had been undertaken by the sample as a whole, with some suggestion of more acquisition by the Corporate Strategic Planners. As expected, the majority of divestiture for the whole sample was businesses in mature and declining markets.

The Corporate Strategic Planners were the largest firms, but other Planning Categories had been growing faster.

Overall, the general patterns do not indicate sharp strategic profiles of firms that do corporate strategic planning against those that do not. On one level this is rather surprising, since one of the major goals of strategic planning is to shape strategy. It is possible, of course, that, from a performance perspective, differences in strategy do not matter, though chapter 11 will show that this is not the case.

Corporate Strategic Planners have no convincing superiority in their strategic posture, though their greater size, greater emphasis on the elements of strategy generally viewed as effective, greater thrust for new products, and broader international scope are important competitive issues. It may be that the corporate role is less important than we believed or that the adaptive orientation of strategic planning is less important than we expected. Perhaps the best explanation is that planning is just one of a number of ways to shape strategy and that firms have other means at their disposal for strategy development. This question is addressed from differing perspectives in chapters 8 and 9.

NOTES

1. Ansoff (1965) discusses the advantages and disadvantages of developing a corporate strategy.

2. Grinyer, Yasai-Ardenaki, and Al-Bazzaz (1980) and Vancil (1979) failed to isolate the expected relationship; however, whereas Rumelt (1974, 1982) identified a nonlinear relationship, these authors tested a linear model.

3. Salter and Weinhold (1979), Bettis (1981), and Bettis and Hall (1982) investigated the different risk implications of related and unrelated diversification.

4. See Hofer (1975) for a review of the extant research on business and corporate strategy.

5. Neither the various portfolio frameworks nor the PIMS program has been immune from criticism, either from the academic community or from the business press. For critiques of portfolio approaches, see, for example, Day (1977), Wind (1982); for a critique of PIMS, see Anderson and Paine (1978); for critiques of both approaches, see Capon and Spogli (1977) and Wensley (1982). For a review of research using the PIMS database, see Ramunujam and Venkatraman (1984).

6. At the finer level of categorization, the dominant firms comprise: 15% – Dominant Vertical, 7% – Dominant Constrained, and 5% – Dominant Linked/Unrelated; Related firms comprise: 27% – Related Constrained and 17% – Related Linked.

Chapter 7

Planning and Organization

7.1 Introduction

We expect, like others who have sought internal consistency in elements of organization (Leavitt 1962, 1965), that the design of a firm's planning system should be related to other important aspects of the organization with which it coexists. The relationship of a planning system to environment and strategy is concerned mainly with the adaptive function of planning. Since planning is itself an element of organizational design, it serves mainly an integrative function with respect to other components of the organization.

The literature on organization is voluminous, and we cannot hope to do justice to the many aspects of organization that may interface with a planning system. Instead, we adopt a selective approach and focus on a few areas that we believe are especially important. We first distinguish between formal organization and organizational climate and review selected bodies of literature in these two areas; in organizational climate we focus mainly on the definitional and measurement issues. As a prelude to chapter 10, in which we investigate relationships of planning to performance, we then briefly review the organization–performance literature (not including planning). These reviews set the stage for presenting our results. We commence by exploring how selected areas of organization structure relate to planning. We then turn our attention to relationships between planning and organizational climate.

7.2 Formal Organization Structure

Formal organization structure is addressed in two separate ways in the literature: structural design variables and underlying structural dimensions. Structural design variables range from broad organization macrostructure (the overarching framework in which the organization functions) to many individual elements of organizational design (departmentalization, resource allocation processes, performance evaluation and reward systems, information processing systems, career paths, and so forth), which fall under the general category of microstructure or operating structure. Structural dimensions, generally associated with the work of the Aston group (e.g., Pugh, Hickson, and Turner 1968), encompass constructs such as centralization, formalization, complexity, and administrative intensity.

The planning system is a midrange organizational design variable functioning within the broad organization macrostructure. The macroorganization may, however, be modified as a result of planning efforts, as in the shift from division to SBU organizations. The planning system also encompasses elements of microstructure. For example, planning systems typically involve the creation of planning departments, which may play an important role in resource allocation decisions. Performance evaluation is often related to goals formulated within the planning process, and information flows are certainly a large part of any type of planning. Planning systems themselves may also be described in terms of such structural dimensions as formalization, centralization, and so forth.

In our review of work on formal organization structure, we discuss both organization macrostructure and microstruture and key structural dimensions; we also explore relationships between organization structure and strategy.

7.2.1 ORGANIZATION MACROSTRUCTURE

Because the macrostructure allocates tasks in prespecified patterns, it provides context for other organizational design variables. It is also a relatively inflexible component of organizational design in the short term. Much research concerned with formal organization structure has been cast in the strategy-structure paradigm developed by Chandler (1962). The two major organizational forms identified by Chandler were the centralized-functional form, and the multidivisional form in which the central office is responsible for long-run strategic decisions and the divisions for short-run operating decisions. In Chandler's work, the centralized-functional form tends to be used by firms with single businesses or business strategies, whereas multidivisional forms are generally used by those companies engaged in product diversification, the last of four diversification stages discussed by Chandler. Scott (1973) later developed a three-stage model of organization structure development, based on work in the United States (Wrigley 1970), United Kingdom (Channon 1973), France (Pooley-Dyas 1972), Germany (Thanheiser 1972), and Italy (Pavan 1972), in which Chandler's two major stages represent his second and third developmental stages.

Williamson (1975), in his work on markets and hierarchies, suggested three organizational forms that characterize large business organizations. The first is in effect the single business unit (the U-form), which is in general functional. Successful single businesses often grow and diversify into multibusiness, divisionalized organizations (M-form) in which elite staffs provide coordination and in which hierarchy replaces market transactions for factor inputs, semifinished products, or even finished goods. The M-form organization should have both adaptive and integrative characteristics, and according to Williamson, when factor or product-market inefficiencies are important, M-form firms should be able to outperform a parallel set of single businesses linked by markets. Finally, Williamson sees the "holding company" or conglomerate, adaptive but not integrative, as a product of frictions in capital markets.

The most comprehensive empirical study of general organization structure of major American companies is probably that of Rumelt (1974), performed in concert with his study of diversification. Rumelt identified five categories of organization structure: functional, functional-with-subsidiaries, product division, geographic division, and holding company. Of these five forms, the geographic division and holding company forms are relatively unimportant; neither accounts for more than 4 percent of *Fortune* 500 firms for any of the three time periods (1949, 1959, 1969) that Rumelt studied. The functional-with-subsidiaries form decreased marginally in importance over this time period, from 13 percent in 1949 to 9 percent in 1969. The most dramatic results are found for the functional and product-division forms of organization. The functional form accounted for 63 percent of Rumelt's sample in 1949 but by 1969 accounted for only 11 percent of the companies. Conversely, the product-division form increased from 20 percent of firms in 1949 to 76 percent in 1969.

As noted in chapter 5, Rumelt concluded that in the first decade of his study (1949–1959) diversification and divisionalization were associated and that the adoption of product-division structures in this period was contingent on the administrative pressures created by diversification. However, he asserted that in later years divisionalization had become accepted as the norm and that managers sought divisionalization less in response to actual administrative pressures than in response to normative theory. On the basis of Rumelt's work, we anticipate finding extensive divisionalization in our sample.

7.2.2 STRUCTURE FOR INTERNATIONAL OPERATIONS

An associated but quite separate body of research has concerned organization structure for international operations, a matter of increasing importance for firms of the type under study. Stopford (1968) traced changes in organizational form of a sample of *Fortune* 500 firms as they expanded overseas and identified three major structural types: international division, geographic-area division, and product division. The first structural change associated with international expansion is generally the addition of an international division to the existing structure, typically a product-division structure. Stopford viewed the international division as a transitional form to be followed later by one of two types of global structure. If the firm's entire diversified product line were taken abroad, the firm would adopt a worldwide product-division structure; if only its dominant businesses were taken abroad, the firm would adopt a geographic-area form of organization. The geographic-area structures are associated with a higher proportion of foreign-based sales than product-division structures (46% of revenues versus 17%); international-division structures are intermediate (21%), as are functional organizations (27%) and mixed forms (31%).

Franko (1974, 1976) identified a quite different organizational form for international operations, common in European multinationals – a domestic functional organization to which is grafted an international holding company, the mother-daughter form. Franko attributed the widespread use of this form in the early 1960s (60 of 71 firms in 1961) to both cultural and competitive environmental factors. He surmised that changing international competitive environments in the 1960s and early 1970s led to its replacement by organizational forms more similar to those employed by American multinationals. However, he found that the international-division form, so popular with American firms, was largely bypassed by the Europeans.

In their excellent summary of development of organization structure, Galbraith and Nathanson (1978, 1979) raised the question of what structural forms are likely to be developed as multinationals increase both their foreign product diversity and their dependence on foreign sales. Building on work by Davis and Lawrence (1977) and

Miles and Snow (1978), they speculated that these new forms would be grid or matrix structures.

Egelhoff (1982) investigated the relationship between organization structure for international operations and various elements of strategy for a sample of 50 successful United States and European multinationals. Sixteen firms had various forms of mixed or matrix structures; the remainder had elementary organization structures—functional, international division, geographic region, or product division. Using an information-processing perspective, he obtained support for a number of hypotheses relating international strategy to the elementary structural forms. Functional-division organizations were found with low foreign product diversity, little difference in product modification between subsidiaries, few foreign subsidiaries, a low level of outside ownership in foreign subsidiaries, and few foreign acquisitions. International divisions occurred with relatively small foreign operations and a low to moderate number of foreign subsidiaries. Geographic regions were associated with large foreign operations, a high level of foreign manufacturing, and a large number of foreign subsidiaries. Product divisions were related to high foreign product diversity, high rate of product change, relatively large foreign operations, and a large number of foreign subsidiaries.[1]

7.2.3 ORGANIZATION MICROSTRUCTURE

The macrostructure provides the institutional framework and the microstructure or operating structure determines actual day-to-day processes and patterns of behavior. Examples of elements of the microstructure cited in a voluminous literature are resource allocation processes and performance evaluation and reward systems. Most studies have been conducted in the context of single-business organizations, so the results must be treated with caution in considering large diversified firms (in our sample), not only because they operate under a special set of constraints (Caves 1980) but also because the elements investigated may not have been the most appropriate dimensions for study in multibusiness organizations. Galbraith and Nathanson (1978, 1979) discussed interrelationships among the various elements of firm microstructure.

An important issue in any discussion of organization structure for multibusiness organizations is the degree of interdependence among the subunits of the organization. At the level immediately below corporate (which we term the second level)—groups, divisions, SBUs, or functions—the degree and type of interdependence reflect the overall pattern of internal resource sharing and work flow within the firm. High degrees of interdependence generate extensive coordination demands and impose pressures for change in the nature of the organization's microstructure.

Among the scholars who have addressed interdependence, both Thompson (1967) and Emery (1969) have developed conceptual frameworks, and Mohr (1971) has studied interdependence at lower levels in the organization. Other views that involve interdependence include information processing (e.g., Tushman and Nadler 1978) and coordination mechanisms (e.g., Van de Ven, Delbecq, and Koenig 1976). Corollary to business interdependence is the degree to which items such as capital equipment, production processes, and marketing systems are specialized. Specialized systems in individual divisions offer the potential for efficiencies, but important coordination problems may result.

High-level interdependence within the organization was addressed in a series of studies by Berg (1965, 1969, 1973) and Pitts (1976, 1980). They examined two types of large firms: those that had diversified either through an active acquisition policy or through internal development. They focused on three microstructural elements:

1) the relationship between the divisions and corporate headquarters;
2) the extent of, and means by which, interaction between divisions was encouraged;
3) the management control system designed to reinforce these choices.

General findings from the studies are that conglomerate diversification (Williamson's holding company) results in small corporate headquarters (implying a decentralization of functional activities such as marketing, production, R&D) and low resource sharing between divisions. Managerial incentive systems are formal and based exclusively on objective measures of divisional performance. Retention of management of acquired businesses is more common than transfer of senior management between divisions. The logic for these findings is that operational requirements in these firms are diverse and individual businesses require considerable technical and managerial autonomy; corporate management's role is to be an allocator of resources according to performance criteria rather than an integrator. Thus Berg (1965:118) notes:

> The corporate officers may not know the businesses of the divisions as well as their counterparts in a diversified major but neither are they

likely to have developed personal, product or organizational ties that can impede economic rational judgments.

Internal diversifiers (Williamson's M-form organizations), by contrast, have large corporate headquarters, implying coordination of functional activities at the corporate level and a high level of resource sharing among divisions. Managerial incentive systems are less formalized, have significant subjective elements, and are based on both corporate and divisional performance. Senior managers are frequently transferred between divisions. For these firms, both lateral and vertical coordination are seen as necessary to achieve economic benefits. Corporate headquarters manages and integrates, both to attain operational synergies and to ensure that division management acts, not in its own self-interest, but in the interest of the firm as a whole.

In this study we focus on three broad areas of microstructure: organization for innovations, degree of resource sharing among second-level units, and degree of organizational specialization. Planning systems have an important role to play in bringing forth innovations, though too rigid a system may stifle entrepreneurial activity. They are also important in ensuring that internal interdependence is managed well, and we expect different levels of resource sharing and organizational specialization to be associated with different types of planning system.[2] For example, Rumelt (1974) concluded that related-constrained firms (those with collections of businesses clustered about key core skills and shared resources) tend to be most successful. The process of strategic planning is one method by which such a set of businesses might be assembled and managed. Furthermore, strategic planning can help manage shared sales and marketing, production, procurement, research and development, and information resources.

7.2.4 STRUCTURAL DIMENSIONS

A number of structural dimensions of organizations have been identified and extensively researched by organization theorists (see, for example, Pugh, Hickson, and Turner 1968). Four main structural dimensions are complexity, administrative intensity, centralization, and formalization (Ford and Slocum 1977), though there are no consistently used measures available that accurately capture all of these constructs.

Complexity refers to the degree of differentiation within an organization and includes elements that are vertical (number of hierarchical levels), horizontal (number of functions, departments, or jobs), spatial (number of operating sites), and personal (degree of personal expertise).

Administrative intensity refers to the extent of support personnel within the organization; it is typically measured either as a simple count or as a ratio of administrative to production personnel.

Centralization relates to the location of formal control in the organization; it is concerned with hierarchy of decision-making authority, as well as the degree of autonomy and participation in organizational decisions.

Formalization is concerned with existence of, and adherence to, rules and procedures in the organization that prescribe the behavior of members.

A great deal of research effort has sought factors upon which these dimensions are contingent; those most frequently considered are size, technology, and environment. (See Ford and Slocum 1977 for a review.) As we noted in chapter 4, a planning system itself may also be described, in part, in terms of similar dimensions.

7.3 Organizational Climate

Besides microstructure and macrostructure, a key characteristic of organization is climate, sometimes called "corporate culture." Although long established in the organization behavior literature, where research was frequently reviewed in the 1970s (e.g., Campbell, Dunnette, Lawler, and Weick 1970; Hellriegel and Slocum 1974; James and Jones 1974; Payne and Pugh 1976), organizational climate has gained much currency in recent years. Popular books by Ouchi (1981), Pascale and Athos (1981), Deal and Kennedy (1982), and Peters and Waterman (1982), which discuss the importance of corporate culture in determining organizational performance, owe an intellectual debt to many earlier organizational climate researchers.

The earliest definition of organizational climate to gain acceptance, developed by Forehand and Gilmer (1964:362), is the set of characteristics describing an organization that:

(1) distinguish the organization from other organizations
(2) are relatively enduring over time
(3) influence the behavior of people in the organization.

This definition was criticized by Tagiuri and Litwin (1968) on the basis that the climate of an organization is interpreted by its members through their perceptual apparatus and that it is these perceptions that affect their attitudes and behavior. They propose the following definition:

> Organization climate is a relatively enduring quality of the internal environment of an organization that (a) is experienced by its members, (b) influences their behavior, and (c) can be described in terms of a particular set of characteristics (or attributes) of the organization (p. 65).

In reviewing a number of definitions of organizational climate, Woodman and King (1978) argued that it is generally considered to be a molar concept, much like personality, and that for a particular organization it has an air of permanence even though it is not unchanging. Climate is regarded as external to the individual; it is perceived individually, and perceptions can be shared by individuals. Although results differ, organizational climate has generally been found to be a determinant of behavior directly as a main effect or in interactions. A number of issues have, however, troubled climate researchers: examples are whether objective or perceptual measures should be employed, whether perceptual measures capture attributes of people or of organizations, and whether organizational climate and job satisfaction can be distinguished from each other.

Over several decades, researchers have developed a bewildering array of instruments with which to measure organizational climate (see Woodman and King 1978 for a partial listing). Despite such efforts, instruments that initially offered promise of high validity have exhibited high variance in factor structure across organization types, and extant scales do not appear to offer high scale validity and reliability across many different organizations (Woodman and King 1978).

Because of the lack of any single instrument, we decided to select apparently appropriate items from extant scales, in addition to developing a few specially for the study. Our selection was governed by a concern to identify items that had broad applicability across an organization and that measure perceptions rather than objective characteristics of organizations – we measured these separately, and they are treated under organization structure. It was, however, difficult in some cases to judge whether a particular item is better treated as a measure of organization structure or of climate. Instruments that supplied significant numbers of items were Payne and Pheysey's (BOCI) (1971), Schneider and Bartlett's (ACQ) (1968, 1970), as well as Johannesson's (1973) study, which employed items from a variety of instruments. Two important instruments were not used:

Halpin and Croft's (OCDQ) (1963), owing to its focus on schools, and Likert's (POC) (1967), because of its close association with the system-4 organization. In total, 51 five-point Likert-type scales were employed.

7.4 Organization and Performance

There exists an extensive literature on the relationship between organization structure and performance of which the literature on corporate organization structure and corporate performance is but a small subset. In the broader literature there is no strong evidence that organization structure contributes to performance or that contingent relationships exist between structure, contextual variables, and performance. Indeed, in a critical review of this literature, which encompasses studies employing both hard and soft performance (but rarely profitability) measures, Dalton et al. (1980) (see also Cummings and Berger 1976), who considered both structural elements (size, subunit size, span of control, flat/tall hierarchy, etc.) and structural dimensions (termed structuring elements) – specialization, formalization, standardization, and centralization – concluded that:

> The literature on structure-performance relationships is among the most vexing and ambiguous in the field of management and organizational behavior. Evaluations and generalizations concerning the nature and directions of these relationships are tenuous.

Notwithstanding the general absence of relationships between organization structure and performance, many authors have suggested that there should be a positive relationship. For example, Likert (1967) proposed that decentralized participative "system 4" structures are more likely to lead to high performance than "system 1" structures that are autocratic or bureaucratic. However, in this vein, Koontz and O'Donnell (1972) argued that as important decisions are decentralized, appropriate organizational mechanisms must be instituted to maintain control over the decentralized operations.

From the few studies that have addressed the corporate organization structure/corporate performance issue, there is a similar lack of findings. In their review, Galbraith and Nathanson (1978, 1979) concluded that:

> It has not yet been demonstrated that structure contributes to economic performance or that firms that have matched strategy with structure perform better than those that have not.

Among the few extant studies is Rumelt's (1974) work, which found that diversified firms with multidivisional organizations (matched) tended to perform better than those with functional organizations (mismatched); these results are, however, generally directional rather than significant. In a partial replication, Channon (1979) found that functional organizations perform better than multidivisional firms and that holding company structures are the poorest performers; a test of strategy/structure fit to performance was not, however, undertaken. Finally, two papers reported some evidence of a relationship between structure and performance. Poensgen (1974) obtained weak evidence that firms organized by profit center perform in a superior manner to those that are not, and Steer and Cable (1978) found that firms with "optimal" organization structures (single business/functional; diversified/multidivisional with separation of corporate and division interests based on time horizon) perform significantly better than those with "nonoptimal" structures (holding company; diversified/functional; diversified/ multidivisional with corporate too involved in divisions).

A more recent study addressing this topic was performed on a sample of British-based organizations by Grinyer, Yasai-Ardekani, and Al-Bazzaz (1980). Their analysis of match between strategy and structure, and financial performance, which "breaks new ground," found little relationship irrespective of which environmental variable was used to subdivide the sample. Although the authors expressed concern with the quality of this analysis on account of their inability to identify performance data for those companies that were divisions or subsidiaries of other corporations, they nonetheless concluded that:

> (these results) cast(s) some doubt ... on the proposition that a good match or fit between strategy and structure promotes more effective coping with environmental pressures.

Overall, the extant research does not support strong direct or contingent relationships between organization structure and performance.

As noted earlier, a number of authors have argued that positive organizational climates should lead to superior performance, though such assertions have not generally been backed up with empirical data. In one study employing data gathered in the context of this study (Capon, Farley, Hulbert, and Lei 1986b), some support was adduced for the "excellence" principles put forward by Peters and Waterman (1982).

7.5 Results: Formal Organization Structure

In this section, we deal with how formal organization structure in our sample relates to planning. We begin by examining general macrostructure and structural dimensions of organizations. We then turn to macrostructure for international operations. Finally, we focus on elements of microstructure: the locus of responsibility for innovation, the extent of resource sharing and other interrelationships between second-level organizational units, and the degree of perceived organizational specialization.

7.5.1 GENERAL MACROSTRUCTURE DESIGN AND DIMENSIONS

Since our sample is multiproduct, multimarket in scope, and since most firms had significant international operations, they had macrostructures (as expected) consisting of some form of divisional or strategic business units. This result is consistent with Rumelt's (1974) finding.

Although there are differences across the sample, all structures are relatively *complex*. All companies indicated that there are second levels with operating profit responsibility. Ninety-six percent reported a third organizational level, but below the third level the percentage drops off sharply; 57 percent report a fourth level, and only 14 percent a fifth level. At each level, the span of control averaged four to five units. No significant differences are found among Planning Categories in number of levels or units, indicating that organizational complexity is not related to corporate strategic planning. Not surprisingly, however, the Corporate and Division Strategic Planners have a significantly larger number of staff units in total reporting at corporate level, an element of *administrative intensity*.

Across the sample there is a good deal of variability in reported levels of *centralization* in decision-making. The Corporate Strategic Planners reported relatively low levels of centralization (high levels of decentralization) whereas the Non-Planners are highly centralized. In particular, second-level operating executives in the Corporate Strategic Planners generally have greater responsibility for both operating decisions and performance than in the other Planning Categories. For the sample as a whole, however, centralization had not increased as firms had grown in size. Notwithstanding these differences, there is overall agreement across the sample that corporate performance is better than it would have been as separate and individual operating units. As regards *formalization*, there is moderate agreement across the sample that the firms are tightly controlled by means of sophisticated control and information systems, a feature that especially characterizes the Corporate Strategic Planners and Non-Planners.

The Boards of Directors of the sample firms meet about 10 times a year on average, with average commitment of outside directors about 15 days; neither measure varies among Planning Categories.

7.5.2 STRUCTURE FOR INTERNATIONAL OPERATIONS

The structures for international operations, classified by self report using the category system developed by Egelhoff (1982), are diverse (table 7.1). In comparison with Egelhoff's results, it should be remembered that Egelhoff selected a sample of known multinationals (United States and European-based) and excluded all firms with less than 15 percent foreign sales. Our results are based on the total sample, a few of which had little or no international business.

The most striking feature is the extent of matrix organization structures (29% versus 14% in Egelhoff's sample), whereas Egelhoff found more mixed structures. Nonmatrix organizations comprise 66 percent of our sample, comparable to the 70 percent of Egelhoff's firms. The most popular form of nonmatrix structure in our sample is the international division followed by the worldwide product division. By contrast, the worldwide product division represents Egelhoff's most popular form, followed by the geographic-area structure (a form we rarely found) and international division. Neither study finds worldwide functional structures to feature very prominently.

Galbraith and Nathanson (1978) suggested that matrix structures may evolve from the elementary structures of worldwide product division and geographic-area structures, which themselves generally result from dismantling an international-division structure. Of special interest in our study is the importance of the worldwide product-division form (39%), either as a pure type (13%) or as an element in a matrix organization (26%). Just as popular is the international-division structure (39%), in pure form for 27 percent of firms and in matrix structures in 12 percent. Joining these two

Table 7.1
Organization for International Operations

	Egelhoff (1982) Percent	Percent of Sample	Corporate Strategic Planners Percent
Matrix Organization			
National subsidiary CEO's and overlapping product division heads report to Company CEO		7	8
International division head and overlapping product division heads report to Company CEO		12	29*
Geographic region heads and overlapping product division heads report to Company CEO		6	0
National Subsidiary CEO's and overlapping worldwide functional heads report to Company CEO		0	0
Worldwide functional heads and overlapping product division heads report to Company CEO		1	0
Worldwide functional heads and overlapping geographic heads report to Company CEO		3	4
	14	29	42
Non-Matrix Organization			
Simple			
Export Department	--	12	0
National subsidiary CEO's report to Company CEO	2	4	0
Worldwide functional heads report to Company CEO	10	5	13*
International division head reports to Company CEO	14	27	17*
Geographic region heads report to Company CEO	20	5	8
Worldwide product division heads report to Company CEO	24	13	13
	70	66	53
Mixed			
International division and non-overlapping product division heads report to Company CEO		3	0
Geographic region heads and non-overlapping product division heads report to Company CEO		1	4
	14[1]	4	4

[1]One structure was based on the size of the foreign subsidiary

*Significant difference among planning groups, $p < .10$

elements together in a matrix form may have advantages in balancing the competing demands for efficiency within the product division, with sufficient coordination for addressing diverse geographic markets.

The Corporate Strategic Planners differ from the sample as a whole in a number of interesting ways. More Corporate Strategic Planners operate with matrix structures than the sample as a whole. Furthermore, 29 percent of the Corporate Strategic Planners use an international/product division matrix combination (the most popular of all forms used by this Planning Category) compared to 12 percent for the overall sample. They also employ the worldwide functional structure more frequently. Conversely, the Corporate Strategic Planners use a simple nonmatrix form less frequently. Especially striking is the relatively infrequent use overall of the international-division structure.

It is tempting to speculate that the advantages of the matrix structure are best realized when combined with a well-developed corporate strategic planning system.[3]

7.5.3 ORGANIZATION FOR INNOVATIONS

Responsibility for new product development, an important element of strategy and a major organizational issue as well, tends to lie with second-level operating units rather than with special organizational units (table 7.2). Generally, there is no difference among Planning Categories in specific activities – new product development, development of new markets for existing products, and screening new product and new market ideas – except that Corporate Strategic Planners are even less likely to delegate the job of new product development to a special unit of the organization.

Across the sample, incentives tend not to be given for entrepreneurial actions, nor does the form and structure of organization encourage such behavior. Rather, it was believed that the organization form and structure encourages conservative management – there were no differences among Planning Categories. On a related issue, the Corporate Strategic Planners and Division Strategic Planners report significantly greater success in obtaining talented scientific personnel than the other planning types.

7.5.4 INTERRELATIONSHIPS BETWEEN SECOND-LEVEL UNITS

Second-level units in our sample report relatively low levels of resource sharing in terms of information, research and develop-

Table 7.2
Organizational Responsibility for New Products and Markets[1]

New Product Development[2]	Sample Mean	Corporate Strategic Planners Mean	Rank
Second-level Operating Units	3.91	4.13	1
Special Corporate Task Forces Oversee	2.41	2.25	4
Special Organization Unit	2.39	2.21	4**
Screening New Product Ideas[2]			
Second-level Operating Units	3.98	4.17	1
Special Organizational Unit	2.22	2.29	2
New Market Development[2] (existing products)			
Second-level Operating Units	4.20	4.25	2
Special Organizational Unit	1.72	1.70	3
Screening New Market Ideas[2]			
Second-level Operating Units	4.04	4.00	3
Special Organizational Unit	2.05	2.29	1

[1]Means on 5-point scale: 1 = disagree, 5 = agree, about where responsibility lies

[2]Significant difference among loci of responsibility***

***p < .01, **p < .05

ment, procurement, production, and sales and marketing resources. Information and R&D are the most shared – sales and marketing the least (table 7.3). There are no significant differences among Planning Categories – a surprise since one benefit of planning should involve resource sharing. Perhaps the trend toward divisionalization and SBU formation has led to this state of affairs, suggesting that firms expect economies of scale and focus associated with particular businesses to outweigh gains from shared resources/synergy.

Two thirds of the companies indicate that they have a policy of procuring internally wherever possible; there are no significant differences among Planning Categories. Transfer pricing systems are reported by 91 percent of companies; the Corporate Strategic Planners are significantly lower (75%), perhaps indicating some substitution of planned resource transfers for internal "markets."

In five key areas of organizational design – marketing systems, production processes, internal communication patterns, capital

Table 7.3
Resource Sharing Among Second-Level Units[1,2]

	Sample Mean	Corporate Strategic Planners Mean	Rank
Information	3.30	3.22	2
Research and Development	3.04	3.11	2
Procurement	2.98	3.12	1
Production	2.27	2.04	5
Sales and Marketing	1.88	1.63	5

[1]Means on 5-point scale; extensive sharing: 1 = disagree, 5 = agree

[2]Significant difference among type of resource***

***p < .01

configuration, and human organization – only moderate levels of specialization are found (table 7.4), with no pattern of differences among Planning Categories.

Table 7.4
Organizational Specialization[1]

	Sample Mean	Corporate Strategic Planners Mean	Rank
Marketing Systems	3.49	3.62	2
Production Processes	3.38	3.44	2
Internal Communication Patterns	3.23	3.25	4
Capital Configuration	3.23	3.32	2
Human Organization	3.17	3.46	1

[1]Means on 5-point scale: 1 = much less specialized, 5 = much more specialized, compared to major competitors

7.6 Results: Organizational Climate

The tremendous amount of recent attention focused on the impact of organizational climate on performance shows that analysis of climate probably requires more value judgments than most other areas. However, these value judgments are seldom made explicit. Peters and Waterman (1982) stressed the importance of entrepreneurial behavior and decentralization as organizational elements contributing to good performance, so we make that a working assumption. Similarly, we assume that a culture that encourages pride, loyalty, and entrepreneurial behavior is superior to one that fosters autocratic rule, bureaucracy, and procedure. Finally, we assume that rewarding performance with pay, praise, and advancement is positive. On the whole, we expect the Corporate Strategic Planners to have organizational climates that reflect these value judgments.

Two analyses of the 51 Likert-scale items used to assess climate are presented in table 7.5:

(1) means on each item for the whole sample indicated by columns, which helps indicate the general importance of that item

(2) position of the 24 Corporate Strategic Planners relative to the other Planning Categories (indicated in the parentheses)

The results are discussed in terms of relative position and tendencies for results to group meaningfully. The comparison of Planning Categories requires the assumption that no systematic intergroup differences in perceived center point of the scales relates to planning per se. Some scales are reoriented as indicated to read from low to high, and the position of the Corporate Strategic Planners defined in terms of more positive climates—e.g., least unfriendly on an unfriendliness scale, least bureaucratic on a bureaucracy scale.

The overall distribution of the items indicates a tendency to centralize about the midpoint on the 5-point Likert scales, indicating positive organizational climates in the sample as a whole:

Average	_Number of Items_
Greater than 4.0	5
3.5 to 4	19
2.5 to 3.5	21
Less than 2.5	6

Making the same assumptions about what is a more positive climate, we can make comparisons of the Corporate Strategic Planners with the rest of the sample:

Rank of Within-Group Means of Corporate Strategic Planners	_Number of Cases_
1	28
2	13
3	8
4	2
5	0

Table 7.5
Patterns in Organization Climate

Overall Means and Positions of Corporate Strategic Planners
(Ranks indicate position involving "better" practice on that item)

Mean less than 2.5[1]	Mean between 2.5 and 3.5	Mean greater than 3.5
There is a strong tendency toward high-risk, high-return investments (1)	New ideas are always being tried out here (1)	People are rewarded in proportion to the excellence of their performance (1)
There is a strong performance-oriented up-or-out job policy (3)	†It is generally clear who has formal authority to make a decision (3)	In promoting managers, there is a strong emphasis on competitiveness and ability to out-perform others (1)
There is a tendency for the company to be over-staffed with personnel (1)*	Unusual or exciting plans are encouraged (1)	In general, there are excellent communications between line managers and planning personnel (1)*
In decision-making there is a great reliance on specially-trained line and staff personnel as distinct from a reliance on personnel with experience (3)	†There is little emphasis on holding fast to tried and true management principles as business conditions change (2)	There is cooperation between people in getting things done (2)
	Financial and operating information flow quite freely throughout the company (1)	†There is much personal loyalty in this company (1)
	Line managers find the services rendered by company planners very helpful (1)*	†The jobs of managers in this company are not highly routine (1)*
	As the company has grown more in size it has grown more impersonal (3)*	Pay is certainly an indication of performance in this company (2)
	When we have acquired companies we have avoided problems of incompatible managerial behavior (3)*	

†Second level managers generally do not need clearance from corporate executives before making major decisions (2)

The degree of complexity faced by the company will eventually limit its power to grow (4)

†Overall, the decision-making style of senior management in this company is not authoritarian (1)*

There is a strong tendency to let the expert have the most say in decision making, even if this means temporarily bypassing formal authority (3)

†People trust each other in this company (1)

†People generally do not just look out for their own interests in this company (2)

Managers have complete written job descriptions for their jobs (1)

There is strong committee-oriented consensus seeking participative decision making (2)

As the company has grown in size, it has achieved more participation in decision making (1)*

There is strong individualistic decision making by the normally responsible executive (2)*

People feel they are their own bosses in most matters (1)

†Few managerial conflicts require top management resolution (2)*

People are proud of being with this company (1)

Senior management jobs are very secure (2)*

Managers typically consult with subordinates on decisions to adopt new programs (1)*

Decision making in this company is participative (1)*

Managers have jobs where something new is happening every day (1)

†Managers do not do the same job in the same way every day (2)

†Managers do not have to follow the same procedures in most situations (3)

†Managers do not have to follow written orders without question (1)

†Managers do not have to follow whatever situation arises (3)

A friendly atmosphere prevails among people in this company (1)

There is emphasis on getting things done even if this means disregarding formal procedures (2)

Table 7.5 Continued

Overall Means and Positions of Corporate Strategic Planners
(Ranks indicate position involving "better" practice on that item)

Mean less than 2.5[1]	Mean between 2.5 and 3.5	Mean greater than 3.5
	A discussion about the latest scientific inventions would be common here (1)	†Managers are seldom told to go through channels (1)
		Senior management has a positive attitude about their jobs (1)
	Management is quick to criticize for poor performance and seldom forgets a mistake (4)	Managers operating styles are allowed to range freely from the very informal to the very formal (1)
	†Managers can generally make decisions without their bosses' approval (2)	There is a strong tendency to promote from within at the senior levels (1)*
		†There are many opportunities for informal conversation between senior and subordinate personnel (2)
		Careful reasoning and clear logic are highly valued here (1)

[1] Means on 5-point scale: 1 = disagree, 5 = agree

( ) Indicates rank of Corporate Strategic Planners

*Significant difference among Planning Categories at p < .05

†Sense of scale reversed for exposition

Furthermore, 14 of the items are significantly different among Planning Categories, with the Corporate Strategic Planners in the superior position in 9 cases, second in 3 cases, and in the worst position in none. This pattern indicates both significant overall differences across the items and superior climate in the Corporate Strategic Planners. It is not possible, however, to establish direction of effect—that is, whether corporate strategic planning tends to improve climate or whether it is adopted in good climates.

Among the 24 items with means for the entire sample that lie well above the midpoint, the scales tend to measure reward for performance, positive feelings toward the firm, cooperation, and individual freedom and responsibility. (Significant in their absence are items involving innovation or entrepreneurship.) The Corporate Strategic Planners score highest on 16 of these items, in 5 cases significantly so, generally averaging at or near 4 on the 5-point scales.

Among the 21 items where sample means position in the midrange (near 3- on 5-point scales), several involve innovation and entrepreneurship; in all cases, the Corporate Strategic Planners are in the highest position. Many of the other items involve control and procedure, and there are no particular patterns among the Planning Categories. One item is of interest: the Corporate Strategic Planners are significantly more likely to think that line managers find planning useful.

Among the six items with means well below the midpoint (scales that the sample firms as a whole feel do not characterize them) are those measuring job policy, need for corporate clearance for major decisions, and limitations on firms' growth. The profile of Corporate Strategic Planners does not generally distinguish them from the other firms on these items, though they are perceived as overstaffed. The item on tendency toward high risk, high return investments falls in this category, meaning that the sample as a whole does not consider itself entrepreneurial; however, the Corporate Strategic Planners are best positioned on this scale.

7.7 Summary

In this chapter we distinguished between two areas of organizational design—formal organization structure and organizational climate. The most interesting finding is the distinct difference in results associated with organization structure (where Corporate Strategic

Planners do not have a sharply different profile) and organizational climate (where Corporate Strategic Planners are clearly different).

All firms in our sample had some sort of divisional structure. Although all structures were relatively complex, a measure of *administrative intensity* was, unsurprisingly, greater for Corporate Strategic Planners. There were considerable differences in degree of *centralization* across the sample, the Corporate Strategic Planners being the most decentralized, the Non-Planners the least. There was moderate agreement regarding *formalization*, Corporate Strategic Planners and Non-Planners being most strongly controlled by sophisticated systems.[4]

Far more matrix organizations for international operations were found in this study than in previous work. Corporate Strategic Planners were more likely to have matrix organizations, in particular the international/product division form. Conversely, they were less likely to have an elemental organizational form, in particular, the international-division form.

Across the sample, new product development tended to be a second-level responsibility rather than to lie with a special organizational unit. Furthermore, incentives were not given for entrepreneurial actions; rather, the organization forms and structures were believed to encourage conservative rather than entrepreneurial management. The firms were only moderately specialized and low levels of resource sharing were found across the sample. However, most firms both procured internally wherever possible and had transfer pricing systems in place, though these systems were somewhat less in evidence for the Corporate Strategic Planners.

Overall, there were few major differences in organization structure among the Planning Categories.

There are, however, patterns in organizational climate that differentiate the Corporate Strategic Planners from the other Planning Categories. It is important to understand that these are relative rather than absolute differences. For example, the sample in general does not consider itself to be authoritarian or bureaucratic; the Corporate Strategic Planners feel themselves less so. On the other hand, the sample as a whole does not consider that entrepreneurial behavior is rewarded, but the Corporate Strategic Planners report it more rewarded.

Similarly, firms in the sample generally consider their climates cooperative and participative. Jobs are considered interesting, and rewards are thought to be tied to performance. In all of these areas, the Corporate Strategic Planners tend to be leaders.

In the midrange are matters dealing with innovation, whether line managers find planning helpful, how tight controls and procedures are, and whether mistakes are tolerated. Among these, the only pattern is that the Corporate Strategic Planners consider themselves more entrepreneurial.

We must confess to being a little surprised by these findings. While there is ample evidence to support the importance of "soft" (informal) organizational variables vis-à-vis "hard" (formal) variables for effective organizational functioning, the very formality of planning procedures in many large companies led us to expect more relationships to formal structure. The pattern of differences for Corporate Strategic Planners on organizational climate measures, however, lends strong support to the views often expressed by practitioners. Many line executives remain skeptical about the value of formal planning per se, tending to view the organizational context within which planning takes place as more important to the quality of the outcomes of the planning process than the formal procedures and approaches embedded in the process itself.

More generally, in reviewing the findings presented in chapters 5, 6, and 7, it must be recognized that relatively few strong relationships have emerged. The role of planning and the planning system as a key variable to organizational functioning is not strongly supported, no matter whether we look to environment, strategy, formal organization structure, or organizational climate. Whether this state of affairs is due to the fairly basic level of analysis employed to date or to the fact that the impact of planning is much less pivotal – or at least more subtle – than was previously believed is yet to be determined. It is to the resolution of these issues that we apply ourselves in the three chapters that follow.

NOTES

1. See Caves (1980) for an economist's perspective on research in strategy, structure and environment.

2. See Lei, Capon, Farley, and Hulbert (1986) for an analysis of differences in planning system design between multinational firms with matrix macrostructures versus those with elementary forms, cast in the framework of Thompson's (1967) types of interdependence.

3. In separate studies we compare characteristics of those multinational firms (foreign sales more than 15% of total sales) with matrix organizations to those

with elementary structures. In Capon, Farley, Hulbert, and Lei (1986a), the focus is on differences in environment, strategy, and organization; in Lei, Capon, Farley, and Hulbert (1986), detailed comparative analysis of the planning systems was conducted.

4. The combination of decentralization and central control, found for the Corporate Strategic Planners, has been previously noted among large multinational firms (Hulbert and Brandt 1980).

PART III

"INTERMEDIATE" MODELS RELATING PLANNING TO ENVIRONMENT, STRATEGY, AND ORGANIZATION

In the three chapters of part II, we focused our analysis on how planning relates to environment, strategy, organization structure, and organizational climate, using an item-by-item analysis involving the Planning Categories developed in chapter 2. This is one extreme of the analytical options – an exhaustive set of univariate analyses. While this approach to analysis produces a detailed fabric, particularly of the Corporate Strategic Planners in relation to the other Planning Categories, it is not easy to recognize overall patterns of complex interrelationships.

At the opposite extreme of analytical options lie attempts to develop informationally exhaustive models like the principal components model of the planning process presented in chapter 4. These analyses have the virtue of keeping the data base intact, but they are rigid and difficult to relate back to the actual measurements.

Between these two extremes lies a practically endless set of options for combining subsets of the measurements in the data base for meaningful analysis. Some of these options focus on only a few of the variables, addressing specific research questions. Some examples of studies at this level of analysis, with self-explanatory titles, are:[1]
are:[1]

1. A Comparison of Corporate Planning Practice in American and Australian Manufacturing Companies (Capon, Christodoulou, Farley, and Hulbert 1984)

2. A Comparison of the Strategy and Structure of United States and Australian Corporations: An Evolutionary Perspective (Capon, Christodoulou, Farley, and Hulbert 1987)
3. Corporate Diversity and Economic Performance: The Impact of Market Specialization (Capon, Farley, Hulbert, and Martin 1987)
4. Organizational Processes and Economic Performance: A Contingency Approach (Wright, and Capon, Farley, and Hulbert 1985)
5. Covariates of Product Innovation: An Empirical Assessment (Capon, Farley, Hulbert, and Lehmann 1986)
6. Environment, Strategy, and Organizational Dimensions in Matrix and Non-Matrix Multinational Firms (Capon, Farley, Hulbert, and Lei 1986a)
7. Corporate Planning Systems in Matrix and Non-Matrix Multinational Firms (Lei, Capon, Farley, and Hulbert 1986)
8. An Empirical Analysis of the 'Excellent' Companies (Capon, Farley, Hulbert, and Lei 1986b)
9. A New Approach to the Testing of Fit in Contingency Theory (Capon, Farley, and Lehmann 1986)

The purpose of the two chapters in part III is to explore some methods of analysis that are "intermediate" in the sense that they do not attempt to exhaust the information available, but they are more global than either univariate analysis or analysis of selected elements of the data base just described. There is, of course, a large combinatorial number of intermediate modeling possibilities involving various segments of the nearly 1,000 measurements available. Two of these options, based almost entirely on multivariate statistical analysis, are developed in this part.

Chapter 8 extends the process of scale development started in chapter 4 for planning to the development of scales summarizing environment, strategy, organization structure, and organizational climate. Correlations of these scales with the planning scales constitute an exercise in such "intermediate" modeling.

Chapter 9 reverses the process by developing multivariate profiles of firms which are "similar" in terms of planning, environment, strategy, organization structure, and organizational climate. Joint membership in the planning groups and the other groups produces profiles of related firms, which constitute a second "intermediate" type of model.

NOTES

1. Items 1 and 2 involve use of an augmented data base from a sample of Australian corporations.

Chapter 8

Scale Structures: Planning, Environment, Strategy, Organization Structure, and Organizational Climate

8.1 Introduction

It is clear that the nearly 1,000 items discussed in chapters 3, 5, 6, and 7 are interdependent. However, attempting cross-tabulation of the individual items to study these interrelationships is simply not feasible because of the relatively small number of observations and because of the combinatorial implications of such cross-tabling. We can, however, develop sets of scales summarizing environment, strategy, organization structure, and organizational climate like those developed for planning in chapter 4. The relationships of these sets of scales to the planning scales developed in chapter 4 can be examined, as can mean scale values for the Planning Categories developed in chapter 2. The summary power of the scales also allows us to expand the analysis from the focus on the Corporate Strategic Planners in chapters 3, 5, 6, and 7, to all five Planning Categories.

8.2 Procedures for Construction and Analysis of Scales

The same procedure used in chapter 4 to develop the planning scales is employed to develop four more sets of scales – environment, strategy, organization structure, and organizational climate.

　　1. A set of scales is assembled for each area (environment, strategy, organization structure, and organizational climate) based on the items discussed in chapters 5, 6, or 7. The assembly procedure, the same as that used to develop the planning scales in chapter 4, involves

choosing a subset of relevant items and summing them. No effort is made to exhaust the items, though all items are considered in making the choices. In some cases, factor analysis is used to help define dimensions and choose items for individual scales. As an example, the 31 of 51 organizational climate items that load heavily on the 7 factors in a factor analysis are used in scales assembled to summarize that construct.

2. Correlations between values on the planning scales developed in chapter 4, and values on each of the scales developed from step 1, are examined in an attempt to develop a feeling for how planning relates to each construct. Since there are 43 planning scales (13 adaptive and 30 integrative), there are 43 correlations in the analysis for each individual scale involving environment, strategy, organization structure, and organizational climate. For each planning scale, we would anticipate about two of these correlations to be significant (α = .05) by chance, so we interpret more than 5 significant correlations between a given scale and the 43 planning scales as indicating some pattern. It is important to remember, however, that these correlations are not independent, so the analysis looks for overall patterns rather than focusing on individual relationships.

3. Mean values of the scales developed in step 1 are calculated for each of the five Planning Categories (chapter 2). Summaries of the rankings of Corporate Strategic Planners on the individual scales, and the counts of significant differences among Planning Categories are used to develop a more coherent and informationally efficient overview of differences among Planning Categories than was possible in chapters 5, 6, and 7.

The procedure is a compromise between detail and parsimony based both on conceptual considerations and on results of an attempt to apply principal components analysis to the problem of scale construction. We hoped at the outset of the study that "soft models" of the sort used in chapter 4 to build a systems model of planning might be useful for developing the other scales as well, since "information-saving" indexing (as represented by the principal components) would allow an objective weighting of all variables used in chapters 5, 6, and 7 to be accomplished with maximal retention of information; the interrelations of these indices could then be used for model construction. This approach worked reasonably well for structuring the soft model of the planning process in chapter 4, but it broke down in dealing with the broader constructs of environment, strategy, organization structure, and organizational climate. A brief discussion of our disappointment with this approach might be useful to others considering a similar approach to analysis.

The "soft model" approach seemed to collapse in the case of the nonplanning variables for two reasons. First, the measures of environment, strategy, organization structure, and organizational climate are so inherently multidimensional that a few principal components could not provide good summaries. For example, the four individual principal components analyses summarizing the 363 environment, strategy, organization structure, and organizational climate measures produce a total of 109 eigenvalues greater than unity. Relatively speaking, the principal components analyses of the planning variables in chapter 4 produced far fewer large eigenvalues. Second, averaging together a relatively small number of bivariately significant variables with a large number of variables insignificant over Planning Categories appeared to wash out all of the interesting patterns. The scale procedure used here is a compromise, involving a search for subgroupings of the variables that are less aggregate than those used in the principal components analysis but that allow prior choice of items to construct more meaningful scales. For the most part, the scales have good properties. In the case of every scale, the constituent items had significant correlations with the scales, and the Chronbach alphas were high, rarely below 0.5. (Occasionally, scales with lower alphas were retained on grounds of theoretical relevance or completeness.)

8.3 Organizational Climate

8.3.1 SCALE DEVELOPMENT

The 51 organizational climate items (chapter 7) are measured with similar Likert-type scales and have a longer history of application than many of the other items used in our study. We describe the process of scale construction for organizational climate in more detail here for both substantive and methodological reasons. Scales developed for environment, strategy, and organization structure follow similar patterns but are described in less detail.

Factor analysis of the organizational climate items was used to suggest an initial structure in the data. The 51 items produce 20 principal components with eigenvalues greater than 1. A scree analysis, combined with assessment on random splitting criteria, indicates that seven significant factors should be retained for varimax rotation. Table 8.1 shows groupings by loadings greater than 0.4. The seven factors can be interpreted as follows:

Table 8.1
Patterns in Factor Analysis of Organizational Climate Items[1]

1. Load on first factor: Entrepreneurialness

New ideas are always being tried out here (.71)[2]
There is a strong tendency toward high-risk, high-return investments (.69)
Unusual or exciting plans are encouraged (.67)
†There is little emphasis on holding fast to tried and true management principles as business conditions change (.44)

2. Load on second factor: Performance Orientation

There is a strong performance-oriented up-or-out job policy (.68)
People are rewarded in proportion to the excellence of their performance (.53)
In promoting managers, there is a strong emphasis on competitiveness and ability to outperform others (.48)
Financial and operating information flow quite freely throughout the company (.45)
†It is generally clear who has formal authority to make a decision (.40)

3. Load on third factor: Line-Staff Interaction

In decision making, there is great reliance on specially-trained line and staff personnel as distinct from a reliance on personnel with experience (.62)
In general there are excellent communications between line managers and planning personnel (.56)
As the company has grown in size it has grown more impersonal (.46)
Line managers find the services rendered by company planners very helpful (.46)
There is a tendency for the company to be overstaffed with personnel (.45)

4. Loan on fourth factor: Organizational Contentment

Senior management jobs are very secure (.75)
†People trust each other in this company (.69)
People are proud of being with this company (.52)
†There are many opportunities for conversation between senior and subordinate personnel (.50)
†People generally do not look out for their own interests in this company (.49)
There is cooperation between people in getting things done (.48)
There is a strong tendency to let the expert have the most say in decision making, even if this means temporarily bypassing formal authority (.48)
When we have acquired companies we have avoided problems of incompatible managerial behavior (.46)
†There is much personal loyalty in this company (.40)

5. Load on fifth factor: Participative Decision Making

   Decision making in this company is participative (.71)
   As the company has grown in size, it has achieved more participation in decision making (.64)
   †Overall, the decision-making style of senior management in this company is not authoritarian (.61)
   There is strong committee-oriented consensus seeking, participative decision making (.54)
   Managers have complete written job descriptions for their jobs (.46)
   Managers typically consult with subordinates on decisions to adopt new programs (.49)

6. Load on sixth factor: Organizational Fluidity

   A friendly atmosphere prevails among people in this company (.64)
   †Managers do not have to follow the same procedures in most situations (.63)
   †Managers do not do the same job in the same way every day (.58)
   †Managers do not have to follow written orders without question (.52)
   †Managers do not have procedures to follow whatever situation arises (.47)
   Managers have jobs where something new is happening every day (.45)

7. Load on seventh factor: Delegated Responsibility

   People feel that they are their own bosses in most matters (.53)
   There is strong individualistic decision making by the normally responsible executive (.55)
   †Second level managers generally do not need clearance from corporate executives before making major decisions (.49)
   There is emphasis on getting things done even if this means disregarding formal procedures (.42)

Do Not Load On Any Factor

   †The jobs of managers in this company are not highly routine
   Pay is certainly an indication of performance in this company
   The degree of complexity faced by the company will eventually limit its power to grow
   †Few managerial conflicts require top management resolution
   A discussion about the latest scientific inventions would be common here
   Management is quick to criticize for poor performance and seldom forgets a mistake
   Management can generally make decisions without their bosses' approval
   †Managers are seldom told to go through channels
   Senior managers have a positive attitude about their jobs
   Managers' operating styles are allowed to range freely from the very informal to the very formal
   There is a strong tendency to promote from within at senior levels
   Careful reasoning and clear logic are highly valued here

[1]All items measured on 5-point scales: 1 = disagree, 5 = agree

[2]Factor loadings

†Sense of scale reversed for exposition

Factor 1 – Entrepreneurialness. This factor indicates the extent to which the company atmosphere encourages openness to new ideas and risk taking.

Factor 2 – Performance Orientation. This factor measures the extent to which the organization is oriented to reward excellence for individual performance in various ways.

Factor 3 – Line-Staff Interaction. This factor indicates how well staff are received by the line organization.

Factor 4 – Organizational Contentment. This factor indicates the extent to which company employees are content with their organization; it is the degree to which they feel secure and trust one another and are loyal to and proud of the organization.

Factor 5 – Participative Decision Making. This factor measures the degree to which decision making is participative rather than authoritarian.

Factor 6 – Organizational Fluidity. This factor indicates the extent to which the organization is seen as organic and environmentally open as opposed to rigidly bureaucratic with extensive procedures to be followed.

Factor 7 – Delegated Responsibility. This factor indicates the degree of delegated responsibility and individual freedom in decision-making.

Next, those items that seemed to capture best the dimensions identified in the factor analysis were selected for the development of scales to summarize organizational climate. The 31 measurements chosen, all 5-point Likert scales, are shown in appendix table A8.1. Seven scales were developed:

Entrepreneurialness is composed of four items and captures the extent to which entrepreneurial behavior is encouraged.

Performance Orientation is measured by three items indicating tight linkages between managerial performance and reward.

Line-Staff Interaction is based on three items that focus on how well line and staff function together.

Organizational Contentment is composed of seven items based on positive feeling for the organization: trust, security, loyalty, cooperation, and pride in the organization.

Participative Decision Making is measured by five items directly related to the extent of participative decision making in the firm.

Organizational Fluidity contains five items involving procedure and formal control. These measure the extent to which the

organization is rule bound. However, the scales were reversed to provide a measure of organizational fluidity.

Delegated Responsibility is composed of four items related
to decentralization of decision making.

The scales are constructed such that high values on each
scale accord with the current received wisdom regarding positive
organizational climates.

8.3.2 ORGANIZATIONAL CLIMATE SCALES AND PLANNING SCALES

Of the 301 correlation coefficients between the 43 planning
scales and the 7 organizational climate scales (table 8.2), 108 (36%)
are significant at α = .05, including 35 of 91 (38%) of the adaptive
correlations and 73 of 210 (34%) of the integrative correlations. Of the
108 significant correlations, only 8 are negative; 6 of these involve the
atmosphere at plan and performance review. All organizational
climate scales show at least some degree of relationship to planning;
the minimum number of significant correlations for an individual
scale is 7, and all but 8 of the planning scales display at least one
significant relationship.

Participative Decision Making shows very strong patterns
of association with planning (27 of 43 correlations significant),
especially with the adaptive scales. It is highly related to strategic and
environmental orientations and to use of planning tools and strategic
criteria in resource allocation decisions. It is also related to formal integration of plans, high levels of information flow, and influence of
both line managers and planners in a process that extends deep into
the organization, is long run in focus, and relaxed as regards performance reviews. There is relatively little prior evidence that planning
and participative management go hand in hand, but here it certainly
appears to be the case.

Organizational Contentment (22 of 43 correlations significant) is associated with a selection of adaptive scales, notably
strategic resource allocation decisions, competitive analysis, and
globalness of planning. It is also related to good functional integration
of planning; good information flow; internal influence and participation, including Board of Directors, CEO, line management and planners; and line acceptance of planning. When contentment is high, atmosphere at both plan and performance reviews is relaxed.

Line-Staff Interaction (17 of 43 correlations significant)
shows especially strong relationships to adaptive scales; high levels of

Table 8.2
Correlations of Planning Scales and Organizational Climate Scales[1]

			Organizational Climate Scales				
Adaptive Planning Scales	Entrepreneurialness	Performance Orientation	Line-Staff Interaction	Organizational Contentment	Participative Decision Making	Organizational Fluidity	Delegated Responsibility
Environmental Orientation							
Environmental Information	-	-	-	-	.32***	-	-
Competitive Analysis	-	.23***	.24***	.21**	.21**	-	-
Strategic Orientation							
"Strategic" Planning	.19**	-	-	-	.27***	.21**	-
Time Horizon	.16**	-	-	-	.33***	-	-
Globalness	.24***	.27***	.27***	.18**	.21**	-	-
Portfolio Change	-	-	-	-	-	-	.18**
Resource Allocation	.21**	.22***	.42***	.24***	.36***	-	-
Planning Tools							
Portfolio Models	-	-	.21**	-	.19**	-	-
Model Use	-	-	.17**	-	.24***	-	-
Resource Allocation Decisions							
Long Run Expense Distinction	-	.21**	.23***	.16**	.21**	-	-
Strategic Criteria	-	.33***	.31***	.20**	.22***	-.20**	-
Plan Comprehensiveness							
Corporate	-	-	-	-	.20**	-	-
Second Level	-	-	-	-	-	-	-
Integrative Planning Scales							
Formal Integration of Plans							
Corporate/Functional	.17**	.24***	.43***	.28***	.27***	-	-
Over-time	-	-	-	-	.29***	-	-
Information Flow							
Top Down	.18**	-	-	.22***	.27***	.18**	-
Internal	-	-	-	.29***	.22***	-	-
Corporate Planning Exchange	-	-	-	-	.19**	-	-
Influence and Participation							
Board of Directors	-	.16**	.19**	.17**	-	.16**	-
CEO	-	-	.26***	.20**	-	-	-
Top Second-Level Line Management	.36***	-	.32***	.23***	.29***	.21**	.23***
Corporate Planning	-	-	-	.16**	.23***	-	-
Internal	-	.25***	-	.23***	-	-	-

	Organizational Climate Scales						
	Entrepreneurialness	Performance Orientation	Line-Staff Interaction	Organizational Contentment	Participative Decision Making	Organizational Fluidity	Delegated Responsibility
Goal and Strategy Formulation Process							
Bottom-Up	-	-	.16**	.16**	.17**	-	-
CEO Negotiation	-	-	-	-	-	-.17**	-
Planning and Line Management							
Relative Staff/Line							
Nature of Planning	-	.17**	-	-	-	-	-
Line View of Planning	.32***	.24***	.27***	.29***	.36***	.17**	.30***
Integrative Value of Planners							
Added Value	-	-	-	-	-	-	-
Planning Group Integration	.37***	.25***	.44***	.33***	.41***	-	.28***
Status and Authority of Planners							
Reporting Importance	.17***	-	-	-	.22***	-	-
Planning Authority	-	-	.26***	-	-	-	-
Formalization of Planning							
Corporate	-	-	-	-	.21**	-	-
Second-level	-	-	-	-	-	-	-
Plan Density Preparation	-	-	-	.16**	-	-	-
Plan Density Review	-	-	-	.18**	.18**	-	-
Plan Distribution Depth	-	.18**	-	-	-	-	-
Planning and Performance Review							
Plan Review Atmosphere	-	-	-	-.32***	-	-	-.19**
Performance Review:							
Atmosphere	-	.18**	-	.21**	-.26***	-.29***	-.25***
Frequency	-	-	-	-	-	-	-
Criteria	.34***	.30***	.20**	.29***	.23***	-	-
Depth	-	-	-	-	-	-	-
Goals							
Use of Goals	.25***	.24***	.17**	.17**	.20**	-	.33***
Goals for Planning	-	-	-	-	-	-	-
Number Significant	12	15	17	22	27	8	7

[1]All tests in this table are 1-tailed.

***p < .01, **p < .05

interaction are related to use of strategic criteria in resource allocation decisions, use of planning tools, competitive analysis, and globalness of planning. As regards the integrative scales, line-staff interaction is associated with good functional integration; influence and participation from the CEO, line management, and planners; overall good integration of the planners; and high levels of planning authority.

Performance Orientation (15 of 43 correlations significant) has identical relationships to the adaptive scales as organizational contentment and is associated with functional integration, internal and CEO influence and participation, use of goals, tense performance reviews yet positive line management view of planning, good planning integration, and long-run orientation.

Entrepreneurialness (12 of 43 correlations significant) is associated with a strategic orientation to planning, commitment of line management to planning, good planning integration, long-run orientation, and use of goals.

Organizational Fluidity (8 of 43 correlations significant) is characterized most strongly by relaxed performance reviews and heavy line management influence and participation.

Delegated Responsibility (7 of 43 correlations significant) is related to resource allocation focus and to similar integrative scales as entrepreneurialness. It is also related to relaxed plan and performance reviews but not to a long-run orientation.

Some interesting patterns are also shown when the focus of analysis is shifted to those planning scales that correlate with several of the organizational climate scales.

Of the adaptive scales, the strongest correlations (number significant) are for resource allocation (6 of 13 significant), "strategic" criteria for resource allocation decisions (5) (including the curious negative relationship with organizational fluidity), and globalness of planning (5). As expected from the earlier discussion, these relationships are focused in the entrepreneurialness, performance orientation, line-staff interaction, organizational contentment, and participative decision-making scales. On the other hand, environmental information and corporate plan comprehensiveness have just one significant relationship each, while portfolio change and second-level plan comprehensiveness have no relationships at all.

The strongest relationships for the integrative scales are top second-level line management influence (6), line view of planning (6), planning group integration (6), use of goals (6), corporate/functional plan integration (5), and performance review criteria (5). Each scale displays only positive significant relationships to the organizational climate scales. In all cases but one, either, or both, delegated responsibility and organizational fluidity is nonsignificant.

As noted, the focus of the negative relationships is atmosphere of plan and performance review. Of the seven significant relationships involving these two scales, six are negative, implying that high values on the planning scales relate to a relaxed atmosphere; for only the performance orientation scale is a tense atmosphere indicated.

Overall, then, there appears to be a strong set of relationships between organizational climate and planning practice. Consistent with current wisdom on planning, positive organizational climates tend to be associated with good planning practice.

8.3.3 ORGANIZATIONAL CLIMATE SCALES AND PLANNING CATEGORIES

The analysis of the Planning Categories (table 8.3) is done both with means of the scales computed from the 31 items and, for comparison in this case, factor scores based on the seven factors (table 8.1). Since the results are quite similar in both cases and the factor scores are more difficult to interpret than the scales, the scores are not discussed further.

Surprisingly, given the results on the individual items in chapter 7, there is only one significant difference for organizational climate scale means across Planning Categories. There are, however, patterns of consistency. The Corporate Strategic Planners are polar in terms of entrepreneurialness, performance orientation, line-staff interaction, contentment, and participation. They are second on organizational fluidity and in respect to delegation. Division Financial Planners and Non-Planners tend also to be polar but in the opposite direction. One of these two Categories is at the end-point on all of the scales. Finally, there is no clear pattern to distinguish between Division Strategic Planners and Corporate Financial Planners in terms of organizational climate.

8.4 Environment

8.4.1 SCALE DEVELOPMENT

Separate factor analyses of the common items used in chapter 5 to characterize both the historic and anticipated-future environment produced practically identical two-factor structures. Just the anticipated-future enviromental items were selected and com-

Table 8.3

Means (and Ranks) of Organizational Climate Scales
by Planning Category

Organizational Climate Scales (computed on chosen 31 items)	Planning Category					Significance among Planning Categories
	Corporate Strategic Planners	Division Strategic Planners	Corporate Financial Planners	Division Financial Planners	Non-Planners	
Entrepreneur-ialness	.23(1)	.14(2)	-.08(3)	-.45(5)	-.44(4)	NS
Performance Orientation	.46(1)	-.07(2)	-.09(3)	-.42(5)	-.13(4)	NS
Line-Staff Interaction	.26(1)	.01(2)	-.03(3)	-.44(5)	-.12(4)	NS
Organizational Contentment	.28(1)	-.12(4)	.18(2)	-.70(5)	-.06(3)	NS
Participative Decision-Making	.63(1)	-.13(4)	-.08(3)	-.05(2)	-1.01(5)	**
Organizational Fluidity	.04(2)	.03(3)	.09(1)	-.07(4)	-.65(5)	NS
Delegated Responsibility	.20(2)	-.13(3)	.21(1)	-.27(4)	-.62(5)	NS
Organizational Climate Scales (computed as factor scores)						
Entrepreneur-ialness	.18(1)	.17(2)	-.12(3)	-.43(5)	-.25(4)	NS
Performance Orientation	.23(1)	.03(2)	-.19(5)	-.01(3)	-.01(3)	NS
Line-Staff Interaction	.02(2)	-.06(3)	.16(1)	-.64(5)	-.46(4)	NS
Organizational Contentment	.24(1)	-.01(3)	-.17(5)	-.08(4)	.16(2)	NS
Participative Decision-Making	.61(1)	-.05(3)	-.13(4)	-.04(2)	-1.12(5)	**
Organizational Fluidity	.05(3)	-.08(4)	.14(2)	.17(1)	-.67(5)	NS
Delegated Responsibility	.22(1)	-.14(3)	.11(2)	-.19(4)	-.24(5)	NS

**Significant at $\alpha = .05$

bined with the set of 10 uncertainty (reverse of confidence) measures to develop an overall factor structure of the anticipated-future environment (table 8.4).

Table 8.4
Patterns in Factor Analysis
of Anticipated-Future Environment[1] Items

	Factor Name		
	Uncertainty	Change	Hostility
Market Conditions			
Growth[2]	-	.65	-
Market Predictability			
Demand[3]	-	-	.77
Major Competitors' Actions[3]	-	-	.68
Factor Input Problems			
Raw Materials & Supplies[4]	-	-	.52
Human Resources[5]	-	-	.42
Financing[5]	-	-	-
Technology Change			
Product[6]	-	.82	-
Process[7]	-	.60	-
Government Regulation Change			
Increase[8]	-	-	-
Uncertainty[9]			
Foreign Economies	.73	-	-
Human Resources	.74	-	-
Social Cultural	.66	-	-
Governmental	.60	-	-
Domestic economy	.60	-	-
Purchased Materials and Components	.74	-	-
Competitive Behavior	.65	-	-
Technology	.64	-	-
Financial Markets	.75	-	-
Industry-Level Demand	.69	-	-
Percent Variance Explained	4.90	1.90	1.82

[1] Next 5 years unless otherwise stated
[2] % of Sales from markets growing in excess of 10% p.a.
[3] % of Sales unpredictable or worse
[4] Significant Availability problems or worse (%)
[5] Difficulty in securing, means on 5-point scale: 1 = no problems, 5 = severe problems
[6] % of Sales in 1990 generated by technology not commercially available in 1980
[7] Means on 5-point scale: 1 = no change, 5 = substantial change, in next 10 years
[8] % of Sales in for which government regulation will increase
[9] All measured on 5-point scales on confidence of having an adequate appraisal of the situation regarding each area: 1 = very confident, 5 = not at all confident

On the basis of these factor analysis results, three scales were constructed to summarize environment. The 17 measurements chosen are shown in appendix table A8.2. The scales are:

Uncertainty involves 10 items that measure the lack of confidence that the firm has an adequate appraisal of the situation in 10 environmental areas.

Change is measured by three items focused on different types of environmental change: product technology, process technology, and market growth.

Hostility is measured by four items that capture the unpredictability of the future demand and competitive environments and the extent of anticipated problems in securing human and raw material resources.

Table 8.5

Correlations of Planning Scales and Environment Scales[1]

Adaptive Planning Scales	Environment Scales		
	Uncertainty	Change	Hostility
Environmental Orientation			
Environmental Information	-.39***	-	-
Competitive Analysis	-.15**	-	-
Strategic Orientation			
"Strategic" Planning	-.24***	-	-
Time Horizon	-	-	-
Globalness	-.15**	-	-
Portfolio Change	-.16**	-	-
Resource Allocation	-	-	-
Planning Tools			
Portfolio Models	-	-	-
Model Use	-.21**	-	-
Resource Allocation Decisions			
Long Run Expense Distinction	-	.16**	-
Strategic Criteria	-	-	-
Plan Comprehensiveness			
Corporate	-	-	-
Second Level	-	-	-
Integrative Planning Scales			
Formal Integration of Plans			
Corporate/Functional	-	-	-
Over-time	-	-	-
Information Flow			
Top Down	-.40***	.15**	.20**
Internal	-	-	-
Corporate Planning Exchange	-	-	-
Influence and Participation			
Board of Directors	-	-	.23***
CEO	-	-	-
Top Second-Level Line Management	-	.15**	-
Corporate Planning	-	-	-
Internal	-	-	-

8.4.2 ENVIRONMENT SCALES AND PLANNING SCALES

Only 16 correlations between the 43 planning scales and the 3 environmental scales (table 8.5) are significantly different from zero. Beneath this general lack of significance is an underlying pattern. Nine of the 16 significant correlations (56%) involve uncertainty and are negative; six of these relate to the adaptive scales. Low uncertainty is related to environmental information gathering, competitive analysis, "strategic" planning, globalness, portfolio change, and model use; it is also related to top-down information flow, long-run performance review criteria and added value of planners. Perceived environmental uncertainty thus appears to be related to an internal as opposed to an external orientation – suggesting that we are observing the result of failure to devote sufficient resources to understanding the environment – hence the perceived uncertainty – rather than an il-

Table 8.5 (continued)

	Environment Scales		
	Uncertainty	Change	Hostility
Goal and Strategy Formulation Process			
Bottom-Up	-	-	-
CEO Negotiation	-	-	-.16**
Planning and Line Management			
Relative Staff/Line			
Nature of Planning	-	-	-
Line View of Planning	-	-	-.21**
Integrative Value of Planners			
Added Value	-.19**	-	-
Planning Group Integration	-	-	-
Status and Authority of Planners			
Reporting Importance	-	-	-
Planning Authority	-	-	-
Formalization of Planning			
Corporate	-	-	-
Second-level	-	-	-
Plan Density Preparation	-	-	-
Plan Density Review	-	-	-
Plan Distribution Depth	-	-	-
Planning and Performance Review			
Plan Review Atmosphere	-	-	-
Performance Review:			
Atmosphere	-	-	-
Frequency	-	-	-
Criteria	-.22***	-	-
Depth	-	-	-
Goals			
Use of Goals	-	-	-
Goals for Planning	-	-	-
Number Significant	9	3	4

[1]All tests in this table are 1-tailed.

***p < .01, **p < .05

logical response on the part of the firm to seek highly uncertain environments.

Between hostile and changing environments only one adaptive scale is significant (high change related to long-run expense distinction in resource allocation). Some pattern can be identified for hostile environments with the integrative scales; high degrees of hostility were related to top-down information flow, board of directors' influence in planning, lack of CEO negotiation in goal and strategy formulation, and a negative view of planning by line management. Under difficult conditions a top-down emphasis seems apparent.

When the analysis is focused on the planning scales, only one scale was related to more than one environmental scale; top-down information flow was positively related to hostility and change but negatively related to uncertainty.

8.4.3 ENVIRONMENT SCALES AND PLANNING CATEGORIES

In general, hostile and uncertain environments are most likely viewed as undesirable, whereas changing environments might well be viewed as positive. Effective planning should enable the firm to avoid undesirable environments but find attractive environments. A contrast between the five Planning Category means for the environment scales, however, reveals no significant patterns (table 8.6). There are some weak directional differences. Corporate Strategic Planners seem to face low uncertainty but high change. The Non-Planners, by contrast, seem concentrated in unchanging and hostile environments.

Table 8.6

Means (and Ranks) of Environment Scales by Planning Category

Environment Scales	Planning Category					Significance among Planning Categories
	Corporate Strategic Planners	Division Strategic Planners	Corporate Financial Planners	Division Financial Planners	Non-Planners	
Hostility[1]	-.03(3)	-.08(2)	-.09(1)	.45(5)	.26(4)	NS
Change[2]	.27(1)	.04(3)	-.16(4)	.12(2)	-.52(5)	NS
Uncertainty[3]	-.12(1)	-.05(2)	.13(5)	.07(4)	-.03(3)	NS

[1] Positive number implies high hostility, negative number implies low hostility

[2] Positive number implies high change, negative number implies low change

[3] Positive number implies high uncertainty (low confidence), negative number implies low uncertainty (high confidence)

8.5 Strategy

8.5.1 SCALE DEVELOPMENT

Similar procedures were employed to develop 10 scales using 31 items, including both realized and intended strategy measures, to summarize strategy. The items are shown in appendix table A8.3. The scales are:

Internal Innovation comprises six items, including commitment of resources to R&D, fraction of corporate revenues from early in the product life cycle, expressed tendencies for innovation, being first to market, at the cutting edge of technology, and a lack of risk aversion in R&D.

Acquisition consists of three items measuring the number and importance of acquisitions since 1974.

Divestiture consists of two items measuring the number and importance of divestitures since 1974.

International Posture consists of two items measuring the importance of sales and manufacturing abroad.

Industrial Goods is a single item measuring importance of sales to industry and government.

Scale comprises two measures of size – sales revenues and number of employees.

International Marketing consists of two items measuring globalness of marketing effort.

Explicit Growth/Share Strategy is based on four items measuring expressed attempts to gain high market shares in growing markets.

New Product Strategy consists of four items measuring the expressed importance of new products.

Explicit Segment Strategy consists of five items that capture the notion of an explicit seeking of market segments and avoiding competitors.

8.5.2 STRATEGY SCALES AND PLANNING SCALES

The 430 correlations between the 43 planning scales and the 10 strategy scales are shown in table 8.7. Of the 430 correlation coefficients, 112 (26%) are significant at $\alpha = .05$, 38 of 130 adaptive correlations (29%) and 74 of 300 integrative correlations (25%); all of the 43 planning scales except 4 are significantly correlated to at least one strategy scale. These patterns are stronger than would be expected by chance. However, the significant relationships cluster on

Table 8.7
Correlations of Planning Scales and Strategy Scales[1]

	Strategy Scales									
Adaptive Planning Scales	Internal Innovation	Acquisition	Divestiture	International Posture	Industrial Goods	Scale	International Marketing	Explicit Growth/Share Strategy	New Product Strategy	Explicit Segment Strategy
Environmental Orientation										
Environmental Information	-	-	-	-	-	.31***	-	.18**	-	-
Competitive Analysis	.16**	-	-	-	-	.26***	-	.36***	-	-
Strategic Orientation										
"Strategic" Planning	-	-	.16**	-	-	.29***	-	.20**	-	-
Time Horizon	.28***	-	-	-.19**	.29***	.36***	-	.25***	-	-
Globalness	-	-	-	.38***	-	.22***	.32***	.22***	.21**	-
Portfolio Change	.22***	-	-	-.22***	.28***	-	-	-	-	-
Resource Allocation	-	-	-	-	-	.26***	-	.42***	-	-
Planning Tools										
Portfolio Models	-	-	-	-	-	-	-	.41***	-	-
Model Use	-	-	-	-	-	.26***	.18**	.17***	-	-.15**
Resource Allocation Decisions										
Long Run Expense Distinction	-	-	-	.21**	-	.27***	-	.19**	.23***	-
Strategic Criteria	.15**	-	-	-	-	-	-	.33***	-	-
Plan Comprehensiveness										
Corporate	-	-	-	-	-	.26***	-	.23***	-	-
Second Level	-	-	-	-	-	-	.17**	.18**	-	-
Integrative Planning Scales										
Formal Integration of Plans										
Corporate/Functional	-	-.19**	-	-	-	.21**	-	.24***	-	-
Over-time	.15**	-	-	-	-	.30***	-	.20**	.25***	-
Information Flow										
Top-Down	.24***	-	-	-	.19**	.38***	-	.18**	-	.15**
Internal	-	-	-	-	-	-	-	-	-	-
Corporate Planning Exchange	-	-	-	-	-	-	-	-	-	-
Influence and Participation										
Board of Directors	-	-	-	-.18**	.21**	-	-	-	-	-
CEO	-	-.21**	-	-	-	.24***	-	.20**	-	-.20**
Top Second-Level Line Management	-	-.15**	-	-	-	.15**	-	.20**	-	-
Corporate Planning	-	-	.15**	-	-	.20**	-	.32***	-	-
Internal	.18**	-	-	-	-	.25***	-	-	-	.16**

	Strategy Scales									
Goal and Strategy	Internal Innovation	Acquisition	Divestiture	International Posture	Industrial Goods	Scale	International Marketing	Explicit Growth/ Share Strategy	New Product Strategy	Explicit Segment Strategy
Formulation Process										
Bottom-Up	–	–	–	–	.17**	–	–	.23***	–	–
CEO Negotiation	.20**	–	–	–	–	–	–	.30***	–	–
Planning and Line Management										
Relative Staff/Line										
Nature of Planning	–	–	–	–	–	–	–	–	–	–
Line View of Planning	.20**	–	-.16**	–	–	–	–	.36***	–	–
Integrative Value of Planners										
Added Value	.19**	–	–	–	.16**	.23***	.21**	.35***	–	–
Planning Group Integration	.17**	–	–	–	–	–	–	–	–	–
Status and Authority of Planners										
Reporting Importance	.22***	–	.17***	–	.19**	.23***	–	.17**	–	–
Planning Authority	–	–	–	–	–	.16**	–	–	–	–
Formalization of Planning										
Corporate	–	–	–	–	–	.22**	–	.19**	–	–
Second-level	–	–	–	–	–	.31***	–	.20**	–	–
Plan Density Preparation	–	-.17**	–	.19**	.17**	.21**	–	–	–	–
Plan Density Review	–	–	–	–	–	.23***	–	-.21**	–	-.16**
Plan Distribution Depth	–	-.17**	–	–	.24***	.21**	–	.16**	–	–
Planning and Performance Review										
Plan Review Atmosphere	–	–	–	-.15**	.15**	–	–	–	–	–
Performance Review:										
Atmosphere	–	–	.16**	–	.19**	–	–	–	–	–
Frequency	–	–	.24***	–	–	.16**	.20**	–	–	.20***
Criteria	.17**	–	–	–	–	–	.25***	.16**	–	–
Depth	–	–	.15**	–	–	–	–	–	–	–
Goals										
Use of Goals	–	–	–	–	–	–	–	.22***	–	–
Goals for Planning	–	–	–	–	–	–	–	–	–	–
Number Significant	13	5	7	7	11	25	6	29	3	6

[1] All tests in this table are 1-tailed.

***p < .01, **p < .05

two strategy scales that account for half of the significant correlations, one realized strategy measure (scale) and one intended strategy measure (explicit growth/share strategy).

Explicit Growth/Share Strategy and *Scale* (29 and 25 respective significant correlations with planning scales) have quite similar profiles with 21 significant scales in common. There are especially strong relationships between explicit growth/share strategy and the adaptive scales; except for portfolio change, each scale has a significant and positive relationship. For scale, nine correlations are positive and significant, and just four (portfolio change, portfolio models, strategic criteria for resource allocation decisions, and second-level plan comprehensiveness) are not significant.

For the integrative scales, the patterns are very similar for both explicit growth/share strategy and scale. However, bottom-up and negotiated goal and strategy formulation, positive line view of planning, long-run performance criteria, and use of goals are positively related to explicit growth/share strategy but not to scale. Internal influence, reporting importance of planners, greater density of plans prepared and reviewed at corporate, and more frequent performance review are positively related to scale but not to explicit growth/share strategy.

Internal Innovation (13 of 43 correlations significant) is related to globalness, a strategic orientation to resource allocation and competitive analysis. It also seems to be associated with organizational openness (CEO negotiation), long-run performance orientation, over-time integration and top-down information flow. Finally, innovation is associated with high reporting levels for planners who add value, are positively viewed by line management, and who are well integrated into the company.

Industrial Goods strategies (11 of 43 correlations significant) have, as expected, long planning horizons and a strategic orientation to resource allocation. The integrative scale correlations are scattered, but there is a tendency for planners to be well integrated into the firm and to have formal authority, for planning to be bottom-up oriented with Board of Directors participation, for there to be extensive preparation and distribution of plans, but with tense plan and performance reviews.

Relationships of the other six strategy scales are much closer to those that might be expected by chance. *Acquisition* (5 of 43 correlations significant) is unrelated to the adaptive scales; *Divestiture* (7 of 43 correlations significant) has just one significant adaptive-scale relationship. For the integrative scales, *Acquisition* is associated with a general lack of planning (all five correlations negative), whereas *Divestiture* is associated with a negative line management view of planning and with high depth, high frequency, and confrontational performance reviews. As expected, *International Posture* (7 of 43 correlations significant) is positively related to globalness and the use of strategic criteria for resource allocation but negatively related to long time horizons and portfolio change in planning; *New Product Strategy* (3 of 43 correlations significant) and *International Marketing* (6 of 43 correlations significant) are each associated with globalness in planning but otherwise they, and *Explicit Segment Strategy*, show little in the way of significant relationships.

Viewed from the perspective of the individual planning scales, the strongest relationships (number significant) for the adaptive scales are for globalness (6), time horizon (4), and strategic orientation to resource allocation (4). For the integrative scales, top-down information flow (5) and planning group integration (5) show most relationship with the strategy scales; over-time plan integration, corporate planning influence, and authority, plan density preparation, and depth of distribution each show four significant relationships.

8.5.3 STRATEGY SCALES AND PLANNING CATEGORIES

Mean values for the strategy scales (table 8.8) show that 3 of the 10 are significantly different among Planning Categories. The

Table 8.8

Means (and Ranks) of Strategy Scales by Planning Category

Strategy Scales	Planning Category					Significance among Planning Categories
	Corporate Strategic Planners	Division Strategic Planners	Corporate Financial Planners	Division Financial Planners	Non-Planners	
Internal Innovation	.24(1)	.21(2)	-.24(3)	-.30(5)	-.29(4)	NS
Acquisition	.20(1)	-.21(4)	.14(2)	.01(3)	-.26(5)	NS
Divestiture	-.07(4)	.13(1)	-.04(3)	.02(2)	-.29(5)	NS
International Posture	.15(2)	.16(1)	-.25(5)	-.18(4)	.13(3)	NS
Industrial Goods Scale	.01(2)	-.02(3)	-.03(4)	.35(1)	-.38(5)	NS
International Marketing	.42(1)	.03(3)	-.17(4)	.11(2)	-.92(5)	**
Explicit Growth/ Share Strategy	.33(1)	.07(3)	-.26(4)	.10(2)	-.43(5)	NS
New Product Strategy	.49(1)	-.06(3)	-.14(4)	.40(2)	-1.32(5)	**
Explicit Segment Strategy	.56(1)	.06(2)	-.35(4)	-.02(3)	-.51(5)	**
	.05(3)	-.13(4)	.07(2)	.22(1)	-.17(5)	NS

**Significant at α = .05

Corporate Strategic Planners fall at the end point on 6 of the 10 scales, including the 3 that show a significant result. The Non-Planners fall at the opposite end point for 5 of these, also including the three that are significant. The Division Strategic Planners fall at, or next to, the same end point as the Corporate Strategic Planners for 4 of the scales, and surprisingly, the Division Financial Planners are also similarly placed for four scales.

The Corporate Strategic Planners are more likely to display an explicit growth/share strategy and articulation of a strategy with strong new product emphasis; they are also more likely to be larger than the other firms. In addition, they both exhibit more acquisition activity and put more effort into internal innovation, as well as international marketing activities; these latter three scales are not significant, however. The Corporate Strategic Planners score low in divestiture (which is not a key element of growth strategy in any case) and on explicit segment strategies (which are not necessarily consistent with a strong strategic posture). By contrast, the Non-Planners score lowest on eight scales and are not above the middle on the other two.

8.6 Organization Structure

8.6.1 SCALE DEVELOPMENT

Eight scales developed from 28 items were used to summarize various aspects of organization structure. As in chapter 7, the topic of organization structure is viewed rather broadly. Since the basic organization of virtually all of the sample firms was divisional along product/market lines (though there were differences in organization for multinational operations), the measures focus mostly on process dimensions. The items are shown in appendix table A8.4. The scales are:

Entrepreneurial Incentives consists of three items relating to entrepreneurial structure and special incentives.

Task Forces comprises five items that capture the use of task forces and special organization units in developing new products and new markets.

Resource Sharing comprises three items measuring sharing of marketing, production, and R&D resources among second-level units.

Interdivisional Communication is based on two items measuring cooperation and information exchange among senior management.

Decentralization is based on two items and measures degree of managerial decentralization.

Insider Influence is composed of five items – four on a tendency *not* to hire from outside and one on a tendency to promote from within.

Organizational Interdependency is based on three items involving internal procurement, transfer pricing, and technological interdependency.

Organizational Specialization is composed of five items measuring the extent of organizational specialization in capital equipment, people, internal communication patterns, marketing systems, and production processes.

8.6.2 ORGANIZATION STRUCTURE SCALES AND PLANNING SCALES

Of the 344 correlations between the 8 organization structure scales and 43 planning scales (table 8.9), 61 (18%) are significant at = .05 – 15 of 104 adaptive scales (14%) and 46 of 240 integrative scales (19%); only 6 of the correlations are negative. Again, the significant correlations cluster, with half involving two organization structure scales – Interdivisional Communication and Organizational Specialization.

Interdivisional Communication (16 of 43 correlations significant) is related to half of the adaptive scales: strategic resource allocation decisions, environmental information gathering, competitive analysis, and globalness of planning. Integratively, it is related to an information-intense, line-oriented planning process and specifically involves functional integration of planning and information flow; line management influence and participation in, and positive view of planning; planning group integration; and extensive plan review under relaxed conditions.

Organizational Specialization (14 of 43 correlations significant) also involves environmental information gathering and globalness in planning, in addition to "strategic" planning. There is much similarity with interdivisional communication as regards the integrative scales, notably in acceptance of planning by line management and information flow; in addition, goals are used and planners add value.

Table 8.9
Correlations of Planning Scales and Organization Structure Scales[1]

	Organization Structure Scales							
	Entre-preneurial Incentives	Task Forces	Resource Sharing	Interdivisional Communication	Decentralization	Insider Influence	Organizational Interdependency	Organizational Specialization
Adaptive Planning Scales								
Environmental Orientation								
Environmental Information	-	-	-	.16**	-	-	-	.19**
Competitive Analysis	-	-	-	.31***	-	-	-	-
Strategic Orientation								
"Strategic" Planning	-	.17**	-	-	-	-	-	.19**
Time Horizon	-	-	-	.33***	-	.19**	-	.18**
Globalness	-	-	-	-	.17**	.18**	-	-
Portfolio Change	-	-	-	.25***	-	-	-	-
Resource Allocation	-	-	-	-	-	-	-	-
Planning Tools								
Portfolio Models	-	-	-	-	-	-	-	-
Model Use	-	-	-	-	-	-	-	-
Resource Allocation Decisions								
Long Run Expense Distinction	-	.27***	-	.32***	-	-	-	-
Strategic Criteria	-	-	-	.27***	-	-	-	-
Plan Comprehensiveness								
Corporate	-	-	-	-	-	-	-.20**	-
Second Level	-	-	-	-	-	-	-	-
Integrative Planning Scales								
Formal Integration of Plans								
Corporate/Functional	-	-	-	.27***	-	-	-	-
Over-time	-	.19**	-	-	-	-	-	.16**
Information Flow								
Top-Down	-	.23***	-	.16**	-	-	.18**	.31***
Internal	-	-	-	.23***	-	-	-	.20**
Corporate Planning Exchange	-	-	-	-	-	-	-	-
Influence and Participation								
Board of Directors	.16**	-	-	-	-	.24***	-	-
CEO	-	-	-	.31***	.20**	-	-	.18**
Top Second-Level Line Management	.22***	-	-	-	-	-	-	-
Corporate Planning								
Internal	-	-	-	.17**	-	.53***	-	.19**

Organization Structure Scales

	Entre-preneurial Incentives	Task Forces	Resource Sharing	Interdivisional Communication	Decentral-ization	Insider Influence	Organizational Inter-dependency	Organizational Special-ization
Goal and Strategy								
Formulation Process								
Bottom-Up	-	-	-	.20**	.18**	-	-	-
CEO Negotiation	-	-	-	-	-	-	-	-
Planning and Line Management								
Relative Staff/Line								
Nature of Planning	.18**	-	.16**	-	.21**	-	-	-
Line View of Planning	-	-	-	.37***	-	-	-	.17**
Integrative Value of Planners								
Added Value	-	-	.19**	-	-	-	.17**	.17**
Planning Group Integration	.16**	-	.16**	.33***	-	.24***	-	.19**
Status and Authority of Planners								
Reporting Importance	-	-	-	-	-	-	-	-
Planning Authority	-	-	-	-	-	-	-	-
Formalization of Planning								
Corporate	-	-	-	-	-	-	-	-
Second-level	-	-	-	-	-	-	.22***	-
Plan Density Preparation	-	-	-	.22***	-	-	-	-
Plan Density Review	-	-	-	-	-	-	-	-
Plan Distribution Depth	-	-	-	-	-	-	-	-
Planning and Performance Review								
Plan Review Atmosphere	-	-	-	-.23***	-	-.20**	-	-.19**
Performance Review:								
Atmosphere	-	-	-	-	-.27***	-	-	-
Frequency	.17**	-	-	-	-	-	-	.32***
Criteria	-	-	-	-	.28***	-	.24***	-
Depth	-	-	-	-	-.24***	-	-	-
Goals								
Use of Goals	.28***	-	-	-	-	-	-	.29***
Goals for Planning	-	-	-	-	-	-	-	-
Number Significant	6	4	3	16	7	6	5	14

[1]All tests in this table are 1-tailed

***p < .01, **p < .05

As with strategy, the bulk of the organization structure scales show no systematic pattern of relationships with planning, though isolated results are suggestive.

Task Forces seem to be used when planning time horizons are many and tend to be long, when long-run expense distinctions are made in resource allocation, and when there is top-down information flow. *Entrepreneurial Incentives* are related to line management influence and participation in, and positive view of planning, and to planning group integration. *Resource Sharing* involves value added by planners and planning group integration. (Neither of these latter two scales has any relationships with the adaptive scales.) *Decentralized Organizations* have influential line managers, make heavy use of goals in a bottom-up planning process (but have no specific goals for planning per se), and have relaxed performance reviews. *Insider Influence* is associated with a strategic orientation to resource allocation, portfolio change, CEO influence and participation, planning group integration, and relaxed planning reviews. Finally, *Organizational Interdependency* is related to the preparation of many (but not necessarily comprehensive) plans, the use of goals, and added value by the planners.

There is a scant pattern of relationship for any planning scales over organization structure scales. None of the adaptive scales is related to more than two organization structure scales. Just five integrative planning scales are related to four or more organization structure scales: top-down information flow (4); line management influence and participation in (4), and positive line view of planning (4); planning group integration (5); and use of goals (4). In addition to the relationships between these scales and interdivisional communication and organizational specialization, four of them are the only ones for which the relationship to entrepreneurial incentives is significant. Finally, 13 of the planning scales have no significant correlation with any of the organization structure scales.

8.6.3 ORGANIZATION STRUCTURE SCALES AND PLANNING CATEGORIES

Differences in patterns of organization structure scales among Planning Categories (table 8.10), like the correlation results just discussed, are rather muddy. Means are significantly different among Categories for only one of eight scales (decentralization); as before, however, the ranks show some patterns.

The Corporate Strategic Planners are in polar position for six of the eight scales; the Non-Planners are in the opposite polar posi-

Table 8.10
Means (and Ranks)
of Organization Structure Scales by Planning Category

Organization Structure Scales	Planning Category					Significance among Planning Categories
	Corporate Strategic Planners	Division Strategic Planners	Corporate Financial Planners	Division Financial Planners	Non- Planners	
Entrepreneurial Incentives	.20(1)	.06(2)	-.02(3)	-.39(5)	-.27(4)	NS
Task Forces	-.01(3)	-.11(4)	.18(2)	.27(1)	-.74(5)	NS
Resource Sharing	-.15(4)	.10(1)	.06(2)	-.03(3)	-.26(5)	NS
Interdivisional Communication	.31(1)	-.11(3)	-.03(2)	-.11(3)	-.18(5)	NS
Decentralization	.29(1)	-.12(4)	.08(3)	.19(2)	-1.07(5)	**
Insider Influence	.24(1)	-.02(3)	.07(2)	-.32(4)	-.58(5)	NS
Organizational Interdependency	-.34(5)	.21(1)	.06(2)	-.12(4)	-.02(3)	NS
Organizational Specialization	.20(1)	.07(2)	-.03(3)	-.34(4)	-.35(5)	NS

**Significant at α = .05

tion for four scales. There is little ordinal difference between the Division Strategic and Corporate Financial Planners, though the Division Financial Planners, as expected, appear most like the Non-Planners.

The Corporate Strategic Planners score highest on entrepreneurial incentives, interdivisional communication, insider influence, specialization, and decentralization but lowest on organizational interdependency. Thus, not only do their operating units have autonomy vertically (from corporate), they also appear relatively free of strong relationships horizontally (with other operating units). The Division Strategic Planners are the most interdependent and engage in the most resource sharing.

8.7 Summary

This chapter developed an overview of the results linking planning to other areas by developing scales that summarize key elements of environment, strategy, organization structure, and organizational climate. These sets of scales were then related to the 43 planning scales developed in chapter 4. Table 8.11 shows that a quarter of the correlations between the planning scales and the other sets of scales are significant. The results are, of course, correlational and not necessarily causal.

Table 8.11
Summary of Significant Correlations
Between Planning and Other Scales

	Number of Scales	Planning Scale Type	Number of Correlations	Number Significant	Percent Significant at α = .05
Environment	3	Adaptive	39	7	18
		Integrative	90	9	10
		All	129	16	12
Strategy	10	Adaptive	130	38	29
		Integrative	300	74	25
		All	430	112	26
Organization Structure	8	Adaptive	104	15	14
		Integrative	240	46	19
		All	344	61	18
Organizational Climate	7	Adaptive	91	35	38
		Integrative	210	73	34
		All	301	108	36
Totals	28	Adaptive	364	95	26
		Integrative	840	202	24
		All	1204	297	25

The strongest results are for organizational climate, for which 36 percent of correlations were significant. To the extent that the majority of correlations is positive, indicating that "good" planning and healthy working environments are correlated, this finding may represent an important side benefit of planning.

Perhaps somewhat surprisingly, the degree of correlation of planning with strategy and organization structure is somewhat less, though certainly stronger than chance. The most surprising result is the lack of relationship to environment; received wisdom would have anticipated stronger relationships, though the findings here are consistent with those in chapter 5. Overall, the degree of relationship of the adaptive and integrative planning scales is comparable. The adaptive relationships are a bit stronger for environment, strategy (unsurprisingly), and organizational climate but are more weakly related to organization structure than the integrative scales.

Viewed from the perspective of the individual planning scales, there are several that are especially strongly related to the other four sets of scales across the board. In the adaptive group, globalness of planning (14), competitive analysis (9), and three scales associated with resource allocation – strategic orientation (12), long-run expense distinction (10), and use of strategic criteria (9) are significant in more than 30 percent of the cases. As regards the integrative scales, top-down information flow (16), influence and participation of line management (14), positive line view of planning (14), planning group integration (16), use of goals (11), long-run performance criteria (11), and corporate/functional integration of plans (9) are also significant more than 30 percent of the time.

Analysis of the scales among the five Planning Categories anticipated that the Corporate Strategic Planners would score "well" on the scales. The results can be summarized as follows:

	Number of Scales	Number of Cases with Corporate Strategic Planners at End Point (& Next to End Point)	Number of Cases with Non-Planners at Opposite End Point (& Next to End Point)	Number of Significant Differences
Environment	3	2(2)	1(1)	0
Strategy	10	6(9)	5(7)	3
Organization Structure	8	6(7)	4(5)	1
Organizational Climate	7	5(7)	1(6)	1
Total	28	19(25)	11(19)	5

The overall patterns indicate a strong tendency for both the Corporate Strategic Planners and Non-Planners to rank at the scale end points, but the resulting profiles are not sharp in terms of statistical differences in mean scale values.

In summary, the results presented in this chapter add an overview to the detailed analyses of chapters 5, 6, and 7. Although information loss occurred in summarizing environment, strategy, organization structure, and organizational climate by means of scales, correlation with the 43 planning scales enabled a more detailed fabric to be constructed as regards both adaptive and integrative elements of planning. The results establish that there are clearly relationships between planning and organizational climate, and to a somewhat lesser extent, between planning and strategy, and organization structure. Environment and planning are not, however, closely related. It is important to remember, of course, that the tests are not at all independent and that it is the overall pattern rather than any particular result that is important.

In the next chapter, we reverse the process and develop groups of firms that are similar in terms of planning, environment, strategy, organization structure, and organizational climate.

Appendices to Chapter 8:

Table A8.1
Organizational Climate Scales

Name	Variables	Notes	α^1
Entrepreneurialness	Attitudes towards risk: a) New ideas tried out here b) High risk, high return investments encouraged c) Unusual or exciting plans encouraged d) Willingness to forego tried and true management principles	Higher value means more entrepreneurial	.75
Performance Orientation	Degree of performance emphasis in job policy: a) Strong performance-oriented up-or-out job policy b) People rewarded in proportion to excellence of performance c) In promotion -- strong emphasis on competitiveness and outperforming others	Higher value means more intense performance emphasis	.54
Line-Staff Interaction	Staff and Line Characteristics in this company: a) There is a reliance on specially trained line and staff rather than experienced personnel b) There are excellent communications between line managers and planning personnel c) Line managers find services of company planners helpful	Higher value means good line-staff cooperation	.66
Organizational Contentment	In this company: a) Senior management jobs are secure b) People trust each other c) People are proud of working here d) People do not just look out for their own interests e) There is cooperation between people to get things done f) The problem of incompatible managerial behavior has been avoided in acquisitions g) People are loyal to the company	Higher value means greater organizational contentment	.77

Table A8.1 (continued)

Name	Variables	Notes	α
Participative Decision-Making	Decision making in this company: a) Is participative b) Has become more participative with growth c) Is non-authoritarian d) Is committee-oriented and consensus seeking e) Typically involves consultation with subordinates to develop new programs	Higher value means greater participative decision making	.76
Organizational Fluidity	In this company managers do not: a) Have to follow the same procedures in most situations b) Do the same job in the same way every day c) Have to follow written orders without question d) Have procedures to follow whatever situation arises e) Have jobs where nothing new is happening every day	Higher value means greater fluidity or less routineness	.67
Delegated Responsibility	In this company: a) People feel they are their own bosses in most matters b) There is strong individualistic decision making by the normally responsible executive c) Second level managers generally do not need clearance from corporate executives before making major decisions d) There is emphasis on getting things done even if formal procedures are disregarded	Higher value means greater delegated responsibility	.71

Table A8.2
Environment Scales

Name	Variables	Notes	α
Uncertainty	Lack of confidence that the firm has an adequate appraisal of the situation in: a) Foreign economies b) Human resources c) Socio-Cultural d) Governmental e) Domestic economy f) Purchased materials and components g) Competitive behavior h) Technological i) Financial markets j) Industry-level demand	Higher value means greater environmental uncertainty	.87
Change	Degree of change in: a) Product technology b) Process technology c) Market growth	Higher value means greater environmental change	.61
Hostility	Lack of predictability of: a) Demand environment b) Major competitors Anticipated problems in securing: a) Raw materials and supplies b) Human resources	Higher value means greater environmental hostility	.46

Table A8.3
Strategy Scales

Name	Variables	Notes	α
Internal Innovation	Company's innovation characteristics: a) % revenues spent on R&D b) % revenues from introduction/growth stages of life cycle Company believes it is: c) Highly innovative d) First to market with new products e) At the cutting edge of technology f) Not risk-averse	Higher value means more highly innovative	.76
Acquisition	Extent of acquisition activity since 1974: a) % sales derived from acquisitions b) Number of acquisitions c) Significant acquisition made	Higher value means greater acquisition orientation	.57

Table A8.3 (continued)

Name	Variables	Notes	α
Divestiture	Extent of divestiture activity since 1974: a) % sales revenue divested b) Number of divestitures	Higher value means greater divestiture orientation	.52
International Posture	Extent of international involvement: a) Percent overseas revenues b) Number of overseas manufacturing subsidiaries	Higher value means greater international orientation	.95
Industrial Goods	Percent revenues from industrial products	Higher value means higher industrial versus consumer orientation	†
Scale	Company size characteristics: a) Number of employees b) 1979 revenues (logarithms of)	Higher value means greater scale	.89
International Marketing	Nature of international marketing activities: a) Major markets sought to sell products and technologies b) New products introduced in world market after U.S.	Higher value means greater international marketing activities	.47
Explicit Growth/ Share Strategy	Characteristics of growth share/strategy. Company seeks situation where it can: a) Achieve economies of scale b) Obtain large market shares c) Have high product differentiation d) Participate in high growth markets	Higher value means more growth/share orientation	.64
New Product Strategy	Characteristics of new product strategy. Company seeks growth by: a) New products in existing markets b) New products in new markets c) Reverse of existing products in existing markets d) Obtaining patent protection	Higher value means greater new product strategy	.60

Table A8.3 (continued)

Name	Variables	Notes	α
Explicit Segment Strategy	Characteristics of segment strategy. Company seeks to: a) Enter markets with few competitors b) Exit markets with many competitors c) Avoid scarce resource positions d) Obtain largest share of segment served e) Has well-defined mission	Higher value means greater segment strategy	.56

Table A8.4
Organization Structure Scales

Name	Variables	Notes	α
Entrepreneurial Incentives	Entrepreneurial nature of structure: a) The organization form and structure encourages entrepreneurial behavior b) There are special incentives for entrepreneurial behavior c) The organization form and structure does not encourage conservative management	Higher value means greater structural and process encouragement of entrepreneurial behavior	.72
Task Forces	Orientation to use special units: a) Special corporate task force oversees new product development Special organizational unit: b) Screens new market ideas c) Screens new product ideas d) Develops new markets for existing products e) Develops new products	Higher value means greater tendency to use special units	.82
Resource Sharing	Extensive sharing of: a) Marketing resources b) Production resources c) R&D resources	Higher value means greater resource sharing	.70
Interdivisional Communication	Relationships between senior managers: a) A great deal of cooperation b) Information freely exchanged	Higher value means greater communication	.72

Table A8.4 (continued)

Name	Variables	Notes	α
Decentralization	Company's decentralization characteristics: a) Little centralization in decision making, most operating decisions are not made at the top b) Level of highest functional line executives	Higher value means greater decentralization	.46
Insider Influence	Extent of internal versus external appointment of senior executives Reverse of company tends to: a) Hire academic consultants b) Hire from close competitors c) Hire from consulting firms d) Hire from other industries and, e) Strong tendency to hire from within	Higher value means greater internal influence	.52
Organizational Interdependency	Organizational characteristics: a) Policy of procuring internally wherever possible b) Formal transfer pricing system in place c) High degree of technological interdependence among second level units	Higher value means greater organizational interdependence	††
Organizational Specialization	Compared to competitors, company is much more specialized in: a) Capital equipment b) Human organization c) Internal communication patterns d) Marketing systems e) Production processes	Higher value means greater organizational specialization	.67

†Single item, α not meaningful

††Scale developed from counts, α not meaningful

[1]Chronbach α

Chapter 9

A Gestalt Perspective
on Planning

9.1 Introduction

In the last six chapters, we examined our sample firms' planning
practices using a deductively developed five-category system of planning sophistication developed in chapter 2. The scheme uses few criteria, but results reported in chapter 2 indicate that it has considerable strategic content. Furthermore, the scheme proved to be robust
in chapters 3 and 4 in capturing both adaptive and integrative dimensions of planning.

　　In recent years a "gestalt" perspective has gained currency
for the study of environment, strategy and organization (see, for example, work by Miller and Friesen 1977, 1978; Hambrick 1983a).
Rather than focus on a series of predetermined dimensions, scales,
or items, seeking to capture the phenomena of interest, with all of the
attendant problems of definition and dealing with correlated
measures, the focus of gestalt analysis is on creating groups of observations that are similar to one another in important ways. (See
McKelvey 1975, 1978 for detailed guidelines for the classification of
organizations.) Gestalts are formed across one element (e.g., environment), as in Hambrick (1983a), or across several simultaneously (e.g.,
environment, strategy, organization, etc.), as in Miller and Friesen
(1977).

　　In this study, an intermediate approach is taken. We use
cluster analysis to develop inductively groups of firms similar in terms
of their planning practices. We also develop groups of similar firms
for each of environment, strategy, organization structure, and organizational climate. The profiles of the planning groups are compared

with the Planning Category system and with each set of the other inductively formed groups (chapter 9); and their performance is also assessed (chapters 10 and 11).

Because of the data-driven nature of group formation, the results in this chapter should be viewed as hypothesis-generating. Nonetheless, for reasons developed in chapters 3 through 8, we anticipate that a firm will show up in corresponding groups in terms of planning, environment, strategy, organization structure, and organizational climate, though, since data from the same firms are used five times in the process, some degree of intercluster correspondence is inevitable. It is also important to recall that, while we are looking at the problem somewhat differently, we are using the same measurements that were used in the earlier chapters.

9.2 Developing the Groups by Clustering

The groups are formed from the scales developed in chapter 4 for planning (43 scales) and in chapter 8 for environment (3), strategy (10), organization structure (8), and organizational climate (7). While it might be preferable to cluster on the basis of individual items instead of scales, the large number of measurements on planning, strategy, organization structure, and organizational climate made such a procedure infeasible. A scree-type criterion was used in each of the five clustering procedures to determine the number of clusters (groups) in a Ward's cluster solution. The profiles of each group were then developed in terms of within-cluster means for the scales used in that set of groups and each group was subjectively given an interpretive name based on general patterns in that group relative to the others in the set. For all scales in each set of groups, the within-group means of the scales are significantly different among groups.

In interpreting the results, it is important to remember that the profiles differ in terms of degree rather than in terms of absolutes, for the means lie on a continuum of standardized scale values.

9.2.1 PLANNING GROUPS

Five planning groups (table 9.1) were formed on the basis of the 43 planning scales developed in chapter 4.[1]

Fully Integrated Planners. This group of 33 firms has the most extensive and well-integrated planning systems. Planning is characterized by an information-rich environment, both internally and externally obtained, and by extensive transmission of information through the firm. Competitive analysis is important,

and there is extensive use of models as part of the planning process. Planning is "strategic," and the planning systems tend to be
oriented to resource allocation. Strategic criteria are employed
for making resource allocation decisions, and planning is performed on a worldwide basis. In these firms, not only does the corporate planning group have great influence and possess a good
deal of formal authority, but also there is excellent communication with line management. Line management feels positive about
the planning process and believes that it too has extensive influence. Heavy commitment is given to planning by senior corporate management, functional plans are well integrated, and
goal-setting is an important management tool.

Extensive Planners. This group of 25 firms has well-
established and formalized planning systems. They have a strategic
orientation to planning and make significant use of portfolio and
other models in the planning process. They produce many and extensive plans, but while they employ moderate levels of environmental information, they tend not to obtain significant information internally. Staff planners report at high organizational
levels but, though heavily involved in the planning process, do not
seem to be particularly well integrated. Line management is
neutral as regards the value of planning.

Seat-of-the-Pants Planners. This group of 32 firms plans
in meager information environments, and there is not good information transmission through the firm. There is little use of
models as planning tools, and the final plans are not extensive.
The planning process is line-driven with moderate CEO influence;
planners do not have significant authority. Formalization of planning is not high, and goals are not used as an important management tool.

Marginal Planners. These 15 firms are below the mean
on virtually every positive planning scale but are higher than the
not-at-all planners. Their information environments are sparse,
they do not use models, there is little corporate commitment to
planning, and the final plans are not extensive.

Not-at-all Planners. These eight firms score at the
negative end point for virtually every planning scale. Their major
distinguishing feature is that goals and strategies are developed
top down and that performance reviews are held frequently.

9.2.2 ENVIRONMENT GROUPS

Three environment groups (table 9.2) were formed on the
basis of the three environment scales developed in chapter 8:

Table 9.1

Within-Group Standardized Scale Means (and Ranks)
of Planning Groups[1]

Adaptive Planning Scales	Fully Integrated	Exten- sive	Seat- of-the- Pants	Marginal	Not-at- all
Environmental Orientation					
Environmental Information	.37(1)	.24(2)	-.13(3)	-.27(4)	-1.36(5)
Competitive Analysis	.54(1)	.13(2)	-.03(3)	-.65(4)	-1.20(5)
Strategic Orientation					
"Strategic" Planning	.41(1)	.34(2)	-.05(3)	-.12(4)	-2.31(5)
Time Horizon	.24(2)	.28(1)	.07(3)	-.21(4)	-1.73(5)
Globalness	.70(1)	-.07(2)	-.25(3)	-.49(4)	-.74(5)
Portfolio Change	.08(3)	.12(1)	.10(2)	.00(4)	-1.09(5)
Resource Allocation	.75(1)	.15(2)	.00(3)	-1.34(5)	-.88(4)
Planning Tools					
Portfolio Models	.19(2)	.50(1)	-.07(3)	-.63(4)	-.78(5)
Model Use	.40(2)	.63(1)	-.39(3)	-.47(4)	-1.18(5)
Resource Allocation Decisions					
Long Run Expense Distinction	.30(1)	.27(2)	-.15(3)	-.47(4)	-.63(5)
Strategic Criteria	.49(1)	.08(2)	.00(3)	-.72(4)	-.80(5)
Plan Comprehensiveness					
Corporate	.22(2)	.61(1)	-.28(3)	-.31(4)	-1.10(5)
Second Level	.22(2)	.58(1)	-.22(3)	-.56(4)	-.75(5)
Integrative Planning Scales					
Formal Integration of Plans					
Corporate/Functional	.78(1)	-.12(3)	-.06(2)	-.94(5)	-.86(4)
Over-time	.37(1)	.12(2)	.00(4)	.12(3)	-2.13(5)
Information Flow					
Top Down	.62(1)	.10(2)	-.34(4)	-.11(3)	-1.34(5)
Internal	.46(1)	-.48(4)	.26(2)	-.57(5)	-.35(3)
Corporate Planning Exchange	.20(1)	.19(2)	.07(3)	-.58(5)	-.55(4)
Influence and Participation					
Board of Directors	.17(2)	.19(1)	.07(3)	-.56(5)	-.48(4)
CEO	.24(2)	.20(3)	.37(1)	-.97(4)	-1.32(5)
Top Second Level Line Management	.56(1)	.03(3)	.05(2)	-.67(4)	-1.25(5)
Corporate Planning	.65(1)	.10(3)	.22(2)	-1.16(4)	-1.55(5)
Internal	.18(2)	-.26(5)	-.15(4)	.35(1)	-.09(3)

High Change. This group of 27 firms is characterized mostly by high levels of change, slightly greater than average hostility, and moderate uncertainty in their environments.

Benign. This group of 53 firms is characterized by low levels of hostility and uncertainty, and relatively low levels of change in their environments.

High Difficulty. This group of 33 firms is characterized by highly uncertain, highly hostile, and relatively slow-changing environments.

Table 9.1 (continued)

	Fully Integrated	Exten- sive	Seat- of-the- Pants	Marginal	Not-at- all
Goal and Strategy					
Formulation Process					
Bottom Up	.31(1)	-.20(3)	.19(2)	-.35(4)	-.71(5)
CEO Negotiation	.13(2)	.28(1)	-.08(3)	-.36(4)	-.47(5)
Planning and Line Management					
Relative Staff/Line	-.16(3)	-.29(5)	.44(1)	-.27(4)	.28(2)
Nature of Planning					
Line View of Planning	.61(1)	.01(3)	.04(2)	-.70(4)	-1.13(5)
Integrative Value of Planners					
Added Value	.36(1)	.08(2)	.05(3)	-.14(4)	-1.65(5)
Planning Group					
Integration	.66(1)	.01(3)	.28(2)	-1.40(5)	-1.16(4)
Status and Authority of Planners					
Reporting Importance	.44(1)	.40(2)	-.43(4)	.07(3)	-1.55(5)
Planning Authority	.47(1)	-.06(3)	.15(2)	-.52(4)	-1.31(5)
Formalization of Planning					
Corporate	.18(2)	.71(1)	-.27(3)	-.43(4)	-1.24(5)
Second level	.33(2)	.38(1)	-.18(4)	.18(3)	-2.21(5)
Plan Density Preparation	.15(2)	.59(1)	-.25(4)	-.18(3)	-1.15(5)
Plan Density Review	.41(1)	.03(3)	-.28(4)	.21(2)	-1.05(5)
Plan Distribution Depth	.32(1)	-.11(3)	-.05(2)	-.15(4)	-.49(5)
Planning and Performance Review					
Plan Review Atmosphere	.10(2)	-.07(3)	-.08(4)	.37(1)	-.51(5)
Performance Review:					
Atmosphere	.17(1)	-.10(4)	-.16(5)	.06(3)	.13(2)
Frequency	.35(1)	.28(2)	-.13(3)	-.34(4)	-1.27(5)
Criteria	.45(1)	-.11(3)	.15(2)	-.71(4)	-.77(5)
Depth	.24(1)	-.05(2)	-.06(3)	-.29(5)	-.06(4)
Goals					
Use of Goals	.52(1)	.36(2)	-.40(3)	-.67(5)	-.40(4)
Goals for Planning	.14(2)	.20(1)	-.08(3)	-.15(4)	-.62(5)
Number of Firms	33	25	32	15	8

[1]Significant differences among groups for each scale at α = .05

9.2.3 STRATEGY GROUPS

Four strategy groups (table 9.3) were formed on the basis of the 10 strategy scales developed in chapter 8.

Innovative Strategists. The 49 firms in this group are characterized by being highly innovative, both in terms of their realized strategies – their new product innovation, and their intended strategies – their efforts with regard to new product development in both existing and new markets; conversely, they tend to eschew acquisitions. They have explicit strategies to seek high shares in high growth markets, have strong international postures, and have moderate levels of divestiture. They tend to be large companies, predominantly in industrial goods.

Segmenters. The major distinguishing characteristic of

Table 9.2

Within-Group Standardized Scale Means (and Ranks)
of Environment Groups[1]

Environment Scales	Environment Groups		
	High Change	Benign	High Difficulty
Uncertainty	.00[2](2)	-.67(3)	1.11(1)
Change	1.01[3](1)	-.29(3)	-.23(2)
Hostility	.46[4](2)	-.75(3)	.79(1)
Number of firms	27	53	33

[1]Significant differences among groups for each scale at α = .05

[2]Higher value means greater environmental uncertainty

[3]Higher value means greater environmental change

[4]Higher value means greater environmental hostility

Table 9.3

Within-Group Standardized Scale Means (and Ranks)
of Strategy Groups[1]

Strategy Scales	Strategy Groups			
	Innovative Strategists	Segmenters	Domestic Status Quoers	Domestic Portfolio Switchers
Internal Innovation	.57(1)	-.21(2)	-.51(3)	-.56(4)
Acquisition	-.34(4)	-.03(3)	.16(2)	1.50(1)
Divestiture	-.07(2)	-.15(3)	-.27(4)	2.42(1)
International Posture	.53(2)	.72(1)	-.85(4)	-.58(3)
Industrial Goods	.31(1)	-.26(3)	-.18(2)	-.46(4)
Scale	.21(2)	.31(1)	-.36(4)	-.18(3)
International Marketing	.24(2)	.60(1)	-.88(3)	-1.14(4)
Explicit Growth/Share Strategy	.51(1)	-.20(2)	-.50(4)	-.20(3)
New Product Strategy	.50(1)	-.91(4)	-.15(2)	-.40(3)
Explicit Segment Strategy	.14(2)	.67(1)	-.38(3)	-.71(4)
Number of firms	49	17	40	7

[1]Significant differences among groups for each scale at α = .05

these 17 firms is that they have explicit strategies of seeking strong positions in market segments, frequently internationally. They tend to be large firms, are in consumer goods, are relatively uninnovative, and engage in acquisition and divestiture activity to only a moderate extent.

Domestic Status Quoers. These 40 firms are the antithesis of the Innovative Strategists. They are uninnovative, domestically oriented, smaller than average firms that engage in moderate levels of acquisition; they do not have explicit corporate strategies.

Domestic Portfolio Switchers. This small group of seven firms is distinguished by the exceptionally high turnover of their portfolios; both their acquisition and divestiture activity are extremely high. They are uninnovative, smaller than average, domestic consumer-goods oriented, and they lack explicit corporate strategies.

9.2.4 ORGANIZATION STRUCTURE GROUPS

Five organization structure groups (table 9.4) were formed on the basis of the eight organization structure scales developed in chapter 8.

Organic. The 23 firms in this group are characterized by highly fluid organization structures. Structure and processes are designed to encourage entrepreneurial behavior, and there are high degrees of decentralization; they exhibit high levels of organizational specialization and moderate levels of interdivisional communication and interdependency.

Decentralized. The most striking features of the 15 firms in this group are the high degree of decentralization and low levels of organizational interdependence and resource sharing. Entrepreneurial behavior is encouraged to a moderate degree, but task forces tend not to be used.

Table 9.4
Within Group Standardized Scale Means (and Ranks)
of Organization Structure Groups[1]

Organization Structure Scales	Organization Structure Groups				
	Organic	Decen-tralized	Homegrown/ Task Forces	Outsider/ Isolated	Centralized Control
Entrepreneurial Incentives	.97(1)	.15(2)	-.11(3)	-.46(4)	-.62(5)
Task Forces	-.25(3)	-.57(5)	.67(1)	-.45(4)	.37(2)
Resource Sharing	-.17(4)	-.90(5)	.04(2)	-.07(3)	1.52(1)
Interdivisional Communication	.32(2)	-.23(4)	.56(2)	-.70(5)	-.20(3)
Decentralization	1.05(1)	.45(2)	-.25(3)	-.26(4)	-1.24(5)
Insider Influence	.30(2)	.20(3)	.62(1)	-1.08(5)	.01(4)
Organizational Interdependency	.19(3)	-1.29(5)	-.11(4)	.37(2)	.68(1)
Organizational Specialization	.79(1)	-.23(4)	-.18(3)	-.47(5)	.41(2)
Number of firms	23	15	34	29	12

[1]Significant differences among groups for each scale of $\alpha = .05$

Homegrown/Task Forces. The 34 firms in this group are characterized by the high degree of influence on key management decisions by longtime organization servants. They tend not to build entrepreneurial behavior into their structures; rather they have a strong tendency to employ special task forces to attack key issues in new business development. There tends to be a high degree of communication across the organization, but resource sharing and interdependence of the different organization units are only moderate.

Outsider/Isolated. The 29 firms in this group are characterized by having neither an organization form that encourages entrepreneurial behavior nor a disposition to use task forces to focus on new business issues. Rather, they rely on obtaining new ideas through their hiring practices and show less tendency to promote from within than all other firms. There tend to be low levels of communication across divisions, yet moderate specialization and interdependence across the organization.

Centralized Control. The 12 firms in this group are managed in highly centralized manners. There is a high degree of organizational interdependence and specialization, yet also high levels of resource sharing between second-level units. There is little structural concern for entrepreneurship.

9.2.5 ORGANIZATIONAL CLIMATE GROUPS

Four organizational climate groups (table 9.5) were formed on the basis of the seven organizational climate scales developed in chapter 8. They differ primarily along dimensions of participativeness.

Table 9.5

Within-Group Standardized Scale Means (and Ranks)
of Organizational Climate Groups[1]

Organizational Climate Scales	Organizational Climate Groups			
	Partici- pative Autonomy	Partici- pative Bureaucracy	Average	Rigid Bureaucracy
Entrepreneurialness	1.23(1)	.17(2)	.08(3)	-.92(4)
Performance Orientation	.78(1)	.36(2)	-.10(3)	-.58(4)
Line-Staff Interaction	-.28(3)	.95(1)	.00(2)	-.75(4)
Organizational Contentment	.93(1)	.53(2)	.08(3)	-1.08(4)
Participative Decision Making	.77(1)	.56(2)	-.06(3)	-.84(4)
Organizational Fluidity	1.29(1)	-.68(4)	.07(2)	-.14(3)
Delegated Responsibility	1.19(1)	.09(2)	-.03(3)	-.66(4)
Number of Firms	15	27	42	29

[1]Significant differences among groups for each scale at $\alpha = .05$

Participative Autonomy. The 15 firms in this group have highly participative, open internal environments with high levels of delegation of responsibility. Entrepreneurial behavior is encouraged, organizational members are content with their positions, and there is a strong tendency to reward on the basis of results.

Participative Bureaucracy. The 27 firms in this group have internal environments that are participative yet have excessive routinization of tasks. Delegated responsibility is moderate, there is significant line-staff interaction, and organizational members are content.

Average. These 42 firms score at about the mean on all of the defining scales. Their climates are somewhat participative, slightly decentralized, and moderately rigid; members are somewhat content; and so forth.

Rigid Bureaucracy. The 29 firms in this group are characterized by authoritarian, nonparticipative, noninteractive, uncooperative, unfriendly types of internal environment. There is little delegation of responsibility, and management tends not to be rewarded on the basis of job performance.

9.2.6 PLANNING GROUPS AND PLANNING CATEGORIES

Table 9.6 shows the relationship between the deductively developed Planning Categories and the inductively developed planning groups. The most striking results are for the Corporate Strategic Planners, Division Financial Planners, and Non-Planners. Twenty-one of 24 (88%) Corporate Strategic Planners fall into either the Fully Integrated or Extensive planning groups; only 1 of 18 of Division Financial Planners and Non-Planners is so classified. The

Table 9.6
Relationship Between Planning Groups and
Planning Categories

Planning Groups (Chapter 9)	Planning Categories (Chapter 2)					
	Corporate Strategic	Division Strategic	Corporate Financial	Division Financial	Non-Planners	Total
Fully Integrated	10	11	11	1	0	33
Extensive	11	8	6	0	0	25
Seat-of-the-Pants	2	11	12	7	0	32
Marginal	1	7	5	2	0	15
Not-at-all	0	0	0	1	7	8
Total	24	37	34	11	7	113

Not-at-All planning group and the Non-Planners category are for practical purposes identical. By contrast, the Division Strategic and Corporate Financial Planners are less clearly classified by the planning groups. However, expected and actual cell sizes are so small that statistical testing is not feasible. The next section develops procedures for collapsing the groups in a substantively useful way that makes further analysis possible.

9.3 Relationships Among the Planning, Environment, Strategy, Organization Structure and Organizational Climate Groups

9.3.1 COLLAPSING THE GROUPS FOR ANALYSIS

The cluster analyses produced five planning groups, three environment groups, four groups each for strategy and organizational climate, and five organization structure groups. As noted, however, even this level of data reduction is insufficient for statistical testing of relationships among the groups, so more data reduction is required. This was done by combining the groups on the basis of substantive similarities, with an eye on making the combinations of roughly equal size. The three environment groups were not collapsed because they did not group naturally, and because they were already large enough for meaningful statistical analysis.

Planning. The 33 Fully Integrated and the 25 Extensive firms (a total of 58) were combined because both have well-developed planning systems. Each group scores highest or next to highest on all adaptive scales (except one), and for 42 of the 60 cases (30 x 2) for the integrative scales. Neither the Marginal planners (15), nor the Not-at-All planners (8), both of which tend to have extreme scale means, has well-developed planning systems. Furthermore, although the 32 Seat-of-the-Pants planners are in the middle position on 12 of 13 adaptive scales and have a more variable pattern for the integrative scales, their scale means are overall closer to the Marginal and Not-at-All planners than the other two groups. The Seat-of-the-Pants, Marginal, and Not-at-All planners (a total of 55) were therefore combined.

Strategy. The 49 Innovative Strategists were combined with the 17 Segmenters (a total of 66), since each group had an explicit strategic focus; the firms are rather large, internationally focused, and somewhat innovative. The remaining 47 firms—Domestic Quoers (40) and Portfolio Switchers (7)—neither of which has explicit strategies, share extreme positions on 7 of the 10 strategy scales.

Organization Structure. Combining groups in this case was particularly difficult because the five groups are quite different; the pattern of means in table 9.4 reflects this disparity. It was finally decided to combine the 23 Organic firms, the 15 Decentralized firms, and the 34 Homegrown/Task Force firms (a total of 72) because of apparent flexibility in decision-making structure. The overall pattern of scale means shows these firms in the leading position on entrepreneurship, interdivisional communication, decentralization, and insider influence. The other group of firms is rather disparate, made up of the 29 Outsider/Isolated firms and the 12 Centralized-Control firms (a total of 41), which seem to lack the same flexibility. These firms share extreme positions on four of eight scales; in particular, they have centralized control of interdependent units.

Organizational Climate. The Organizational Climate groups tend to divide into relatively participative and nonparticipative groups. The 15 Participative Autonomous and 27 Participative Bureaucratic firms (a total of 42) share highest values on five of seven organizational climate scales (table 9.5) and have organizational climates consistent with the management principles proposed by Peters and Waterman (Capon, Farley, Hulbert, and Lei 1986b). The 71 Average (42) and Rigidly Bureaucratic (29) firms score at the low end of five of the seven climate scales.

9.3.2 RELATIONSHIP OF COLLAPSED PLANNING, STRATEGY, ORGANIZATION STRUCTURE, ORGANIZATIONAL CLIMATE, AND ENVIRONMENT GROUPS TO PLANNING CATEGORIES

There are good reasons for believing that the inductively derived groupings from this chapter should be related to the Planning Categories developed in chapter 2 and used throughout this book. In the case of each grouping, the individual groups are defined in terms of a set of scales; the defining constituents are the items discussed in chapters 3, 5, 6, and 7. In those chapters, many items were shown to vary significantly among Planning Categories. For planning, strategy, and organizational climate, the relationships were quite strong, whereas for environment and organization structure, fewer relationships were found with the Planning Categories. Chapter 8 also showed that the planning scales themselves were strongly related to the Planning Categories.

Table 9.7

Relationships of Collapsed Planning, Environment,
Strategy, Organization Structure and Organizational
Climate Groups with Planning Categories

Groups (Chapter 9) Planning Groups**	Planning Categories (Chapter 2)			Division Financial and Non-Planners	Total In Collapsed Groups
	Corporate Strategic	Division Strategic	Corporate Financial		
A. Fully-Integrated and Extensive	21†	19	17	1	58
B. Seat-of-the-Pants, Marginal and Not-at-All	3	18	17	17††	55
Environment Groups					
A. High Change	7†	8	5	7	27
B. Benign	12	20	16	5	53
C. High Difficulty	5	9	13	6††	33
Strategy Groups**					
A. Innovative Strategists and Segmenters	17†	25	13	11	66
B. Domestic Status Quoers, Domestic Portfolio Switchers	7	12	21	7††	47
Organization Structure Groups**					
A. Organic, Decentralized and Homegrown/ Task Forces	21†	19	24	8	72
B. Outsider/Isolated, and Centralized Control	3	18	10	10††	41
Organizational Climate Groups**					
A. Participative Bureaucracy and Autonomy	15†	10	13	4	42
B. Average and Rigidly Bureaucratic	9	27	21	14††	71
Total in Categories	24	37	34	18	113

**Differences significant at α = .01

†Anticipated membership for Corporate Strategic Planners

††Anticipated membership for Division Financial Planners and Non-Planners

Joint membership in the Planning Categories and these collapsed groups (as noted above, environment was not collapsed) is
shown in table 9.7, along with hypotheses about joint membership. In
the Planning Categories, the firms that do neither corporate nor
strategic planning, and that had been shown to be otherwise similar to
each other in chapters 3 to 8 (11 Division Financial Planners and 7
Non-Planners) are also combined because of small sample sizes.

Planning. As expected from table 9.6, a significant relationship is found between the Planning Categories and Planning
groups. Table 9.7 shows correspondence between the Corporate
Strategic Planners and the group composed of the Fully Integrated and Extensive planners. Similarly, the Division Financial Planners and Non-Planners correspond to the planning group
made up of Seat-of-the-Pants, Marginal and Not-at-All planners.
The 37 Division Strategic Planners and 34 Corporate Financial
Planners divide about evenly between the two planning groups,
indicating that neither has succeeded consistently in setting up
planning systems that have classic characteristics associated with
"good" planning. Division Strategic Planners omit corporate integration and Corporate Financial Planners omit the adaptive
function.

Environment. We expect that firms attempt to seek
High Change environments where new opportunities abound but
avoid High Difficulty environments; systematic planning may
help them do this. We have no hypothesis regarding Benign environments. Consistent with results from earlier chapters, there
were no significant differences in the three environment groups
across the Planning Categories, though there was some suggestion that the Corporate Financial Planners were less likely to be
in the High Change environment group.

Strategy. By hypothesis, the Corporate Strategic Planners should tend to be Innovative Strategists or Segmenters, and
Non-Planners and Division Financial Planners should be Domestic Status Quoers or Portfolio Switchers; the other two Planning
Categories are expected to be in between. A significant relationship is found between the Planning Categories and Strategy
groups, and table 9.7 confirms the expected pattern for the Corporate Strategic Planners. The Division Strategic Planners tend
to resemble the Corporate Strategic Planners, whereas the Corporate Financial Planners do not. The Division Financial Planners and Non-Planners, however, tend to be Innovative Strategists or Segmenters, although they use a route other than plan-

ning to achieve this purpose. This result will have some implications for our study of performance in chapter 10.

Organization Structure. Somewhat surprisingly, in view of our earlier results, significant differences are found between the Planning Categories and the Organization Structure groups. There is a tendency for the Corporate and Division Strategic Planners to have Organic, Decentralized, or Homegrown/Task Forces, whereas Division Financial Planners and Non-Planners tend to have less flexible Outsider/Isolated or Centralized Control organizations.

Organizational Climate. A significant relationship was found between Planning Categories and Organizational Climate groups. The Corporate Strategic Planners tend to have participative climates, whereas firms in the other Planning Categories do not – not surprisingly for the Corporate Financial Planners, Division Financial Planners and Non-Planners, but somewhat surprisingly for the Division Strategic Planners. The contrast between the two types of Strategic Planners further underlines the suggested weakness of the division mode of planning.

Overall Patterns. The results of the analysis of Planning Categories and the inductively-derived groupings show clear patterns; significant differences were found across firm groupings for planning, strategy, organization structure, and organizational climate, though not for environment. Looked at from the perspective of the Planning Categories, the strongest profiles are for the "best" and "worst" Planning Categories – Corporate Strategic Planners and Division/Financial/Non-Planners respectively.

The Corporate Strategic Planners are sharply defined as either Fully Integrated or Extensive Planners. They are most often characterized as Innovative Strategists or Segmenters; they are relatively large firms with strong international postures and explicit strategies. They are likely to be operating within organization structures characterized as Organic, Decentralized, or Homegrown/Task Forces and with organizational climates that are Participative.

By contrast, those firms that do neither Corporate nor Strategic Planning fall into those groups with ineffective or, at best, Seat-of-the-Pants planning. They tend to have organization structures that are extreme in terms of centralization and nonparticipative organizational climates. However, strategically they tend to be Innovative Strategists or Segmenters.

Perhaps the most interesting patterns involve the Division Strategic Planners, which we expected to share many of the characteristics of Corporate Strategic Planners, and Corporate

Financial Planners, which we expected to be quite different. The results, however, are much more mixed. The Corporate Financial Planners have the more flexible organization structures, and neither category has a particularly participative climate. In terms of planning groups, neither the Division Strategic nor Corporate Financial Planners have sharp profiles, though the Division Strategic Planners are more likely to be Innovative Strategists or Segmenters.

9.3.3 RELATIONSHIPS OF PLANNING GROUP MEMBERSHIP TO ENVIRONMENT, STRATEGY, ORGANIZATION STRUCTURE, AND ORGANIZATIONAL CLIMATE GROUPS MEMBERSHIP

Patterns of common group membership may be useful in developing an overview profile of how planning relates jointly to environment, strategy, organization structure, and organizational climate. This section examines such patterns but in doing so takes explicit account of uncertainty inherent in the process by which the groups were developed.

The process of assigning observations (firms) to groups in the cluster analyses involves uncertainty about in which group a particular observation belongs. In general, for each cluster analysis there is a nonzero probability that an observation belongs to each group, and assignment is typically based on the highest probability – a process that in effect makes zero-one assignments on the basis of the highest probability. However, the process involves some loss of information. For example, an observation with a probability of .51 of belonging to a group is treated identically to one with a probability of 0.99 of belonging to that group.

This section uses a newly developed methodology to analyze relationships among probabilities of group membership that avoids the information loss problem (Capon, Farley, and Lehmann 1986).[2] The probabilities of membership are estimated by using five discriminant functions – one for each grouping (planning, environment, strategy, organization structure, organizational climate) – and by using the sets of scales as the independent variables. Since the groups were defined by clustering the scales, it is no surprise that the discriminant functions classify the respective groups with very little error. More important for our purposes, however, is the result that the majority of observations have a probability of .8 or more of belonging to one group, and virtually none have a largest probability of less than .5. In other words, within-group profiles discussed earlier in this chapter are in fact rather sharp and group assignment relatively unambiguous.

Relationships of the likelihoods (probabilities) of planning group memberships and likelihoods of memberships in the environment, strategy, organization structure, and organizational climate groups are investigated by correlation analysis (table 9.8). The correlations in the table are calculated over the 113 firms for probabilities of each firm belonging to each group shown in tables 9.1 to 9.5. A positive (or negative) correlation indicates that a firm tends to belong (or not belong) to both a planning group and one of the environment, strategy, organization structure, or organizational climate groups.

Table 9.8

Correlations of Probabilities of Membership in the Five Planning Groups with Probabilities of Membership in Respective Environment, Strategy, Organization Structure, and Organizational Climate Groups

| | Planning Groups | | | | |
Other Groups	Fully Integrated	Extensive	Seat-of-the-Pants	Marginal	Not-at-all
Environment					
High Change	.11	-.05	-.12	.10	-.04
Benign	.13	.01	-.06	-.11	.02
High Difficulty	-.25***	.02	.17*	.05	.04
Strategy					
Innovative Strategists	.18**	.17*	-.13	-.20**	-.11
Segmenters	-.11	.02	.11	-.09	.08
Domestic Status Quoers	-.19**	-.12	.09	.22***	.08
Domestic Portfolio Switchers	.16*	.14	-.08	.11	-.07
Organization Structure					
Organic	.02	.06	-.02	.01	-.05
Decentralized	.03	-.13	.03	.09	-
Homegrown/Task Force	.10	.06	-.02	-.08	-.11
Outside/Isolated	-.14	.01	-.04	.11	.16*
Centralized Control	.03	-.04	.08	-.12	.02
Organizational Climate					
Participative Autonomy	.15	-.08	-.08	.01	.02
Participative Bureaucracy	.42***	-.05	-.15	-.24***	.08
Average	-.17*	.17*	.19**	-.17*	-.08
Rigidly Bureaucratic	-.34***	-.08	.01	.41***	.16*
Number of Firms	33	25	32	15	8

***p < .01, **p < .05, *p < .10

In interpreting the correlations, it is important to remember that the tests are not independent, for the correlations are calculated by using probability distributions that sum to one over each set of groupings for each observation (McGuire, Lucas, Farley, and Ring 1968). Furthermore, the correlations are computed by using data on the same firms repeatedly, so the results should be interpreted as directional. The analysis should also be viewed as exploratory, for no hypotheses are developed in regard to expected sign or magnitude. Overall (table 9.8), there is some pattern, which generally motivates further attention to how environment, strategy, organization structure, organizational climate, and planning relate.

Environment Groups. The 15 correlations between probabilities of membership in planning and environment groups show that there is little pattern, except that Fully Integrated planners are evidently not found in difficult environments while Seat-of-the-Pants planners are—perhaps as a result of poor planning.

Strategy Groups. Of the 20 correlation coefficients relating the strategy groups and the planning groups, a number are significant. Innovative Strategists tend to be Fully Integrated or Extensive planners but not Marginal planners. By contrast, Domestic Status-Quoers tend to be Marginal planners but not Fully Integrated Planners. Domestic Portfolio Switchers also tend to be Fully Integrated Planners, probably indicating planning attention needed for portfolio management. There are no patterns for Segmenters.

Organization Structure Groups. In the case of planning and organization structure, only 1 of the 25 correlation coefficients is even weakly significant. There appears to be little or no relationship between firms' planning systems (as defined by the clustering procedures) and their organization structures.

Organizational Climate Groups. The strongest relationships in this stream of analysis are found between the organizational climate groups and the planning groups. The Fully-Integrated Planners usually have Participative-Bureaucratic climates but tend not to have Rigidly Bureaucratic or Average climates. Conversely, the Marginal planners tend to have Rigidly Bureaucratic climates but neither Participative Bureaucracies nor even Average climates. Both the Extensive and Seat-of-the-Pants Planners tend to have Average climates, perhaps indicating a weakness in implementation for the Extensive planners. Finally, the Not-at-All-planners tend to be Rigidly Bureaucratic.

9.3.4 JOINT MEMBERSHIP IN COLLAPSED GROUPS

The results in table 9.7 and the pattern of correlations in table 9.8 suggest that we attempt to probe more deeply into patterns of joint group membership. This is accomplished both by using the collapsed classifications from table 9.7 and by characterizing the collapsed groups.

We were able in chapters 2, 3 and 4 to develop a profile of "good" planning on the basis that it should contain certain characteristics; planning that does not contain these characteristics can be thought of as "bad" planning. On the basis of this profile we may label the Fully Integrated and Extensive planners, which both have well developed planning systems, as "good," and the Seat-of-the-Pants, Marginal and Not-at-All planners as "bad."

By contrast, in chapters 5 through 8 we have in general avoided attempting to label any particular environment, strategy, organization structure, or organizational climate as either "good" or "bad." There were two reasons for this decision. First, the notion of contingency pervades the study of these aspects of management—decisions regarding one aspect depend upon decisions regarding other aspects; for example, for a firm facing a particular business environment there is a certain type of strategy and certain organizational configuration that is most likely to be found and/or is most appropriate from a performance standpoint. The second reason has to do with cultural assumptions; for example, to an American an open and participative organizational climate might seem desirable; to an Easterner this may seem chaotic.

Nonetheless, drawing on those earlier chapters and using some value judgments, we are able to make a rough cut at what might be considered to be "good" strategy, organization structure and organizational climates generally speaking, in terms of the collapsed groupings in table 9.7. Thus, Peters and Waterman would no doubt view participative organizational climates as "good." Ansoff would probably view the Innovative Strategists and Segmenters as exhibiting "good" strategy, and Organic, Decentralized and Homegrown/Task Force organization structures would probably also be viewed as "good." We make these judgments ("A" groups in table 9.7 as "good"), and investigate the actual distribution of firms with various combinations of "good" and "other" organizational characteristics compared to chance distributions.

Analysis of the combinations of "good" and "bad" planning with membership of the "good" and "other" strategy, organization structure and organizational climate groups were conducted considering two, three, and four variables at a time.

On the level of pairs, significant relationships are found between planning and both strategy and organizational climate, but not for organization structure (table 9.9). This is consistent with the correlational analysis in section 9.3.3. "Good" planning tends to coexist in firms with "good" strategies and organizational climates; "bad" planning tends to coexist with the less attractive strategies and organizational climates.

Table 9.9
Joint Occurrence of Firms in Collapsed Groups:
Planning Versus Strategy and Organization

Strategy	Planning Fully Integrated and Extensive	Others	Significant Differences among Groups
Innovative Strategists and Segmenters	39	27	**
Others	19	28	
Organization Structure			
Organic, Decentralized, Homegrown/Task Forces	40	32	NS
Others	18	23	
Organizational Climate			
Participative (Autonomy and Bureaucracy)	31	11	**
Others	27	44	

**α = .05.

More detailed analysis of group membership three and four at a time reveals a disproportionate occurrence of "good" planning with "good" strategy, organization structure and organizational climate, especially in High Change and Benign environments. By contrast, firms with "bad" planning and with "other" strategies, organization structures and organizational climates tend to concentrate in High Difficulty environments. Of course, the cell sizes are extremely small at this level, and these results should only be considered as suggestive.

A specific result that is of interest concerns the two polar four-fold combinations of "good" planning, strategy, organization structure and organizational climate, and "bad" planning and "other" strategy, organization structure and organizational climate, aggregated across environment. The marginal probabilities from table

9.7 imply that, under assumptions of independence, 8 firms should have "good" planning, strategy, organization structure and organizational climate; in fact we observe 20 firms with this combination. Similarly, the combination of "bad" planning with the "other" categorization of strategy, organization structure, and organizational climate should occur 5 times under independence; in fact it occurs for 11 firms.

These results indicate the presence of contingencies, but they appear quite complex, operating at several levels at once. Furthermore, firms appear to seek out extreme combinations and avoid intermediate combinations, which might in fact involve contradictory elements. Our analysis of financial performance in subsequent chapters sheds additional light on this phenomenon.

9.4 Summary

This chapter attempted to gain insight into planning practice and its relationships to environment, strategy, organization structure, and organizational climate by grouping firms inductively into relatively homogeneous groups for each organizational component. The process essentially reversed the analytic procedure of the earlier chapters, which concentrated on how items differ over Planning Categories; here the focus was on groups of similar firms derived empirically.

Despite the intuitive appeal and potential benefits of this procedure, it is important to be aware of its shortcomings. First, of course, it is highly empirical, and the "naming" of the various firm groupings is subjective. Second, the five sets of groups (planning, environment, strategy, organization structure, organizational climate) are made up of the same firms, so the possibility exists that a significant amount of measurement error is correlated over the sets of groups. Third, and related to the second point, available sample sizes are so small and the phenomena so complex that hold-out sampling for reliability is not feasible. Fourth, the basic approach was through clustering of observations, with its inherent arbitrariness in terms of choice of number of clusters and their interpretation. Fifth, the groups are defined in terms of scales rather than raw measurements, injecting yet another level of problem with interpretability. Finally, the same firms are used here as were used in the analyses of chapters

3 through 8, so the results should be viewed as basically cor-
roborative.

Despite all these caveats, the grouping process provides
profiles that relate in some interesting ways. Corporate Strategic
Planners tend to have integrated, or at least extensive, centrally
managed planning systems, which operate in relatively open decision-
making systems in relatively participative organizational climates.
They tend to be larger, internationally oriented firms that develop explicit strategies and are mostly innovative. The firms that are neither
Corporate nor Strategic Planners (Division Financial Planners and
Non-Planners) have rather ad hoc planning, if they have any at all, and
have less organic decision-making systems housed in rigid
bureaucracies. They do, however, tend to resemble the Corporate
Strategic Planners as regards their strategies. The firms we have
classified as Corporate Financial Planners (which lack strategic content in their plans) and the Division Strategic Planners (which do not
carry the rigor of strategic resource allocation to the corporate level)
have less clear tendencies in terms of group membership, though both
tend to have bureaucratic climates. The Division Strategic Planners
tend to resemble the Corporate Strategic Planners in their strategy
making, whereas Corporate Financial Planners tend to be smaller,
domestically oriented, noninnovative firms lacking explicit strategies.

The analyses that examined the various relationships using
just the inductively developed groupings were similarly instructive.
Evidence of relationships between planning and strategy, and between planning and organizational climate was supported, but not between planning and either environment or organization structure.
The distribution of firms in various possible combinations of groups
was far from random, indicating the presence of contingencies.
However, these contingencies appear to be quite complex, operating
at several levels at once. For example, there was a tendency for firms
to cluster in the cell defined by "good" planning, strategy, organization structure, and organizational climate, especially in Benign and
High Change environments.

As we said in the introduction to this chapter, however, the
results should be considered primarily as hypothesis-generating for
future studies attempting to profile firms in terms of *joint*
characteristics such as planning, environment, strategy, organization
structure, and organizational climate. Our results indicate that such
work is likely to be productive.

NOTES

1. Standard Deviations of scales, within groups, are found in appendix III.

2. An extension of this methodology for analysis of performance contingencies (Capon, Farley, and Lehmann 1986) has advantages over other methodologies (Lorsch and Morse 1974, Pennings 1975, Dewar and Werbel 1979).

PART IV

INTEGRATION

We conclude with two integrative chapters. In chapter 10 we investigate the impact of planning on performance from several points of view. In the final chapter of the book, we pull together the various strands of results from the earlier chapters and highlight the implications of our findings for both management practice and future research.

Chapter 10

Planning
and Performance

10.1 Introduction

Planning has potential qualitative benefits, many of which have been discussed in earlier chapters. In the final analysis, however, the value of any management practice is best assessed in terms of identifiable economic impact. Since return-on-investment (ROI) was the target measure cited most frequently in our inquiries regarding goals, this chapter approaches the assessment of planning through its impact on one closely related measure of ROI – return-on-capital (defined in 10.3.1).

Studies of the impact of any managerial practice on financial performance can be divided into two basic types: universalistic and contingent. In universalistic studies, the direct impact of a single major construct is investigated. For example, the PIMS studies of strategy that relate market share, market growth, capital intensity, and other factors to profitability fall into this category (Schoeffler, Buzzell, and Heany 1974; Buzzell, Gale, and Sultan 1975). By contrast, contingency studies investigate the extent to which two or more constructs taken together affect profitability. Here, the key notion is "fit." For example, a particular strategy should "fit" a particular organizational design if good performance is to occur (e.g., Pennings 1975; Wright, Capon, Farley, and Hulbert 1985; Fredrickson and Mitchell 1984).

This chapter has a primarily universalistic outlook; we focus on the direct impact of planning on performance, though contingent relationships are also investigated in section 10.13.

10.2 Previous Studies of the Value of Planning

10.2.1 OVERVIEW

The 1970s saw publication of various studies investigating the direct impact of planning on financial performance (generally of U.S. companies). Armstrong (1982), for example, made 15 plan/no plan comparisons drawn from the 12 studies listed in table 10.1 and concluded that stockholders benefit from formal planning in 10 cases but that informal planning is superior in 2 cases. He suggested that planning is most helpful for setting objectives and monitoring performance, especially when organizations are attempting to make major changes (see also Greenley 1986 and Rhyne 1986).

Not surprisingly, problems arise in any effort to isolate the impact of a single management practice from the myriad of complex and often interacting factors that affect a firm's performance. Indeed, the nature of findings on the effectiveness of planning has shifted noticeably over time. Early research tended to find positive economic benefits from planning, whereas later research was less clear. Among the studies that found economic benefits were those of Ansoff, Avner, Brandenburg, Portner, and Radosevich (1970) for firms with significant acquisition programs; Eastlack and McDonald (1970) for a sample of *Fortune* 500 firms; Gershefski and Harvey (1970) for a small sample of petroleum firms; Thune and House (1970) for firms in the drug, chemical, and machinery industries; Herold (1972) for drug and chemical companies; and Karger and Malik (1975) (Malik and Karger 1975) first for chemical and drug and then for electronics and machinery companies. On the other hand, studies by Denning and Lehr (1971, 1972) and Grinyer and Norburn (1974, 1975) on U.K. companies, by Kudla (1978) on a *Fortune* 500 sample, by Kallman and Shapiro (1978) (Shapiro and Kallman 1978) on firms in the motor freight industry, and by Robinson and Pearce (1983) on small banks, cast serious doubts on whether planning produces positive performance benefits.

The apparent conflict in these results becomes less surprising when the studies are examined in detail in terms of research design, such as conceptualization of planning, researcher bias, performance measures, data quality, and data analysis. In this section, 16 studies of planning are investigated in some detail to illustrate problems in these areas (table 10.2).

Table 10.1
Research Results on Planning[1]

Study [Time Span]	Description	Improved Stockholder Return for Formal Planners?
Van de Ven (1980) [1973-1975]	9 planners versus 5 non-planners in introduction of community child care programs.	Yes
Ansoff et al. (1970) [1947-1966]	Acquisitions by 22 planners versus 40 non-planners.	Yes*
Thune and House (1970) [1958-1965]	A: Drug, chemical and machinery industries 9 planners versus 9 non-planners. B: Food, oil and steel industries 8 planners versus 10 non-planners	Yes* ?
Herold et al. (1972) [1962-1969]	Drug and chemical industries 5 planners and 5 matched non-planners (Extension of Thune and House, 1970)	Yes
Kudla (1980-1981) [1960-1975]	78 planners versus 51 non-planners from Fortune 500	Yes
Harju (1981, pp. 112-113) [1976-1979]	12 planners with commitment versus 31 lacking either formal planning or commitment or both.	Yes*
Karger and Malik (1975) Malik and Karger (1975) [1964-1973]	19 planners versus 19 non-planners among chemical, drug, electronics and machinery industries	Yes
Wood and LaForge (1979, 1981) [1972-1976]	Survey of banks, interview plus questionnaire 27 planners versus 9 non-planners	Yes*
Kallman and Shapiro (1978) [1965-1974]	298 firms in motor freight industry 5 levels of planning examined	Yes
Grinyer and Norburn (1975) [1966-1977]	In-depth interviews with 91 executives from 21 companies in the U.K.	?
Leontiades and Tezel (1980) [1971-1977]	61 companies from Fortune 1000 largest industrial firms	?
Fulmer and Rue (1974) [1972-1977]	A: Durable goods, 33 planners versus 20 non-planners	Yes
Rue and Fulmer (1973) [early 1970s]	B: Non-durable goods, 108 planners versus 41 non-planners C: Service industries, 27 planners versus 40 non-planners	No No

*Statistically significant

[1]Source: Armstrong, 1982

Table 10.2
Review of Planning/Performance Studies

Study [Timespan]	Sample Size Results (Total) Site	Final Sample Demographics	Planning Categories (#s)	Data Collection	Response Rate (%/#)
Ansoff et al. (1970) [1947-1966]	62(412) USA	Significant acquirers	Extensive(22)[10] Minor(40)	Mail Q. Compustat	23
Eastlack & McDonald (1970) [late 1960's]	211(N/A) USA	Fortune 500+ HBR subscribers	Strategic(N/A)[7] Others(N/A)	Mail Q.	21
Gershefski & Harvey (1970) [late 1960's]	15[1](1900) USA	Petroleum Firms	Formal(N/A)[6] Informal(N/A)	Q. hand distribution	48/17[16]
Thune & House (1970) [1955-1965]	36[2](145) USA	Sales Revs. $75M	Formal(17)[8] Informal(19)	Mail Q.	63/25[17]
Denning & Lehr (1971 1972) [1967]	328(350) UK	Top 300 U.K. Industrial Firms	Planners(71)[13] Non(41) Other(216)	Mail Q.	50
Herold (1972) [1962-1969]	(10) USA	Medium and large firms in the drug and chemical industry	Planners(5) Nonplanners(5)	Mail Q.	N/A
Rue & Fulmer (1973) Fulmer & Rue (1974) [early 1970s]	386(1333) USA	Durables(151) Nondurables (168) Services(67)[5]	Impoverished (132)[11] Primary(24) Pro Forma(156)	Mail Q. Compustat	29
Grinyer & Norburn (1974) [1966-1977]	21(N/A) UK	L5M-L25M	Progressive Predictive(74) No Categories[12]	Personal Interview	N/A
Karger & Malik (1975) Malik and Karger (1975) [1964-1973]	38[3](273) USA	Sales Revs. $50M-$500M[4]	FILRAP(19)[9] Non(19)	Mail Q. Value Line SEC/Co. Reports	33/14[18]

Study [Timespan]	Sample Size Results (Total) Site	Final Sample Demographics	Planning Categories (#s)	Data Collection	Response Rate (%/#)
Kallman & Shapiro (1978) Shapiro & Kallman (1978) [1965-1974]	298	Motor Freight Industry	Not described	N/A	N/A
Wood & LaForge (1979 1981) [1972-1976]	92(150)	Large U.S. Banks	Planners (26) Non-Planners (9) Partial Planners (6) Control Group (20	Personal Q.	61
Leontiades & Tezel (1980) [1971-1977]	61(300) USA	Fortune 500	Ratings of Importance & Contribution of Planning	Mail Q.	20
Kudla(1980 1981) [1960-1975]	129(557) USA	Fortune 500+ 57 Strategic Planners	Complete(161)[14] Incomplete(116) Non(51)	Mail Q. CRSP	59/23[19]
Harju(1981, pp. 112-113) [1976-1979]	43	Big and medium Finnish firms	Planners (12) Nonplanners (31)	Mail Q. Telephone follow up	N/A
Robinson & Pearce (1983) [1977-1980]	50(85)	Small U.S. Banks	Formal (12) Non-Planners (38)	Personal Q.	59
Welch(1984) [1975-1979]	49(380) USA	Major Industrial Firms	Strategic Planners(33)[15] -Corporate(19) -Division(14) Nonplanners(16)	Mail Q.	32/13[20]

Table 10.2 (continued)

Study	Performance Measures 2T-22	Respondent	Significance Tests	Findings
Ansoff et al. (1970)	A'',B'',C'', N'',E'',O,D', P'',Q'', M',K',R,	Acquisition Exec, Staff analyst	Yes	Extensive planners outperform minor planners on most measures Post vs. Preacquisition results better for extensive than minor planners.
Eastlack & McDonald (1970)	A,E'	"CEO"	No	High Performers, CEO's more active in strategic planning, selective in implementation.
Gershefski & Harvey (1970)	A,B	Planning Executive	No	Formal Planners; faster growth in sales & net income
Thune & House (1970)	A,C,D,E,F	"CEO"	Yes	Formal Planners outperform informal on C.E.F. Post vs. Preformal Planners on A,D,E.
Denning & Lehr (1971 1972)	BB+	CEO+	Yes	No significant differences: Right direction results.
Herold(1972)	A,B	N/A	No	Formal planners outperform informal planners.
Rue & Fulmer (1973) Fulmer & Rue (1974)	A,B,S,T	Corporate Executive	No	Nonplanners no different from other firms. Nonplanners outperform other firms in Services.
Grinyer & Norborn (1974)	U'	Directors	Yes	Better performance if more formal communication channels & more information used. No difference for other items.
Karger & Malik (1975) Malik & Karger (1975)	A,B,C,E,F,G, H,I,J,K,L,M	N/A	Yes	Planners outperform non-planners on most measures.

Study	Performance Measures^{2}T^{22}	Respondent	Signi-ficance Tests	Findings
Kallman & Shapiro (1978) Shapiro & Kallman (1978)	A,B,C,S,T	N/A	No	Planners do not outperform non-planners.
Wood & LaForge (1979 1981)	B',E'	CPO	Yes	Planners outperform nonplanners.
Leontiades & Tezel (1980)	C,E',F',M,A	CEO CPO	Yes	High & Low performance firms did not differ on planning ratings.
Kudla(1980 1981)	V',W',X',Y'	N/A	Yes	No differences complete vs. nonplanners.
Harju(1981, pp. 112-113)	E',U'	CEO	Yes	Planners outperform nonplanners.
Robinson & Pearce (1983)	B,E,U	CEO	Yes	Planners do not outperform non-planners.
Welch(1984)	H'	"CEO"	Yes	Strategic planners outperform non-planners. Corporate planners outperform division planners.

Notes for Table 10.2

1. Subset of respondents; petroleum firms only.

2. Subset of respondents; drug(6), chemicals(6), machinery(6), steel(6), oil(7), food(5).

3. Subset of respondents; chemicals & drugs(10), electronics(15), machinery(13).

4. From 6 industry groups: apparel, food, drugs, chemicals, electronics, machinery.

5. From 5, 5, & 6 individual industrial groupings respectively.

6. Formal Planners: 1. Set Corporate goals 3 years in future; 2. Action Programs to achieve goals.

7. Strategic Planners: undefined.

8. Formal Planners: 1. Set Corporate Strategy & goals 3 years in future; 2. Specific Action Programs, projects, procedures to achieve goals.

9. Formal Integrated Long Range Planning (FILRAP): 1. Written 5 year plans for total organization, each division, each plant; 2. Expanded 1-2 year plans; 3. Group effort to produce plans and full distribution.

10. Acquisition Planner: Explicit Statement and ranking of corporate objectives. Operational Planners: Procedures for acquisition search, evaluation & budget allocation.

11. 1. Impoverished Planners: No formal long range planning process; 2. Primary Planners: Written documented 3 year plan. Includes specification of objectives, goals and selection of long run strategies; 3. Pro Forma Planners: Same as Primary Planners plus pro forma financial statements and other quantitative projections; 4. Progressive Predictive Planners: Same as Pro Forma Planners, plus procedures to anticipate/detect errors in, failures of the plan and to prevent/correct them. Also, some attempt to account for factors outside the immediate environment at the firm.

12. No overall categories developed. Different aspects of Planning examined: Formality, Agreement on Objectives, Perception of DIM roles, Channels of Information, Items of Information.

13. Planners: Formal Planning sequence for at least 3 years into the future; Other than Planners: Some planning activity.

14. Complete Planners: Written Long Range Plan for at least 3 year horizon; quantity, goals and objectives, prepare pro forma financial statements. Mechanisms for scanning external environment, systematic planning for virtually all facets of operations, procedures for monitor/control vs. plan; Incomplete Planners: Written Long Range Plan for at least 3 year time horizon but not all requirements of complete planners; Nonplanners: No formal Long Range planning process.

15. Strategic Planners: Long Term financial objectives, obtained and
     used environmental information, identified and analyzed strategic
     options, evaluated resource constraints, planned courses of action.
     Centralized Planners: Conducted strategic planning at corporate
     level. Decentralized Planners: Conducted strategic planning at
     division level (not at corporate). (Most non-strategic planners met
     all criteria except gathering environmental information.)

16. Overall response rate 17 percent, 323 firms. Basis for results was
     petroleum firms, 15 in sample.

17. Overall response rate 63 percent, 92 firms, 54 formal & 2 informal
     planners discarded; final sample 36 firms, 17 formal, 19 informal.

18. Overall response rate 33 percent, 90 firms. All 14 food & apparel
     firms discarded; plus 38 firms from chosen industries, final sample
     38 firms.

19. Overall response rate 59 percent. All incomplete planners & 83
     complete planners discarded.

20. Strategic Planners & Nonplanners chosen so that some industries
     represented at 4-digit SIC code level. Of 123 useable responses, 74
     responses discarded.

21. Performance Measures: Growth in: A. Sales, B. Net Income, C. EPS,
     D. Stock Price, E. ROE, F. EPC., G. Sales PS, H. Cash Flow PS,
     I. Book Values PS, J. Operating Margin, K. Dividend/Net Income,
     L. Capital Spending PS, M. P/E Ratio, N. Total Assets, O. Dividends
     PS, P. Debt/Equity, Q. Common Equity, R. Price/Equity, S. Earnings/
     Sales, T. Earnings/Total Capital, U. Earnings/Net Assets, V. Stock
     Returns, W. Stock Price & Dividends, X. Residuals from market
     portfolio, Y. Beta. Mean or Level -- As above with prime ('); Mean
     & Growth -- As above with double prime ("); Deviation from Trend
     -- As above with plus (+).

22. Across studies growth is measured over various time periods; 3, 5,
     10 years; in a variety of ways, Mean Annual Growth, Simple % change,
     trend line.

10.2.2 CONCEPTUALIZATION OF PLANNING

As shown in chapters 2, 3, and 4, planning has many dimensions, yet tests of planning/performance hypotheses have generally used relatively simple operationalizations of planning. In all studies except Grinyer and Norburn (1974, 1975), whose work focused on several aspects of planning, and Welch (1984), the hypothesis tested was whether a single category of "planning" companies outperformed a single "other" category of companies – typically designated nonplanners. Ansoff et al. (1970), Gershefski and Harvey (1970), Karger and Malik (1975) (Malik and Karger 1975), Thune and House (1970), Wood and LaForge (1979, 1981), Harju (1981), and Robinson and Pearce (1983) all used a single planning category. Others, though developing multiple planning categories conceptually, tested a simple plan/no plan hypothesis, either by collapsing groups (Fulmer and Rue 1974, Rue and Fulmer 1973) or by omitting categories from the analysis (Denning and Lehr 1971, 1972; Kudla 1980).

It is difficult for a single "planning" measure or category, whether developed beforehand or formed later, to capture characteristics of planning such as, for example, mundane and repetitive versus insightful, intuitive versus formal, short- versus long-range, high- versus low-quality, organizational subunit versus corporate, operational versus strategic, integrative versus nonintegrative. Furthermore, we might expect planning in a highly structured, operations-based, financially driven, and tightly controlled planning system to differ significantly in terms of impact from a loose, intuitive, strategically oriented process driven by subunit management. Finally, many studies group companies into industries with plan/no plan comparisons made within a particular industry. This approach is at odds with the notion that a key task of strategic planning at the corporate level is to decide what businesses to be in, including selection of technologies, markets, raw material suppliers, and so forth.[1]

10.2.3 PERFORMANCE MEASURES

Economic performance measures are diverse and in some cases numerous, ranging from 22 in the Ansoff et al. (1970) study, through 13 in Karger and Malik (1975) (Malik and Karger 1975), to 1 in the Grinyer and Norburn (1974) study. Some measures employed, such as debt/equity ratio (mean), dividends/net income (mean and growth rate), and capital spending per share (growth rate) are closer to being direct results of managerial decisions than they are economic performance per se. Some authors rely on external assessments such as stock price (mean and growth rate), stock returns (mean and growth rate), and Beta (Kudla 1980, 1981), but these are more measures of investors' anticipations of future performance (or value) than of past or present performance. Meanwhile, potentially important elements of performance are often overlooked; for example, variability in performance is addressed in only two studies.

The multiple performance measures used in some studies are inevitably intercorrelated. While multiple measures are useful, the dimensionality of performance and the issue of which dimensions are affected by planning is often ignored. Finally, all studies except Denning and Lehr (1972), which found "some evidence that 'planning' companies tend to have a higher rate of technological change than the remainder," focused solely on measures of economic performance, even though a number of authors – notably Ang and Chua (1979), Armstrong (1982), Denning and Lehr (1971), and Hulbert and Brandt (1980) – documented noneconomic benefits of planning. (See King

1983 for a detailed discussion of various criteria by which planning systems could be evaluated.)

10.2.4 BIASED PRIORS, DATA QUALITY, AND ANALYSIS

The adoption of planning and acceptance of the attendant costs of its development and implementation are no doubt predicated on the assumption that planning will provide economic benefits. Studies of planning and performance might start with a favorable bias toward proving the point. For example, Karger and Malik (1975:60) stated:

> (this) research was motivated to so strongly establish the positive benefits of planning that the practice of planning in industry would increase significantly.

Their conclusion that planners outperform nonplanners is based on analysis of 38 companies from the chemical and drug, electronics, and machinery industries. Data from 38 other companies in these industries were discarded, as were data from all 16 firms in the apparel and food industries.

Thune and House (1970) based their results for the positive impact of planning on a sample of 36 firms that "were carefully selected" from 92 respondent companies. Among those discarded were 54 companies that were formal planners by the authors' own definition. Similarly, Gershefski and Harvey (1970) claimed significant superiority of their 4 formal planning companies versus 11 others in the petroleum industry. They also displayed directional effects for chemical and manufacturing firms, claiming insufficient sample size for significance. There is no explanation of why 15 chemical or 52 manufacturing firms constituted inadequate sample sizes, while 15 petroleum firms were sufficient, nor why data from the remaining 241 companies from a variety of other industries were not discussed.

Given discarding and nonresponse, the effective response rates in the studies are often quite low, seldom above 25 percent; yet nonresponse bias was typically not checked. (All but three studies collected data via mail questionnaire.)

A number of studies used no statistical tests and based conclusions on inspection of the data. Furthermore, the studies typically investigated the relationship between planning and performance and did not consider the possibility that results may have been due to omitted variables, despite the fact that Rumelt (1974) and studies based on the PIMS data base (Buzzell, Gale, and Sultan 1975; Schoeffler, Buzzell, and Heany 1974), together with research in the industrial organization literature, have shown that a variety of factors may mediate, moderate, or otherwise contribute to planning-performance relationships. The exceptions to this procedure appeared in work by Fulmer and Rue (1974), who noted that the planning category of the firms is correlated with size, and in studies by Thune and House (1970) and by Herold (1972), who based their results on analyses of companies roughly comparable in size. However, contingent relationships were rarely examined in these studies.

10.2.5 SUMMARY

The foregoing discussion suggests that significant problems pervade studies in the planning-performance literature. Corroborating evidence is provided by Armstrong (1982), who rated the 12 studies he reviewed on Terpstra's (1981) scale of evaluation for organizational behavior research. He obtained an average score of 1.5 against an ideal score of 6; the average score of Terpstra's 52 organizational behavior studies is 3.0. Armstrong concluded that across all studies the methodology employed is poor but that variation on this dimension is not related to the finding of relationships between planning and performance. He concluded that, overall, there is support for a positive relationship between planning and performance.[2]

10.3 Measures of Performance

10.3.1 ISSUES IN SELECTION OF MEASURES

This chapter focuses on economic performance. However, several different measures of economic performance are available. Measures may be absolute (e.g., sales, profit, market value of the firm) or return (e.g., profit/sales, profit/capital, cash flow/net assets). Measures may be internal (e.g., sales, profit/sales) or external (e.g., market value of the firm, stock price). The measure may be annual, a mean over some longer period, or a growth rate. Variability may be measured about the mean, or about trend, for a number of time periods.

Our basic outlook is that sample firms attempt to maximize long-term profitability; they do so by trying to control a shorter term proxy – return-on-capital ROC. ROC is defined as net profit + ½ (interest on long-term debt)/(long-term debt + net worth); net profit is defined as net (after tax) income before extraordinary gains or losses and net worth as common + preferred stockholders equity, including intangibles (Bernhard 1959). This measure captures the firm's ability to produce operating profit from invested capital and corresponds closely to the measure (return-on-investment) most frequently used by our sample to set their goals at the corporate and lower levels.

The choice of time span for the performance measurements raises several issues that result from the fact that the impact of planning on performance is unlikely to be instantaneous. Simple contemporary analysis, while necessary, must therefore be combined with analysis over a longer time period. In addition, study of variability in performance is best done with longitudinal analysis. On the one hand, a long time span makes random events in an individual year less likely to dominate performance. On the other hand, the greater the time span, the more likely that either the system or its environment will change. In addition, the sample size is more likely to be reduced by acquisition and merger, over a longer time period.

A balancing of these issues led us to two spans of measurement. The first involved measurements for two single years, 1979 (approximately concurrent with data collection) and 1981 (involving a two-year lag). Second, a five-year period centered in 1979 was used to calculate mean returns and variability about a simple growth trend for that period.[3] A measure of variability is important since we have indications of significant differences in risk aversion among Planning Categories (chapters 7 and 8); risk-averse managers may stray far from optimality (Jagpal and Brick 1982) even if there is agreement between corporate and divisions about the nature of risk aversion (Jagpal and Farley 1984).

In interpreting the results of these multiple analyses, it is important to understand that the individual measures are far from independent, as is shown by the simple correlations among them:

| | Return on Capital 1977–1981 | | |
	Mean	*Standard Deviation About Trend*	*1979 ROC*
Standard Deviation About Trend	− .48***		
1979 ROC	.84***	− .03	
1981 ROC	.78***	− .54***	.44***

***p < .01

Variability is negatively related to mean return (preliminary analysis also showed this relationship for the 1970-79 time period), indicating that high returns do not simply result from a set of risky businesses[4].

10.3.2 RELATIONSHIP OF RETURN-ON-CAPITAL AND OTHER FINANCIAL INDICATORS

Using return-on-capital to measure performance makes substantive sense and, as noted above, corresponds to measures used by most of our sample to express both quantitative goals and evaluate managers' performance. However, other measures (e.g., based on cash flow and net worth) could also have been used. Further, growth in various performance indicators and variability may also be important. In fact, 42 percent of the sample has goals expressed in terms of some sort of growth measure, though none has goals based on variability in performance.

As table 10.3 indicates, mean ROC is significantly and positively related to mean return-on-sales, mean relative cash flow, and is practically identical to mean return-on-net worth. A pattern of similarity also emerges between the measure of variability used here (standard deviation about trend in ROC) and other measures of variability of returns, about both mean performance and performance trend.[5] Neither mean ROC nor variability in ROC is strongly related to various measures of growth in return, chiefly because there is no consistent pattern of growth in the return indices, though high growth of ROC and return-on-net worth is associated with low variability in ROC. Finally, there is little relationship between the mean and variability of ROC and unadjusted growth and variability measures based on absolute indicators such as sales, net profits, and cash flow. This indicates that we are not merely studying a scale phenomenon.[6] Significance does, however, emerge when the absolute measures are adjusted by dividing by their mean values.

10.4 Tests of Planning/Performance Relationships

Five approaches are available to assess the impact of planning on performance:

1. Performance of planners versus nonplanners on the basis of self-reports (chapter 2)
   a. Full sample in 1979

Table 10.3
Correlations of Return-on-Capital Measures to Other
Financial Indicators (1977-1981)

Return Indicators	Return on Capital (percent) (1977-1981)	
	Mean	Variability about Trend[1]
Mean		
Return on capital	1.00	-.48***
Return on net worth	.94***	-.60***
Return on sales	.79***	-.41***
Cash flow on sales	.63***	-.37***
Variability about Mean		
Return on capital	-.45***	.93***
Return on net worth	-.53***	.94***
Return on sales	-.19**	.53***
Cash flow on sales	-.14	.40***
Variability about Trend		
Return on capital	-.48***	1.00
Return on net worth	-.53***	.95***
Return on sales	-.25**	.57***
Cash flow on sales	-.17*	.42***
Growth[2]		
Return on capital	.18***	-.44***
Return on net worth	.22**	-.47***
Return on sales	.06	-.16*
Cash flow on sales	.09	-.16*
Absolute Indicators		
Growth		
Sales	.13[2] .06[3]	-.03[2] .08[3]
Net profits	.20** .15	-.17* -.30***
Cash flow	.21** .31***	-.13 -.24***
Variability about Trend		
Sales	-.05 -.21**	.18* .32***
Net profits	-.12 -.52***	.35*** .64***
Cash flow	-.12 -.55***	.34*** .56***

[1]The operational definition of variability for results in this table is
standard deviation.

[2]Annual growth rate determined by regression analysis in this column.

[3]Annual growth rate determined by regression analysis divided by mean
in this column.

***p < .01, **p < .05, *p < .10

    b. Before/after measures on subsample with an identifiable date of start-up for planning

2. Performance of planning groupings:
    a. Deductively developed Planning Categories (chapter 2)
    b. Inductively developed Planning groups (chapter 9)
    c. Combination deductive/inductive (combinations of a and b)

3. Performance as related to planning process summary measures ("Soft Model" scores from chapter 4)

4. Performance by firms using particular adaptive and integrative planning function elements (planning scales from chapter 4)

5. Planning practices of firms which perform well (developed in this chapter)

To our knowledge, this is the most exhaustive set of bases for testing planning-performance relationships yet attempted. Hypotheses about what the relationships should be in each case are discussed in connection with each test.

    Of course, the tests are not independent, because they repeatedly use the same data and occasionally the same items. Furthermore, chapter 2 shows correspondence between the deductively developed five-group Planning Category system and self-reports on planning; chapter 4 shows correspondence to the various elements of both the adaptive and integrative functions of planning. Chapter 9 shows that the inductively developed planning groups correspond closely to the Planning Categories in chapter 2.

10.5 Presence/Absence of Planning: Self Reports

10.5.1 NATURE OF THE TESTS

    This approach to conceptualizing planning provides the closest link to most previous work that has tested planning/performance relationships. As a working hypothesis, firms with corporate planning systems should make better decisions than firms with either decentralized planning systems or no planning at all, and hence achieve better long-run returns. This is, however, stated as a weak hypothesis, for, as indicated earlier in this chapter, the richness of planning is not captured with a simple dichotomy.

    Self-report tests were made both on a cross-sectional basis for the entire sample and longitudinally for a subset of the sample for which the starting date for planning could be estimated to have been between 1973 and 1976 on the basis of self-reports.

10.5.2 RESULTS OF TESTING CORPORATE PLANNERS VERSUS NON CORPORATE PLANNERS

All respondents were asked:

"Does your company develop a formal corporate plan (or plans) on a regular basis?"

Seventy firms responded affirmatively and 43 responded negatively. The earnings patterns of self-designated "planners" and "nonplanners" are:

	Return on Capital (percent)			
	1977-1981			
	Mean	Standard Deviation about Trend	1979	1981
Self-Declared Planners	11.09	1.46	12.40	10.39
Self-Declared Nonplanners	11.03	1.78	12.19	11.16

None of these differences is significant.

10.5.3 RESULTS OF TESTS OF PERFORMANCE BEFORE AND AFTER PLANNING

An ideal research design for assessing the impact of planning would be to identify a group of firms that plan, pinpoint the time when they started, and assess performance before and after that point as compared to a control group of nonplanners assessed at the same points in time (or, better yet, manipulate this variable by assigning some firms to plan and others not to).

However, such an approach is difficult to execute in practice. First, few firms start planning at the same time (and even fewer would permit their planning activities to be manipulated in a field experiment). Second, personnel changes and short organizational memories make it difficult to pinpoint the timing of critical events in the past. Indeed, implementation of planning is often a process that takes an extended period of time instead of being an instantaneous event for which the date can be identified. Third, it is not absolutely clear from self-reports who plans and who does not.

Nonetheless, some interesting directional evidence on planning and performance is available for a subset of our sample that both claim to be planners and to have begun planning during the 1970s. In order to make before-and-after performance comparisons, a firm was selected for the subsample only if it had operated both with and without planning for at least three years of that decade – that is, only if planning started between 1973 and 1976, inclusively. This allows for t-tests of differences in preplanning and postplanning ROC involving the period from 1970 to 1979, but barely, on account of few within-group data points.

Of 19 firms that meet these very restrictive requirements, 9 have significantly higher mean ROC in the postplanning period, 5 have higher mean ROC (but not significantly), and 5 have lower mean ROC in the postplanning period. Mean ROC for the entire sample is slightly but not significantly higher in the 1977–1981 time frame as against the 1970–79 period. Of course, our sample of 19 firms which adopted corporate planning at particular times is limiting, so a more precise comparison against real "controls" is difficult. This result should be viewed as at best directional, owing to selectivity (only about a fifth of our sample is included), to problems of self-reporting, and to extremely small within-period sample sizes used to develop the t-tests.

10.6 Deductively Developed Planning Categories

In chapter 2, we developed a five-group Planning Category system that provides a richer conceptualization than the plan/no plan dichotomy.

10.6.1 NATURE OF THE TEST
The deductive approach employs the five categories of planning:

Corporate Strategic Planners. These 24 companies exhibit the most sophisticated form of planning with a significant strategic dimension to their planning at both corporate and lower levels. The corporate plan is a document that takes a corporate perspective and is not just an agglomeration of lower level plans.

Division Strategic Planners. These 37 companies do not develop a formal written plan that takes a corporate perspective. However, strategic planning is conducted at lower levels in the organization. Thus, the planning system focuses on the development of a series of lower level strategic plans, with little or no corporate perspective.

Corporate Financial Planners. These 34 companies develop a formal written corporate plan. However, neither it, nor lower level plans are strategic; rather the focus is on financial planning – the development of pro forma budgets and so forth – based on a series of assumptions about the future environment.

Division Financial Planners. These 11 companies do not develop formal corporate plans, and none of their planning is strategic. They do develop a series of lower level financial plans. There is, however, no evidence that these lower level financial plans are assembled into a corporate financial plan in any way more complex than adding up the budgets.

Non-Planners. These 7 companies show no evidence of any corporate- or division-level planning system, be it either strategic or financial.

The hypothesis regarding these planning Categories is that greater sophistication of the planning system is associated with better performance. This rather clearly designates the Corporate Strategic Planners best by hypothesis and the Non-Planners worst. However, ordering the other categories is more complex. We conclude, first and most importantly, that strategic planners will perform better than financial planners and, second that corporate planners will perform better than division planners. The rationale for the first conclusion is that, since strategic planners are adaptive and environmentally oriented in their planning, and since they engage in formal processes for thinking through key strategic issues and resource allocation priorities, they are more likely both to identify attractive opportunities and threats and to take appropriate action. Financial planners, being less adaptive, more internally oriented, and heavily focused on financial projections, are less likely to make good strategic decisions. Second, Corporate Planners are expected to perform better than Division Planners since a corporate perspective should offer advantage over independent subunit perspectives, regardless of whether the planning is strategic or financial. The argument for Division Strategic Planners outperforming Corporate Financial Planners is less clear, but our judgment is that the benefits of an adaptive and environmentally oriented strategic focus, albeit at the second level, should outweigh the integrative benefits of corporate financial planning. An additional argument is that corporate financial planning may lead to strong centralized control and stifle innovation at the division level. The anticipated ordered performance was thus: Corporate Strategic > Division Strategic > Corporate Financial > Division Financial > Non-Planners.

10.6.2 RESULTS

The most surprising result (table 10.4) is that the performance of the Non-Planners is superior to all other groups for all three ROC measures, though none of these differences is significant. However, the Corporate Strategic Planners outperform the other Categories that plan in terms of higher returns and lower variability. (They also have the lowest standard deviation about trend overall.) Furthermore, both strategic groups outperform both financial groups on most measures.

Table 10.4
Performance (and Ranks)
for Deductively Developed Planning Categories

Planning Category†	Number of Firms	Return on Capital (percent)			
		1977-81			
		Mean	Standard Deviation about Trend	1979	1981
Corporate Strategic	24	12.0(2)	.89(1)	12.7(2)	11.6(2)
Division Strategic	37	11.2(3)	1.54(2)	12.2(4)	10.1(4)
Corporate Financial	33	10.5(4)	1.93(4)	12.4(3)	10.0(5)
Division Financial	11	9.2(5)	1.92(3)	10.6(5)	10.3(3)
Non-Planners	7	13.2(1)	2.03(5)	14.0(1)	14.7(1)
(Non-Planners††	6	10.4	2.31	11.5	12.1)

†Order of categories represents hypothesized performance order;
1-tailed tests

††Results when one firm which performed particularly well is removed for special circumstances

Two further sets of analyses were performed. First, three sets of covariates were introduced to control for other important factors that might systematically affect returns:

Scale   – measured by 1979 sales, to see if the results were just due to size

Diversification – number of 2-digit SIC codes in which the firm was operating, to see if diversity was also a factor in performance

           – four dummy variables representing the broad diversification categories of Rumelt's (1974) scheme (single business, dominant business, related business, unrelated business)

Maturity — proportion of 1979 company sales reported to be in mature or declining product categories, to see if age of product mix explained differences in performance

The results produced virtually identical results in terms of ordering of Planning Category performance. The covariates were insignificant and had no systematic pattern of effects on performance over Planning Categories.

Second, the Non-Planners were examined in more detail for explanation of their superiority. The Non-Planners are an unusual group of firms, operating in several industries, whose relatively mature product lines were enjoying particular popularity and, in some cases, had done so for some time. One Non-Planner consistently earned exceptionally high returns-on-capital, well over twice the grand 1977-1981 mean for *all* firms in our sample. When this firm was removed, the order relationships changed (last line on table 10.4), and most importantly, the Corporate Strategic Planners are the best performers on all four measures. The Non-Planners, however, still outperform the Divisional Financial Planners. Again, these differences are not significant.

Finally, tests of a variety of other performance measures generally failed to identify significant effects (table 10.5). Since

Table 10.5

Significance of Additional Performance Tests for Deductively Developed Planning Categories

	Mean	Standard Deviation	Growth[1] Rate	Standard Deviation about Trend	1979	1981
			1977-1981			
Return-on-Capital	No†	No	No	No†	No†	No†
Return-on-Equity	No	No	No	No	No	No
Return-on-Sales	No	Yes**	No	Yes**	No	Yes**
Cash Flow-on-Sales	No	Yes**	No	Yes**	No	No
Sales	No	No	No	No	No	No
Net Profit	No	No	No	No	No	No
Cash Flow	No	No	No	No	No	No

[1]Annual growth rate determined by regression analysis.

†See Table 10.4

**Significant differences among groups, $\alpha = .05$

several of these measures are highly correlated with mean and standard deviation about trend of return-on-capital, this is perhaps unsurprising. In particular, none of the five-year mean or growth rate measures, nor the 1979 measures, produced significance. However, both standard deviation and standard deviation about trend, of both return-on-sales and cash flow-on-sales, and 1981 return-on-sales, were significant.

Table 10.6 reveals monotonic relationships for four of these five measures; Corporate Strategic Planners have the least variability, and Non-Planners the most variability, on each of the four measures of this type. Consistent with the return-on-capital results, Non-Planners have the highest 1981 return-on-sales; Corporate Strategic Planners are roughly equivalent to Division Financial Planners and higher than the other two categories.

Table 10.6
Planning Category Means (and Ranks)
for Significant Performance Measures

	1977-1981				1981
	Return on Sales		Cash Flow on Sales		Return
		Standard		Standard	on
	Standard	Deviation	Standard	Deviation	Sales
Planning Category[1]	Deviation	about Trend	Deviation	about Trend	
Corporate Strategic	.69(1)	.42(1)	.67(1)	.42(1)	5.43(3)
Division Strategic	1.21(2)	.68(2)	1.19(2)	.65(2)	4.74(4)
Corporate Financial	1.39(3)	.80(3)	1.40(3)	.80(3)	4.60(5)
Division Financial	1.53(4)	1.03(4)	1.55(4)	1.05(4)	5.49(2)
Non-Planners	2.85(5)	1.96(5)	3.46(5)	2.44(5)	9.91(1)

[1]Each performance measure significant at $\alpha = .05$

10.7 Inductively Developed Planning Groups

A somewhat richer definition of planning groups is provided by the inductive approach presented in chapter 9. Although this classification is less satisfactory in some ways than the deductive approach, since it depends solely on statistical criteria, it has the advantage of grouping firms according to many measures about their planning rather than the handful of criteria used in chapter 2.

10.7.1 NATURE OF THE TEST

The inductive approach produced the following five groups empirically (chapter 9):

Fully Integrated Planners. This group of 33 firms has the most extensive and well-integrated planning systems. Planning is characterized by an information-rich environment, both internally and externally obtained, and by extensive transmission of information through the firm. Significant competitive analysis is performed, and there is extensive use of models as part of the planning process. Planning is "strategic," and the planning systems tend to be oriented to resource allocation. Strategic criteria are employed for making resource allocation decisions, and planning is performed on a worldwide basis. In these firms, not only does the corporate planning group have great influence and possess a good deal of formal authority, but also there is excellent communication with line management. Line management feels positive about the planning process and believes that it too has extensive influence. Heavy commitment is given to planning by senior corporate management, functional plans are well integrated, and goal-setting is an important management tool.

Extensive Planners. The 25 firms of this group have well-established and formalized planning systems. They have a strategic orientation to planning and make significant use of portfolio and other models in the planning process. They produce many and extensive plans, but whereas they employ moderate levels of environmental information, they tend not to obtain significant information internally. Staff planners report at high organizational levels but, though heavily involved in the planning process, do not seem to be particularly well integrated – line management is neutral as regards the value of planning.

Seat-of-the-Pants Planners. This group of 32 firms plans in meager information environments, and there is not good information transmission through the firms. There is little use of models as planning tools, and the final plans are not extensive. The planning process is line-driven with moderate CEO influence, and planners do not have significant authority. Formalization of planning is not high, and goals are not used as an important management tool.

Marginal Planners. These 15 firms are below the mean on virtually every positive planning scale but higher than the Not-at-All Planners. Their information environments are sparse, they do not use models, there is little corporate commitment to planning, and the final plans are not extensive.

Not-at-All Planners. These eight firms score at the negative end point on the scale for virtually every planning scale item. Their major distinguishing feature is that goals and strategies are developed top down and that performance reviews are held frequently.

Some measure of validation of the deductive Planning Category system is provided by the fact that it shares common characteristics with the inductive groupings (chapter 9). However, because the inductive groups were developed from the many planning scales, they involve much more of a feeling of what it takes to make planning work.

Our working hypothesis for the inductive Planning grouping System is that Fully Integrated planners should outperform Extensive planners, Extensive planners should outperform Seat-of-the-Pants planners, and all three should outperform the remaining two groups. The basis for these hypotheses was that the Fully Integrated planners appear to embody what is generally accepted as the best characteristics of planning. Their information environments (external and internal) are rich, they perform extensive analysis, use strategic criteria for resource allocation decisions, and plan on a worldwide basis. Functional plans are well integrated, goal setting is an important management tool, and though the corporate planning group is very influential, there is heavy line involvement in the planning process. Extensive planners appear to operate in poorer information environments, especially internally; there is less line management involvement; and the planning systems are overall less well integrated into the organization than those of the Fully Integrated planners. Both groups have, however, better systems than Seat-of-the-Pants planners, which have meager information environments, little information transmission, little use for models, moderate corporate commitment, and limited final plans. Neither the Marginal nor Not-at-All planners do any planning to speak of, and so it is hard to separate them.

10.7.2 RESULTS

The performance results for these inductive groups (table 10.7) show that once again the Nonplanning group (Not-at-All planners) has the best results for all three ROC measures. The most sophisticated planning group, the Fully Integrated planners, has the second highest mean and the second lowest variability in returns; results for the Extensive planners are similar. The Seat-of-the-Pants planners performed least well overall; however, none of the results for these comparisons is significant. When the same high-performing Not-at-All planner was removed, as in the previous analysis, this group dropped from first position to fourth on the mean and 1979 ROC measures.

Table 10.7
Performance (and Ranks) for Inductively
Developed Planning Groups

Planning Group†	Number of Firms	Return on Capital (percent)			
		1977-81			
		Mean	Standard Deviation about Trend	1979	1981
Fully Integrated	32	11.7(2)	1.47(2)	12.6(3)	11.2(3)
Extensive	25	11.6(3)	1.38(1)	12.7(2)	10.9(4)
Seat-of-the-Pants	32	9.5(5)	1.83(4)	11.4(5)	8.6(5)
Marginal	15	11.3(4)	1.49(3)	12.4(4)	11.6(2)
Not-at-all	8	12.8(1)	1.85(5)	13.6(1)	14.6(1)
(Not-at-all††	7	10.4	2.07	11.4	12.4)

†Order of groups represents hypothesized performance order; 1-tailed tests

††Results when one firm which performed particularly well is removed.

In chapter 9 we collapsed the Fully Integrated and Extensive planners into a group of "good" planners, and the Seat-of-the-Pants, Marginal and Not-at-All-planners into a "bad" planners group. An extreme test of performance relationships selected the 20 highest and 20 lowest performers in terms of five-year mean ROC, and investigated their distribution among the "good" and "bad" planning groups. The results are not significant, although the best performers are somewhat more likely to be Fully Integrated or Extensive planners.

Planning Group	20 Best Performers (Highest 5-year ROC)	20 Worst Performers (Lowest 5-year ROC)	Remaining 72 firms
Fully Integrated or Extensive	12	8	37
Seat-of-the-Pants, Marginal or Not-at-All	8	12	35

10.8 Combination Deductive/Inductive Planning Groups

The deductively developed Planning Categories and the inductively developed Planning groups are closely related, though they are not identical. Since each has good and bad points, the two systems were combined to produce a new sixfold deductive/inductive combination system.

10.8.1 NATURE OF THE TEST

The deductive category scheme was first collapsed across the corporate/financial dimension to form three groupings: strategic, financial, Non-Planners. Five of the six categories of the combination scheme were formed from the intersection of groups in the two category systems and are named accordingly; the Not-at-All/Non-Planners group was formed from the union of these two groups. The six categories are Fully Integrated/Strategic (21), Extensive/Strategic (19), Seat-of-the-Pants-Marginal/Strategic (21), Fully Integrated-Extensive/Financial (18), Seat-of-the-Pants-Marginal/Financial (26), Not-at-All/Non-Planners (8). The hypothesized order of performance, related to the anticipated directions for the two underlying systems discussed in sections 10.6 and 10.7, is indicated in table 10.8.

10.8.2 RESULTS

The results are similar to those for the two planning classifications considered separately (table 10.8). The Not-at-All/Non-Planners group performs bests on ROC; the most sophisticated planning group, Fully Integrated/Strategic, has the second highest mean and the lowest variability in performance. The Seat-of-the-Pants-Marginal/Financial group performs least well in each test, especially for 1981 ROC, where a significant difference was observed. Interestingly, the Extensive/Strategic planners also perform poorly. Removal of the one high-performing Not-at-All/Non-Planner produced results similar to those in tables 10.4 and 10.5.

Removal of the one high-performing Not-at-All/Non-Planner produced results similar to those in tables 10.4 and 10.5.

Table 10.8
Performance (and Ranks) for Combination
Deductive/Inductive Planning Categories

Planning Group†	Number of Firms	Return on Capital (percent)			
			1977-81		
		Mean	Standard Deviation about Trend	1979	1981**
Fully Integrated/Strategic	21	12.3(2)	.89(1)	13.0(2)	11.7(3)
Extensive/Strategic	19	10.7(5)	1.85(4)	12.0(5)	8.9(5)
Seat-of-the-Pants -- Marginal/Strategic	21	11.4(4)	1.17(2)	12.1(4)	11.2(4)
Fully-Integrated-Extensive/Financial	17	11.8(3)	1.63(3)	12.9(3)	12.7(2)
Seat-of the-Pants -- Marginal/Financial	26	9.1(6)	2.17(6)	11.4(6)	8.2(6)
Not-at-All/Non-Planners	8	12.8(1)	1.85(4)	13.6(1)	14.6(1)

†Order of groups represents hypothesized performance order, 1-tailed tests

**Significant differences among groups, $\alpha = .05$

10.9 Adjusted Return Performance Measure

The results from the three grouping systems just described are not significant, though they are more or less consistent. The Non-Planners did well on return but poorly on variability, whereas the Corporate Strategic Planners did well on both. We therefore constructed a measure of return performance adjusted by variability (mean ÷ standard-deviation-about trend), which is an index of a firm's ability simultaneously to achieve high returns and low variability of returns.

The results of analyzing the three grouping systems by the adjusted return performance measure are displayed in table 10.9. Significant differences across firm grouping were obtained for both the deductive and the combination deductive/inductive schemes, but the substantive conclusions remain relatively unchanged from the nonadjusted results.[7]

In particular, the Corporate Strategic Planners and the

Table 10.9
Return Performance Adjusted by Variability†

Deductive Planning Categories	Return on Capital (percent) 1977-81 Mean ÷ Standard Deviation about Trend
Corporate Strategic	29.2**
Division Strategic	15.8
Corporate Financial	13.2
Division Financial	7.3
Non-Planners	22.5
(Non-Planners††	12.8)
Inductive Planning Groups	
Fully-Integrated	20.1
Extensive	21.7
Seat-of-the-Pants	12.8
Marginal	12.3
Not-at-all	21.9
(Not-at-all††	13.5)
Combination Category System	
Fully Integrated/Strategic	31.5**
Extensive/Strategic	13.9
Seat-of-the-Pants-Marginal/Strategic	17.1
Fully Integrated/Extensive/Financial	15.3
Seat-of-the-Pants-Marginal/Financial	9.1
Not-at-all/Non-Planners	21.9
(Not-at-all/Non-Planners††	13.5)

†Order of groups represents hypothesized performance orders; all tests
1-tailed.

††Results when one firm which performed particularly well is removed
for special circumstances.

**Significant among groups at α = .05

combination Fully Integrated/Strategic planners outperform all other
groups.

10.10 Planning Process Summary Measures

In chapter 2, a process perspective on planning comprising seven constituent building blocks was introduced. In chapter 4, a "soft" model
based on these building blocks showed that a consistent structure of
relationships existed among the first principal components for the

seven groupings that classified the 501 planning measures on our 113 firms.

10.10.1 NATURE OF THE TEST

The set of seven groupings involves three basic elements. The first dimension involves three types of input to the planning process:

Information Inputs – the type of data collected externally and internally, the resources spent obtaining it, its perceived usefulness, the extent to which it is transmitted through the organization.

Planning Tools – the types of models and conceptual frameworks employed in planning, where they are employed, the breadth of use.

Planning Organization – those persons who are involved in the planning process, their degree of, and involvement in, the process, and the organizational arrangements involved in planning.

Two process elements were identified for the second dimension:

Planning Activities are the what and how of planning. They include the degree to which resource allocation decisions are part of the planning process, the criteria employed, effort on acquisitions, divestitures, and so forth.

Organizational Planning Environment deals with the manner in which the planning departments function and interact with other areas of the organization, including relationships between planning and line management.

Finally, two output elements were identified:

Planning Process Outputs comprise the plans themselves – their existence, their content, and so forth.

Planning Process/Performance Interface is concerned with what happens after the plans are produced. It deals with the evaluation processes of organizational performance versus planned goals and represents the key feedback component of the planning system.

To check how elements of the planning process are related to performance, the first principal components from each group were correlated with the four performance measures. Our working hypothesis was that the greater the intensity of firm efforts on each dimension of the planning process, the better the economic performance should be.

10.10.2 RESULTS

There is a general pattern of lack of significance in the results. Of the 28 correlations (7 principal components by 4 performance measures) only 1 is significantly different from zero at $\alpha = .05$ (table 10.10).

Table 10.10

Correlations Between Performance and First Principal
Components Summarizing Planning Process Variable Groups (Ch.4)[1]

First Principal Component Describing:	Return on Capital (percent) 1977-81			
	Mean	Standard Deviation about Trend	1979	1981
Planning Inputs				
Information Inputs	-.03	-.04	-.04	.06
Planning Tools	.12	-.12	.06	.18**
Planning Organization	.06	.03	.11	.04
Planning Process				
Planning Activities	-.02	.01	.03	.06
Organizational Planning Environment	-.08	.09	-.02	-.04
Planning Outputs				
Planning Process Outputs	.05	-.11	.04	.10
Planning Outputs/Performance Interface	.04	.08	.09	.07

[1]All tests in this table are 1-tailed

**$\alpha = .05$

There are, however, some qualitative patterns. Of the 21 correlations of mean and annual ROC with the planning measures, 15 are positive—6 of 7 with the 1981 and 5 of 7 with the 1979 performance measures. This provides some weak evidence that across-the-board practice of what is popularly thought of as "good" planning may have some general positive influence on performance. There is no such pattern in seven correlations involving the five-year mean or the variability.

10.11 Planning Function Elements

In chapter 4, we developed a series of 43 scales involving planning, 13 of which measure adaptive elements and 30 of which measure integrative elements of planning.

10.11.1 NATURE OF THE TEST
Tests were made by correlating the 4 performance indices with the 13 adaptive and 30 integrative scales. In general, we anticipated positive relationships between these elements and financial performance, especially for the adaptive elements. An adaptive perspective, we felt, could only bring positive benefits (for reasons discussed earlier); emphasis on integration would be likely to have positive benefits, unless it led to an extreme stifling of innovative thinking, in which case it could lead to poor performance. These tests might also help pinpoint elements of adaptation and integration that have particularly consistent impact on performance.

10.11.2 RESULTS
The results again indicate a pattern of insignificance (table 10.11). For the adaptive scales, only six correlations are significant at $\alpha = .05$, and none of these are in the anticipated direction. Indeed, of the 52 correlations with the adaptive scales, only 20 are in the anticipated direction. Of the 120 integrative correlations, 16 are significant at $\alpha = .05$; however, only one is in the anticipated direction. In total, only 30% of correlations with the integrative scales have the expected sign. Finally, the five summary scales, developed from the 13 adaptive and 30 integrative scales in section 4.4, show no stronger relationship to performance.

Regressions using all 43 scales simultaneously as independent variables show little explanatory power for the scales as a group:

| | Return on Capital (percent) | | | |
| | 1977-1981 | | 1979 | 1981 |
	Mean	Standard Deviation About Trend		
p-Level of F Ratio Measuring Goodness of Fit	0.22	0.55	0.25	0.21
Number of Significant Regression Coefficients ($\alpha = .05$) of 43	4	3	5	4

Integration

Table 10.11
Correlations Between Performance
and Planning Function Elements (Ch.4)

Adaptive Planning Scales	Return on Capital (percent) 1977-81			
	Mean	Standard Deviation about Trend	1979	1981
Environmental Orientation				
Environmental Information	-.09	.03	-.09	-.07
Competitive Analysis	.02	.03	.10	-.11
Strategic Orientation				
"Strategic" Planning	-.02	-.14	-.07	-.04
Time Horizon	-.11	.13	-.05	-.09
Globalness	.07	-.09	.03	.02
Portfolio Change	-.11	-.02	-.16**	-.03
Resource Allocation	-.20**	-.03	-.28***	-.09
Planning Tools				
Portfolio Models	-.08	.03	-.02	-.15**
Model Use	.09	-.17**	.02	-.05
Resource Allocation Decisions				
Long Run Expense Distinction	.03	.07	.02	.05
Strategic Criteria	-.08	.02	-.04	-.15**
Plan Comprehensiveness				
Corporate	.01	.04	.06	-.10
Second Level	.02	-.08	.00	-.05
Integrative Planning Scales				
Formal Integration of Plans				
Functional	-.07	.05	-.05	-.07
Over-time	-.06	-.02	-.05	-.09
Information Flow				
Top-Down	.08	-.13	.01	.06
Internal	.07	-.03	.08	-.03
Corporate Planning Exchange	-.16**	.00	-.17**	-.08
Influence and Participation				
Board of Directors	-.09	.03	-.17**	-.10
CEO	-.07	.00	-.04	-.18**
Top Second Level Line Management	-.04	.02	-.03	-.10
Corporate Planning	-.18**	.01	-.17**	-.21**
Internal	.10	.02	.12	-.01

Table 10.11 (continued)

Integrative Planning Scales	Return on Capital (percent) 1977-81			
	Mean	Standard Deviation about Trend	1979	1981
Goal & Strategy Formulation Process				
Bottom-Up	-.17**	-.07	-.17**	-.11
CEO Negotiation	.04	-.01	.04	-.01
Planning and Line Management				
Relative Staff/Line	-.05	-.03	-.09	-.01
Nature of Planning				
Line View of Planning	-.06	-.09	-.07	-.12
Integrative Value of Planners				
Added Value	.00	.02	.04	-.10
Planning Group Integration	.02	-.04	.02	-.08
Status & Authority of Planners				
Reporting Importance	.15**	-.10	.10	.10
Planning Authority	-.15**	.03	-.16**	-.16**
Formalization of Planning				
Corporate Planning	-.01	-.06	.01	-.06
Second Level	.05	-.16**	-.01	.01
Plan Density Preparation	-.03	.03	.01	-.02
Plan Density Review	-.02	-.05	-.04	.03
Plan Distribution Depth	-.04	-.01	-.05	-.09
Planning/Performance Review				
Plan Review Atmosphere†	-.06	-.09	-.13	.02
Performance Review:				
Atmosphere†	.01	-.11	-.05	.07
Frequency	-.14	.10	-.05	-.31***
Criteria	.03	-.07	.04	0
Depth	-.13	.07	-.09	-.13
Goals				
Use of Goals	-.15	-.02	-.17**	-.10
Goals for Planning	-.04	-.04	-.05	-.02
Scale Synthesis				
Adaptive				
Comprehensiveness	-.04	-.04	-.08	-.04
Depth	-.04	-.01	-.02	-.13
Integrative				
Influence and Integration	-.15	.02	-.15	-.20**
Formalization	.01	-.09	.03	-.03
Authoritarian	.06	.04	.11	.01

[1]All tests in this table except † are 1-tailed

***α = .01, **α = .05

Overall, these results indicate no relationship between performance and the scales describing adaptive and integrative functions of planning.

10.12 Planning Practices of Firms Which Perform Well

So far, this chapter has indicated at best a marginal relationship between planning and performance. It seems natural at this point to attempt to sharpen the results by comparing planning as it is practiced by the firms that do perform particularly well with planning by the firms that perform less well. We do this analysis in the spirit of hypothesis generation for later studies rather than as an effort to produce definitive results, both because the process (reversing the analytical approaches developed in chapters 3 and 4) is basically data driven and because the tests are on correlated items. This approach should help increase our ability to find patterns, but at the same time it increases chances of finding relationships that in fact are spurious.

10.12.1 NATURE OF THE TEST

To attempt to identify patterns in individual measurements about planning that differ for firms that perform particularly well, the sample was divided into approximate thirds (high, medium, and low performers) on 1979 ROC, 1981 ROC, mean ROC (1977-1981), and variability about 1977-1981 trend. Univariate tests were performed across these groups on the 501 variables, which had been divided into the same 7 planning process building blocks used for the "soft" model in chapter 4 and for the performance tests in section 10.10. Because this work is exploratory, the significance level here is 10 percent rather than 5 percent used elsewhere throughout this book.

The high, medium, and low performing groups show very distinct differences in performance:

| Performance Group | Return on Capital (percent) | | | |
| | 1977-1981 | | 1979 | 1981 |
	Mean	Standard Deviation about Trend		
High	16.1	0.5	16.7	15.9
Medium	10.7	1.1	11.8	10.9
Low	5.2	3.2	7.9	6.5

The high performers earned more than twice as much return-on-capital as the low performers. Variability about trend is much greater for high variability (presumably poorer) performers than for high performers. Of course, the same firms are not necessarily included in high performing groups in all cases, though the vast majority are in corresponding groups.

10.12.2 RESULTS

Table 10.12 summarizes the results on planning and performance both overall and for the seven building blocks used in the process model of planning. The patterns indicate that the elements of planning are not associated with variability in performance. Some-

Table 10.12

Patterns of Significance for Items Comprising Performance Groups

Number of variables with significant
differences among the three profitability
groups ($\alpha = .1$)

| Variable Group | Number of Items in Group | Return of Capital (percent) 1977-1981 | | | | Number of Non-Monotonic Relationships |
		Mean	Standard Deviation about Trend	1979	1981	
Planning Inputs						
Information Inputs	27	1	0	0	0	0
Planning Tools	54	7	3	13*	13*	5
Planning Organization	106	20*	8	8	16*	7
Planning Process						
Planning Activities	146	26*	8	19*	38*	14
Organizational Planning Environment	58	5	6	2	13*	4
Planning Outputs						
Planning Process Outputs	69	5	2	5	5	3
Planning Outputs/ Performance Interface	41	6	8	4	6	6
	501	70	35	51	91*	39

*Significantly greater number of items are significant than would be expected by chance using a binomial approximation, $\alpha = .1$.

what stronger patterns occur for the three measures of return on capital, though many of these are nonmonotonic. None of our theoretical work or literature reviews suggest that we would find a large number of nonmonotonic relationships here. Furthermore, there is only a weak pattern of consistency over the four performance measures, indicating even more the tentativeness of our conclusions. The following discussion should be interpreted in light of the fact that the elements of the planning system are interrelated, as is shown by the pattern of linkages among elements of the "soft" model of planning system in chapter 4. The discussion keys on broad patterns rather than on differences of specific items.

10.12.2.1 The Significant Variable Groups

Four of the seven variable groups contain a significant number of items that are different for high and low performers on at least one performance measure. High performance in terms of return-on-capital is generally associated with the use of planning tools (2 performance measures), planning activities (3) and with organizational issues – planning organization (2) and organizational planning environment (1).

Planning Tools (table 10.13). The tools associated with strategic planning are one of its most visible and publicized elements. The measurements of planning tools focus on portfolio-type models and their applications (previous and anticipated-future use), as well as on other types of models and computer systems.

At a general level, the high performers appear to apply in practice one of the key results underlying most portfolio models – seeking high market shares in their served markets. On the other hand, the high performers are less frequent users of formal tools of strategic planning overall, and in fact it is the low performers that generally anticipate future use of the tools. The high performers do, however, appear to use portfolio models in greater depth, though this may be changing over time. Whereas the sample is generally familiar with use of models and other computer tools for planning, their use does not appear to have influenced performance to a significant extent, though high performers tend to employ strategy-linked computer systems. These results do not necessarily negate the general usefulness of these planning tools, but they do have implications for firms hoping that their adoption will provide a "quick fix" for lagging performance.

Planning Organization (table 10.14). Planning personnel in the most profitable firms appear to be better trained and more experienced, and the planning system appears more "home grown" and

Table 10.13
Performance and Planning Tools: Significant Relationships†

	Return on Capital (percent) 1977-1981			
	Mean	Standard Deviation about Trend	1979	1981
Portfolio Models				
Future use expected of:				
A. D. Little Portfolio Models	L			L
BCG Model			L	
GE Matrix				L
Ansoff categories				L
PIMS	L		L	L
Previous use of:				
BCG Model			·	L
PIMS			L	L
Attempt to get largest share in served market	H		H	H
Portfolios used for:				
Cash flow	L			L
Resource allocation				L
Competitors				L
Customers			H	L
Suppliers			H	
At lower levels			H	
Other Models				
Models used:				
Number operational		H		
Econometric			M††	
Forecasting and budgeting			L	
Forecasting (second level)		H		
Financial (second level)		H		
Corporate planning			H	
Computer Systems				
Computer systems used:				
Linked strategy model	H		H††	H
Analysis of performance			M††	
Linked corporate and second-level planning models	M††			
Linked corporate and second-level decision models			L	M††
Linked data management	H			

†H, M, L indicates that high values of that measurement are associated with high (H), medium (M) or low (L) performance on the respective performance index.

††Non-monotonic

Table 10.14

Performance and Planning Organization: Significant Relationships†

	Return on Capital (percent) 1977-1981			
	Mean	Standard Deviation about Trend	1979	1981
Management Involvement in Planning				
The Board is influential in developing:				
Objectives	M,L			
Strategy	M,L			
Approval	M,L	M,L	L	
Format of plan		L		
The CEO is personally involved in:				
approval of plan	L			L
The CEO has relatively great influence on:				
assumptions in plan		L		
setting planning objectives	M††			
approval of final plan	M††	M††		L
format of the plan	M††			L
second level missions	M††			
Strategies are developed by the CEO	H			H
Line influence on:				
planning assumptions		L		
strategies	M			M
The Planning Department				
The Planning Department has influence on:				
corporate goals	L			
second-level goals	L		L	L
assumptions in the plan	M††			L
setting objectives				L
approval of plans	L			L
corporate strategy				L
second level strategy				L
Planners:				
feel a chance to advance			H,M	
have graduate training	H		H	H
have staff experience		L		
have experience in personnel		M††		

†H, M, L indicates that high values of that measurement are associated with high (H), medium (M) or low (L) performance on the respective index.

††Non-monotonic

Table 10.14 (continued)

| | Return on Capital (percent) 1977-1981 | | | |
	Mean	Standard Deviation about Trend	1979	1981
There are other professionals in the department:				H
Operations research specialists				L
Marketing specialists				L
People stay long in planning jobs				L
Decisions influenced by:				
academics		L		
consultants			L	
executives from other industries			L	
Second-level planners:				
exist	H			
have been with the firm a long time	H			
Key information comes from:				
line personnel for planning	H			
corporate planning for second-level goals	L			
second-level managers for second-level goals	H			
Outsiders				
Consultants validate:				
divestiture decisions			M	
acquisition decisions			M	

†H, M, L indicates that high values of that measurement are associated with high (H), medium (M) or low (L) performance on the respective performance index.

less "off the shelf," or designed by consultants. The CEO sets strategy in high performing firms and is involved broadly in planning in the moderate performers; broad involvement of the planning department is characteristic of firms that perform less well. Furthermore, there is greater involvement of line managers in setting strategies in moderately performing firms and greater propensity to provide information for setting their own goals for high performers. Although the results are sketchy, broad involvement in planning by the CEO and line management, with the planners supporting rather than planning, appears to be associated with higher performance.

Planning Activities (table 10.15). The measures in this category involve corporate and lower-level goals, the benefits that the firm expects from planning, investment criteria, the focus of planning effort, and how planning is executed, coordinated, and controlled. The classic association of high performance and CEO development of goals and strategies is present here, as well as an indication of the importance of competitive analysis and a view that second-level goals help extend product life cycles. Otherwise the patterns of association

Table 10.15
Performance and Planning Activities: Significant Relationships†

| | Return on Capital (percent) 1977-1981 | | | |
	Mean	Standard Deviation about Trend	1979	1981
Goals				
Goals are set by the CEO	H			H
Second-level goals are developed:				
by aggregating third-level goals	L			
in negotiation with central management			L	L
Change in Goals likely to be brought about by:				
competitive changes				H
poor performance	L	H	L	L
Second-level goals:				
are used as rationing devices	L		L	L
are a major influence on corporate goals	M††			
are set by second level management				M
have different financial demands	H			
improve long-range resource allocation		M††		L
help extend product life cycles	H	H		H
help auditing	L		L	
help knowledge sharing and storing	M††			M††

†H, M, L indicates that high values of that measurement are associated
with high (H), medium (M) or low (L) performance on the respective
performance index.

††Non-monotonic

are neither consistent nor indicative that planning has major
organizational impact. None of the most visible potential benefits of
planning seem to be associated with performance, nor does effort
devoted to those things that planning does best seem to help performance in a consistent manner. Among characteristics of high performance is an apparent dependence on financial as opposed to strategic
criteria and a global approach to strategy development.

Organizational Planning Environment (table 10.16). These
items are significant only in the case of 1981 return on capital. Line
managers in finance and manufacturing support planning in the high
performers, and the atmosphere at plan review tends to be relaxed.

Table 10.15 (continued)

| | Return on Capital (percent) 1977-1981 | | | |
	Mean	Standard Deviation about Trend	1979	1981
Benefits of Planning				
Corporate planning adds value in:				
R&D		H		
Raw material procurement		L		
Financial management				L
Human resources				L
Marketing			H	
Planning:				
helps avoid risk				L
assures best use of scarce resources		H		L
encourages business development				L
helps identify financing needs	L	L	L	L
develops better financial data	M††			
suggests new business opportunities	M††	H	H	
Importance of Criteria for Judging Businesses				
Forecast net operating profit				L
Earnings/share projections				L
Market share forecasts				L
Market growth forecasts				L
Forecast ROI	L		L	L
Resource need forecasts	L		L	L
Short-term cash flow	L		L	L
Criteria Used for Business Investment:				
Not affected if market and GNP grow at same rate	H			H

†H, M, L indicates that high values of that measurement are associated with high (H), medium (M) or low (L) performance on the respective performance index.

††Non-monotonic

10.12.2.2 The Nonsignificant Variable Groups

The other three variable groups show only chance patterns of association with performance. The following discussion should thus be considered as merely suggestive of potentially useful areas for future research.

Information Inputs. Only one item has a significant relation to performance. (It is that downward transmission of forecasts characterizes firms with high average rates of return.) Chapter 3 indicates relatively little effort overall devoted to quality information, and this result may simply indicate that relatively inadequate information characterizes all of our firms.

Table 10.15 (continued)

| | Return on Capital (percent) 1977-1981 | | | |
	Mean	Standard Deviation about Trend	1979	1981
Criteria Used in Business Investment (continued)				
Differ for different market growth rates	L			
Differ for units with different ROI	M††			
Different criteria in different industries			L	
More weight on financials in slow growth markets			L	
Planning Effort				
Effort is devoted to macro-forecasts			M††	
Competitive analysis:				
is done by corporate planning			H	H
focuses on product analysis			H	H
focuses on cost structure				L
Effort is devoted by Planning to help:				
Develop corporate goals				L
Corporate strategies				L
Quality of thinking				L
Developing and writing plan				L
Second level goal formulation				L
Integrating corporate and second level plans				L
Developing second level strategies		M††		L

†H, M, L indicates that high values of that measurement are associated with high (H), medium (M) or low (L) performance on the respective performance index.

††Non-monotonic

Planning Process Outputs (table 10.17). The high performers appear to have corporate plans that are rich and comprehensive, as well as multiple, goal-oriented second-level plans.

    Planning Outputs/Performance Interface (table 10.18). Again, a picture of the use of plans as guideposts as opposed to control devices by the high performers emerges. Performance is more tightly checked against the plan by low performing firms, which also have a greater tendency to tie compensation to short-term performance.

Table 10.15 (continued)

| | Return on Capital (percent) 1977-1981 | | | |
	Mean	Standard Deviation about Trend	1979	1981
Coordination				
Short- and long-term plans developed simultaneously	M††			M††
Human resources linked to corporate plan			L	
Long range plans developed independently				H
Marketing coordinated with corporate plan			H	L
Acquisition planning done by Corporate Planning			L	
Corporate planning is coordinated with production and marketing planning	M		L	
Review of Plans				
Corporate Planning has authority:				
In revision of second level plans	M††		L	
To accept and reject second level plans	M††			
To develop review procedures	M††			L
Globalness				
Production strategies are developed worldwide	H			
Marketing strategies are developed worldwide	H,M			

†H, M, L indicates that high values of that measurement are associated with high (H), medium (M) or low (L) performance on the respective performance index.

††Non-monotonic

10.13 Planning/Performance Contingency Relationships

Contingent/performance studies seek to explain organizational performance by means of the concept of "fit," in contrast to the universalistic/performance focus taken thus far in this chapter. Research in the universalistic tradition seeks direct relationships between planning and performance. Contingency theory states that "it depends." For example, the contingency theorist believes that a particular type

Table 10.16
Performance and Organizational Planning Environment:
Significant Relationships†

	Return on Capital (percent) 1977-1981			
	Mean	Standard Deviation about Trend	1979	1981
Plan review atmosphere is:				
Relaxed		M††		H
Confrontational				L
Tense	L			
Planning is resisted by:				
Finance	L		L	L
Manufacturing	L			L
Problems in planning are:				
Organizational	M††			
Procedural		H		
with Uncertainty				H
Second level planner reports to operating officer	H		H	
Second level management is involved in planning department				L
Feeling of teamwork in planning department				L
Poor definition of chains of command in planning				M††
Line management views planning:				
as a way to satisfy corporate	L			
as a way to develop action programs				L
as a creative exercise				L
Planning faces changing problems				M††
People familiar with portfolio ideas				L
Access to plan for:				
senior staff		L		
second level management		L		
Second level managers are involved in corporate strategy		H		L

†H, M, L indicates that high values of that measurement are associated with high (H), medium (M) or low (L) performance on the respective performance index.

††Non-monotonic

of planning demands a particular organization structure or strategy for optimum performance, rather than there being one best way to plan.

Much research in the past 10 years has been framed in the contingency tradition. Among the many studies are Lawrence and Lorsch (1967), Pennings (1975), and Child (1975) on environment and organization structure; Hambrick and Lei (1985) on environment and strategy; and Wright, Capon, Farley, and Hulbert (1985) on strategy and organizational processes.

Table 10.17
Performance and Planning Process Outputs:
Significant Relationships†

| | Return on Capital (percent) 1977-1981 | | | |
	Mean	Standard Deviation about Trend	1979	1981
Corporate plan:				
Updated annually			H	
Update more frequently			M††	M††
Comprehensiveness			H	
Contains Market analysis			H	
Contains second-level strategies		L		
Contains mission				L
Contains environmental analysis	H		H	
Contains forecasts and budgets	L			
Second-level plans:				
Number	H			H
Contain goals and objectives	H			H
Budgets integrated into long range plan				H,M
Contain contingencies		L		
Third level plans are prepared	M††			

†H, M, L indicates that high values of that measurement are associated with high (H), medium (M) or low (L) performance on the respective performance index.

††Non-monotonic

Relatively few studies directly address contingent effects in planning/performance relationships. Although they do not investigate such relationships explicitly, both Thune and House (1970) and Fulmer and Rue (1974) (Rue and Fulmer 1973) claim a positive economic impact of planning for some industry and product groups but not for others. Furthermore, a comparison of Robinson and Pearce's (1983) study of small banks, which found no relationship between planning and performance, with Wood and LaForge's (1979, 1981) study of large banks, in which a significant positive relationship is identified, suggests that size may be an important mediating variable. Finally, in associated work on the comprehensiveness of strategic decision processes, Fredrickson (1984) found a positive relationship between comprehensiveness and performance in stable environments, whereas Fredrickson and Mitchell (1984) found a negative relationship in unstable environments.

326 Integration

Table 10.18
Performance and Planning Outputs/Performance Interface:
Significant Relationships†

| | Return on Capital (percent) 1977-1981 | | | |
	Mean	Standard Deviation about Trend	1979	1981
Corporate goals provide motivation				H
Goal failure caused by:				
Wrong goals	H			
Competition	L			L
Regulation	L	L	L	
Environment	L			
Failure to reach goals caused by:				
Technological change		H		
Organization structure		H		
Incentive compensation:				
Subjective at Second Level	M††	L		
Based on short-term project at second level			M††	
Stock options			L	L
Based on Long-Range Goals	L			
Performance review:				
Involves numerical procedures		M††		
Involves corporate goals		M††		
Second Level goals			L	L
Involves achievement of strategic objectives				L
Plan review:				
Involves considerable effort	M††			
Is monthly		M††		H

†H, M, L indicates that high values of that measurement are associated
with high (H), medium (M) or low (L) performance on the respective
performance index.

††Non-monotonic

Investigation of contingencies in our case would involve examination of the extent to which planning, in combination with environment, strategy, organization structure, and organizational climate, leads to superior performance.

10.13.1 NATURE OF THE TEST

Performance contingencies were investigated by seeking significant interactions between the Planning Category system and the four sets of scales dealing with environment, strategy, organization structure, and organizational climate. The approach was a two-way (5x2) ANOVA with five levels of planning category (Corporate Strategic, Division Strategic, Corporate Financial, Divisional Financial, Non-Planners) and two levels (high/low) on each scale obtained by median splits. The 28 scales and four performance measures provided a total of 112 tests. Other approaches to fit that involve the Planning groups (chapter 9) are discussed in chapter 11. In this "interaction" approach to the examination to fit (Drazin and Van de Ven 1985, Van de Ven and Drazin 1985), we looked for significant interaction effects in the ANOVA.

10.13.2 RESULTS

The four sets of probabilities for the interactions, one each for the four performance measures, are displayed in table 10.19. Twenty-one of the 112 interactions are significant at $\alpha = .05$ in these bivariate tests. The significant results are associated with main ef-

Table 10.19

P-Values for Performance Interactions of Planning Category System
with Environment, Strategy, Organization Structure,
and Organizational Climate Scales

| | Return on Capital (percent) | | | |
| | 1979-1981 | | | |
	Mean	Standard Deviation about Trend	1979	1981
Environment				
Uncertainty	.91	.66	.96	.39
Change	.84	.38	.87	.78
Hostility	.14	.35	.57	.18
Strategy				
Internal Innovation	.85	.62	.85	.83
Acquisition	.03	.01	.05	.29
Divestiture	.96	.55	.73	.97
International Posture	.03	.05	.17	.11
Industrial Goods	.50	.20	.65	.67
Scale	.00	.34	.00	.07
International Marketing	.99	.19	.82	.37
Explicit Growth/Share Strategy	.90	.95	.79	.25
New Product Strategy	.13	.15	.30	.24
Explicit Segment Strategy	.00	.58	.01	.03
Organization Structure				
Entrepreneurial Incentives	.58	.44	.89	.23
Task Forces	.00	.72	.00	.05
Resource Sharing	.05	.06	.05	.86
Interdivisional Communication	.64	.59	.26	.85
Decentralization	.67	.42	.40	.60
Insider Influence	.00	.51	.01	.05
Organizational Interdependency	.32	.58	.79	.08
Organizational Specialization	.96	.99	.89	.69
Organizational Climate				
Entrepreneurialness	.99	.85	.93	.89
Performance Orientation	.00	.20	.01	.01
Line-Staff Interaction	.90	.09	.71	.52
Organizational Contentment	.35	.53	.59	.66
Participative Decision Making	.42	.21	.49	.69
Organizational Fluidity	.50	.52	.66	.48
Delegated Responsibility	.41	.92	.19	.91

fects (not reported here) and cluster in the planning and strategy, and planning and organization structure interactions. There are no significant planning and environment interactions. The results indicate the presence of some contingencies, but they do not support two-way contingency theory as a complete explanation.[8]

10.14 Summary

This chapter examines the relationship of planning to performance in a number of ways; generally little relationship is found. We acknowledge that the results from the different approaches are related since the same data are used repeatedly.

Our goal was to exhaust as nearly as possible the options for assessing the impact of planning on performance, given the data available to us. We have made a rather exhaustive attempt to assess the impact of planning on return on capital; we looked at contemporaneous return, lagged return, mean return, and variability in return. We were unable to find a systematic, significant impact of planning on ROC or variability of ROC, though various measurements of planning were employed: self-reports; deductive, inductive, and combination planning category systems; planning process summary measures; and planning function elements. At most, there are some weak indications that better planning practice may be associated with better performance and some even weaker indications that it may reduce variability. Taking mean return and variability in return together, however, the strongest result obtained was for a rate of return adjusted by variability in which the more sophisticated planners in general performed somewhat better.[9] The relative paucity of results should not, however, be taken as an indication that planning is of no benefit, though it does indicate that planning, even if practiced "well" according to conventional wisdom, is not a quick fix for low returns. In addition, there was only very weak evidence of impact of two-way contingent relationships (interactions) between planning, and environment, strategy, organization structure, and organizational climate on performance.

On the other hand, there do appear to be characteristics of planning, particularly those involving organization, associated with firms that perform relatively well in terms of mean ROC. Belief in the key strategic elements underlying portfolio analysis (high growth and high share) is associated with high performance, even though use of the portfolio tools themselves is not. Planning by the high performers is more professional and involves more participation by line management. Plans in firms which perform well are only loosely linked together; plans are used as guideposts rather than as control devices, and review, while regular, is relatively casual. These results are consistent with the conclusions of Peters and Waterman (1982) (among others) that planning is best viewed as one means to the end of developing more effective strategies.

Finally, these results should be seen in the context of the extant research on the relationships between organization and performance, which we noted in chapter 7. The evidence for relationships between organization structure variables, whether direct or contingent, and performance is not strong. In this light, perhaps it is too much to expect that a midrange organization design variable such as planning would be directly related to performance. Furthermore, as we discussed in the beginning of this chapter, there is some reason to believe that missionary zeal of some researchers may have been, in part, responsible for some of the positive planning-performance results found in earlier studies.

Our reviews of performance-related studies in chapters 5, 6, and 7 suggest that the determinants of performance are extremely complex, though there is some indication that strategy has a larger role to play than environment, planning, or organization. In chapter 11 we explore some more complex relationships between planning and performance, simultaneously considering environment, strategy, organization structure, and organizational climate.

NOTES

1. A few of the more recent studies have, however, attempted to capture more of the complexity of planning. Wood and LaForge (1979) and Leontiades and Tezel (1980) each tested relationships in which three levels of planning comprehensiveness were identified (including nonplanners), and Kallman and Shapiro (1978) identified five different planning levels. Welch (1984) distinguished between strategic planning at the corporate level and at the division level, and Grinyer and Norburn (1974) focused on different aspects of planning.

2. There has been some controversy over Armstrong's use of Terpstra's evaluation scale (Foster 1985, Armstrong 1986).

3. One firm was dropped from the performance analyses on account of its exceptionally low ROC and high variability in ROC throughout the period. It experienced particular idiosyncratic turmoil at this time. When included, it caused a major distortion

in the results, and in the cases of the Planning Category and Planning group analysis it shifted the orders in a major way. It was classified as a Corporate Financial Planner and Fully Integrated planner respectively.

4. See Bowman (1980) for the first of a series of papers (including Figenbaum and Thomas 1986) which discuss findings of positive association between return and risk.

5. Variability about growth trend was used, rather than variability about the mean, to avoid penalizing firms that were experiencing changes in profitability. Growth trend, determined from simple linear regression, was used rather than year-to-year changes to avoid problems associated with negative numbers and observations around the zero point. For absolute performance measures, an adjusted growth trend, obtained by dividing the simple growth trend by the mean, was also employed.

6. Factor analysis of these items produced a clean four-factor solution. The factors were (1) variability (about mean and trend) of return measures, (2) variability about trend, and growth of absolute measures, (3) growth of return measures, (4) mean of return measures.

7. The standard deviations of the adjusted performance measures for the groupings in each case were, in order: Planning Categories – 45.9, 14.7, 15.4, 4.4, 27.2, Planning groups – 36.4, 28.4, 12.4, 12.8, 25.2, Combination Planning groups – 48.6, 15.6, 13.2, 17.4, 10.6, 25.2.

8. Note that these tests were for two-way planning/performance contingencies. It is possible that some higher order interactions may be present; this possibility is investigated in chapter 11.

9. The results are consistent with a "good firm-level strategic management" explanation of findings of positive association between return and risk (Bowman 1980, Figenbaum and Thomas 1986).

Chapter 11

Summary and Synthesis

Our aim in this chapter is to summarize the results of the study and to attempt to synthesize them. We do not try to document each result in detail but rather highlight and pull together the major findings. Detailed results are available in the chapters noted throughout this summary. We follow with documented suggestions for future research and with managerial implications of our findings.

11.1 An Overview of the Study

The central focus of this study is on the planning practices of major manufacturing corporations headquartered in the Eastern half of the United States. We had reason to believe that U.S. firms were more likely to have developed planning systems than firms located elsewhere and that the manufacturing sector, because of high capital intensity compared with other sectors, was in the lead in terms of advanced forms of planning. By focusing our attention on a sample drawn from the *Fortune* 500, we hoped to be able to study the most sophisticated planning practices.

Few of the firms in our sample frame refused to participate, so nonresponse bias was not a problem. Interviews were held with the chief corporate planner (or with an executive with similar responsibilities) and with one assistant in each of the 113 sample firms. Our results thus reflect the views of planning personnel and should be seen in that light. Planning personnel were, however, the most appropriate group of interviewees for a detailed study of planning, though we would have liked to validate the responses by interviewing others in the organizations. Limited resources put the trade-off between more observations per firm versus more firms solidly on the side of more firms for this phase of our work.

The questionnaires, which required almost a year to develop and pretest, were based on intensive study of the literature on management in general and on planning in particular. The questionnaires contained approximately 500 measurements on all phases of planning. In addition, we were interested in the relationships between firms' planning systems and their environments, strategies, organization structures, and organizational climates, so nearly 400 additional measures were taken in these areas. Financial performance data came from *Value Line.* (Appendices I and II contain, respectively, descriptions of how the questionnaires were developed and the questionnaires themselves.)

Analysis was performed on a number of levels – with the individual measurements (chapters 3, 5, 6, and 7), with scales developed as summary measures (chapters 4 and 8), and with statistical groupings of similar firms (chapter 9). In general, the results from all approaches to analysis were similar, so our descriptive summaries of planning (section 11.2), of the relationships between planning and environment, strategy, organization structure, and organizational climate (section 11.3), and of how planning relates to performance (section 11.4) blend results from the several analytic streams. A more quantitative summary follows (section 11.5), which also includes a description of how our results fit into major streams of research on management.

11.2 How Do the Firms Plan?

11.2.1 CLASSIFICATION OF PLANNING

Seventy of our 113 firms reported that they did longer term corporate planning. However, our assessment of the planning literature (chapter 2) made it clear that a simple Plan-No Plan dichotomy would not capture the complexity of actual planning practices. A method of classifying firms' planning was developed, using criteria designed to answer three questions (chapter 2):

1. Does the firm plan at all?
2. Does the firm's planning involve added value at the corporate level, or does planning basically take place at lower levels?

3. Can the firm's planning be characterized as strategic on the basis of the contents of its plans and on the criteria used in decision-making for long-run benefits, or is planning mainly financially oriented? Strategic criteria include such factors as market growth and strength of the firm's business position.

Based on these questions, a classification scheme for longer term planning consisting of five categories was developed. Corporate Strategic Planners, the most advanced, do strategic planning at the corporate level; Division Strategic Planners plan strategically but do not add significant value to their plans at the corporate level; Corporate Financial Planners plan at the corporate level, but their planning is characterized by a heavy emphasis on financial projections and budgets; Division Financial Planners are similarly characterized by heavy emphases on financial issues, but they do not integrate the lower level plans at the corporate level; the Non-Planners do not plan at all. Application of the criteria to the 113 sample firms resulted in the following categorizations:

Planning Categories	Number of Firms
Corporate Strategic Planners	24
Division Strategic Planners	37
Corporate Financial Planners	34
Division Financial Planners	11
Non-Planners	7

Several self-reported "corporate planners" in fact planned only at lower levels, and their "corporate" plans consisted primarily of lower level plans bound together. Several other firms that claimed to do strategic planning in fact operated complex financial budgeting systems that had few characteristics of real planning, save investment of great effort. A few firms made it clear that they did no long-term planning.

Another method of classifying planning systems and practices based on statistical clustering of similar firms (chapter 9) produced a related five-group empirical classification of planning.

Finally, a "soft" model of planning produced a logical flow – that is, a structure of inputs (information, planning tools, planning organization) seemed to feed into the planning process (planning activities, organizational planning environment) to produce a series of plans implemented and later reviewed against actual performance (chapter 4).

11.2.2 HAS THE RECEIVED WISDOM ON PLANNING
BEEN IMPLEMENTED?

In general, it appears that much of the conventional wisdom on planning has been at least partially implemented (chapter 3). The firms that planned at all generally committed significant human and financial resources to planning, though proportionately less than similar firms based elsewhere – in Australia, for example.

The chief corporate planner generally had a long record of service with the company but by and large had limited experience with planning. Planning personnel were generally happy with their jobs, though they did not expect planning to be a career path. Their influence on the planning process was considerable, both through control of administrative matters such as format and schedule and of planning content by control of assumptions used in planning. The goals and objectives of planning were, however, only moderately clear. Although they tended to report to the most senior levels in the firm, the chief corporate planners reviewed and criticized lower level plans rather than having the authority to accept or reject them.

The most important influence on planning was the CEO, particularly in terms of setting goals and objectives, developing strategies, and approving the final plan. Boards of directors had little influence. Senior line management was in general very influential, especially for developing second-level missions and setting second-level goals. Negotiation characterized the goal and strategy formulation process of many firms, and line management was, on the whole, reported to be positive about planning.

Forecasting effort for planning was focused in the traditional areas of near-term industry demand and the domestic economy, and these forecasts were the most extensively transmitted to lower levels. Much less effort went into forecasting (and transmitting data on) sociocultural, technological, and human resource environments. Competitive analysis was not a major activity of corporate planning. Surprisingly, the much-discussed conceptual frameworks for developing strategic plans (such as various portfolio models) were viewed as having relatively little influence, and formal decision models and computer systems were by no means universally employed.

Planning was, however, viewed as having improved firms' resource allocation processes and as having aided in dealing with uncertainty and risk. In general, firms made budgetary distinctions between expenditures for short-run and long-run benefits. Criteria for evaluating capital expenditure proposals contained elements associated with contemporary strategic planning (e.g., market growth market share), as well as considerable emphasis on the track record of managers supporting the proposal. However, conventional financial criteria still appear to be the dominant force in capital decisions.

Firms claimed to put more effort into long-range planning (mostly with five-year time horizons) and into acquisition and divestiture planning, than into operational planning. Planning was not, however, generally global, and contingency planning was rare. Many second-level plans were prepared in standard formats, but coordination of different types of plan was limited for both functional plans (except financial) and for plans with different time horizons.

Most firms required some sort of formal analysis of variance between plan and actual performance. Incentive compensation schemes were mostly present for second-level managers; achieving short-term profits or other short-term goals dominated long-term measures such as achieving strategic objectives.

Not surprisingly, the 24 Corporate Strategic Planners have been particularly effective in developing planning practices that come closest to those desirable under the received wisdom about "good" planning. Corporate Strategic Planners devote more effort to forecasting and internal transmission of data, though they too focus their efforts on near-term industry demand and on the domestic economy rather than on broader social and other environmental factors. They are the most extensive users of all analytical planning devices, especially portfolio models for which usage is the greatest for the sample, though still modest. The Corporate Strategic Planners put more effort into long-range planning, tend to plan for longer time horizons, and are more global in their planning. However, like the others, they do little contingency planning.

The resource allocation decisions of the Corporate Strategic Planners are especially well integrated into the planning process, and these firms feel that planning has aided in dealing with uncertainty and risk. For the Corporate Strategic Planners, planning is a device by which conflicting expectations are resolved; it is an adaptive, evolving learning activity that plays a central role in the firm's communication network. The Corporate Strategic Planners are the heaviest users of strategic criteria in resource allocation decisions, but even they use financial criteria extensively.

The Corporate Strategic Planners coordinate their various plans to a greater degree than the other firms do, and planning personnel seem better integrated into the organization. Line managers in these firms spend the most time on long-range planning and seem particularly positive about planning; they are also more familiar with contemporary planning ideas and take an active interest in the output and recommendations of the corporate planning group. Although the CEO is heavily involved in the planning process in the Corporate Strategic Planners, bottom-up planning and negotiation characterize both goal and strategy formulation.

Review of performance against plan is more regular for the Corporate Strategic Planners, and performance criteria in general are more heavily emphasized. However, even for these firms, short-term criteria tend to dominate longer term considerations.

11.2.3 HOW DOES PLANNING HELP?

Planning helps the firm both to *adapt* to environmental change, as well as to *integrate* operations, to encourage units to pull toward corporate goals and to gain from synergies (chapter 4). Overall, the Corporate Strategic Planners have both the most adaptive and most integrative planning systems. Corporate Strategic Planners demonstrate adaptation by preparing the most nearly comprehensive plans at both corporate and lower levels of the organization. They gather more environmental information, do more competitive analysis, and use models to analyze data. They have a strategic and global orientation to planning and use multiple and strategic criteria for resource allocation. Although the patterns are less strong for integrative measurements, the Corporate Strategic Planners show good integration of corporate and functional plans, substantial internal information flows, broad participation in planning (especially from line management) in a negotiation-oriented planning process, good integration of planners who report at high levels, a positive view of planning by line management, formalized systems at corporate and lower levels, and regular reviews of plans and goals.

11.3 The Context of Planning: Relationships Between Planning and Environment, Strategy, Organization Structure, and Organizational Climate

A comprehensive study of planning must consider the context – that is both the external environment and the organization structure and organizational climate with which the planning system interfaces. A study of planning must also examine strategy, probably the major output of planning.

11.3.1 HOW DOES PLANNING RELATE TO THE ENVIRONMENT?

Taken as a whole, our results do not indicate a strong link between planning and the environment. All firms tended to agree about key features of historical and anticipated demand, competitive climate, and input factors (financial, human, and raw material) (chapter 5). There is some evidence that firms with more advanced planning systems are more confident about anticipating their future environments, and the Corporate Strategic Planners tended to have greater confidence than the other firms (chapter 8). The Corporate Strategic Planners also tended to operate in environments characterized by market change and product/technological change and to have more dominant market positions than other firms. Finally, "good" planning (chapter 9) was associated with avoidance of difficult environments.

These are at best weak results, however, and they certainly do not support the existence of the strong interactions (contingencies) between environment and planning suggested by many authors.

11.3.2 HOW DO PLANNING AND STRATEGY RELATE?

There is, however, a stronger relationship between planning and strategy. Since the study is cross-sectional, we cannot say that a particular type of planning leads to a particular type of strategy, but we can say that a particular type of planning and a particular type of strategy tend to occur together. The Corporate Strategic Planners differed from the other firms in several important ways, including the fact that they were larger (chapters 6 and 8).

Corporate Direction. Although there were no differences regarding missions, Corporate Strategic Planners were more likely than other firms to have qualitative goals. They were also more likely to have specific quantitative goals and to adjust them more frequently, especially for inflation (chapter 6).

Market and Entry Strategy. Corporate Strategic Planners were most likely to espouse popular strategic theories of seeking high market shares, high growth markets, product differentiation, scale economies, and patent protection (chapters 6 and 8). They invested more resources in R&D required for internal innovation. They had a greater tendency to seek new products and new markets and a lesser tendency to focus on older products for existing markets, even though this was the most popular growth strategy for the sample overall. They anticipated even more emphasis on new products and new markets in the future. They tended to be neither late entrants nor fast followers in growing markets, viewing themselves as first-to-market and at the cutting edge of technology.

Diversification. Corporate Strategic Planners did not differ markedly from the other firms in terms of industry mix, though there was a tendency for them to be less involved in raw and semifinished materials and more involved in capital goods (chapter 6). They were marginally more likely to obtain revenues from products early in the life cycle and to follow a diversification strategy involving closely related businesses.

International Posture. Across the entire sample, approximately a quarter of sales revenues were generated abroad, slightly more for the Corporate Strategic Planners. The Corporate Strategic Planners were, however, more spread out around the world for production and sales, consistent with their greater aggressiveness to market existing products and technologies abroad (chapters 6 and 8).

Acquisition and Divestiture. The sample as a whole had been active in both acquisition and divestiture; Corporate Strategic Planners made more acquisitions of greater overall size.

Overall, planning and strategy are related. The firms that do more advanced planning tend to be larger, to focus on new products, to seek growth markets and economies of scale, and to diversify internationally. These appear to be managed strategic differences, rather than just historical accidents.

11.3.3 HOW DO PLANNING AND ORGANIZATION STRUCTURE RELATE?

We found only scattered relationships between planning and organization structure. (All firms in our study were divisionalized, so there was little opportunity to examine radically different organizational forms.) Corporate Strategic Planners were not different from the other firms in terms of numbers of organizational levels or numbers of organizational units at each level (chapter 7). They did not differ in how they organized for new products or in the degree of interdivisional resource sharing. Corporate Strategic Planners were more likely to employ matrix structures internationally, product/international division structures in particular. Corporate Strategic Planners had good interdivisional communication and tended toward organizational specialization (chapter 8). Overall, though, advanced planning systems neither determine nor are determined by particular types of organization structure.

11.3.4 HOW DO PLANNING AND ORGANIZATIONAL CLIMATE RELATE?

Organizational climate is more related to planning than organization structure. On the basis of several approaches to measurement, the Corporate Strategic Planners had more entrepreneurial climates, strong performance orientation, good line-staff interaction, organizational contentment and loyalty, participative decision making, and organizational fluidity. It is useful to notice, though, that the sample did *not* in general consider itself entrepreneurial. Firms with marginal planning systems or none at all tended to be rigidly bureaucratic (chapter 9).

Overall, firms embracing more advanced planning practices generally enjoy more "positive" climates. We are inclined to speculate that the increased communication and openness of internal environment that flows from an advanced planning system results in more positive organizational climates, though this is conjecture.

11.3.5 SUMMARY

The overall pattern of relationships between planning and environment, strategy, organization structure, and organizational climate is mixed; 'some patterns are quite strong and others quite weak.

Despite the popularity of contingency notions in the organization literature, we found little evidence of interaction of environment and planning system design. In chapter 5, we suggest the possibility of managerial choice, slack resources, and competitive pressure as factors that lead to a particular planning system design. On the basis of our results, there is every reason to believe that the major force driving design of planning systems is received wisdom about effective planning, as modified by firms' particular needs.

Relationships of planning to organization structure are also weak. Somewhat stronger relationships are found between planning and organizational climate, and planning and strategy. Advanced planning systems tend to be found with more positive organizational climates and with growth-oriented strategic thrusts. In neither case, however, can we be sure of the direction of the relationships. The coexistence may simply reflect the fact that such companies are populated with more accomplished managers, though there is little in the literature to indicate a systematic tendency of such managers to congregate.

11.4 Does Long-Term Strategic Planning Pay?

Regardless of the relationships between planning and external and internal aspects of the firm, a more important issue for managers is how planning affects economic performance. This is the key question that our study was designed to address. The unfortunate fact is that we cannot provide a definitive answer (chapter 10).

From a strictly statistical perspective, the Corporate Strategic Planners did not earn significantly greater returns-on-capital (annual or five-year average) than the other Planning Categories, though they did have higher returns than other Categories that embraced any type of corporate or strategic planning. (The Non-Planners performed best, though when one extraordinarily high-performing Non-Planner was removed, the Corporate Strategic Planners also outperformed the Non-Planners.) We used other approaches to try to identify planning-performance relationships, including self-reports, statistical groupings of similar firms, and various measures of planning. These produced no clearer patterns.

These results should, however, be interpreted in the light of the demanding nature of statistical criteria. The inherent variability in the performance measurements would require a 3 percent superiority in return-on-capital to produce statistical significance for one Planning Category. Such a large effect would be likely to produce wholesale copying of successful planning practices. Furthermore, unlike most studies of planning-performance relationships, we have not attempted to control for such key factors as industry differences, which no doubt produce variability in returns across firms. We made this choice because we believe that a key task of strategic planning is choice of markets and industries, so study of strategy and planning within one industry is overly narrow in our view.

Nonetheless, based on the average firm, profit differences for the Corporate Strategic Planners outweigh the budget of the average planning department. Of course, the planning department budget understates the resources committed to planning, many of which are the opportunity costs of line managers' time; on the other hand, managers in these large multimarket, multiproduct firms would have to commit time to resource allocation decisions even in the absence of a planning system, so these opportunity costs are probably in the main unavoidable.

We did find a somewhat clearer tendency, though still not statistically significant, for the Corporate Strategic Planners to have lower variability in return-on-capital. If risk aversion enters into the resource allocation of firms like these (and risk aversion did seem to characterize the sample in general), the impact of lower variability in performance may be important. On the basis of one measure, Corporate Strategic Planners earned significantly higher returns adjusted for variability than all other Categories that did any planning and more than the Non-Planners.

Finally, there was little evidence of any interactions between planning and environment, strategy, organization structure, or organizational climate that systematically affected performance. This is an important result, given the currency of contingent theories of planning.

11.5 Synthesis

This section develops a quantitative summary of results to support the general discussion earlier in the chapter. Patterns in results from Planning (chapter 3), Environment (5), Strategy (6), and Organization Structure and Organizational Climate (7) are assembled from bivariate analyses based on individual measurements. This extensive array of measurements also forms the basis for sets of scales (chapters 4 and 8), and in turn for "similar" groups of firms based on clusters of the scales (chapter 9). We need to be sure both that our measurement is appropriate and that our "empirical results" are not based on randomly significant findings. We have addressed these issues by attempting synthesis in terms of design of measurements, in summaries of statistical tests on individual items, and in terms of patterns in scales formed from those items. We also synthesize our results on how planning affects performance. We then put the results in context of four major research traditions.

11.5.1 MEASUREMENT AS SYNTHESIS
In a broad sense, the whole study is an exercise in synthesis. The original goal was to gain insight into the impact of planning. The literature on planning was carefully surveyed (chapter 3) to form the

basis for the 501 questionnaire items that comprise the description of planning. While we could not hope to measure other key phenomena in such detail, we nonetheless developed nearly 400 measures to calibrate key components of environment (literature review in chapter 5), strategy (review in chapter 6), and organization structure and organizational climate (reviews in chapter 7). In total, these measurements constitute the broadest single simultaneous synthesis involving all these areas that we know of.

We have also attempted to take an eclectic view of how planning is practiced in large U.S. corporations; how it relates to environment, strategy, organization structure, and organizational climate; and how it impacts performance. While certain new results emerged, the pattern of bivariate findings is generally consistent with other studies of management and firm performance. There are, however, a number of problems that we candidly recognize. We have attempted to explore the possibility of spurious relationships or intervening variables, though much remains to be done along these lines. We have also been careful to note that the various analyses are partially based on the same measurements, so overinterpretation of results is a concern. In addition, the relatively small sample size (113) compared to the number of measurements (nearly 1,000) was a continuing problem.

The possibility of measurement error abounds, despite the effort invested in establishing appropriate measurement procedures from the various contributing literatures. Similarly, errors of omission are possible, though we feel it unlikely (because of our extensive use of the literature) that whole areas of explanation for our results have been omitted. Final shortcomings are that our measurements are seen through the eyes of the planners and that validation of their responses by line managers was not possible. However, whereas the planners' view may be myopic, by the very nature of their jobs they must (or at least should) take a broad view of the firm's business and also have their fingers on important corporate pulses.

11.5.2 PATTERNS OF SIGNIFICANCE IN TESTS ON PLANNING

Our first step is to establish that our general results discussed earlier in this chapter do not simply come from keying in on a subset of results that are significant merely by chance. We approach this problem through assessment of overall patterns of results. For most individual measurements on planning, there were prior bases (as discussed in chapters 1 and 2) to expect that Corporate Strategic

Planners would be at extreme points in distributions (e.g., strategic planners should be more open to information from the environment, should be more likely to use portfolio and other models). Table 11.1 contains a summary count of results of bivariate tests in chapter 3, along with analysis of the positions and patterns of significance in differences between Corporate Strategic Planners and the other Categories.

Table 11.1
Patterns of Results for Corporate Strategic
Planners on Planning Items and Scales

Planning Items	Total	Number of Variables With Hypotheses Indicating Order of Planning Categories	With Corporate Strategic Planners in Expected Extreme Position	With Corporate Strategic Planners in Expected Extreme Position and Significant Differences among Planning Categories
Planning Inputs				
Information Inputs	27	27	19*	11**
Planning Tools	54	50	19*	10**
Planning Organization	106	76	24*	19**
Planning Process				
Planning Activities	146	121	63*	24**
Organizational Planning Environment	58	37	12*	6**
Planning Outputs				
Planning Process Outputs	69	54	24*	7**
Planning Outputs/Performance Interface	41	30	12*	4**
Planning Scales				
Adaptive	13	13	10*	10**
Integrative	30	28	19*	11**
Summary Based on Factor Scores of Adaptive and Integrative Scales	5	4	4*	4**

*Significantly more than would be expected by chance using a rank test, $\alpha = .05$.

**Significantly more than would be expected by chance using a binomial approximation, $\alpha = .05$.

The overall patterns indicate results stronger than random, so the individual substantive results discussed in chapter 3 do not appear to reflect merely a search among a large number of relationships for that handful that are significant by chance. There is little doubt that pattern exists in the results, though by no means were all of our expectations confirmed for the null hypothesis of no difference among Planning Categories is accepted for the majority of items.

That so many expectations were not supported may be partly due to difficulties with the basic Planning Category scheme developed in chapter 2, though experiments with alternative schemes (e.g., with the self-reports discussed in chapters 2 and 10) produced less than satisfactory results. Also, both the phenomena we are trying to measure and the interrelationships among them are extraordinarily complex.

To deal with these problems of complexity in the analysis of individual items, we summarized key phenomena by developing scales from sets of items. Scales tend to stabilize results, and it is much easier to manage analysis of the smaller group of summary scales than the items from which the scales were developed. The scales also allowed us to examine the other Planning Categories in more detail, particularly the Non-Planners. A total of 43 scales were developed to summarize planning (chapter 4), 13 involving adaptive elements of planning and 30 involving integrative elements. Again, table 11.1 shows that Corporate Strategic Planners tend to occupy extreme positions on these scales. The results are certainly not random and are somewhat stronger than those for individual items, in part no doubt due to the tendency of scales to stabilize results.

Finally, of 5 summary planning scales developed from the 43 planning scales using factor analysis, 4 have Corporate Strategic Planners in the expected extreme positions and significance across the Planning Category System. Corporate Strategic Planners have the most adaptive and integrative planning systems. As regards the other categories, Corporate Financial Planners tend to have integrative planning, whereas Divisional Strategic Planners tend to have rather adaptive planning systems.

11.5.3 PLANNING AND ENVIRONMENT, STRATEGY, ORGANIZATION STRUCTURE, AND ORGANIZATIONAL CLIMATE

Paralleling the results on planning (section 11.5.2), a similar count of tests involving environment (chapter 5), strategy (chapter 6), and organization structure and organizational climate (chapter 7) is shown in table 11.2. As with the planning items, the Corporate Strategic Planners tend to occupy polar positions in a nonrandom pattern.

Table 11.2
Patterns of Results for Corporate Strategic Planners on Items
and Scales Measuring Environment, Strategy, Organization Structure,
and Organizational Climate

Individual Items	Total	With Corporate Strategic Planners in Extreme Position	With Corporate Strategic Planners in Extreme Position and Differences Significant among Planning Categories
Environment (Chapter 5)	31	14*	4
Strategy (Chapter 6)	92	32*	17**
Organization Structure (Chapter 7)	32	14*	4
Organizational Climate (Chapter 7)	51	28*	9**
Scales (Chapter 8)			
Environment	3	2*	0
Strategy	10	6*	3**
Organization Structure	8	6*	1
Organizational Climate	7	5*	1

*Significantly more than expected by chance using a rank test, α = .05

**Significantly more than expected by chance using a binomial approximation, α = .05

Scales were also developed from these items for environment (3 scales), strategy (10), organization structure (8) and organizational climate (7). Again, the Corporate Strategic Planners tend to occupy the extreme positions. As with planning, these results with the scales are also somewhat stronger than with the individual items, no doubt again related to the stabilization property of the scales. Again, however, there were no significant results for many items and scales.

An obvious implication of these mixed results is that, in a large set of studies, each attempting to focus on a bivariate hypothesis involving individual measurements of the type described here, many individual studies are doomed to failure. However, a whole collection of such successful and unsuccessful studies may weave a fabric of overall significance if their results can be assembled and considered as

Table 11.3
Patterns of Results for Planning and Performance

Tests Involving Classifications	Rankings on 5 Performance Measures
Deductively-Developed Planning Categories (5 groups from Chapter 2)	
Corporate Strategic	Rank first or second on all measures
Non-Planners	Rank first on three measures
Corporate Financial and Division Financial	No ranking higher than third; one or other ranks last on four measures
Inductively-Developed Planning Groups (5 groups from Chapter 9)	
Fully Integrated	No ranking lower than third; rank second on two measures
Extensive	Rank first on one measure; second on two measures
Not-at-All	Rank first on four measures
Seat-of-the-Pants	Rank last on three measures
Combination of Deductive and Inductive Planning Categories (6 combined groups from Chapter 9)	
Fully Integrated/Strategic	Rank first or second on four measures
Seat-of-the-Pants--Marginal/ Financial	Rank last on all measures

a set of imperfect replications of related studies (Farley, Lehmann, and Ryan 1982).

The results in tables 11.1 and 11.2 are best considered an approximation as they are based on the assumption of inter-item independence. However, the items in each variable group, while highly multidimensional (see, for example, discussion of the principal components of the seven groups of planning variables in chapter 4) are, in fact, not independent of one another. Furthermore, the individual significance tests used as the basis for tables 11.1 and 11.2 are generally bivariate or at most the result of two-way ANOVAs. Summary multivariate tests using all items are desirable, but not feasible, since the number of observations is so much smaller than the number of variables. Also infeasible is meaningful use of holdout samples since the number of observations is small (113) and the number of Corporate Strategic Planners even smaller (24).

Table 11.3 (continued)

Tests Involving Summary Indices	Number of Relationships with Performance Tested	Number Significant at α = .05
Planning Process Elements		
7 Principal Components (Chapter 4)	28	1
Planning Scales		
(Chapter 4)		
Adaptive	52	6
Integrative	120	16*

Tests for Differences on Different Items
for High, Middle and Poor Performers

Number of Groups	Number of Item Groups with Significant Number of Differences	Number of Tests Using These Item Groups	Number of Significant Tests at α = .10
7	4	16	8

*Significantly different than would be expected by chance under binomial approximation, α = .05.

11.5.4 PLANNING AND PERFORMANCE

We tried seven different ways to test the impact of planning on short- and medium-term performance, measured as return-on-capital, variability of return-on-capital, and return-on-capital per unit of variability. No clear statistical pattern emerged, though there were some interesting tendencies (chapter 10).

In three tests that grouped firms into planning classes, companies that did not plan on average outperformed all others. When one firm with a strong consumer franchise in one family of products is removed from the analysis, the superiority of Non-Planners fades. Nevertheless, that firm is in the sample and this conclusion is important.

On the other hand, in each of the tests (which are not, of course, independent), firms with "good" planning practices generally outperformed other planning groupings on most of the measures of performance that were used (table 11.3). Although the results were not significant, the consistency of higher performance from the better planners inclines us to believe that a real but weak performance phenomenon does exist.

We cannot say so much for tests involving statistical summaries of planning (chapter 4), either for the principal components from seven planning process groupings or for the planning scales.

Test results tend to be insignificant, and sign patterns are not at all consistent.

Finally, firms that perform well are similar in planning to firms that perform less well. However, in general, planning by the high performing firms was less bureaucratic, focusing more on organizational issues and less on the technical aspects of planning.

Our overall conclusion is that the relationships between planning and performance are weak at best but that there seems to be a tendency for better planning practice to be related to better performance.

11.5.5 SYNTHESIZING RESULTS IN TERMS OF RESEARCH PERSPECTIVE

Parts of our results fit into each of four different traditions of management research. The traditions involve pairings of perspective and objective:

Perspective:

Universalistic – there is a "best" way to plan, regardless of the situation. The research seeks such an "optimal" way to plan.

Contingent – the best way to plan depends on, for example, the nature of the environment. The research focuses on combinations (usually pairings) of conditions for good planning.

Objective:

Occurrence – this type of research seeks to describe how and when certain types of planning occur.

Performance – this type of research seeks to link planning with performance.

The four pairings of perspective and objective form traditions of management research. Figure 11.1 shows a summary of results related to these four types of research, together with the relevant chapters in the book.

11.5.5.1 Universalistic/Occurrence

Universalistic/occurrence studies focus on a single substantive area, in our case on planning. Examples of managerial research in this tradition are Chandler's (1962) development of a model of organizational growth, Wrigley's (1970), Rumelt's (1974) categorization of firms by means of frameworks of diversification, Hambrick's (1983a) study of environments, and the many studies referenced in chapter 2 that have measured various elements of company planning systems.

Many of the results presented in the book are of this type.

Objective of the Research	
Occurrence	Performance
Description of planning or its relationships other than performance	Detecting determinants of performance

Research Perspective

Universalistic	Universalistic/Occurrence	Universalistic/Performance
There is a "best" way to plan	Detailed description of planning reveals several distinct kinds of corporate and strategic planning (Chapters 3, 4 and 9)	There is only limited evidence that planning is related to performance (Chapter 10)
Contingent	Contingent/Occurrence	Contingent/Performance
The best way to plan depends on other things, such as environment or strategy	Significant differences in planning relate to strategy and organizational climate (Chapters 6, 7, 8 and 9), but less so to corporate environment or to organization structure (Chapters 5, 7, 8 and 9)	There is some evidence of complex partial relationships involving planning and performance, contingent on strategy and organization structure but not on environment or organizational climate (Chapter 10)

Figure 11.1

Summary of Results by Research Type

In chapter 3, we described planning practices for the sample, showing that 24 Corporate Strategic Planners (the most sophisticated group of our five-Category system of planners) were quite different. In chapter 4 we took more informationally efficient approaches by developing a soft model of the planning process and a series of planning scales based on the individual measurements on planning. Again, the Corporate Strategic Planners were quite different, but we were also able to show how Strategic Planners differ generally from Financial Planners and how Corporate and Division Planners also differ. Finally, in chapter 9, we took account of potential interrelationships in planning practices by statistically developing a set of Planning groups using the planning scales; these groups turned out to be quite similar to the Planning Categories developed in chapter 2.

11.5.5.2 Contingent/Occurrence

Contingent/occurrence studies seek to understand the relationships between two (sometimes more) elements (e.g., planning and environment) in terms of occurrence but do *not* consider performance. Research that falls into this category includes the work of Burns and Stalker (1961) on environment and organization structure, of Woodward (1965) on technology and organization structure, and of Chandler (1962), Channon (1973), Pavan (1972), Pooley-Dyas (1972),

Thanheiser (1972), and Miles and Snow (1978) on strategy and organization structure.

Our work in this tradition examined the set of relationships between planning and, respectively, environment (chapter 5), strategy (chapter 6), and organization structure and organizational climate (chapter 7). In chapter 8 we extended our analysis of these relationships by using summary scales. Finally, in chapter 9, we examined the relationships between inductively developed planning groups and similar groups based on environment, strategy, organization structure, and organizational climate. In general, we found planning related to strategy and organization climate, less so to organization structure, and (surprisingly), even less so to environment.

11.5.5.3 Universalistic/Performance

In this research tradition, choosing the "best" way to plan implies that good performance will follow. The work reviewed in chapter 10 on the direct relationship between planning and performance is primarily in this tradition. Much of the work of early management theorists (e.g., Taylor 1911, Fayol 1949, Weber 1947) also falls into this category, as does much of the empirical research on organization structure and performance reviewed by Dalton et al. (1980). Empirical work on corporate strategy and performance is included in the stream, notably studies that seek to link diversification strategy to performance (e.g., Rumelt 1974, 1982; Christensen and Montgomery 1981). Much of the work with the PIMS data base in which various business-level strategies are directly linked to financial performance (Schoeffler, Buzzell, and Heany 1974; Buzzell, Gale, and Sultan 1975) is also in this tradition, as is Peters and Waterman's (1982) volume on "excellent" companies. Chapter 10 primarily took a universalistic approach to the study of planning and performance. We sought to understand direct relationships between planning and performance at the levels of individual planning measures, planning scales, and for both the deductive Planning Category and inductive Planning group systems. In general, we found little hard statistical evidence of such universalistic relationships, though the sophisticated planners performed marginally better.

11.5.5.4 Contingent/Performance

Research in the contingent/performance stream seeks to explain performance by means of "fit". In its strong form, contingency theory states that, rather than choices on individual elements (e.g., planning and environment) determining performance, the individual elements must "fit" for good performance to be achieved. In a weaker form, contingency theory says that certain combinations of levels of two elements should bring returns over and above their additive individual effects. Discussions of contingencies often seem to confuse the stronger and weaker forms of the theory. There is little empirical work on planning in this tradition, though there is some in the PIMS studies combining, for example, impact of market share and product quality on performance.

In chapter 10, we found little evidence of performance contingency relationships involving planning and environment, and planning and organizational climate. There is some weak evidence of performance contingency relationships between planning and strategy, and planning and organization structure. Later in this chapter, we broaden our concept of contingency relationships in discussion of needs for future research. Results indicate only limited evidence of the existence of planning-performance contingencies of the type characterized in the literature.

11.6 Implications for Future Research

We view this study both as substantive research on strategic planning and as the beginning of system-level analysis of complex management practices, of which planning is only one. We have attempted to take a broad view of parts of the organization and the environment that interface with planning and that, together with planning, may affect longer term performance of large multiproduct, multimarket U.S. manufacturing corporations. Our effort to be broad probably led us to measure too many things and in excessive detail. A side benefit is, however, that the items in the questionnaires (appendix II) have now been used in practice and are available for use in replication and extension of the whole or parts of our study. Furthermore, almost half of the items in the questionnaires are not specific to planning and may be useful for study of various aspects of management and performance of large multiproduct, multimarket firms. As a result, we offer a set of suggestions for future research that, we believe, is unusually detailed and well documented.

11.6.1 FOLLOW-UP REPLICATIVE STUDY OF PLANNING

We need more work to validate and calibrate our results. The data we used are idiosyncratic views of managers in senior planning positions at one point in time. We need to investigate how planning develops over time to identify changes in companies' planning practices and, more precisely, the causes of those changes. Further-more, we need to corroborate our findings from other points of view – particularly from senior line managers and CEOs, who have been shown here to be the keys to successful planning.

The intriguing preliminary results about the few Non-Plan-ners (especially the single extraordinarily high performing firm) in our sample deserve follow-up in detail, presumably with a sample of firms further down in the *Fortune* list of companies. In particular, the means by which they develop and implement their strategies is of significant interest.

The wave of megamergers and strategic alliances that ac-companies the publication of this book makes some detailed clinical work attractive. We know, for example, that firms with quite dif-ferent approaches to planning are combining. We do not know what the surviving mode of planning will or should be.

Finally, the importance of strategic planning extends beyond application to large manufacturing firms based in the United States. For example, the rapid shifts that have accompanied de-regulation in some U.S. service industries such as banking, tele-communications, and airlines may produce conditions where massive shifts in resources, often across industry, must be accomplished quick-ly, in contrast to manufacturing, which may have the luxury of mov-ing more slowly. Similarly, only a minority of the world "500" manufacturing firms is U.S. based, and only cursory information is available about corporate or strategic planning in impmortant non-U.S.-based corporations. We also know little about the planning prac-tices in smaller firms.

11.6.2 FOLLOW-UP STUDIES ON PLANNING

Of course, all of the obvious deficiencies inherent in attempting to use a cross-sectional design to study a dynamic process are operative here. Our results apply to a particular point in time, though our hope is that identification of planning practice in early 1980, a time of considerable economic turmoil and high interest rates, offers a useful benchmark for comparison to a time when planners might face a calmer environment in the short term. Standard cross-sectional research paradigms tend to bias research in the direction of seeking contemporaneous effects. In our performance tests we have tried to take a somewhat broader window (up to five years), but we are very much aware that there is considerable uncertainty about not only how, but also when, planning affects performance.

An illustration of this problem is available in a comparison made in 1984 of the seven firms that did no planning in 1980 against the 24 Corporate Strategic Planners.

The Non-Planners. It is no surprise that some of our firms did no corporate or long-range planning; it is a surprise that there are only seven Non-Planners and that as a category they outperformed the other Planning Categories during the period of study. While few, they are diverse, including firms whose businesses are principally in consumer package goods, industrial products, raw and semifinished materials, and services. They do not have "superstar" book-author CEOs, but they are represented on the Peters-Waterman roster of "excellent" firms. As mentioned earlier, they are smaller, and they tend to be managed in a relatively tight, hierarchical, nonparticipative manner. They violated not only accepted wisdom on planning but also other premises of "modern" management of organizations.

However, by 1984 the seven Non-Planners offered a somewhat different picture. Three had disappeared by merger, one under duress. (Two of the 11 Division Financial Planners had also disappeared by merger.) The remaining four had nominal revenue increases averaging 35 percent for the five-year period 1979-1984 – an annual rate of growth of about 6 percent. The one firm identified in chapter 10 as an exceptional performer continued to earn in excess of 20 percent return-on-capital over the period, but the other three averaged less than 5 percent; for two of these, the 1979 ROC was the highest achieved in the 1974-1984 period.

The Corporate Strategic Planners. The 24 Corporate Strategic Planners are more diverse, representing a broad spectrum of industrial and consumer products and services. They are also represented on the Peters-Waterman "excellent" firms list. For these firms, 1984 was in many ways similar to 1979. Twenty-two of the 24 were still operating normally, 1 had filed for bankruptcy, and 1 disappeared in merger in the intervening period. Seven had higher returns-on-capital in 1984 than in 1979, 15 had lower returns, but none made a loss. Revenues had increased 54 percent for the group, an annual growth rate of about 9 percent and significantly more than for the Non-Planners. None earned as high a rate of return as the best performing Non-Planner.

The comparison is, of course, flawed, for we do not know to what extent the planning configurations we identified in 1980 were still in place in 1984. However, we have no evidence from the press to suggest either wholesale embracing of planning by Non-Planners or wholesale abandonment by Strategic Planners.

At a minimum, though, these results are intriguing and call

for follow-up in new time periods. Such follow-up should attempt some sort of longitudinal analysis to calibrate a reasonable time frame for research on the impact on performance of a major managerial innovation like planning. It appears that even three to five years is inadequate for this purpose.

11.6.3 FOLLOW-UP STUDY ON IMPACT OF ENVIRONMENT, STRATEGY, ORGANIZATION STRUCTURE, AND ORGANIZATIONAL CLIMATE ON PERFORMANCE

The primary thrust of this study was an evaluation of the impact of planning on performance. However, as a dividend, we can also do preliminary analysis of how environment, strategy, organization structure, and organizational climate affect returns. This is a dividend, since these other elements were measured primarily as covariates of planning. We plan to follow up these complex relationships in more detail, but we present some preliminary results here. This is not the major purpose of our book, but the preliminary results provide some clear guidance for future research on environment, strategy, organization structure, and organizational climate.

Our preliminary approach was to correlate the scales developed in chapter 8 with the four performance measures used in chapter 10. Some interesting relationships are obtained (table 11.4) and the patterns are:

Scales	Number of Scales	Number of Correlations of Scale with Performance Measures	Number of Significant Correlations
Environment	3	12	5
Strategy	10	40	14
Organization structure	8	32	10
Organizational climate	7	28	3

These are not just chance patterns, even though the performance measures are correlated. Rather, the results should be viewed in the context of parallel results with the planning scales; only 6 of 52 correlations of adaptive scales and 16 of 120 integrative scales were significant in similar tests, with signs of the correlations showing an inconsistent pattern.

Of the 28 correlations involving variability in ROC, only 5 are significant, whereas 27 of the 84 correlations involved with mean 1977-1981, 1979 and 1981 return-on-capital are significant. Environ-

Table 11.4

Relationship of Environment, Strategy, Organization Structure
and Organizational Climate Scales (Chapter 8) to Performance

| | Return-on Capital (percent) | | | |
| | 1977-81 | | | |
	Mean	Standard Deviation about Trend	1979	1981
Environment Scales				
Uncertainty	.12	-.18**	.06	.05
Change	.27***	-.15	.28***	.13
Hostility	-.21**	.15	-.11	-.36***
Strategy Scales				
Internal Innovation	.29***	-.17*	.30***	.13
Acquisition	.17*	-.24**	.05	.17*
Divestiture	-.15	-.05	-.25***	.01
International Posture	.36***	-.22**	.32***	.23***
Industrial Goods	-.17*	.03	-.22***	-.06
Scale	.09	.00	.09	.05
International Marketing	-.02	.03	.06	.12
Explicit Growth/Share Strategy	-.09	-.09	-.04	-.17*
New Product Strategy	.06	-.02	.02	.02
Explicit Segment Strategy	.01	.08	.15	-.15
Organization Structure Scales				
Entrepreneurial Incentives	.13	-.12	.09	.03
Task Forces	.04	.04	.13	.02
Resource Sharing	-.01	.12	.01	-.11
Interdivisional Communication	.07	.04	.17*	.09
Decentralization	.09	-.07	.14	.16*
Insider Influence	-.15	.08	-.13	-.16*
Organizational Interdependency	-.21**	.10	-.17*	-.23***
Organizational Specialization	.27***	-.18**	.21**	.22***
Organizational Climate Scales				
Entrepreneurialness	.16*	-.10	.17*	.07
Performance Orientation	.11	.01	.17*	.14
Line-Staff Interaction	-.03	.03	.11	-.02
Organizational Contentment	.06	.10	.12	.05
Participative Decision Making	-.09	.03	-.09	-.11
Organizational Fluidity	.00	-.06	.00	.07
Delegated Responsibility	.06	-.13	-.01	.11

***p < .01, **p < .05, *p < .10

ment, strategy, organization structure, and organizational climate apparently affect return more than they do risk. Furthermore, there are patterns of consistency:

- Changeable *environments* are associated with high returns whereas hostile environments are associated with low returns.
- *Strategy* matters. Internal innovation, global operations, and acquisition are associated with high returns; they are also associated with low variability despite the fact that all can be thought of as "risky." That lower returns are associated with industrial goods is probably a reflection of the classic pattern involving capital intensity.

- *Specialized Organization Structure* is associated with high returns and low variability. Interdependence of organizational units is associated with low returns, a result that may have bearing on the ever-present search for "synergy."
- *Organizational climate* seems to matter less, though entrepreneurialness and performance orientation exhibit some positive association with return.

The management literature in general stresses "contingent" or interaction effects among environment, strategy, organization structure and organizational climate, so these should be examined, in addition to the main effects, to develop a clearer structure of causation underlying the correlations. We have some preliminary indications of how the pieces fit together, and it appears that the direct effects of individual factors outweigh the interactions among them. An analysis of variance of all of the scales in table 11.3 produced the following results:

	Percent of variability in 1977-1981 mean ROC explained by the scales
Environment (3 scales)	1%
Strategy (10 scales)	16%
Organization Structure (8 scales)	10%
Organizational Climate (7 scales)	2%
Shared explanatory power not attributable to a single factor	16%
Total variance explained (R^2)	45%

Only strategy is significant. In addition, despite the overall stronger results from the direct effects, the shared variance does indicate the presence of some contingent effects.

In an additional analysis, analysis of variance with interactions of all orders was used to examine the combined effects of planning, environment, strategy, organization structure and organizational climate on five-year mean ROC using the empirically-derived firm groupings from chapter 9. The only significant main effect again involved strategy; the combined group of Innovative Strategists and Segmenters earned 2.5 percent more on capital than the Domestic Status Quoers and Domestic Portfolio Switchers. Only one of the 26 interactions (many of the cells were null) was significant. A 5-way in-

teraction of firms in High-Change environments, using Fully Integrated or Extensive planning, that were Innovative Strategists or
Segmenters, that had Organic, Decentralized or Home Grown/Task
Forces for organization structures and that had either Participative
Bureaucracy or Participative Autonomy organizational climates
earned 1.6 percent more on their capital than the other firms did. This
result is, however, highly tentative, for there are only five firms that
fit this particular profile. That so many interactions were not significant casts doubt on contingency theories, although clearly much more
work is needed in this area.

11.7 Implications for Managerial Practice

The major purpose of this study was to advance the state of
knowledge about planning and about its effects. Nonetheless, we
think that a number of prescriptive implications flow from our results
and that these are important to practitioners. Many of our findings fit
well with the anecdotal experiences related to us by managers who
have wrestled with attempting to initiate formal planning processes
or to modify existing approaches to planning that have proven unsatisfactory.

   We commence our review of managerial implications by
focusing on what strategic planning is and what it does. We try to put
planning into perspective as regards performance implications and
look at what seems to make for "good" and "bad" planning. We then
set priorities for performance improvement – in other words, implications of our study for the manager dedicated to improving effectiveness. In our discussion, we take some license in combining our
results with those of others without ponderous reference. We also include some conjectures based on combining our experience with the
results.

11.7.1 WHAT IS STRATEGIC PLANNING?

   In our view, strategic planning is long-term (five-year or
more) planning that weighs heavily on criteria other than rigid financial
bases (ROI or discounted cash flow) in plotting the mix of future
businesses. Strategic criteria may include market growth and market
position, competitive conditions, strength of management, or how a
business "fits" with other businesses. In other words, strategic planning considers not only the quantity but also the quality of future
earnings. Strategic planning has a substantial environmental orienta-

tion and has the largest potential payoff at the corporate level, where interdivisional resource trade-offs must be made.

Many companies (and indeed many authors) seem to confuse corporate strategic planning with long-term financial planning and budgeting and with strategic planning at the divisional level.

11.7.2 DO YOU "NEED" STRATEGIC PLANNING?

Planning is not necessary for good performance nor is it a guarantee of good performance. Of the 112 companies in our sample that were operating under reasonably normal conditions, 7 did neither corporate nor strategic planning and on average they outearned the others in our sample during the period of study. However, only one of these seemed to have developed a solid strategy with long-term prospects for profitability.

Of the other 105 companies, only 24 did corporate strategic planning as we view it, and they had the highest mean and least variable returns-on-capital of all the planners. Companies with divisional strategic planning performed next best, and companies that did only financial planning performed less well.

The differences in return on capital between the groups were about 1 percent, and the differences do not clear conventional standards of statistical significance; significance would require a difference of nearly 3 percent ROC – a level practically impossible to expect from one single practice like strategic planning. However, 1 percent return for the average firm in our sample is $20M, substantially more than the marginal cost of implementing strategic planning.

11.7.3 PUTTING PLANNING IN PERSPECTIVE

Waves of fashion seem to surge through management, become the fad of the moment, and pass away – sometimes without even a trace (*Business Week* 1986). Jack Welch of General Electric once described the process as pendulum-like, swinging from one technique or concept to another, often too far, before swinging back. One hopes that the best from each new vogue remains a permanent addition. As regards planning, our study makes clear that more is not necessarily better. Whereas we have been able to identify some fairly definite benefits associated with planning, it has also become clear that not all planning is "good" and that the qualitative distinctions we drew were, in fact, terribly important.

For example, a planning process with a strong financial and budgetary orientation seems to be less efficacious than one that is more externally focused, dealing with the adaptive criteria and issues we identified in the study. Some companies now take pains to separate strategic planning from the budgeting process, echoing in their actions the belief that "when the numbers come in, the thinking goes out." This view may be a little extreme, but our results would certainly suggest a wariness with planning that has a financial focus. In one sense, this finding might be adduced as support for the movement toward "strategic" planning that occurred during the 1970s.

Our results also suggest the merits of adding value to planning at the corporate level. Research on strategy has long suggested the importance of the corporate element, and it is encouraging to find support in this study of planning. Stock market theorists should also take some solace in this view, though the finding that so few of the sample actually did much corporate strategic planning probably adds fuel to those who criticize much corporate diversification.

Our results should generally lead managers totally skeptical of the value of planning to think again. While it is clear that much planning effort is not productive, it is also evident that some of the best planning is practiced in high performing companies. Many of these firms had a considerable history of good results, sound strategy, and an admirable organizational climate. Thus, while effort into planning per se does not guarantee improved performance, good planning tends to be associated with better strategies and improved performance profiles.

11.7.4 "GOOD" PLANNING

We found no simple formula for planning, but we were able to conclude that the "best" plans are probably developed in firms with respected central planning staffs who report high in the organization and with divisional planning specialists who report to a high level of divisional management. Confidence of line management is critical, as are clear goals and decision criteria *other than* simple financial measures like discounted cash flow. This is not a simple state to achieve, and a good planning system probably takes five years to set up and get working properly.

It is fairly easy to identify forces that work strongly against good planning. The most important is probably a strong tendency of American firms to compensate senior managers on the basis of short-term financial performance. This works against any effort to promote strategic thinking, which good planning should do. Strategic planning takes a good deal of time and effort from line managers and good professional overseers; lack of either of these is likely to shackle planning. Most problems with planning seem to be organizational and people based. Technical planning problems seem less important, though we have indications that too little longer term competitive or customer analysis is available to management. Oddly, very little contingency planning is done, even though strategic planning is meant to deal with environmental changes that threaten market positions.

A number of other considerations tend to be signs of "good" and "bad" planning. They are relatively easy to spot when they are looked for. Many are organizational, and few involve technical aspects of planning. A list meant to be suggestive rather than exhaustive might include:

"Good" Signs	*"Bad" Signs*
• Planning deals with long-run strategic matters	• Planning deals mainly with short-term, operational issues
• Resource allocation decisions are integrated into the planning process	• Resource allocation decisions are made separate from the planning process
• Contemporary strategic planningtools are employed in the planning process	• Contemporary strategic planning tools are either not used or are given excessive weight in the planning process
• Significant effort is put into environmental forecasts, particularly for the longer term	• Internally generated forecasts form the basis for plans
• CEO takes active part in review of plans	• Planning is the domain of a senior financial manager
• Line managers see value in planning	• Line managers see planning as a wasteful exercise
• Line managers put considerable effort into long-run planning	• Line managers leave planning to specialists
• Information for planning flows freely through the organization	• Information for planning does not flow freely
• The goal and strategy formulation process is characterized by negotiation and a bottom-up orientation	• The goal and strategy formulation process is characterized by a top-down, autocratic orientation
• There is a small corporate staff and small planning staffs in each division	• There is a large central planning staff but no planning specialists in the divisions

- The corporate planning process generally involves some modification of divisional plans
- Finished plans contain both words and numbers
- Individual plans are integrated with each other
- Formal planning tools are understood but used only as needed
- Atmosphere at plan and performance review is appropriate to the situation and occurs as needed
- The planning cycle is flexible, depending on features of the business

- Corporate planning takes the divisional plans pretty much as given
- Finished plans consist largely of numbers
- Individual plans are stand-alone documents
- Formal planning tools are applied rigidly
- Review of the plan is tense and confrontational, occurring in a rigid time cycle
- The planning cycle is a rigid, annual ritual

11.7.5 SETTING THE FRONTIER FOR PERFORMANCE IMPROVEMENT

Although the primary focus of the study was planning, we were also able to investigate the relationship of a variety of other variables to both planning and corporate performance. Included were environment, strategy, organization structure, and organizational climate.

In general, neither environment (surprisingly) nor organization structure (less surprisingly) related much to planning. The best of the planners did seem to have a more entrepreneurial climate, though the sample as a whole did not consider itself particularly entrepreneurial. The relationship to strategy, was, however, convincingly supported. Many who watched the growth and spread of formal planning systems in the 1970s were apprehensive about results. Our study suggests that "good" planning is certainly associated with higher quality strategies, but it by no means follows that formal planning is the only way to develop good strategy or that good strategies will necessarily evolve from elaborate formal planning systems.

As regards performance, the preliminary strategy results suggest some broad patterns. Strong multinational presence and focus on new ventures tend to pay off over the long haul. There is also tangential evidence that the economies of focus may on average outweigh those of scale, though industry parameters, not included in this study per se, could be important qualifiers. Of all the major elements included in the study, further research focused on strategy would seem likely to be the most productive.

11.8 "The New Breed of Strategic Planner"

Just as this book was coming together into final form, *Business Week* (1984) published a cover story on changes in corporate planning with a subheadline "Number-Crunching Professionals Are Giving Way to Line Managers." The essence of the story was that, despite the efforts we have described to involve line management in developing and implementing strategic plans, many firms have found that their planners are isolated from reality and as a result are ineffective. In particular, planning by formula (using the portfolio procedures, for example) was criticized, as were assumptions that shifts of assets among businesses can be achieved quickly and easily. In many cases, the article continued, line managers are increasingly given planning responsibilities, often with minimal staffs.

The appearance of this article caused us to contemplate how our results related to this new version of "received wisdom" about planning. To us, the events reported by *Business Week* are on the one hand puzzling and on the other not. Puzzling is the emphasis that the article put on portfolio models, which we found to be familiar but relatively unimportant in planning practice. Further, we found that our planning executives were in general experienced managers who had spent considerable time with their companies. Planning systems we identified as strategic also appeared to have many of the "good management" characteristics cited by the *Business Week* article. Internal product development, as well as acquisition and divestiture, follow reasonable courses in terms of product life cycle expectations. Strong positions in attractive markets were a consistent goal, particularly of the Corporate Strategic Planners.

Less puzzling is the fact that many companies are dissatisfied with their planning systems. We have seen that many firms that believe they do corporate strategic planning in fact plan only lower down in the organization, and many others create complex budgets rather than real strategic plans. We found that planning systems in general do not take a particularly broad view in terms of environmental forecasting, and the lack of contingency planning no doubt is related to the many surprises (most of them unpleasant) discussed by *Business Week*. We found a relatively weak connection between operating plans (which should be closer to "real world" issues) and strategic plans, and we found planners relatively uninterested in the "shared resources" that often provide synergies among sets of businesses. We also found that rotation of line management through planning assignments is rare, creating more potential for planners and line managers to drift apart.

The prescriptions for improvement suggested by *Business Week* included having planners report to senior managers of operating units to encourage strategic thinking by managers. On the basis of our results, this reporting relationship is characteristic of second-level planners of better performing companies, but reporting relationships alone are almost certainly not causal. Indeed, the idea looks in the wrong direction, for it sounds like a prescription for a divisional focus for planning. In many companies line managers do not think strategically, because, in general, they are neither motivated nor compensated to do so. Our results indicate that senior line managers spend less than 10 percent of their time on longer term issues, of which developing business strategies is only one part. They are generally compensated on short-run performance, rather than on performance judged from a strategic perspective. The dispersal of planning activities throughout the organization, while possibly useful in the short run for the operating units, will probably defeat the development of integrated longer term corporate-level strategies. The dispersal could also shorten the time focus of planning (already not long) and further discourage contingency planning. The remedies for deficiencies in longer term planning, like many other general issues involved in management of American industry, appears to lie deeper than in the planning systems themselves. In summary, we echo the subheading of a recent article in *Harvard Business Review* – "There's nothing wrong with formal strategic planning – if you do it right" (Gray 1986).

11.9 Conclusion

This book has been a kind of odyssey that was begun as an investigation of corporate planning as a key explainer of differences of performance of large multiproduct, multimarket U.S. manufacturing firms. Through a series of steps, we broadened focus to include the key roles of environment, strategy, organization structure, and organizational climate. It is clear that planning, even if executed well, is not a certain route to improved performance. Effective strategy can evolve in a variety of ways, and formal planning is best viewed as one of a series of options for developing effective strategy. This result, which forms the basis for our suggestions for future research, is more or less a dividend from our analysis, since measurements about environment, strategy, and organization were originally collected essentially as covariates in the main study of planning. Nonetheless, there is much more work to be done, both to chart the evolution of corporate and strategic planning and to investigate relationships of environment, strategy, and organization, both singly and in concert, to corporate financial performance.

Appendix I

Research Methodology

A.1 Introduction

Development of methodology and survey instruments for research of the type described in this book was not a straightforward task. First, the subject of interest is itself, at most, in adolescence. There has been relatively little broad-based empirical research dealing with strategic planning, even though there is a fairly large body of literature on planning in general. Second, our approach was intentionally broad, necessitating measurement of a wide variety of environmental, strategic, organizational, planning, and other variables, often representing constructs difficult to operationalize. This approach was necessary to meet the goals discussed in chapter 1, but it also meant that we had to deal with large questionnaires with a relatively restricted number of question items per construct. These problems have been successfully overcome in other research, but the precision of measurement often achieved by item redundancy, with which specialist researchers prefer to attack narrower topics, must sometimes be sacrificed. Third, as we noted in chapter 1, some formidable analytical problems are often created by data bases of the type we use here – e.g., large numbers of variables with relatively few observations. However, the relatively new analytic methods that we used were helpful in coping with these problems. These methods are well suited for dealing with complex systems characterized by measurement error and were therefore ideal for the task that we attempted.

A.2 Instrument Design and Testing

In this section, we describe the major stages of the instrument development and testing process; the stages are shown in figure A1, which is a flowchart of the whole sequence of activities.

Each stage is now briefly described.

A.2.1 DEVELOP PRELIMINARY MODEL
Figure A2 shows the preliminary model used to structure the study. It reflects a belief that both the need for strategic planning and the nature of the process that evolves are dependent on the environment in which the firm operates.

A.2.2 REVIEW RELEVANT LITERATURE
We reviewed the appropriate literature in more detail in relevant chapters of the book proper. However, the literature review was an illuminating and vital part of the whole study since it covered a very broad range of topics, including work in areas such as organizational behavior, industrial economics, business policy, planning, corporate strategy, international business and others. Naturally, the search process was deliberately selective, but work in all of these areas had a significant effect on the final design.

A.2.3 REVIEW WITH ADVISOR GROUP
The advisor group for the study consisted of practitioners personally involved in strategic planning and was primarily composed of management consultants. We had several motives in working with such a group. First, in dealing with a fairly novel development in management practice, it seemed sensible to draw upon the knowledge of those who had considerable experience in the area and had worked with systems of the type to be studied. Second, and not unrelated, was our knowledge that since strategic planning was an area of great topical interest, the executives we were likely to survey had almost certainly already been bombarded by academic researchers and questionnaires. We therefore felt it essential that our methodology and instruments clearly reflect sound knowledge and understanding of the area and its problems. At all cost, we wished to avoid appearing like naive academic researchers and producing a ruinous response rate. Subsequent events were to prove the soundness of this reasoning.
The early review process produced a number of benefits, the most important of which was a sharpening of the focus of the study.

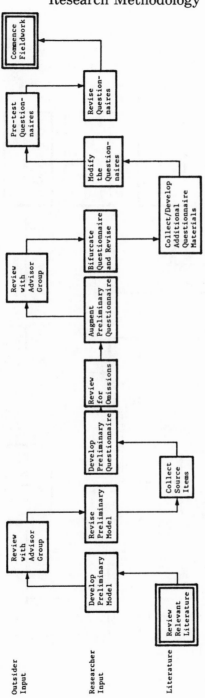

FIGURE A1

Instrument Design And Testing

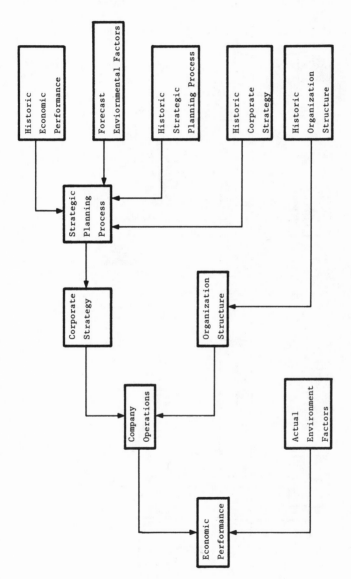

FIGURE A2

Preliminary Model Linking Current and Historical
Elements of Environment, Strategy, Planning, Organization
Structure and Performance

There was emerging agreement that we should focus primarily on planning systems and the formal plans themselves rather than on the content of strategy decisions per se. While this had been our intent, it was not always clear in our preliminary documentation. This issue was to arise again later in the instrument development process, but it was at this point that we made our key decision. Although the questionnaire was subsequently expanded to include questions dealing with the content of strategy, this area was not a primary concern of the study. Other comments were instrumental in revision of the preliminary model.

A.2.4 COLLECT SOURCE ITEMS

In a broad study of this type, it should be evident that we drew upon a wide variety of sources—both in theoretical development and in questionnaire construction. In developing questions on goals and objectives, the work of both Cyert and March (1963) and Bower (1970) was helpful. In the strategy area, we relied upon concepts and measures developed by a variety of authors, including, among others, Ansoff (1965); Child (1972); Henderson (1979); Schoeffler, Buzzell, and Heany (1974); Buzzell, Gale, and Sultan (1975); Rumelt (1974); and Chandler (1962).

The planning process itself has also been the subject of a considerable amount of theorizing and empirical research. In terms of information collection and analysis, we developed questions based on a variety of frameworks and approaches, using concepts presented by Day (1977), Hussey (1978), Hofer and Schendel (1978), Aguilar (1967), and Keegan (1980). The planning system was also covered in depth, and both concepts and measures were drawn from the work of Vancil, Aguilar, and Howell (1968); Vancil and Lorange (1975); Khandwalla (1973); Ringbakk (1969); and Steiner (1979).

Development of objectives, strategies, and plans obviously takes place within an organizational context, and it was in this area, with its strong tradition of empirical research, that we found the most useful and immediately applicable measures upon which we could draw. In the measurement of informal aspects of organization, items were drawn or developed from the work of Johannesson (1973), Payne and Pheysey (1971), Schneider and Bartlett (1968, 1970), and Woodman and King (1978). Other useful sources in organization included Williamson (1975); Pugh, Hickson, and Turner (1968); and Mintzberg (1973). In the international area we drew on the work of Stopford and Wells (1972), Hulbert and Brandt (1980), and Egelhoff (1982).

A.2.5 DEVELOP PRELIMINARY QUESTIONNAIRE

The next step was to develop a preliminary questionnaire. For the most part, this first questionnaire consisted of a compilation of the items (modified and otherwise) derived from previous research.

A.2.6 REVIEW FOR OMISSION

Comparison of the first questionnaire with the model constructs enabled identification of areas which were underrepresented or nonexistent as regards questionnaire items. For example, in chapter 1 we identified the use of certain techniques of strategic planning as one of the key elements in defining how strategic the company's planning process was. No directly usable questions dealing with this topic were generated by the literature search, and there were other such areas.

A.2.7 AUGMENT PRELIMINARY QUESTIONNAIRE

We then set about augmenting the first questionnaire so as to generate an appropriate representation of questionnaire items. Wherever possible, items were written in structured form in order to facilitate subsequent coding and data processing.

A.2.8 REVIEW WITH ADVISOR GROUP

This was one of the most crucial and productive meetings of the preparation sequence. The advisor group had many suggestions for item modification and questionnaire augmentation, as might be expected. More importantly, however, was the resultant decision on data collection strategy.

The choice of respondent had never been easy. At one point, we had considered interviewing the chief executive. However, with the narrowing of research focus onto formal planning systems, it was decided that the chief planning officer (typically VP-Corporate Planning) might be the best interviewee. Other problems, however, remained. We had to face up to the fact that in many companies, a substantial amount of the planning activity takes place at the divisional or business unit level. To gain an understanding of planning at this level, however, would have necessitated multiple interviews per company. Either we should interview at each division/business unit, or we would need some kind of representative sample of divisions/business units from each company on a comparable basis. Both alternatives would have demanded an enormous number of interviewing hours – more than our manpower budget could accommodate – and both were therefore rejected.

As we discussed the questionnaire with the advisor group, however, it became evident that we wanted to gather too much information and had far too many questions for a single respondent. It was at this point that we decided to split the questionnaire and seek two respondents per company. There was an enthusiastic response to this concept, and the principle for the bifurcation was established as follows.

A.2.9 BIFURCATING THE QUESTIONNAIRE

Upon examining the questionnaire items more closely, it became clear that they fell into two basic categories. One class of questions was those that could clearly be answered only by the corporate planner. These were questions that, for example, sought personal attitudes or opinions on issues or that demanded substantive insights on the working of the planning process that only the chief planner would possess. Many of the other questions did not, however, need such a respondent, for they dealt with matters of descriptive fact; these answers could easily be provided by someone in the Corporate Planner's staff, rather than the planner. It was on this basis, then, that the preliminary questionnaire was bifurcated, with the tentative plan that we would seek two interviews per company. The first, with a corporate planning staff member, would focus on more descriptive matters, while the second, with the chief corporate planner, would focus on some of the key issues in the study. The first interview would also serve to further brief the interviewers for their encounter with the senior planning officer.

A.2.10 COLLECT/DEVELOP ADDITIONAL QUESTIONNAIRE MATERIALS

Having split the original questionnaire into two parts, we were able to add some questions while eliminating still others. The bifurcation of the original questionnaire, combined with the addition and deletion of items, necessitated a reflowing of each questionnaire, as well as insertion of additional instructions. This accomplished, we were ready for pretesting.

A.2.11 PRETEST QUESTIONNAIRES

The initial pretests of the questionnaire were performed with persons known to the researchers who were working in corporate or strategic planning departments. None of these interviewees was working for companies that would be included in the sample. Subsequent pretesting was conducted with persons in similar positions and companies but who were not previously known to the researchers.

A.2.12 REVISE QUESTIONNAIRES

A final round of revisions was made iteratively as a result of the pretest interviews. Most of the changes were relatively minor changes in wording, and occasional logical problems were dealt with in similar fashion. The two final questionnaires are reproduced in appendix II.

A.3 Data Collection Procedures

There were four major components of the data collection procedure. The first involved the selection and training of interviewers; the second was the task of establishing contact with sample companies and setting up an interview schedule; the third was, of course, the interviewing process itself; the final stage was the follow-up sequence with respondents. These stages are now described in more detail.

A.3.1 INTERVIEWER SELECTION AND TRAINING

The choice of interviewers for this project was crucial. Obviously, given the level of respondents and the complexity of the subject matter, interviewer competence was essential. We were faced with a variety of choices, including options such as hiring junior management consultants or using industrial market researchers who were accustomed to interviewing high-level executives. In the end, we chose a different alternative, but one we feel – *ex post* – was the best choice we could have made.

The market research company that was to manage the data collection process agreed that they currently had no suitable interviewers on their staff. In conversation, however, they mentioned that in the past they had successfully trained well-educated individuals (particularly students) in a fairly short period of time and had found them to be very successful interviewers. This was the model we chose to work with; we rejected the notion of using temporarily unemployed or retired business executives as interviewers in favor of hiring MBA students.

The prospective interviewers were carefully chosen on the basis of academic achievement, maturity, and interest in the subject area. They were offered the training experience, the opportunity to interview some of the top planners in the country, as well as pay! On this basis we were able to hire two full-time MBA students (who took a term off from their program in order to participate) and one part-time student who was taking a reduced course load.

A.3.2 RESPONDENT CONTACT SEQUENCE

To attain good cost control required fairly intensive use of interviewer's time, as well as suitable routing – particularly on trips to the Midwest. In addition, the busy schedules of target interviewees meant that we should call sufficiently in advance of desired interviewing time to permit appointments to be made.

The first stage was to send a letter with individualized introduction, signed by the Dean of the Graduate School of Business, requesting that the corporate planner and his company participate in the study (exhibit A1). The telephone contact that ensued was typically preceded by one to three unsuccessful attempts to reach him/her (the planner would be out of town on business or, more frequently, in a meeting).

When finally reached, the planner was given a rather standard introduction, as follows:

> This is Professor Pardew[1] from the Graduate School of Business. I am working with Professors Capon, Farley, and Hulbert on a study of strategic planning practices in leading corporations. Our Dean, Boris Yavitz, recently sent you a letter describing the study in general terms and asking your company to participate. Have you seen that letter yet?

Most had seen the letter and wanted to have the study described in more detail (e.g., what are you looking to find out, how much time will it take, etc.). Confidentiality provisions were among the concerns of some, though surprisingly few.

The largest fraction at this point agreed to participate and acceded to our request that they, along with another member of the planning staff, be interviewed.

A number of companies said they were simply too busy and that we should try them later. Others wanted time either to think the request over or clear the agreement with their superiors. A few said that no, they did not want to participate.

Generally the conversation concluded with agreement on dates and times for the interviewers or a decision that their secretary would confirm the availability of the second person to be interviewed and get back to us. Interviewees were told the nature of certain factual material that was required and were asked to prepare this before the interview.

Columbia University in the City of New York | *New York, N.Y.* *10027*

GRADUATE SCHOOL OF BUSINESS   URIS HALL

OFFICE OF THE DEAN

March 27, 1980

Dear

I am writing to ask you to participate in an important study dealing
with the contemporary practice of corporate planning and its impact on
organization and market performance. The project is part of the Columbia
Business School's major commitment to the area of strategy, and we
anticipate that the results will impact on the practice of management as
well as all aspects of our teaching, including MBA and executive programs.

Your organization has been chosen in a sample of leading Fortune 500
firms. Participation will involve two interviews in your offices. The
first interview will be with an experienced member of your staff who
will be asked to provide background material on the organization and the
environment it faces. The second interview will be with you personally.

The questionnaires have been carefully developed to reflect the state of
advanced thinking in the field and have been pretested with corporate
planners of other leading corporations. No questions involving internal
financial performance will be asked, and you will receive copies of all
publications which result from the study.

The study is under the direction of Professors Noel Capon, John Farley
and James Hulbert of our faculty. A member of the research team will be
calling you to schedule the interviews and answer any questions you
might have. I would very much appreciate your willingness to be a participant
in this study.

Sincerely

Boris Yavitz
Dean

BY:eb:zs

Exhibit A1

Once dates and times had been agreed upon, a confirmation letter indicating who would be coming to conduct the interview and reiterating previous arrangements was mailed, with a copy to the second person being interviewed. A day or so before the scheduled date, a reminder call was placed to the interviewee or his/her secretary.

A.3.3 INTERVIEWING PROCESS

Personal interviews were held in respondents' offices over a period of four months' lapsed time. Respondents were given an unmarked questionnaire, and the interviewer recorded responses on another questionnaire, along with verbatims, side comments and observations.

A.3.4 RESPONDENT FOLLOW-UP SEQUENCE

Following the completion of both interviews, a thank-you letter from the Dean was sent to each participant. Subsequently, in late autumn 1980, each participating company was contacted to announce that preliminary results would be announced in the first Abraham Shuchman Memorial Seminar, to be held in early 1981. Response from the survey participants was modest, but a good number of sample companies sent at least one person to the seminar.

A.4 Data Preparation

All items were punched and verified. Marginal distributions of all items were inspected for nonfeasible values and corrections made. Five questionnaires were checked in totality with virtually no errors found.

A.5 Summary

In this appendix, we have reviewed the basic elements of the methodology used for this study. The questionnaires were developed by using existing questionnaire items where possible, augmented by additional questions – all of which were screened via an advisory group and pretesting.

Data collection procedures were, we believe, an effective yet economical solution to the problems posed by this extensive and complex survey. The virtues of insisting on personal interviews became evident as we progressed through the study and the analysis, and the wealth of information that resulted permitted a much richer study than would otherwise have been the case.

NOTES

1. The principal of the market research firm was also an Adjunct Professor at Columbia Business School.

Appendix II

The Questionnaires

Questionnaire I

Graduate School of Business
Columbia University

Survey of Corporate Planning Practice

Thank you for agreeing to participate in this survey of corporate planning practice of major United States corporations. In this questionnaire we shall be asking a series of questions about both your corporate planning process, and company operations, strategy and organization. All responses which you provide will, of course, remain confidential. For analysis purposes they will be combined with responses from other corporations. In order to make it easier to respond to some of the questions, we have grouped them into the following broad categories.

  I. Company Goals
  II. Corporate Strategy
 III. The Planning System
 IV. Making Resource Allocation Decisions
  V. Organization Climate and Structure

Company: _____

Interviewee: _____ Job Title: _____

Interviewer: _____

             Time started: _____

             Time ended: _____

Card _ _ _ _ 201 (1-7)

1

I. COMPANY GOALS

A. In this section we would like to ask some questions about the setting of goals at the <u>corporate</u> <u>level</u>.

1. Can you please tell us the <u>quantitative</u> goals which serve guiding roles in decisions that are strategic for the company as a whole?

___(8)
___(9)
_____ ___(10)
_____ ___(11)
_____ ___(12)
_____ ___(13)
_____ ___(14)

2. a. Are the goals noted above adjusted for inflation?

        Yes   No   (15)
       (15-1)   (15-0)

b. Are any of the goals noted above dominant?

        Yes   No (go to 2.d.)   (16)
       (16-1)   (16-0)

c. Which are dominant?

_____ ___(17)
_____ ___(18)
_____ ___(19)
_____ ___(20)
                                 ___(21)

d. Do you also have formal <u>qualitative</u> goals?

                                 (22)
        Yes   No (go to Q.3)
e. Please specify the main ones: (22-1) (22-0)

_____ ___(23)
_____ ___(24)
_____ ___(25)
_____ ___(26)
_____ ___(27)
_____ ___(28)

3. a. When is the last time that there was a significant change in either the <u>type</u> of corporate goal or the <u>level</u> of goal or goals?

                               19_____
                               (29-30)
b. What was changed at that time?

   <u>Goal</u>   <u>Change</u>

_____ (31) _____ (32)

_____ (33) _____ (34)

_____ (35) _____ (36)

c. How important were the following reasons for bringing about these changes?

	Not at all Important				Very Important	
Changes in top management	1	2	3	4	5	(37)
New competitive conditions	1	2	3	4	5	(38)
Technological breakthroughs	1	2	3	4	5	(39)
Unsatisfactory performance	1	2	3	4	5	(40)
Other _____	1	2	3	4	5	(41)

_____

2

	Failed to achieve				Exceeded goals	
4. a. Since 1974, would you say that your company has in general exceeded or failed to achieve its key goals?	1	2	3	4	5	(42)

	Not at all important reason				Very important reason	
b. What do you think are the reasons for that performance:						
Appropriateness of goals	1	2	3	4	5	(43)
Managerial performance	1	2	3	4	5	(44)
Political, regulatory action	1	2	3	4	5	(45)
Competition	1	2	3	4	5	(46)
Organization structure	1	2	3	4	5	(47)
Economic environment	1	2	3	4	5	(48)
Technological change	1	2	3	4	5	(49)

	Not at all influential				Very influential	
5. a. How influential were the following in setting your present corporate goals?						
Outside members of the Board of Directors	1	2	3	4	5	(50)
Chief Executive Officer	1	2	3	4	5	(51)
Top Corporate Management	1	2	3	4	5	(52)
Corporate Planning Department	1	2	3	4	5	(53)
Second Level line managers	1	2	3	4	5	(54)

b. Which of the following best reflects your company's process for setting corporate goals?

Set for the company by the CEO	
Set for the company by a Board of Directors group	$\overline{(55-1)}$
An aggregation of the goals developed by second level management	$\overline{(56-1)}$
A negotiation process between a top management/BOD group and second level management	$\overline{(57-1)}$
A negotiation process between the CEO and second level management	$\overline{(58-1)}$
	$\overline{(59-1)}$

6. To what extent do your corporate goals serve an important role in each of the following areas?

	Do not serve this role			Serve an important role		
Evaluation of past performance	1	2	3	4	5	(60)
Communication to external publics	1	2	3	4	5	(61)
Evaluation of second level objectives	1	2	3	4	5	(62)
Monitor current performance	1	2	3	4	5	(63)
Used to activate contingencies	1	2	3	4	5	(64)
Provide challenge and motivation	1	2	3	4	5	(65)

3

7. How do you believe that your corporate reputation has changed in the past five years?

	Less favorable			More favorable		
a. As viewed by our customers	1	2	3	4	5	(66)
b. As viewed by the general public	1	2	3	4	5	(67)

B. In this section, we would like to ask you some questions about the setting of goals at the second level.

1. How influential were the following in setting your present second level goals?

	Not at all influential			Very influential		
Outside members of the Board of Directors	1	2	3	4	5	(68)
Chief Executive Officer	1	2	3	4	5	(69)
Top Corporate Management	1	2	3	4	5	(70)
Corporate Planning Department	1	2	3	4	5	(71)
Second level line managers	1	2	3	4	5	(72)

	Not important use			Very important use		
2. How are second level goals used in your company?						
As a major influence on final corporate goals	1	2	3	4	5	(73)
As rationing devices for capital and other resources	1	2	3	4	5	(74)
As standards to evaluate business unit performance	1	2	3	4	5	(75)
As a basis for formally determining an incentive portion of managerial compensation	1	2	3	4	5	(76)

NEW CARD __ __ __ __ 202 (1-7)

3. Which of the following best reflects your company's process for
setting second level long range goals?

Set for second level units by corporate management or CEO	(8-1)	(8)
An aggregation of goals developed by third level management	(9-1)	(9)
A negotiation process between corporate management and second level management	(10-1)	(10)
A negotiation process between CEO and second level management	(11-1)	(11)
Set by second level management	(12-1)	(12)

4. a. Do all second level operating units have identical performance goals?

Yes   No (go to 4.c.) (13)
(13-1)   (13-0)

   b. (If yes) What is the unit of measure?

___(14)

_____ ___(15)

_____ ___(16)

(go to Q. 5)

4 ___(17)

4. c. (If no) What are the reasons for setting different goals, on   ___(18)
what basis are they set, and what are the units of measure?   ___(19)

_____ ___(20)

_____ ___(21)

_____ ___(22)

   d. Who provides the key information which results in the setting of   ___(23)
different second level goals?   ___(24)

Corporate line management	____ (25-1)	(25)
Corporate planning	____ (26-1)	(26)
Second level line management	____ (27-1)	(27)
Third level line management	____ (28-1)	(28)

Appendix II

	Not at all important			Very important		
5. In measuring the overall performance of second level managers, how important is:						
Quality of their planning effort	1	2	3	4	5	(29)
Implementation of planned strategy	1	2	3	4	5	(30)
Achievement of strategic objectives	1	2	3	4	5	(31)
Achievement of short-term profits	1	2	3	4	5	(32)

6. How are second level managers held responsible for <u>variances</u> between <u>plan</u> and <u>actual</u> performance?

No attempt made to analyze differences	_____(33-1)	(33)
No formal procedures for analysis, but explanation of significant differences expected	____(34-1)	(34)
Written narrative explanation of differences required	____(35-1)	(35)
Quantitative analysis of causes of differences required	____(36-1)	(36)

7. a. Do you have an incentive compensation scheme for second level <u>line</u> <u>managers</u>?

                                <u>Yes</u>   <u>No</u> (go to Q. 8) (37)

  b. (If <u>yes</u>) Is the incentive compensation (37-1) (37-0)
based on progress achieved in meeting
their <u>long range goals</u>?

                                       (38)
                              <u>Yes</u> <u>No</u>
                             (38-1) (38-0)

  c. How is the incentive compensation computed for these second level managers?

    _____ ___(39)

    _____ ___(40)

    _____ ___(41)

    _____ ___(42)

	Very poor			Very good		
8. Overall, how do you assess the <u>quality</u> of second level <u>long range goals</u>:	1	2	3	4	5	(43)

New card _ _ _ _ 203 (1-7)

5

II. CORPORATE STRATEGY

In this section we would like to discuss a number of elements of your corporate strategy.

A. First we have some questions about corporate mission.

1. What is the current mission statement for your company as a whole? (If more than one, please state all.)

_____

_____

_____

No current mission definition (indicate if appropriate) _____(8-1)(8)
                                                         (go to Section B)

2. a. Has this mission been changed in the
      past five years?   (9)
                                    ‾Yes‾ ‾No‾ (go to Q. 3)
                                    (9-1) (9-0)

   b. (If yes) When was it changed?   19____   (10-11)

   c. What changes were made in your mission statement at that time?

                                                           ___(12)
      _____   ___(13)
                                                           ___(14)
      _____   ___(15)
                                                           ___(16)
      _____

   d. Why was the mission changed? (Indicate whichever are appropriate.)

      Company developed new capabilities   ____(17-1) (17)
      New CEO   ____(18-1) (18)
      Political or Regulatory actions   ____(19-1) (19)
      New members of Board of Directors   ____(20-1) (20)
      Recommendations from line management   ____(21-1) (21)
      Unsatisfactory past performance   ____(22-1) (22)
      Recommendations from corporate plan-
                     ning department   ____(23-1) (23)
      Other_____   ____   (24)

3. Do you expect that your current mission will still be applicable
   in 1985?   (25)
            ‾Yes‾   ‾No‾
            (25-1) (25-0)

B. Now we would like to ask some questions about product/market strategy.

One way to classify options for seeking growth is shown below.

	Existing Products	New Products (to the company)
Existing Markets	a	c
New Markets (to the company)	b	d

1. How important was each of these product/market combinations in your corporate strategy over the last five years, regardless of whether they were pursued internally or via acquisitions.

	Not at all important			Very important		
a. Growth via existing products in existing markets	1	2	3	4	5	(26)
b. Growth via introducing existing products into new markets	1	2	3	4	5	(27)
c. Growth via introducing products new to the company into existing markets	1	2	3	4	5	(28)
d. Growth via introducing products new to the company into new markets	1	2	3	4	5	(29)

2. How important do you think each of these will be in your corporate strategy over your long range planning horizon?

a. Growth via existing products in existing markets	1	2	3	4	5	(30)
b. Growth via introducing existing products into new markets	1	2	3	4	5	(31)
c. Growth via introducing products new to the company into existing markets	1	2	3	4	5	(32)
d. Growth via introducing products new to the company into new markets	1	2	3	4	5	(33)

C. Now we have a number of general questions about your corporate strategy.

	Disagree			Agree		
1. An explicit part of our corporate strategy is to:						
a. Attempt to exit from markets with large numbers of competitors	1	2	3	4	5	(34)

b. Seek to enter markets with <u>small numbers of competitors</u>   1   2   3   4   5   (35)

c. Seek situations where we can attain <u>large shares</u> of <u>served markets</u>   1   2   3   4   5   (36)

7

	Disagree				Agree	
d. Seek to enter <u>high growth markets</u>	1	2	3	4	5	(37)
e. Seek situations where <u>product differentiation</u> is important	1	2	3	4	5	(38)
f. Seek situations were <u>patents</u> are important	1	2	3	4	5	(39)
g. Seek situations where <u>economies of scale</u> are significant	1	2	3	4	5	(40)
h. Seek situations requiring <u>low capital intensity</u>	1	2	3	4	5	(41)
i. Seek to enter or develop <u>service businesses</u>	1	2	3	4	5	(42)
j. Seek situations where <u>scarce resources</u> are important	1	2	3	4	5	(43)
k. Vertically integrate <u>backward</u> toward sources of supply	1	2	3	4	5	(44)
l. Vertically integrate <u>forward</u> toward final markets	1	2	3	4	5	(45)

2. From our company's experience, it is generally most profitable to have the largest share of the market or segment we are serving.   1   2   3   4   5   (46)

3. Our company's senior management is satisfied with the company's present corporate strategy.   1   2   3   4   5   (47)

4. As you know, we asked you earlier about the process for developing <u>corporate goals</u>. Now we wish to focus on the development of <u>corporate strategy</u>.

In your company, corporate strategy is: (indicate only one)

   a. Developed for the company by the CEO   ____(48-1)   (48)

   b. Developed for the company by a Board of Directors group.   ____(49-1)   (49)

   c. An aggregation of strategies developed by second level management.   ____(50-1)   (50)

   d. A negotiation process between top management/BOD and second level management.   ____(51-1)   (51)

   e. A negotiation process between the CEO and second level management.   ____(52-1)   (52)

5. Our next area of concern is international strategy and operations
   To what extent is each statement representative of your company's
   experience?

	Disagree			Agree		
a. Generally we introduce new products in overseas markets after we do so in the U.S.	1	2	3	4	5	(53)
b. Despite the dollar devaluation, our foreign competition is tougher than it ever was.	1	2	3	4	5	(54)
c. We are consciously shifting toward exporting and away from overseas manufacture.	1	2	3	4	5	(55)
d. We engage in major modifications of our products and programs to penetrate foreign markets.	1	2	3	4	5	(56)
e. Increasing, we find that new products and technologies appear first in foreign markets.	1	2	3	4	5	(57)
f. The U.S. government offers adequate support for American business overseas.	1	2	3	4	5	(58)
g. Generally, we seek foreign markets in which we can market our existing products and technologies.	1	2	3	4	5	(59)
h. Our procurement strategies are developed on a world-wide basis.	1	2	3	4	5	(60)
i. Our production strategies are developed on a world-wide basis.	1	2	3	4	5	(61)
j. Our marketing strategies are developed on a world-wide basis.	1	2	3	4	5	(62)
k. All of our corporate planning is conducted on a world-wide basis.	1	2	3	4	5	(63)
l. All of our second level planning is conducted on a world-wide basis.	1	2	3	4	5	(64)

6. Next, we are interested in identifying the degree of influence of
   different persons on key strategic decisions within your company.

   The extent of influence currently being exercised on key strategic
   decisions by the following personnel is as follows:

	No influence			A great deal of influence		
a. Senior executives promoted from within the organization	1	2	3	4	5	(65)
b. Senior executives hired in from close competitors	1	2	3	4	5	(66)
c. Senior executives hired in from different industries	1	2	3	4	5	(67)

d. Senior executives hired from consulting companies	1	2	3	4	5	(68)
e. Senior executives hired from academic institutions	1	2	3	4	5	(69)
f. Consulting firms	1	2	3	4	5	(70)
g. Academic consultants	1	2	3	4	5	(71)

9

D. **Our final questions on corporate strategy deal with acquisitions and divestitures.**

1. **Have you made any significant acquisitions since January 1974?**

Yes (72-1) No (72-0) (go to Q.3) (72)

2. a. To what extent did outside consultants pay a role in your acquisition decisions

Not at all important ___ Very important

1 2 3 4 5 (73)

b. Generally, outside consultants validated decisions already made rather than spearheaded them.

Disagree ___ Agree

1 2 3 4 5 (74)

3. Do you expect acquisitions to play a role in your corporate strategy over the next five years?

No role at all ___ Significant role

1 2 3 4 5 (75)

4. Have you divested, liquidated, or otherwise eliminated any important operations since January 1974?

Yes (76-1) No (76-0) (go to Q.6) (76)

5. a. To what extent did outside consultants play a role in your divestiture decisions?

Not at all important ___ Very important

1 2 3 4 5 (77)

b. Generally, outside consultants validated decisions already made rather than spearheaded them.

Disagree ___ Agree

1 2 3 4 5 (78)

6. Do you expect divestitures to play a role in your corporate strategy over the next five years?

No role at all ___ Significant role

1 2 3 4 5 (79)

New card __ __ __ __   204 (1-7)

10

III. THE PLANNING SYSTEM

A. In this section of the questionnaire we would like some information
on the role of the corporate planning group and the functioning
of the long range planning process in your company.

1. First, we would like you to assess how much effort is expended by
Corporate Planning in each of the following activities:

	No effort			High degree of effort		
a. Helping corporate management formulate goals and objectives	1	2	3	4	5	(8)
b. Helping corporate management formulate strategy	1	2	3	4	5	(9)
c. Improving the quality of strategic thinking of corporate management	1	2	3	4	5	(10)
d. Developing and writing the corporate plan	1	2	3	4	5	(11)
e. Helping second level management formulate goals and objectives	1	2	3	4	5	(12)
f. Helping second level management formulate strategy	1	2	3	4	5	(13)
g. Improving the quality of strategic thinking by second level management	1	2	3	4	5	(14)
h. Reviewing and evaluating second level plans.	1	2	3	4	5	(15)
i. Integrating second level plans with the corporate plan	1	2	3	4	5	(16)
j. Assess the overall effectiveness of planning process	1	2	3	4	5	(17)
k. Defining the guidelines, formats and timetables for planning activity	1	2	3	4	5	(18)
l. Monitoring and controlling progress versus plans	1	2	3	4	5	(19)
m. Helping management with acquisition plans	1	2	3	4	5	(20)
n. Helping management with divestiture plans	1	2	3	4	5	(21)
o. Developing macro-forecasts of the economy, financial markets, political environment, etc.	1	2	3	4	5	(22)
p. Preparing specific studies	1	2	3	4	5	(23)

q. Helping management with identifi-
cation of financing needs   1   2   3   4   5   (24)

r. Developing better accounting and
financial data for strategic planning   1   2   3   4   5   (25)

s. Reorganizing the company around
better-defined business units   1   2   3   4   5   (26)

t. Identifying areas of new business
opportunity   1   2   3   4   5   (27)

11

2. Next, we are interested in finding out more about the planning process in your company. To what extent do you agree with each of the following statements?

In this company, the planning process:	Disagree				Agree	

a. is a device to assure that
conflicting expectations are resolved   1   2   3   4   5   (28)

b. plays a central role in the
organization's communication network   1   2   3   4   5   (29)

c. is a means of organizational
conflict resolution   1   2   3   4   5   (30)

d. involves a great deal of bargaining   1   2   3   4   5   (31)

e. is a means for systematically
dealing with uncertainty   1   2   3   4   5   (32)

f. is a means of ensuring that
specialized knowledge is stored
and available to the whole organization   1   2   3   4   5   (33)

g. enables the company to avoid un-
acceptably high levels of risk   1   2   3   4   5   (34)

h. is often characterized by
distortion of data   1   2   3   4   5   (35)

i. has constrained the strategic risk
taking behavior of lower level
managers   1   2   3   4   5   (36)

j. is a key device for allocating
corporate resources throughout the
company   1   2   3   4   5   (37)

k. assures that scarce resources are
allocated to high yield uses   1   2   3   4   5   (38)

l. has improved the company's long
range resource allocation decisions   1   2   3   4   5   (39)

m. has had a measurable positive effect
on sales and profits   1   2   3   4   5   (40)

n. is necessary to sequence future
activities   1   2   3   4   5   (41)

o. plays an important role in
auditing ongoing activities   1   2   3   4   5   (42)

p. encourages development of new
businesses by combining expertise
and resources from lower level units   1   2   3   4   5   (43)

                                                  12

3.   We are also interested in some of the coordination issues involved
in planning. To what extent do you agree with each of the following
statements for your company?

	Disagree				Agree	

a. Marketing activities are closely
coordinated with corporate planning.   1   2   3   4   5   (44)

b. Human resource planning is closely
coordinated with corporate planning.   1   2   3   4   5   (45)

c. Financial planning is closely
coordinated with corporate planning.   1   2   3   4   5   (46)

d. Manufacturing planning is
closely coordinated with corporate
planning.   1   2   3   4   5   (47)

e. Corporate planning gets a great
deal of resistance from our sales
and marketing people.   1   2   3   4   5   (48)

f. Corporate planning gets a great
deal of resistance from our
financial people.   1   2   3   4   5   (49)

g. Corporate planning gets a great
deal of resistance from our
manufacturing people.   1   2   3   4   5   (50)

h. Very high quality information for corporate planning is
obtained from:

     sales and marketing   1   2   3   4   5   (51)

     finance   1   2   3   4   5   (52)

     accounting   1   2   3   4   5   (53)

     manufacturing   1   2   3   4   5   (54)

i. The second level strategies
which emerge from our planning
process are definitely implemented.   1   2   3   4   5   (55)

j. One of the corporate planning
department's major functions is to
act as an agency for assembling
financial reports.   1   2   3   4   5   (56)

13

4. These questions deal with the emphasis and direction of your corporate
    planning effort. To what extent do you agree with each of the following?

	Disagree			Agree		
a. Competitive analysis is primarily the responsibility of our <u>sales</u> and <u>marketing</u> people.	1	2	3	4	5	(57)
b. Competitive analysis is a major activity of the <u>corporate planning</u> department.	1	2	3	4	5	(58)
c. Competitive analysis is a major activity of our <u>second level</u> <u>management</u>.	1	2	3	4	5	(59)
d. In our company, a great deal of effort is expended in attempting to identify competitor's cost structures	1	2	3	4	5	(60)
e. Overall, our company focuses its competitive analysis on competitive product analysis.	1	2	3	4	5	(61)
f. Attaining the largest share of served markets should be a major objective of corporate strategy	1	2	3	4	5	(62)
g. Our planning effort is an adaptive, evolving, learning activity.	1	2	3	4	5	(63)
h. Our planning effort is a fairly routinized activity.	1	2	3	4	5	(64)
i. In the planning process in this company, all key personnel contribute their fair share of effort	1	2	3	4	5	(65)
j. In this company, daily routine drives out planning effort	1	2	3	4	5	(66)
k. Long range resource allocation decisions are made as an integral part of the corporate planning process.	1	2	3	4	5	(67)

6. With regard to performance of the corporate
    planning group:

a. Specific performance goals have been clearly established.	1	2	3	4	5	(68)
b. Numerical or quantified procedures are used extensively to measure performance.	1	2	3	4	5	(69)

7. Do you receive reports detailing the
    performance of corporate planning?   (70)

                                    <u>Yes</u>   <u>No</u> (go to Section B)
    (If <u>yes</u>) How frequently?   (70-1) (70-0)

                        _____ per year.   (71-72)

14

B. Now we would like your views on the roles of various corporate personnel in the planning process, and your perceptions of their attitudes toward planning.

	Not at all involved			Very involved		
1. To what extent is the CEO personally involved in:						
a. the development of corporate goals	1	2	3	4	5	(73)
b. the development of alternative corporate strategies	1	2	3	4	5	(74)
c. the evaluation and approval of the corporate plan	1	2	3	4	5	(75)
d. having planning accepted as a philosophy in this company	1	2	3	4	5	(76)

	Very few sr. executives feel this way			Most sr. executives feel this way		
2. To what extent to Senior Line Executives believe that the purpose of planning is:						
a. to identify external opportunities and threats	1	2	3	4	5	(77)
b. to develop our corporate strategy and long range planning policies	1	2	3	4	5	(78)
c. to develop a set of action programs and operating plans	1	2	3	4	5	(79)
d. to provide a frame of reference for the operating budget	1	2	3	4	5	(80)
			NEW CARD			205(1-7)
e. to satisfy corporate and get them off my back	1	2	3	4	5	(8)
f. a mind stretching, creative exercise	1	2	3	4	5	(9)

3. Outside the normal planning cycle, how much time per week do senior line executives spend working on longer term planning problems?

Less than 1 hour	_____	(01)	(10-11)
1 - 5 hours	_____	(02)	
6 -10 hours	_____	(08)	
11 -15 hours	_____	(13)	
16 or more hours	_____	(18)	

4. With regard to the Board of Directors:	Negative			Strongly Supportive		
a. How supportive is the Board with respect to corporate planning activity?	1	2	3	4	5	(12)

	Not involved			Very involved		
b. How involved is the Board in corporate planning activity?	1	2	3	4	5	(13)

15

5. How influential are each of the following groups with regard to the six corporate planning areas listed?

	Not at all influential			Very influential		
a. Outside members of the Board of Directors						
1 format of the corporate plan	1	2	3	4	5	(14)
2 assumptions used in the final corporate plan	1	2	3	4	5	(15)
3 objectives embodied in the final corporate plan	1	2	3	4	5	(16)
4 strategies embodied in the final corporate plan	1	2	3	4	5	(17)
5 approval of the final corporate plan	1	2	3	4	5	(18)
6 development of missions for second level units	1	2	3	4	5	(19)
b. Chief Executive Officer						
1 format of the corporate plan	1	2	3	4	5	(20)
2 assumptions used in the final corporate plan	1	2	3	4	5	(21)
3 objectives embodied in the final corporate plan	1	2	3	4	5	(22)
4 strategies embodied in the final corporate plan	1	2	3	4	5	(23)
5 approval of the final corporate plan	1	2	3	4	5	(24)
6 development of missions for second level units	1	2	3	4	5	(25)
c. Corporate Planning Department						
1 format of the corporate plan	1	2	3	4	5	(26)
2 assumptions used in the final corporate plan	1	2	3	4	5	(27)
3 objectives embodied in the final corporate plan	1	2	3	4	5	(28)
4 strategies embodied in the final corporate plan	1	2	3	4	5	(29)
5 approval of the final corporate plan	1	2	3	4	5	(30)
6 development of missions for second level units	1	2	3	4	5	(31)

d. Top Second Level Line Managers

1 format of the corporate plan	1	2	3	4	5	(32)
2 assumptions used in the final corporate plan	1	2	3	4	5	(33)
3 objectives embodied in the final corporate plan	1	2	3	4	5	(34)
4 strategies embodied in the final corporate plan	1	2	3	4	5	(35)
5 approval of the final corporate plan	1	2	3	4	5	(36)
6 development of missions for second level units	1	2	3	4	5	(37)

16

6. To what extent does the Corporate Planning department have the authority to:

	No authority			Complete authority		
a. obtain substantive revisions in second level plans	1	2	3	4	5	(38)
b. obtain procedural revisions in second level plans	1	2	3	4	5	(39)
c. review and criticize second level plans	1	2	3	4	5	(40)
d. accept and reject second level	1	2	3	4	5	(41)

C. Now we have questions on inter-relationships in planning.

1. With which five people outside your group do you have the most contact in your job? Title	2. How often do you exchange planning information with them? Never Always	3. How much do they influence the content of the final corporate plan? Not at all Extensively
1._____ (42-43)	1 2 3 4 5 (52)	1 2 3 4 5 (57)
2._____ (44-45)	1 2 3 4 5 (53)	1 2 3 4 5 (58)
3._____ (46-47)	1 2 3 4 5 (54)	1 2 3 4 5 (59)
4._____ (48-49)	1 2 3 4 5 (55)	1 2 3 4 5 (60)
5._____ (50-51)	1 2 3 4 5 (56)	1 2 3 4 5 (61)

Making Resource Allocation Decisions   17

NEW CARD _ _ _ _ 206 (1-7)

A. We would like to discuss the procedures by which you make your
long range resource allocation decisions.

1. Do you make a budgetary distinction between resources required
to maintain current activities and those which will produce
long run benefits:

| no distinction   very clear
                                          distinction

a. for capital expenditures   1 2 3 4 5   (8)

b. for research and development   1 2 3 4 5   (9)
   expenditures

c. for market development   1 2 3 4 5   (10)
   expenditures

2 How important are the following criteria in evaluating expenditure
proposals which are expected to yield long run benefits?

| totally   very
                unimportant   important

a. Track record of unit requesting   1 2 3 4 5   (11)
   funds

b. Track record of manager of unit   1 2 3 4 5   (12)
   requesting funds

c. Impact on earnings per share   1 2 3 4 5   (13)

d. Forecast return on investment   1 2 3 4 5   (14)

e. Impact on company resource needs 1 2 3 4 5   (15)

f. Forecast net operating profit   1 2 3 4 5   (16)

g. Short term cash flow benefits   1 2 3 4 5   (17)

h. Discounted cash flow analysis   1 2 3 4 5   (18)
   (e.g. internal rate of return)

i. Present market share position   1   2   3   4   5   (19)

j. Forecast market share growth   1   2   3   4   5   (20)

k. Growth of market for which   1   2   3   4   5   (21)
   expenditure is requested

l. Forecast sales growth   1   2   3   4   5
                                           (22)

m. Other (please specify)

    _____   1   2   3   4   5   (23)

    _____   1   2   3   4   5   (24)

18

3. How would these criteria differ (if at all) if the market growth was <u>about equal</u> to <u>real GNP</u> growth?

                                               ___(25)

_____ ___(26)

                                               ___(27)

_____ ___(28)

4. How would the criteria differ (if at all) if the market growth rate was <u>significantly greater</u> than <u>real GNP</u> growth?

                                               ___(29)

_____ ___(30)

                                               ___(31)

_____ ___(32)

B. In the last few years several <u>approaches to strategy development</u> have widely discussed and disseminated.

   1. To what extent have each of the following groups or their ideas influenced the <u>content</u> of your <u>corporate strategies</u> in the last 5 years?

                      <u>no influence</u>   <u>very great influence</u>

a. Profit Impact of Market
   Stategy (PIMS) of the
   Strategic Planning Institute
   in Cambridge   1   2   3   4   5   (33)

b. Product portfolio approach
   developed by the Boston
   Consulting Group.   1   2   3   4   5   (34)

c. Product-market fit analyses
   sometimes associated with
   Igor Ansoff.   1   2   3   4   5   (35)

d. Policy matrices such as those
   developed by Shell Chemical,
   General Electric and McKinsey   1   2   3   4   5   (36)

e. A.D. Little Strategy Center
   Concept   1   2   3   4   5   (37)

f. Pragmatic approach to portfolio
   and strategy analysis as advo-
   cated by Booz Allen   1   2   3   4   5   (38)

                                                           19

2. To what extent do you currently believe these approaches will
   influence your corporate strategies in the next five years?

                             no influence   very great influence

a. Profit Impact of Market
   Strategy (PIMS) of the
   Strategic Planning Institute
   in Cambridge.   1   2   3   4   5   (39)

b. Product portfolio approach
   developed by the Boston
   Consulting Group   1   2   3   4   5   (40)

c. Product-market fit analyses
   sometimes associated with
   Igor Ansoff   1   2   3   4   5   (41)

d. Policy matrices such as those
   developed by Shell Chemical,
   GeneralElectric and McKinsey   1   2   3   4   5   (42)

e. A.D.Little Strategy Center
   Concept   1   2   3   4   5   (43)

f. Pragmatic approach to portfolio
and strategy analysis as advo-
cated by Booz Allen   1   2   3   4   5   (44)

3. To what extent are the other people in your company who are actively
   involved in planning familiar with the ideas we have just discussed?

not at all familiar with			very familiar with and are using	

                                       1   2   3   4   5   (45)

4A. Do you develop policy or portfolio matrices at the corporate level?

                                                                     (46)
                 _____   _____
                 (46-1)yes   no(46-0)
4B Is portfolio analysis used at lower levels in the organization?

                 _____   _____   (47)
                   yes   no
                  (47-1)   (47-0)

        (If no to both 4A and 4B , go to Section V.)

                                         20

5. Policy matrices and/or portfolio analyses are used:

                         never used   extensively used

a. As a guide to setting
   resource allocation priorities   1   2   3   4   5   (48)

b. To analyze competitors   1   2   3   4   5   (49)

c. To analyze customers   1   2   3   4   5   (50)

d. To analyze suppliers   1   2   3   4   5   (51)

e. As a cash flow management   1   2   3   4   5   (52)
   tool

New card _ _ _ _ 207 (1-7)
21

VI. ORGANIZATION CLIMATE AND STRUCTURE

Now we have some questions about the climate in which planning takes place
in the organization.

1. To what extent do you agree with each of the following statements
about risk?

	Disagree			Agree		

a. New ideas are always being tried out
here.   1   2   3   4   5   (8)

b. Unusual or exciting plans are
encourage   1   2   3   4   5   (9)

c. There is a strong tendency toward
high risk, high return investments   1   2   3   4   5   (10)

d. The organization form and structure
encourage entrepreneurial behavior.   1   2   3   4   5   (11)

e. There are special incentives for
entrepreneurial behavior.   1   2   3   4   5   (12)

2. How characteristic of your company is each of the following statements
about planning?

	not at all characteristic			very Characteristic		

a. The "chain of command" for planning
is poorly defined.   1   2   3   4   5   (13)

b. When plans are reviewed in the company,
the atmosphere is generally:

   i. relaxed   1   2   3   4   5   (14)

   ii. tense   1   2   3   4   5   (15)

   iii. confronting   1   2   3   4   5   (16)

c. When performance is reviewed against
the plan in this company, the atmosphere
is generally:

   i. relaxed   1   2   3   4   5   (17)

   ii. tense   1   2   3   4   5   (18)

   iii. confronting   1   2   3   4   5   (19)

d. Goals and objectives for the corporate
planning department are clear to everyone.   1   2   3   4   5   (20)

e. Management takes an active interest in
the output and recommendations of the
planning department.   1   2   3   4   5   (21)

f. Second level line management takes an
active interest in the output and recom-
mendations of the planning department.   1   2   3   4   5   (22)

g. There is a feeling of teamwork in the
corporate planning department.   1   2   3   4   5   (23)

22

3. We would like your opinion on your <u>managers</u> and the relations among them.

<u>Disagree</u>   <u>Agree</u>

a. There is a great deal of cooperation
   between senior managers.   1   2   3   4   5   (24)

b. Senior management has a positive
   attitude about their jobs.   1   2   3   4   5   (25)

c. There is great centralization in
   decision making with most operating
   decisions made at the top.   1   2   3   4   5   (26)

d. A great many conflicts require top
   management resolution   1   2   3   4   5   (27)

e. In general, there are excellent
   communications between line managers
   and corporate planning people.   1   2   3   4   5   (28)

f. Line managers find the services
   rendered by company planners very helpful.   1   2   3   4   5   (29)

g. Information is exchanged freely between
   management in this company.   1   2   3   4   5   (30)

h. There are few opportunities for
   informal conversation between senior
   and subordinate personnel   1   2   3   4   5   (31)

i. Managers' operating styles are
   allowed to range freely from the very
   informal to the very formal.   1   2   3   4   5   (32)

j. Managers in this company typically consult
   with their subordinates on decisions
   to adopt new programs.   1   2   3   4   5   (33)

k. The jobs of managers in this company
   are highly routine.   1   2   3   4   5   (34)

l. There is tight formal control of most
   operations by means of sophisticated
   control and information systems.   1   2   3   4   5   (35)

m. When we have acquired companies, we
   have avoided the problem of incompatible
   managerial behavior.   1   2   3   4   5   (36)

4. Please indicate your agreement with each of these statements about
   <u>managerial performance</u>.

a. People are rewarded in proportion to the
   excellence of their performance.   1   2   3   4   5   (37)

b. Management is quick to criticize for poor performance and seldom forgets a mistake.   1   2   3   4   5   (38)

c. Pay is certainly not an indication of performance in this company.   1   2   3   4   5   (39)

d. There is a strong performance-oriented up-or-out job policy.   1   2   3   4   5   (40)

e. In promoting managers, there is a strong emphasis on competitiveness and ability to outperform others.   1   2   3   4   5   (41)

f. There is a strong tendency to promote from within at senior levels.   1   2   3   4   5   (42)

23

5. To what extent do you believe that people in the management hierarchy:

		Disagree			Agree		
a.	feel they are their own bosses in most matters	1	2	3	4	5	(43)
b.	can take little action until their boss approves a decision	1	2	3	4	5	(44)
c.	have complete written job descriptions for their jobs	1	2	3	4	5	(45)
d.	do the same job in the same way every day	1	2	3	4	5	(46)
e.	have procedures to follow, whatever situation arises	1	2	3	4	5	(47)
f.	have jobs where something new is happening every day	1	2	3	4	5	(48)
g.	are constantly told they should go through proper channels	1	2	3	4	5	(49)
h.	follow written orders without question	1	2	3	4	5	(50)
i.	must follow the same procedures in most situations	1	2	3	4	5	(51)

6. We are also interested in <u>your reactions</u> to decision making styles, and whether or not you agree with the following statements:

		Disagree			Agree		
a.	It is sometimes unclear who has the formal authority to make a decision.	1	2	3	4	5	(52)
b.	Second level line executives have to get clearance from corporate executives before making any major decisions.	1	2	3	4	5	(53)
c.	In decision making, there is great reliance in specially trained line and staff personnel as distinct from a reliance on personnel with experience.	1	2	3	4	5	(54)
d.	There is strong individualistic decision making by the normally responsible executive.	1	2	3	4	5	(55)
e.	There is an emphasis on getting things done, even if this means disregarding formal procedures.	1	2	3	4	5	(56)
f.	There is strong committee oriented consensus seeking, participative decision making.	1	2	3	4	5	(57)
g.	There is a strong emphasis on holding fast to tried and true management principles despite many changes in business conditions.	1	2	3	4	5	(58)
h.	The organization form and structure encourages the development of conservative management.	1	2	3	4	5	(59)

24

		Disagree			Agree		
i.	Overall, the decision making style of senior management in this company is authoritarian.	1	2	3	4	5	(60)
j.	Decision making in this company is participative.	1	2	3	4	5	(61)
k.	There is a strong tendency to let the expert in a given situation have the most say in decision making; even if this means temporarily bypassing formal authority.	1	2	3	4	5	(62)

7. Now, we have a few general questions relating to your company.

a. A friendly atmosphere prevails among
   people in this company.   1   2   3   4   5   (63)

b. There is cooperation among people in
   getting things done.   1   2   3   4   5   (64)

c. There isn't much personal loyalty in
   this company.   1   2   3   4   5   (65)

d. People are proud of belonging to this
   company.   1   2   3   4   5   (66)

e. People in this company really do not
   trust each other enough   1   2   3   4   5   (67)

f. In this company, people pretty much
   look out for their own interests   1   2   3   4   5   (68)

g. A discussion about the latest scientific
   inventions would be common here.   1   2   3   4   5   (69)

h. Careful reasoning and clear logic are
   highly valued here.   1   2   3   4   5   (70)

i. Senior management jobs are very secure.   1   2   3   4   5   (71)

j. There is a tendency for the company to be
   overstaffed with personnel.   1   2   3   4   5   (72)

k. Financial and operating information flow
   quite freely throughout the company.   1   2   3   4   5   (73)

l. The degree of complexity faced by the
   company will eventually limit its power
   to grow.   1   2   3   4   5   (74)

m. The responsibility for operating decisions
   is assigned to second level operating units.   1   2   3   4   5   (75)

n. Our performance as a company is much better
   than it would be as separate and individual
   operating units.   1   2   3   4   5   (76)

o. Second level operating executives have full
   performance responsibility.   1   2   3   4   5   (77)

p. As this company has grown in size, it has:
   i.   grown more impersonal   1   2   3   4   5   (78)
   ii. become more centralized   1   2   3   4   5   (79)
   iii. achieved more participation in
         decision making.   1   2   3   4   5   (80)

   NEW CARD _ _ _ _ 208

q. This company is a loosely divisionalized
   structure.   1   2   3   4   5   (8) (1-7)

25

Finally, we conclude the interview with a few questions about yourself.

1. How long have you been with this company? _____ years. (9-10)

2. How long have you been involved in corporate
planning activities? _____ years. (11-12)

3. How many years of line or staff responsibility have you had in
each of these areas?

	Line Responsibility		Staff Responsibility	
Accounting	_____	(13-14)	_____	(27-28)
Finance	_____	(15-16)	_____	(29-30)
Marketing	_____	(17-18)	_____	(31-32)
Production	_____	(19-20)	_____	(33-34)
Planning	_____	(21-22)	_____	(35-36)
Personnel	_____	(23-24)	_____	(37-38)
Other	_____	(25-26)	_____	(39-40)

4. What is your educational background?

BS/BA
_____ _____ _____ ___(41)

Yes No Field ___(42-43)
(41-1) (41-0) (42-43)

MBA ___(44)
_____ _____ _____

Yes No School ___(45-46)
(44-1) (44-0) (45-46)

Other graduate training ___(47)
_____ _____ _____
Yes No Field ___(48-49)
(47-1) (47-0) (48-49)

5. Do you have any special training related to planning? ___(50)
_____ _____
Please specify:_____ Yes No
(50-1) (50-0)
_____

6. How would you rate your chances for advancement in this organization?

Poor Excellent

1 2 3 4 5 (51)

7. How would you rate your chances for advancement overall?

Poor Excellent

1 2 3 4 5 (52)

8. Overall, how satisfied are you with your job?

Not at all   Very
satisfied   satisfied

    1   2   3   4   5   (53)

We thank you for participating in the survey. You will of course
receive copies of all papers developed from this project, and we shall
advise you when the book summarizing the results is published.

Appendix II

Questionnaire II

Graduate School of Business
Columbia University

Survey of Corporate Planning Practice

Thank you for agreeing to participate in this survey of corporate planning practice of major United States corporations. In this questionnaire we shall be asking a series of questions about both your corporate planning process and company operations and strategy. All responses which you provide will, of course, remain confidential. For analysis purposes they will be combined with responses from other corporations. In order to make it easier to respond to some of the questions, they have been grouped into the following broad categories.

    I.   Operating and Planning Structure

    II.   Organization of the Planning Effort

    III.   The Corporate Environment

    IV.   Corporate Operations and Strategy

Company: _____

Interviewee: _____
                                   Job Title

Interviewer: _____

Time Started: _____

Time Ended: _____

I.   OPERATING STRUCTURE

A.   We would first like some information about your Company's operating
organization structure.

1.   Would you please provide me with an organization chart of the
upper levels of the company?

2.   (If no to Q1) Then could you please sketch the three top levels
on a sheet of paper? We are interested in the organizational
positions and relationships, not the names of the people.
Please be sure to identify:
i.   structure of divisionalization
ii.   the organization for international operations
iii. functional officers (and what types) at the corporate level
iv.   the position of corporate planning

3.   Please identify the various organizational levels of
operating responsibility which exist in your company at the
present time. The following table is an example to show what
we have in mind.

Example

Level Number	Organizational Unit	Number of Units at Each Level
1	Corporate	1
2	Groups or Sectors	3
3	Divisions	6
4	Businesses	50
5	Product Lines	200

YOUR COMPANY

Level Number	Organizational Unit	Number of Units at Each Level	
1	8-10		(8-10)
2	11-14		(11-14)
3	15-18		(15-18)
4	19-22		(19-22)
5	23-28		(23-28)

4.   What is the highest level of functional line executives
(e.g., production, sales) in the company?

                                                              (29)

5.   Are the second level units as we have just defined
them profit centers?   Yes   No   (30)
                                        (30-1) (30-0)

6.   What is the lowest level of profit center? _____

                                                              (31)

7. Do you have a formal system of
transfer pricing within your company?   (32)

                                                     Yes   No (go to 7b)
                                               (32-1) (33-1)

	All of the time				None of the time	
a. Are both price and quantity negotiated simultaneously?	1	2	3	4	5	(33)

b. Is there a policy of procuring
internally wherever possible?   (34)

                                                  Yes   No
                                            (34-1) (34-0)

                                                     2

8. We would also like to get some idea of the degree to which company
activities are proprietary and highly specialized.

Compared to your major competitors, to what extent is your company
(as a whole) highly specialized in its:

		Much less specialized			Much more specialized		
a.	Capital Equipment	1	2	3	4	5	(35)
b.	Production Processes	1	2	3	4	5	(36)
c.	Marketing Systems	1	2	3	4	5	(37)
d.	Human Organization	1	2	3	4	5	(38)
e.	Internal Communication patterns	1	2	3	4	5	(39)

9. We want to identify how your company is organized for international
operations. Do you use any kind of matrix structure for this
purpose?   (40)

                        Yes   No (go to 9b)
                      (40-1)   (40-0)

a. Which single description best describes your organization for   (41-6)
international operations: (42-6)

National subsidiary CEO's and overlapping product
division heads report to Company CEO   _____ (43-1) (43)

International division head and overlapping
product division heads report to Company CEO   _____ (44-1) (44)

Geographic region heads and overlapping product
division heads report to Company CEO   _____ (45-1) (45)

National subsidiary CEO's and overlapping world-
wide functional heads report to Company CEO   _____ (46-1) (46)

Worldwide functional heads and overlapping
product division heads report to Company CEO   _____ (47-1) (47)

Worldwide functional heads and overlapping
geographic heads report to Company CEO   _____ (48-1) (48)

                                                    (go to 10)

b. Which single description best describes your
    organization for international operations?

Export department   _____ (49-1) (49)

National subsidiary CEO's report to Company CEO   _____ (50-1) (50)

Worldwide functional heads report to Company CEO   _____ (51-1) (51)

International division head reports to Company CEO   _____ (52-1) (52)

Geographic region heads report to Company CEO   _____ (53-1) (53)

Worldwide product division heads report to Company CEO _____ (54-1) (54)

Mixed organization:

  International division and non-overlapping product
  division heads report to Company CEO   _____ (55-1) (55)

  Geographic region heads and non-overlapping
  product division heads report to Company CEO   _____ (56-1) (56)

                                  3

10. Now we have a few questions about company ownership.

a. On what exchanges are company shares traded? New York ___ (57-1) (57)
                                                  American ___ (58-1) (58)
                                     International
                                          (list) ___ (59-1) (59)
                                            Other
                                          (list) ___ (60-1) (60)

b. Do senior executives have stock option plans?
                                                  Yes   No   (61)
                                                 (61-1) (61-0)

c. Have you been subject to a takeover since 1974?
                                                  Yes   No   (62)
                                                 (62-1) (62-0)

d. Has the company had any stockholder suits since '74?
                                                  Yes   No   (63)
                                                 (63-1) (63-0)

e. Are sales revenue forecasts part of your public
    reporting?   Yes   No   (64)
                                                 (64-1) (64-0)

f. What is the age of your chief executive officer? _____ years   (65-66)

g. How frequently does your board meet?   _____   (67-68)
                                                  times per yr.

h. Approximately how many days per year is an
    outside board member expected to spend with the
    company?   _____ days.   (69-71)

11. In question 3 you identified the major second level operating units for the company. We now would like to ask a few questions about the inter-relationships among these units. For your convenience, we have arranged these questions as a series of statements. Would you please indicate the extent to which you agree with each of them for your company?

	Disagree			Agree		
Our second level units offer products and services competing directly with those of other second level units.	1	2	3	4	5	(72)
Some of our second level units subsidize losses in other units for extended periods of time.	1	2	3	4	5	(73)

Among our second level units, there is extensive sharing of:

sales and marketing resources	1	2	3	4	5	(74)
research and development resources	1	2	3	4	5	(75)
procurement resources	1	2	3	4	5	(76)
production resources	1	2	3	4	5	(77)
information resources	1	2	3	4	5	(78)

There is a high degree of technological interdependency among our second level units.	1	2	3	4	5	(79)

New card _ _ _ _ 102   (1-7)

4

II. ORGANIZATION OF THE PLANNING EFFORT

A. We would now like some information on the extent to which your company is engaged in Corporate Planning.

1. Does your company develop a formal corporate plan (or plans) on a regular basis?   (8)

    Yes   No
    (go to Q3)
    (8-1) (8-0)

2. (If no to Q1) Does your company develop a series of formal lower level plans on a regular basis?   (9)

    Yes   No (go to III, pg.16)
    (9-1) (9-0)

3. For what time horizons does your company develop a formal corporate plan (or lower level plans if no corporate plan)?

    _____   _____   _____
    Years   Years   Years
    (10-11)   (12-13)   (14-15)

4. What is the relationship between these plans? (Please check __one.__)

Prepared independently and not coordinated. ____ (16-1)

Longer range plan prepared first, shorter range plan
fit into long range plan. ____ (17-1)

Shorter range plan prepared first, longer range plans
are then extended. ____ (18-1)

Shorter range plan prepared first, longer range plans
are then modified from previous year. ____ (19-1)

Short and long range plans prepared simultaneously. ____ (20-1)

5. Which of the plans noted in Q3 would you consider the key
guiding __long range__ plan for the corporation? _____ years. (21-22)

6. In which year did you first develop a formal corporate long
range plan? 19____ (23-24)

7. Do you group second level units for planning the same way as they
are grouped for operations? (25)

Yes No (go to Section B, pg. 6)
(25-1) (25-0)

(If __yes__ to Q7) We would like to know the extent to which your operating
organization is engaged in planning. We are interested only in your
long range planning effort, as you responded in question 5 above.

8. In this question we shall refer to your responses to question 3,
page 1, the organization description. We would like to start with
your __second__ organizational level, those units immediately below
corporate.

a. Please indicate the types of plan that are prepared by a
typical second level organization unit and reviewed at the
corporate level.

Type of Plan	Number of Plans of this type	Reviewed at corporate level?
1 _____ (26-27)	_____ (36-37)	_____ (38)
2 _____ (28-29)	_____ (39-40)	_____ (41)
3 _____ (30-31)	_____ (42-43)	_____ (44)
4 _____ (32-33)	_____ (45-46)	_____ (47)
5 _____ (34-35)	_____ (48-49)	_____ (50)

5

b. When did you first <u>start</u> formal long range planning at the second
level: 19___ And <u>with</u> this configuration of plans? 19___.   (51-52)
       (51-52)   (53-54)   (53-54)

c. What problems are you currently experiencing specifically by planning
with this configuration? What changes in planning do you expect
to implement to deal with these problems?

                                                              —(55)

                                                              —(56)

                                                              —(57)

                                                              —(58)

                                                              —(59)

                                                              —(60)

9. We would like to ask questions now about your <u>third level</u> of planning,
those <u>long range</u> plans which form the basis for <u>the second</u> level plans
which <u>are</u> reviewed at the corporate level.

a. Please indicate the types of third level plans that typically form the
basis for those second level plans.

Type of second level plan	Type of third level plan	Number of third level plans
1_____	_____	_____
	_____	_____
	_____	_____
	_____	_____
2_____	_____	_____
	_____	_____
	_____	_____
	_____	_____
3_____	_____	_____
	_____	_____
	_____	_____
	_____	_____
4_____	_____	_____
	_____	_____
	_____	_____
	_____	_____
5_____	_____	_____
	_____	_____
	_____	_____
	_____	_____

b. Overall, how do you assess the extent of <u>integration</u> of your <u>second</u> and <u>third</u> level plans?

Not at all integrated				Highly integrated	
1	2	3	4	5	(61)

6

10. Now we would like to ask some questions about the <u>fourth</u> level of planning.

   a. Is there a fourth level of <u>long range integrated business planning</u> in your company?

   <u>Yes</u>   <u>No</u> (go to Section D, pg. 8)   (62)
   (62-1) (62-0)

   b. About how many of these fourth level plans are developed <u>in total</u> in your company?

   Number   (63-65)

   c. Are the fourth level planning units profit centers?   ___   ___   (66)
                                                             Yes   No
   (proceed to Section D, pg. 8)   (66-1) (66-0)

B. In that case, we would like to examine what we call the <u>second</u> level of planning, those units immediately below the corporate level, but <u>only</u> those for which <u>long range</u> plans are developed.

1. We would like to know what you call these second level planning units, the manner in which they are defined and the number of units of each type.

   (Examples of names: SBU's, Divisions, Sectors)
   (Examples of bases for definition: product, plant, geographic area, market, function, resource, etc.)

Type of second level planning unit	Bases for second level planning unit definition	Number of such units
_____	_____	_____
_____	_____	_____
_____	_____	_____
_____	_____	_____
	Total	_____

2. What are the major reasons that the particular configuration of
(a) definitions you described above was chosen? (e.g., common competitors, customers, facilities, etc.)

_____   ___(67)
_____   ___(68)
_____   ___(69)
_____   ___(70)
_____

(b) Are second level plans reviewed at the corporate level? ___ ___   ___(71)
                                                             Yes   No
                                                         (71-1)   (71-0)

3. When did you first start formal long range planning at the second
level?   19____   And with this configuration of plans?   19____
             (72-73)   (74-75)   (72-73)

4. Are these second level planning units profit centers?   (74-75)
                                                          Yes   No
                                                      (76-1) (76-0)   (76)

5. What problems are you currently experiencing specifically as a
result of using this configuration for planning? Do you expect
the planning or organization structures to change in order to
deal with these problems? If so, how?

_____ ___(77)

_____ ___(78)

_____ ___(79)

_____ ___(80)

                                    New card __ __ __ __ 103   (1-7)

                                                                 7

C. Now we would like to examine what we call the third level of planning;
i.e., those units immediately below the second level, but only those
for which long range plans are developed.

   1. We would like to know what you call these third level planning
      units, the manner in which they are defined and the number of units
      of each type per second level planning unit.

      (Examples of names: SBU's, Divisions, Sectors, Product Groups)
      (Examples of bases for definition: product, plant, geographic area,
                                       market, function, resource, etc.)

Type of second level planning unit	Type of third level planning unit	Bases for third level planning unit	# of units
1._____	_____	_____	___
	_____	_____	___
	_____	_____	___
	_____	_____	___
2._____	_____	_____	___
	_____	_____	___
	_____	_____	___
	_____	_____	___
3._____	_____	_____	___
	_____	_____	___
	_____	_____	___
	_____	_____	___

4._____   _____   _____   ____
              _____   _____   ____
              _____   _____   ____
              _____   _____   ____

5._____   _____   _____   ____
              _____   _____   ____
              _____   _____   ____
              _____   _____   ____

2. What are the major reasons that the particular configuration of
definitions you described above was chosen? (e.g., common competitors,
customers, facilities, etc.)

_____   ___(8)
_____   ___(9)
_____   ___(10)
_____   ___(11)
                                                    ___(12)

3. When did you first start long range planning at the third level?   19___ (13-14)
And with the present configuration?   19___   (13-14)
                          (15-16)
                                                    (15-16)

4. What problems are you currently experiencing specifically as a result
of using this configuration of planning? Do you expect the planning or
organization structures to change in order to deal with these problems?
If so, how?

_____   ___(17)
_____   ___(18)
_____   ___(19)
_____   ___(20)
                                                    (21)

New card __ __ __ __   103   (1-7)

8

5. Are these third level planning units profit centers?   (22)
                          Yes   No
                          (22-1)   (22-0)

6. We would like to ask some questions about the fourth level of
planning.

a. Is there a fourth level of long range integrated business
planning in your company?
                          Yes   No (go to Q.7)   (23)
                          (23-1) (23-0)

b. (If yes to Q.6a) About how many of these fourth level plans are
developed in total in your company?
                          Number   (24-26)

c. Are the fourth level planning units profit centers?   (27)

$$\overline{\text{Yes}} \quad \overline{\text{No}}$$
(27-1) (27-0)

7. Now a more general question: do the personnel who are responsible for preparing plans typically have operating responsibility also?

    a. At the second level   (28)

$$\overline{\text{Yes}} \quad \overline{\text{No}}$$
(28-1) (28-0)

    b. At the third level   (29)

$$\overline{\text{Yes}} \quad \overline{\text{No}}$$
(29-1) (29-0)

D. In this section we are seeking data on the <u>information inputs</u> employed in the <u>corporate planning function</u>.

1. Please indicate how much effort or resources were expended by corporate planning in each of the following forecasting areas over the last five years. Also indicate whether or not external inputs were purchased from other organizations.

Area	No Effort				Great Deal of Effort		Were External Forecasts Purchased? Yes	No
Domestic economy	1	2	3	4	5	(30)		
							(31-1)	(31-0)
Foreign economies	1	2	3	4	5	(32)		
							(33-1)	(33-0)
Technological	1	2	3	4	5	(34)		
							(35-1)	(35-0)
Governmental (legislative, regulatory)	1	2	3	4	5	(36)		
							(37-1)	(37-0)
Social and/or cultural factors	1	2	3	4	5	(38)		
							(39-1)	(39-0)
Purchased materials or components	1	2	3	4	5	(40)		
							(41-1)	(41-0)
Human resources (e.g., manpower forecasts)	1	2	3	4	5	(42)		
							(43-1)	(43-0)
Financial markets	1	2	3	4	5	(44)		
							(45-1)	(45-0)
Industry-level demand	1	2	3	4	5	(46)		
							(47-1)	(47-0)
Competitive	1	2	3	4	5	(48)		
							(49-1)	(49-1)

9

2. How confident are you that you have an adequate appraisal of the situation in each of the following areas?

Area	Not at all confident				Very confident	
Domestic economy	1	2	3	4	5	(50)
Foreign economics	1	2	3	4	5	(51)

Technological	1	2	3	4	5	(52)
Governmental (legis- lative, regulatory)	1	2	3	4	5	(53)
Social and/or cultural factors	1	2	3	4	5	(54)
Purchased materials or components	1	2	3	4	5	(55)
Human resources	1	2	3	4	5	(56)
Financial markets	1	2	3	4	5	(57)
Industry-level demand	1	2	3	4	5	(58)
Competitive	1	2	3	4	5	(59)

3. For a number of companies, early in the planning process, corporate planning departments provide forecasts to the second level. To what extent are forecasts, which corporate were responsible for developing or purchasing, transmitted to the second level in one form or another for each of the following forecast areas:

Area	Never Transmitted			Extensive Transmission		
Domestic economy	1	2	3	4	5	(60)
Foreign economies	1	2	3	4	5	(61)
Technological	1	2	3	4	5	(62)
Governmental	1	2	3	4	5	(63)
Social and/or cultural factors	1	2	3	4	5	(64)
Purchased materials or components	1	2	3	4	5	(65)
Human resources	1	2	3	4	5	(66)
Financial markets	1	2	3	4	5	(67)
Industry-level demand	1	2	3	4	5	(68)
Competitive	1	2	3	4	5	(69)

4. If the forecasts which corporate planning purchased were not available, how severe would the impact be on:

	No Impact			Severe Impact		
a. the quality of your corporate planning effort	1	2	3	4	5	(70)
b. the quality of your second level planning effort	1	2	3	4	5	(71)

5. How difficult would it be for the <u>second level</u> units to obtain <u>for themselves</u> the information they currently receive from corporate planning?

Very difficult				Very easy	
1	2	3	4	5	(72)

E. In this section we are interested in the extent to which your company has developed models or computer systems to serve as aids to <u>corporate planning</u>.

1. First, to what extent have models been used for corporate planning purposes?

No use made whatsoever			Extensive use made		
1	2	3	4	5	(73)

(go to Q.3)

New card _ _ _ _ 104 (1-7)

2. Which models are now <u>operational</u> in the department?

Used Regularly?

	Yes	No
1._____ (8)	‾(9-1)‾	‾(9-0)‾
2._____ (10)	(11-1)	(11-0)
3._____ (12)	(13-1)	(13-0)
4._____ (14)	(15-1)	(15-0)

How <u>useful</u> have these models been?

Not at all useful			Very useful		
1	2	3	4	5	(16)

3. Describe briefly any computer systems which provide current information on performance for planning purposes.

___(17)

_____ ___(18)

_____ ___(19)

_____ ___(20)

_____ ___(21)

___(22)

4. With respect to <u>second level</u> planning, what is your perception of the use of models?

No use made whatsoever			Extensive use made		
1	2	3	4	5	(23)

(go to Q.6)

5. Which models are now <u>operational</u> in second level units?

		Used Regularly?	
		Yes	No
1.	_____(24)	(25-1)	(25-0)
2.	_____(26)	(27-1)	(27-0)
3.	_____(28)	(29-1)	(29-0)
4.	_____(30)	(31-1)	(31-0)

11

6. Do you have any computer systems which link the <u>corporate</u> planning
   system with second level units?   (32)
   If yes, please describe briefly. (32-1) (32-0)
                                       Yes   No   ___(33)
   _____   ___(34)
   _____   ___(35)
   _____   ___(36)
   _____   ___(37)
   _____   ___(38)

F. In this section we have some questions about the resources that your
   company devotes to planning at both the corporate and second levels.

   1. First, we have some questions about the <u>composition</u> of your <u>corporate
      planning</u> department.

      a. How many professional (non-clerical) personnel comprise the
         corporate planning department?
                              _____
                               number

      b. Please classify (approximately) your available professional personnel
         in corporate planning in terms of their skills. (Give full time
         equivalents if applicable.)

planning specialists	_____	(39-41)
economists	_____	(42-44)
forecasters	_____	(45-47)
computer (information) speciclists	_____	(48-50)
operations research specialists	_____	(51-53)
marketing specialists	_____	(54-56)
financial specialists	_____	(57-59)
legal	_____	(60-62)
R & D	_____	(63-65)
manufacturing	_____	(66-68)
other (please specify)	_____	(69-71)
TOTAL	_____	= X from Q.1a above

c. On average, how long to corporate planning personnel stay in
corporate planning jobs? _____ years.   (72-73)

2. What, in rough terms, is the annual direct cash budget (excluding
allocations) of the corporate planning department? $_____   (74-79)

3. To what extent are line personnel   No   Extensive
rotated through the corporate   rotation   rotation
planning department?
                                          1   2   3   4   5   (80)

4. We would like to know the specific reporting relationship of the
Corporate Planner.
                                                   New card __ __ __ __ 105 (1-7)
The chief corporate planner's
immediate supervisor is: Chairman/President   _____   (8)

                                Treasurer/Controller   _____   (9)

                                Corporate executive
                                vice president   _____   (10)

                                other (please specify)   _____   (11)

                                _____

                                                              12

5. Now we would like some information on your second level planners.

   a. Does the company have specialized planning personnel at the
      second level?
                          Yes   No (go to Q.8)   (12)
                         (12-1)   (12-0)

   b. (If yes to 5a) How many second level planning units are there
      in your company?
                              _____   (13-16)
                                 number

   c. Across all second level planning units, how many planning personnel
      does your company have?
                              _____ of specialized people   (17-21)
                                 number

   d. On average, how long do personnel stay in second level planning
      jobs? _____ years   (22-23)

   e. Is there a career path for planning personnel, within planning,
      in your company?
                          Yes   No   (24)
                         (24-1)   (24-0)

6. To what extent are line personnel   No   Extensive
rotated through the second level   rotation   rotation
planning units?
                                         1   2   3   4   5   (25)

7. Typically, the top second level planner's immediate supervisor is:

                       the senior second level operating officer   _____ (26)

                       a subordinate second level operating officer _____ (27)

                       the corporate planner   _____ (28)

                       the second level controller   _____ (29)

                       other _____   _____ (30)

8. Please indicate the three most frequent functional backgrounds of planners in your company.

1._____(31) 2._____(32) 3._____(33)

G. In this section we are interested in the <u>outputs</u> of the planning process.
   (If no corporate plan, go to G 4.)

I. First, we would like to focus on the <u>corporate long range plan</u> or its equivalent.

1. a. How often is this plan updated?
   (please check one)

more than once a year	____	(34)
every year	____	(35)
less than once a year	____	(36)

   b. And is this done:

   <u>regularly</u>   <u>as needed</u>
   (37)   (38)

2. a. How frequently is progress reviewed against this plan? (please check one)

monthly	____	(39-1)
quarterly	____	(39-4)
six monthly	____	(39-6)
annually	____	(39-12)
less than once a year	____	(39-18)

   b. And is this done:

   <u>regularly</u>   <u>as needed</u>
   (40)   (41)

13

3.. Would you please provide us with a copy of the Table of Contents of your 1979 corporate <u>long range</u> plan? Alternatively, would you please list the major headings and number of pages devoted to each (excluding exhibits)?

No. of Pages

_____   _____
_____   _____
_____   _____
_____   _____
_____   _____
_____   _____
_____   _____
_____   _____
_____   _____
_____   _____
_____   _____

4. When in each year does the formal corporate planning cycle,

   a. start? _____   (42-43)

   b. end? _____   (44-45)

5. To what extent does corporate planning provide added value <u>over and above</u> the completed second level plans, in each of the following areas?

	Corporate planning provides no added value			Corporate planning provides major added value		
Financial	1	2	3	4	5	(46)
Human resources	1	2	3	4	5	(47)
Research and development	1	2	3	4	5	(48)
Markets	1	2	3	4	5	(49)
Organizational structure	1	2	3	4	5	(50)
Raw material requirements	1	2	3	4	5	(51)
Competitive analysis	1	2	3	4	5	(52)

6. How would you characterize the extent to which <u>corporate</u> planning effort is spent on the following types of activity:

	No effort				Extensive effort	
Short term emergency planning	1	2	3	4	5	(53)
Action planning or operational planning for 1 to 3 years into the future	1	2	3	4	5	(54)
Formalized contingency planning	1	2	3	4	5	(55)
Long range (5 to 10 year) planning	1	2	3	4	5	(56)
'What kind of company do we want to be in 10-20 years' type of planning	1	2	3	4	5	(57)
Acquisitions	1	2	3	4	5	(58)
Divestitures	1	2	3	4	5	(59)

14

7. Please indicate which organizational personnel have access to the <u>current</u> <u>corporate</u> <u>plan</u> or <u>key</u> <u>guiding</u> <u>long</u> <u>range</u> <u>plans</u> for the company.

    ___(60)

_____ ___(61)

_____ ___(62)

_____ ___(63)

_____ ___(64)

G. II. Now we would like to focus on the outputs of the <u>second level</u> planning process.

1. Does your company prepare second level long range business plans?

    (65)

          <u>Yes</u>   <u>No</u> (go to Q.7)
          (65-1)   (65-0)

2. a. How often are these plans updated? (please check one)

          more than once a year   ___   (66)

          every year   ___   (67)

          less than once a year   ___   (68)

b. And is this done:

$\overline{\text{regularly}}$ $\overline{\text{as needed}}$
    (69)   (70)

3. a. How frequently is progress reviewed
   against this plan?   more than once a year ____ (71)
   (please check one)
                                         every year   ____ (72)

                                         less than once a year ____ (73)

   b. And is this done:

   $\overline{\text{regularly}}$ $\overline{\text{as needed}}$
       (74)   (75)

4. Has the company developed a standardized format for these second
   level plans?
                                                                      (76)
                            $\overline{\text{Yes}}$ $\overline{\text{No}}$ (go to Q.5)
                            (76-1)   (76-0)

   a. (If yes) Approximately what percentage of the plans in fact
   conform to this format?
                    _____ percent.   (77-78)

5. To what extent are the annual budgets for the second level units
   integrated with the long range plans of those units?

               Not at all   Very
               integrated   integrated

                 1   2   3   4   5   (79)

6. We are interested in the structure of the most common type of second
   level business plan. Would you please provide us with a copy of the
   Table of Contents of the most common type of second level business plan?
   Alternatively, please list the major headings and the number of pages
   devoted to each (excluding exhibits) in a typical 1979 plan.

                                              No. of Pages

   _____   _____
   _____   _____
   _____   _____
   _____   _____
   _____   _____
   _____   _____
   _____   _____
   _____   _____
   _____   _____

                                    New card ____ ____ ____ ____ 106   (1-7)
                                                             15

7. Now, more generally, we have some questions about formal contingency
   plans.

   a. Does your company develop formal contingency plans as part of its
   long range planning effort?

                    $\overline{\text{Yes}}$ $\overline{\text{No}}$ (go to Section III, pg.16)   (8)
                    (8-1)   (8-0)

b. At what levels are major contingencies
developed? (please check as appropriate)

Corporate only	_____	(9)
Second level only	_____	(10)
Both corporate and second level	_____	(11)

c. Are the major variables in your
contingency plans:

Uncontrollable environmental factors only   (12)

<u>Yes</u>   <u>No</u>
(12-1)   (12-0)

Controllable strategic actions only   (13)

<u>Yes</u>   <u>No</u>
(13-1)   (13-0)

Both of the above   (14)

<u>Yes</u>   <u>No</u>
(14-1)   (14-0)

16

III. THE CORPORATE ENVIRONMENT

The questions in this section deal with the environments within
which planning takes place.

A. Demand Environments

1.a.

We would like to assess the degree to which the demand faced by
your operating units has been predictable over the past 5 years.
Approximately what percent of your company's sales fell into
each of the following categories over the past five years?

The demand environment has been:

Highly predictable	_____ percent	(15-16)
Predictable	_____ percent	(17-18)
Fairly predictable	_____ percent	(19-20)
Unpredictable	_____ percent	(21-22)
Highly unpredictable	_____ percent	(23-24)
Total	100 percent	

1.b.

We would like you to assess the degree to which the total demand
which will be faced by your operating units is predictable. Please
estimate the percent of your company's sales volume which falls
into each of the following categories for the long term planning
horizon.

The demand environment will be:

Highly predictable	_____ percent	(25-26)
Predictable	_____ percent	(27-28)
Fairly predictable	_____ percent	(29-30)
Unpredictable	_____ percent	(31-32)
Highly unpredictable	_____ percent	(33-34)
Total	100 percent	

1.c.
   How confident are you in the   Not at all   Very
   responses which you provided   Confident   Confident
   to question 1.b.?   1   2   3   4   5   (35)

2.a.
We would also like to get an estimate of the real growth of the
markets in which your company has competed over the past five years.

Approximately what percent of
your sales were in markets
growing at real rates of:

Over 20% per year	_____ percent	(36-37)
10 - 20% per year	_____ percent	(38-39)
5 - 10% per year	_____ percent	(40-41)
0 - 5% per year	_____ percent	(42-43)
Declining markets	_____ percent	(44-45)
Total	100 percent	

17

2.b.
We would now like you to assess the real growth of markets in
which you expect to compete over your long range planning horizon.

What percent of your sales
do you expect to be in markets
growing at real rates of:

Over 20% per year	_____ percent	(46-47)
10 - 20% per year	_____ percent	(48-49)
5 - 10% per year	_____ percent	(50-51)
0 - 5% per year	_____ percent	(52-53)
Declining markets	_____ percent	(54-55)
Total	100 percent	

2.c.
   How confident are you in the   Not at all   Very
   responses which you provided   Confident   Confident
   to question 2.b.?   1   2   3   4   5   (56)

B. Competitive Environments

1. We would like to classify the competition which your operating units face. What percent of your company's total sales volume is achieved in each of the following competitive environments?

More than twice the volume
of second competitor, and
other competition minor _____ percent (57-58)

3 to 7 major competitors:

you are market leader _____ percent (59-60)

you are not market leader _____ percent (61-62)

More than 7 major competitors:

you are market leader _____ percent (63-64)

you are not market leader _____ percent (65-66)

Total 100 percent

2.a.

Over the past five years, what percent of your sales volume fell into categories in which your major competitors' actions were:

Highly predictable _____ percent (67-68)

Predictable _____ percent (69-70)

Fairly predictable _____ percent (71-72)

Unpredictable _____ percent (73-74)

Highly unpredictable _____ percent (75-76)

Total 100 percent

2.b. New card _ _ _ _ 107 (1-7)

Over your long range planning horizon, what percent of your sales volume do you expect to be in categories for which major competitors actions will be:

Highly predictable _____ percent (8-9)

Predictable _____ percent (10-11)

Fairly predictable _____ percent (12-13)

Unpredictable _____ percent (14-15)

Highly unpredictable _____ percent (16-17)

Total 100 percent

18

2.c.
How confident are you in the
responses which you provided
to question 2.b.?

	Not at all confident				Very confident	
	1	2	3	4	5	(18)

C. Technological Environments

1.a.
We would like your assessment of the degree of technological change which has taken place in the industries in which your company has operated over the previous ten years. What percent of this year's sales will be generated by products dependent on technology which did not exist or was not commercially feasible in 1970? (please check one)

Less than 5% of total sales	_____	(19-20)
5 - 15% of total sales	_____	(21-22)
15 - 30% of total sales	_____	(23-24)
30 - 50% of total sales	_____	(25-26)
Over 50% of total sales	_____	(27-28)

1.b.
What percent of sales in 1990 will be generated by products dependent upon technology which does not exist or is not commercially feasible today?

Less than 5% of total sales	_____	(29-30)
5 - 15% of total sales	_____	(31-32)
15 - 30% of total sales	_____	(33-34)
30 - 50% of total sales	_____	(35-36)
Over 50% of total sales	_____	(37-38)

1.c.
How confident are you in the responses which you provided to question 1.b.?

Not at all confident   Very confident

1   2   3   4   5   (39)

2.a.
To what extent have your company's production processes been changed by the introduction of new technology since 1970?

No technological changes in production processes   Substantial technological changes in production processes

1   2   3   4   5   (40)

2.b.
To what extent do you think your company's production processes in 1990 will be technologically different from those in use today?

1   2   3   4   5   (41)

2.c.
How confident are you of the responses which you provided in Q.2.b.?

Not at all confident   Very confident

1   2   3   4   5   (42)

D. Governmental Environments

1.a.
We would like your assessment of the extent of government regulation of your company's business over the past five years. What percent of your company's sales volume has been:

Highly government regulated	_____ percent	(43-44)
Somewhat government regulated	_____ percent	(45-46)
Not at all government regulated		
	_____ percent	(47-48)
Total	100　percent	

1.b.
Over your long range planning horizon, what percent of your sales volume will fall into categories for which government regulation will:

Increase	_____ percent	(49-50)
Stay the same	_____ percent	(51-52)
Decrease	_____ percent	(53-54)
Total	100　percent	

1.c.
How confident are you in the responses which you provided in question 1.b.?

Not at all Confident			Very Confident		
1	2	3	4	5	(55)

E. Resource Environments

1.a.
Within the past few years, concerns have been raised about the long term availability of resources. What percent of your raw material and component supplies fell into the following categories over the last five years:

No availability problems	_____ percent	(56-57)
Some availability problems	_____ percent	(58-59)
Significant availability problems		
	_____ percent	(60-61)
Severe availability problems	_____ percent	(62-63)
Total	100　percent	

1.b.
What percent of your raw material and component supplies will fall into the following categories over your long range planning horizon:

No availability problems	_____ percent	(64-65)
Some availability problems	_____ percent	(66-67)
Significant availability problems		
	_____ percent	(68-69)
Severe availability problems	_____ percent	(70-71)
Total	100　percent	

1.c.
How confident are you in the
responses which you provided
in question 1.b.?

Not at all Confident			Very Confident		
1	2	3	4	5	(72)

20

2.a.
Considering your company's human
resource needs as a whole, to
what extent have you had problems
in securing and retaining the
necessary personnel during the last
five years:

No problems			Severe problems		
1	2	3	4	5	(73)

2.b.
To what extent do you anticipate
problems in securing and
retaining personnel over your
long range planning horizon:

1	2	3	4	5	(74)

2.c.
How confident are you in the
responses which you provided
in question 2.b.?

Not at all Confident			Very Confident		
1	2	3	4	5	(75)

3.a.
Considering your company's
financing needs, to what extent
have you had problems in securing
the necessary funds over the
last five years:

No Problems			Severe problems		
1	2	3	4	5	(76)

3.b.
To what extent do you anticipate
problems in securing the
necessary funds over your long
range planning horizon:

1	2	3	4	5	(77)

3.c.
How confident are you in the
responses which you provided
in question 3.b.?

Not at all Confident			Very Confident		
1	2	3	4	5	(78)

New card _ _ _ _ (1-7)

21

IV. CORPORATE OPERATIONS AND STRATEGY

A. In this section we would like some information on corporate operations.

1. Can you please give us the line of business breakdown that you
provide to the SEC, with the percentages of 1979 corporate revenues
in each category?   (If this information is provided from the
annual report or 10K, go to Q.2)

_____

_____

_____

_____

2. What percent of 1979 corporate revenues were generated in the following?

Services

Retail and/or Wholesale Distribution	_____ percent	(8-9)
Other Services	_____ percent	(10-11)

Consumer Products Manufacturing

Durable Products	_____ percent	(12-13)
Non-durable Products	_____ percent	(14-15)

Industrial/Commercial/Governmental
Products Manufacturing

Capital Goods	_____ percent	(16-17)
Raw or Semi-finished Materials	_____ percent	(18-19)
Components for incorporation into Finished Products	_____ percent	(20-21)
Supplies or other Consumable Products	_____ percent	(22-23)

Total   100   percent

3. Approximately what portion of your corporate sales revenue is value added by your firm? (Value added is total sales revenues minus outside purchases, and tends to be low for trading firms, high for vertically integrated manufacturing firms.)

Value added is   Value added is
less than 10% of   over 70% of
sales revenues   sales revenues

1   2   3   4   5   (24)

4. In your company's major businesses, would you say that you are, in general, more or less vertically integrated than your major competitors?

Much less   Much more
vertically   vertically
integrated   integrated

1   2   3   4   5   (25)

This card
continues on p. 23
of the questionnaire

New card __ __ __ __ 109 (1-7)

22

5. Can you please identify the industries in which your company participates. Please circle where appropriate.

I

Code

AGRICULTURE, FORESTRY, & FISHING

01	Agricultural Production of Crops	(8-1)
02	Agricultural Production of Live-stock	(9-1)
03	Agricultural Services	(10-1)
04	Forestry	(11-1)
05	Fishing, Hunting, Trapping	(12-1)

MINING

10	Metal Mining	(13-1)
11	Coal Mining	(14-1)
13	Oil and Gas Extraction	(15-1)
14	Nonmetallic Minerals, Except Fuels	(16-1)

CONSTRUCTION

15	General Building Construction	(17-1)
16	Heavy Construction	(18-1)
17	Special Trade Contractors	(19-1)

MANUFACTURING

20	Food and Kindred Products	(20-1)
21	Tobacco Manufactures	(21-1)
22	Textile Mill Products	(22-1)
23	Apparel & Other Textile Products	(23-1)
24	Lumber and Wood Products	(24-1)
25	Furniture and Fixtures	(25-1)
26	Paper and Allied Products	(26-1)
27	Printing and Publishing	(27-1)
28	Chemicals and Allied Products	(28-1)
29	Petroleum & Coal Refining	(29-1)
30	Rubber & Misc. Plastic Products	(30-1)
31	Leather and Leather Products	(31-1)
32	Stone, Clay & Glass Products	(32-1)
33	Primary Metal Industries	(33-1)
34	Fabricated Metal Products	(34-1)
35	Machinery, Except Electrical	(35-1)
36	Electric and Electronic Equipment	(36-1)
37	Transportation Equipment	(37-1)
38	Instruments and Related Products	(38-1)
39	Other Manufacturing	(39-1)

TRANSPORTATION & PUBLIC UTILITIES

40	Railroad Transportation	(40-1)
41	Local & Interurban Passenger Transit	(41-1)
42	Trucking & Warehousing	(42-1)
43	Water Transportation	(43-1)
44	Transportation by Air	(44-1)
46	Pipe Lines, Except Natural Gas	(45-1)
47	Transportation Services	(46-1)
48	Communication	(47-1)
49	Electric, Gas, & Sanitary Services	(48-1)

Code

WHOLESALE TRADE

50	Wholesale Trade -- Durable Goods	(49-1)
51	Wholesale Trade -- Non-durable Goods	(50-1)

RETAIL TRADE

52	Building Materials & Garden Supplies	(51-1)
53	General Merchandise Stores	(52-1)
54	Food Stores	(53-1)
55	Automotive Dealers & Service Stations	(54-1)
56	Apparel and Accessory Stores	(55-1)
57	Furniture & Home Furnishings Stores	(56-1)
58	Eating and Drinking Places	(57-1)
59	Other Retail	(58-1)

FINANCE, INSURANCE, AND REAL ESTATE

60	Banking	(59-1)
61	Credit Agencies Other than Banks	(60-1)
62	Security, Commodity Brokers & Services	(61-1)
63	Insurance	(62-1)
65	Real Estate	(63-1)
67	Holding & Other Investment Offices	(64-1)

SERVICES

70	Hotels and Other Lodging Places	(65-1)
72	Personal Services	(66-1)
731	Advertising Services	(67-1)
732	Credit Services	(68-1)
734	Building Services	(69-1)
737	Computer & Data Processing Services	(70-1)
739	Other Business Services	(71-1)
74	Auto Repair, Services, & Garages	(72-1)
78	Motion Pictures	(73-1)
79	Amusement & Recreation Services	(74-1)
80	Health Services	(75-1)
82	Educational Services	(76-1)
83	Social Services	(77-1)
89	Engineering & Architectural Services	(78-1)

OTHER (Please Specify)

90	_____	(79-1)
91	_____	(80-1)
92	_____	
93	_____	
94	_____	
95	_____	

6. We should like information on the geographic bases of your company's operations.

   a. Which parts of the world account for over one percent of your sales and production volume? (Please indicate whichever apply.)

	Sales		Production	
United States & Canada	1	(26-1)	1	(27-1)
Central & South America	2	(28-1)	2	(29-1)
Africa	3	(30-1)	3	(31-1)
Western Europe	4	(32-1)	4	(33-1)
Eastern Europe	5	(34-1)	5	(35-1)
Middle & Near East	6	(36-1)	6	(37-1)
India & Pakistan	7	(38-1)	7	(39-1)
Far East	8	(40-1)	8	(41-1)
Australia & New Zealand	9	(42-1)	9	(43-1)

   b. What percent of sales take place outside the U.S.? (exports and overseas manufactured) _____ percent   (44-45)

   c. How many manufacturing subsidiaries do you have outside the United States? _____ number   (46-48)

   d. What percent of these subsidiaries are wholly owned?

                                           _____ percent   (49-50)

7. We have two questions about personnel.

   a. What is the approximate number of employees in the company? (U.S. and overseas)   Total _____   (51-55)

   b. What is the corporate budget for training and development of personnel? $ _____   (56-60)

8. What is the size of the 1979 annual budget for capital expenditures?

                              $ _____   (61-70)

B. In this segment, we have some questions which are oriented around the concept of the product class life cycle.

   1. Could you please estimate the fraction of total corporate revenues in 1979 from each of the following stages:

      Introductory Stage: Primary demand for product class just starting to grow; products or services still unfamiliar to many potential users   _____ percent (71-72)

      Growth Stage: Demand growing at 10% or more annually in real terms; technology and/or competitive structure still changing   _____ percent (73-74)

Maturity Stage: Products or services familiar to
vast majority of prospective users; technology and
competitive structure reasonably stable _____ percent (75-76)

Decline Stage: Weaker competitors exiting; real
sales volume declining. _____ percent (77-78)

Total 100 percent

24

2. Has the company made any significant acquisitions since January 1974?

(79)
Yes No (go to Q. 3)
(79-1) (79-0)

a. Of those acquisitions, what percent of their revenues when
acquired were from the: NEW CARD _ _ _ _ 110 (1-7)

Introductory Stage	_____ percent	(8-9)
Growth Stage	_____ percent	(10-11)
Maturity Stage	_____ percent	(12-13)
Decline Stage	_____ percent	(14-15)
Total	100 percent	

b. How many individual acquisitions has your company made
since January 1974? _____ number   (16-18)

c. What dollar sales volume would you attribute to those acquisitions
in 1979 $_____   (19-26)

3. To what extent is your company's acquisition planning subsumed under
your corporate planning process?

Not at all   Totally
1   2   3   4   5   (27)

4. Have you divested, liquidated or otherwise eliminated any important
operations since January 1974?   (28)

Yes   No (go to Q. 5)
(28-1) (28-0)

a. Of those operations, what percent of their revenues when
divested were from the:

Introductory Stage	_____ percent	(29-30)
Growth Stage	_____ percent	(31-32)
Maturity Stage	_____ percent	(33-34)
Decline Stage	_____ percent	(35-36)
Total	100 percent	

b. How many separate divestitures has your company made since
January 1974? _____ number   (37-39)

c. If you had retained those units, what would you expect their
1979 sales to have been? $_____   (40-46)

5. a. Do you undertake a regular review of business units to identify
      abandonment possibilities?

                          ‾Yes‾   ‾No‾   (47)
                         (47-1) (47-0)
   b. To what extent is your company's divestiture planning subsumed
      under your corporate planning process?

               Not at all   Totally
                   1   2   3   4   5   (48)

6. In new product and service introductions, how often is your company:

   First-to-market with new   Never   Always
   products and services   1   2   3   4   5   (49)

   Early follower of initial
   entrants in fast-growing
   new markets   1   2   3   4   5   (50)

   Later entrants in established
   but still growing markets   1   2   3   4   5   (51)

   Entrants in mature, stable
   markets   1   2   3   4   5   (52)

   Entrants in declining markets   1   2   3   4   5   (53)

   At the cutting edge of techno-
   logical innovation   1   2   3   4   5   (54)

                                                           25

7. Now we would like to ask some questions about how your products are
   managed over their life cycles. Please indicate the extent to which
   you agree with each of the following statements for your company:

                                Disagree   Agree

   a We develop plans for products
      which span their expected life
      cycle.   1   2   3   4   5   (55)

   b We organize special corporate
      task forces to oversee the devel-
      opment of new products.   1   2   3   4   5   (56)

   c Development of new markets for
      existing products is the respon-
      sibility of our second-level
      operating units.   1   2   3   4   5   (57)

   d New product development is the
      responsibility of a special
      organizational unit of our company. 1   2   3   4   5   (58)

   e New product development is part
      of the responsibility of our second
      level operating units.   1   2   3   4   5   (59)

   f The life cycle of most of our
      new products seems to be getting
      shorter and shorter   1   2   3   4   5   (60)

g Screening of new product ideas is
   part of the responsibility of our
   second level operating units.   1   2   3   4   5   (61)

h Screening of new market ideas is
   part of the responsibility of our
   second level operating units.   1   2   3   4   5   (62)

i Development of new markets for
   existing products is part of a
   special organizational unit.   1   2   3   4   5   (63)

j We are making a conscious attempt
   to stretch the life cycle of our
   new products.   1   2   3   4   5   (64)

k Screening of new product ideas
   is the responsibility of a special
   organizational unit of our company.   1   2   3   4   5   (65)

l Screening of new market ideas is
   the responsibility of a special
   organizational unit.   1   2   3   4   5   (66)

8. Today, what do you think is the average expected life cycle of a new
   product introduced by your company?
                                    _____ years   (67-68)

9. What do you think is the average expected time for development of a
   new product in your company, from idea/invention to market introduction?
                                    _____ years   (69-70)

10. For how many years do you expect new products introduced by your
    company to return greater than average profits?

                                    _____ years   (71-72)

                                                              26

C. In this final section of the questionnaire, we would like to obtain
    some information on your research and development emphasis.

    Please note that we define these activities broadly to include applicable
    engineering expenditures.

    1. To what extent do you agree with the following statements:

                                        Disagree   Agree

    a This company considers itself to
       be highly technically innovative.   1   2   3   4   5   (73)

    b The emphasis of our RD & E expenditures
       is highly applied.   1   2   3   4   5   (74)

    c Our RD & E effort tends to avoid
       high risk activity.   1   2   3   4   5   (75)

    d This company prefers to seek growth
       via acquisitions rather than internal
       RD & E.   1   2   3   4   5   (76)

e Currently, we are successful in ob-
taining talented scientific personnel   1   2   3   4   5   (77)

f One of the key responsibilities of
corporate planning is to help focus
our RD & E effort around defined
opportunity areas.   1   2   3   4   5   (78)

                      NEW CARD   —— —— —— — 111 (1-7)

2. a. On the average, over the past five years, what percent of corporate
revenues have been allocated to RD & E activities?

                         _____ percent   (8-9)

    b. Of the allocations, what was the split between new product RD & E
and process RD & E?

              New product   _____ percent   (10-11)

                 Process   _____ percent   (12-13)

                  Total   100   percent

3. a. Is your company a member of an R&D consortium?

                                       (14)

                         Yes   No
                      (14-1) (14-0)

    b. If yes, what percent of your R&D budget is involved?

                         _____ percent   (15-16)

We thank you for participating in the survey. You will of course
receive copies of all papers developed from this project, and we shall
advise you when the book summarizing the results is published.

Appendix III

Tables of Standard Deviations

Table AIIIa
Within-Group Standardized Scale Standard Deviations
of Groups formed in Chapter 9

	Planning Groups				
Adaptive Planning Scales	Fully Integrated	Exten- sive	Seat- of-the- Pants	Marginal	Not-at- all
Environmental Orientation					
Environmental Information	.90	.88	.77	1.14	1.07
Competitive Analysis	.82	.76	.81	.96	1.10
Strategic Orientation					
"Strategic" Planning	.83	.71	.90	.42	0
Time Horizon	1.05	.89	.89	.42	.56
Globalness	.90	.87	.89	.69	1.24
Portfolio Change	1.04	.92	.81	.80	.92
Resource Allocation	.90	.74	1.05	1.08	.83
Planning Tools					
Portfolio Models	1.09	.69	1.04	.69	.76
Model Use	.71	1.07	.86	.80	.56
Resource Allocation Decisions					
Long Run Expense Distinction	1.04	.82	.90	.93	1.26
Strategic Criteria	.73	.47	.77	1.07	1.23
Plan Comprehensiveness					
Corporate	.91	.92	.98	.89	.20
Second Level	.96	1.01	1.04	.56	0
Integrative Planning Scales					
Formal Integration of Plans					
Corporate/Functional	.82	.91	.72	.80	.95
Over-time	.78	.98	.78	.76	.42
Information Flow					
Top Down	1.04	.78	.81	.83	.45
Internal	.73	1.11	.77	1.07	1.23
Corporate Planning Exchange	.86	.79	.82	1.35	1.48
Influence and Participation					
Board of Directors	.83	.97	.74	1.02	1.32
CEO	.78	.67	.54	1.14	1.71
Top Second Level Line Management	.99	.51	.82	.90	1.13
Corporate Planning	.65	.58	.68	.95	.97
Internal	.31	.71	.71	1.07	.83

Table AIIIa (continued)

	Planning Groups				
	Fully Integrated	Exten-sive	Seat-of-the-Pants	Marginal	Not-at-all
Goal and Strategy Formulation Process					
Bottom Up	.82	1.24	.81	.96	1.10
CEO Negotiation	1.08	.96	1.05	.86	.59
Planning and Line Management					
Relative Staff/Line	.50	.14	1.74	.17	.24
Nature of Planning					
Line View of Planning	.81	.72	.87	1.06	1.01
Integrative Value of Planners					
Added Value	.89	.77	1.02	.97	0
Planning Group Integration	.54	.50	.73	.89	1.37
Status and Authority of Planners					
Reporting Importance	.77	.83	.95	.84	.75
Planning Authority	.65	1.60	.85	1.13	1.04
Formalization of Planning					
Corporate	.94	.74	1.03	.99	0
Second level	.64	.44	.95	.83	.66
Plan Density Preparation	.97	1.05	.98	.65	.98
Plan Density Review	1.20	.82	.91	.38	1.11
Plan Distribution Depth	1.17	.60	.95	1.12	1.06
Planning and Performance Review					
Plan Review Atmosphere	.87	1.62	1.00	1.24	.88
Performance Review:					
Atmosphere	.93	1.12	.90	1.08	1.22
Frequency	.97	1.05	.98	.98	.65
Criteria	1.08	.99	.92	1.01	.80
Depth	.90	.97	1.13	.97	1.03
Goals					
Use of Goals	.84	.86	1.06	.65	.92
Goals for Planning	1.08	1.11	.92	1.08	.82

Table AIIIb

	Environment Groups		
Environment Scales	High Change	Benign	High Difficulty
Uncertainty	.81	.60	.43
Change	.63	.70	.71
Hostility	.69	.40	.66

Table AIIIc

	Strategy Groups			
Strategy Scales	Innovative Strategists	Segmenters	Domestic Status Quoers	Portfolio Switchers
Internal Innovation	1.14	.56	.59	.67
Acquisition	1.03	.72	.82	.74
Divestiture	.82	.52	.48	1.86
International Posture	.92	.73	.48	.46
Industrial Goods	.74	.96	1.13	1.47
Scale	1.06	.95	.88	.68
International Marketing	.91	.47	.98	.30
Explicit Growth/Share Strategy	.68	1.00	1.06	.83
New Product Strategy	.77	.88	.96	1.05
Explicit Segment Strategy	.86	.96	1.03	.84

Table AIIId

Organization Structure Scales	Organization Structure Groups				
	Organic	Decen-tralized	Homegrown/ Task Forces	Outsider/ Isolated	Centralized Control
Entrepreneurial Incentives	.80	1.08	.68	.86	.68
Task Forces	.94	.44	.53	.97	1.11
Resource Sharing	.74	.31	.74	.97	.68
Interdivisional Communication	1.05	.66	.47	1.00	.85
Decentralization	.69	.65	.60	.87	.53
Insider Influence	.53	.62	.37	1.04	.66
Organizational Interdependency	.83	.56	1.15	.56	.57
Organizational Specialization	1.25	.96	.67	.70	.84

Table AIIIe

Organizational Climate Scales	Organizational Climate Groups			
	Partici-pative Autonomy	Partici-pative Bureaucracy	Average	Rigid Bureaucracy
Entrepreneurialness	.81	.65	.84	.70
Performance Orientation	.82	.80	.81	1.14
Line-Staff Interaction	1.10	.57	.73	.87
Organizational Contentment	.62	.61	.68	.96
Participative Decision Making	.60	.61	.81	1.08
Organizational Fluidity	.52	.75	.72	1.10
Delegated Responsibility	.92	.83	.89	.74

References

Abell, Derek F. and John S. Hammond. 1979. *Strategic Marketing Planning.* Englewood Cliffs, NJ: Prentice-Hall.

Abernathy, William J. and Kenneth Wayne. 1974. "Limits of the Learning Curve." *Harvard Business Review* (September-October) 52: 109-119.

Abou-Zeid, R. 1974. "A Study of the Approaches and Systems Used by Top Management Executives in Selected Companies for Organizational Goal Identification." Ph.D. Dissertation, University of Texas, Austin.

Ackerman, Robert W. 1970. "Influence of Integration and Diversity on the Investment Process." *Administrative Science Quarterly* (September) 15: 341-351.

Ackoff, R. L. 1981. *Creating the Corporate Future.* New York: John Wiley.

Adamson, Joel. 1980. "Corporate Long Range Planning Must Include Procurement." *Journal of Purchasing and Materials Management* (Spring) 16: 25-32.

Aguilar, Francis J. 1967. *Scanning the Business Environment.* New York: Macmillan.

Aguilar, Francis J., Robert A. Howell, and Richard F. Vancil. 1970. *Formal Planning Systems 1970: A Progress Report and Prospectus.* Cambridge, Mass.: Harvard University Press.

Al-Bazzaz, Shawki and Peter Grinyer. 1980. "How Planning Works in Practice – A Survey of 48 U.K. Companies." *Long Range Planning* (August) 13: 30-42.

Aldrich, Howard. 1979. *Organizations and Environment.* Englewood Cliffs, N.J.: Prentice-Hall.

Allen, Stephen A. 1978. "Organizational Choices and General Manager Influence Networks in Divisionalized Companies." *Academy of Management Journal* (September) 21: 341-365.

Anderson, Carl R. and Frank T. Paine. 1975. "Managerial Perceptions and Strategic Behavior." *Academy of Management Journal* (December) 18: 811-823.

Anderson, Carl R. and Frank T. Paine. 1978. "PIMS: A Reexamination." *Academy of Management Review* (July) 3: 602-612.

Andrews, K.R. 1971. *The Concept of Corporate Strategy*. Homewood, Ill.: Dow Jones.

Ang, James S. and Chua, Jess H. 1979. "Long Range Planning in Large United States Corporations – A Survey." *Long Range Planning* (April) 12: 99-102.

Ansoff, H. Igor. 1965. *Corporate Strategy*. New York: McGraw-Hill.

Ansoff, H. Igor and John M. Stewart. 1967. "Strategies for a Technology-Based Business." *Harvard Business Review* (November-December) 45: 71-83.

Ansoff, H. Igor, Jay Avner, Richard G. Brandenburg, Fred E. Portner, and Raymond Radosevich. 1970. "Does Planning Pay? The Effect of Planning on Success of Acquisitions in American Firms." *Long Range Planning* (December) 3: 2-7.

Argyris, C. 1973. "Personality and Organization Theory Revisited." *Administrative Science Quarterly* 18: 141-167.

Armstrong, J. Scott. 1982. "The Value of Formal Planning for Strategic Decisions: Review of Empirical Research." *Strategic Management Journal* (July-September) 3: 197-211.

Armstrong, J. Scott. 1986. "The Value of Formal Planning for Strategic Decisions: Reply." Working Paper, The Wharton School.

Athreya, M. 1970. "Planning as Integration," In Jay W. Lorsch and Paul R. Lawrence, eds. *Studies in Organization Design*. Homewood, Ill.: Richard D. Irwin, pp. 168-186.

Austin, Douglas V. and Thomas J. Scampini. 1984. "Long Term Strategic Planning: Part 2." *Bankers Magazine* (January-February) 167: 61-66.

Ball, Leslie D. 1982. "MIS Strategic Planning: You Can Be Captain of the Ship." *Infosystems* (May) 29: 32-38.

Bandeen, Robert A. 1984. "Strategic Planning at Crown Life." *Managerial Planning* (May-June) 32: 4-7, 51.

Banks, Robert L. and Steven C. Wheelwright. 1979. "Operations vs. Strategy: Trading Tomorrow for Today." *Harvard Business Review* (May-June) 57: 112-120.

Barber, John M. and Richard M. Kelly. 1981. "The Corporate Planner and The Community." *Planning Review* (July) 9: 14-18.

Bass, Frank M. 1973. "Market Structure and Profitability – Analysis of the Appropriateness of Pooling Cross-Sectional Industry Data." Paper no. 424, Krannert Graduate School of Industrial Administration, Purdue University.

Bass, Frank M., Philippe Cattin, and Dick Wittink. 1978. "Firm Effects and Industry Effects in the Analysis of Market Structure and Profitability." *Journal of Marketing Research* 15: 3-10.

Beard, Donald W. and Gregory G. Dess. 1979. "Industry Profitability and Firm Performance: A Preliminary Analysis on the Business Portfolio Question." *Proceedings,* Academy of Management (August), pp. 123-127.

Beard, Donald W. and Gregory G. Dess. 1981. "Corporate-Level Strategy, Business-Level Strategy, and Firm Performance." *Academy of Management Journal* (December) 24: 663-688.

Beattie, D.L. 1980. "Conglomerate Diversification and Performance: A Survey and Time Series Analysis." *Applied Economics* (September) 12: 251-273.

Berg, Norman A. 1965. "Strategic Planning in Conglomerate Companies." *Harvard Business Review* (May-June) 43: 79-92.

Berg, Norman A. 1969. "What's Different About Conglomerate Management." *Harvard Business Review* (November-December) 47: 112-120.

Berg, Norman A. 1973. "Corporate Role in Diversified Companies." In Bernhard Taylor and Keith MacMillan, eds. *Business Policy: Teaching and Research.* New York: John Wiley, pp. 296-347.

Bernhard, Arnold. 1959. *The Evaluation of Common Stocks.* New York: Simon and Schuster.

Bettis, Richard A. 1981. "Performance Differences in Related and Unrelated Diversified Firms." *Strategic Management Journal* (October-December) 2: 379-393.

Bettis, Richard A. and William K. Hall. 1982. "Diversification Strategy, Accounting Determined Risk, and Accounting Determined Return." *Academy Management Journal* (June) 25: 254-264.

Bhatty, Egbert F. 1981. "Corporate Planning in Medium-Sized Companies in the U.K." *Long Range Planning* (February) 14: 60-72.

Boston Consulting Group. 1972. *Perspectives on Experience.* Boston: The Boston Consulting Group.

Bouamrene, M.A. and R. Flavell. 1980. "Airline Corporate Planning – A Conceptual Framework." *Long Range Planning* (February) 13: 62-69.

Boulton, William R., Stephen G. Franklin, William M. Lindsay, and Leslie W. Rue. 1982a. "How Are Companies Planning Now? A Survey." *Long Range Planning* (February) 15: 82-86.

Boulton, William R., Stephen G. Franklin, William M. Lindsay, and Leslie W. Rue. 1982b. "Strategic Planning: Determining the Impact of Environmental Characteristics and Uncertainty." *Academy of Management Journal* (September) 25: 500-509.

Bourgeois, L. J., III. 1978. "Economic Performance and Dominant Coalition Agreement on Means Versus Ends in Second Order Strategy Making." *Proceedings,* Academy of Management (August), pp. 101-105.

Bourgeois, L.J., III. 1980. "Strategy and Environment: A Conceptual Integration." *Academy of Management Review* (January) 5: 25-39.

Bower, Joseph L. 1970. *Managing the Resource Allocation Process.* Boston: Harvard Business School Press.

Bowman, Edward H. 1980. "A Risk/Return Paradox for Strategic Management." *Sloan Management Review* (Spring) 21: 17-31.

Brandt, W. K., James M. Hulbert, and Raimar Richers. 1980. "Pitfalls in Planning for Multinational Operations." *Long Range Planning* (December) 13: 23-31.

Brown, Arnold. 1983. "Everywhere Planners Are in Pain." *Long Range Planning* (June) 16: 18-20.

Brown, Alvin. 1945. *Organization.* New York: Hibbert.

Brown, James R., Robert F. Lusch, Harold F. Koenig, Terrence T. Kroeten, and Steven W. Pharr. 1985. "Using Key Informants in Marketing Channels Research: A Critique and Some Preliminary Guidelines." Working Paper, University of Nebraska-Lincoln.

Burns, Tom and G. M. Stalker, 1961. *The Management of Innovation*. London: Tavistock.

Business Week. 1975. "Corporate Planning: Piercing Future Fog in the Executive Suite." (April 28), pp. 46-54.

Business Week. 1984. "The New Breed of Strategic Planner." (September 17), pp. 62-68.

Business Week. 1985. "Splitting Up." (July 1), pp. 50-55.

Business Week. 1986. "Business Fads: What's In – And Out." (January 20), pp. 52-61.

Buzzell, Robert D., Bradley T. Gale, and Ralph G. M. Sultan. 1975. "Market Share – A Key to Profitability." *Harvard Business Review* (January-February) 53: 97-106.

Camillus, John C. 1975. "Evaluating the Benefits of Formal Planning Systems." *Long Range Planning* (June) 8: 33-40.

Camillus, John C. 1980. "Corporate Planning System – Too Much of a Good Thing?" *Managing* 19: 36-37.

Camillus, John C. 1982. "Reconciling Logical Incrementalism and Synoptic Formalism – An Integrated Approach to Designing Strategic Planning Processes." *Strategic Management Journal* (July-September) 3: 277-283.

Campbell, John P., Marvin D. Dunnette, Edward E. Lawler III, and Karl E. Weick, Jr. 1970. *Managerial Behavior, Performance, and Effectiveness*. New York: McGraw-Hill.

Capon, Noel, John U. Farley, and James M. Hulbert. 1980. "International Diffusion of Corporate and Strategic Planning Practices." *Columbia Journal of World Business* (Fall) 15: 5-13.

Capon, Noel, Chris Christodoulou, John U. Farley, and James M. Hulbert. 1984. "A Comparison of Corporate Planning Practice in American and Australian Manufacturing Companies." *Journal of International Business Studies* (Fall) 15: 41-54.

Capon, Noel, Chris Christodoulou, John U. Farley, and James M. Hulbert. 1987. "A Comparison of the Strategy and Structure of United States and Australian Manufacturing Corporations: An Evolutionary Perspective." *Journal of International Business Studies* (Spring) 18:51-74.

Capon, Noel, John U. Farley, and James M. Hulbert. 1985. "Characteristics of 'Good Performing' Companies." Working Paper, Columbia University.

Capon, Noel, John U. Farley, James M. Hulbert, and David Lei. 1986a. "Environment, Strategy, and Organizational Dimensions in Matrix and Nonmatrix Multinational Firms." Working Paper, Columbia University.

Capon, Noel, John U. Farley, James M. Hulbert, and David Lei. 1986b. "An Empirical Analysis of the 'Excellent Companies'." Working Paper, Columbia University.

Capon, Noel, John U. Farley, James M. Hulbert, and Donald R. Lehmann. 1986. "Covariates of Product Innovation: An Empirical Assessment." Working Paper, Columbia University.

Capon, Noel, John U. Farley, and Donald R. Lehmann, 1986. "A New Approach to the Testing of Fit in Contingency Theory." Working Paper, Columbia University.

Capon, Noel, John U. Farley, James M. Hulbert, and Elizabeth Martin. 1987. "Corporate Diversity and Economic Performance: The Impact of Market Specialization." *Strategic Management Journal*, in press.

Capon, Noel and James M. Hulbert. 1985. "The Integration of Forecasting and Strategic Planning." *International Journal of Forecasting* 1:123-133.

Capon, Noel and Joan Spogli. 1977. "Strategic Marketing Planning: A Comparison and Critical Examination of Two Contemporary Approaches." in B.A. Greenberg and D.W. Bellenger, eds. *Contemporary Marketing Thought*, 41: 219-223. Chicago: American Marketing Association.

Carlson, Thomas S. 1978. "Long-Range Strategic Planning: Is It for Everyone?" *Long Range Planning* (June) 11: 54-61.

Carter, John R. 1977. "In Search of Synergy: A Structure-Performance Test." *The Review of Economics and Statistics* (August) 59: 279-289.

Cattin, Philippe and Dick Wittink, 1976. "Industry Differences in the Relationship Between Advertising and Profitability." *Industrial Organization Review* 4: 156-164.

Caves, Richard E. 1980. "Industrial Organization, Corporate Strategy and Structure." *Journal of Economic Literature* (March) 18: 64-92.

Caves, Richard E., Michael E. Porter, and A. Michael Spence. 1980. *Competition in the Open Economy: A Model Applied to Canada*, Cambridge, Mass.: Harvard University Press.

Chandler, Alfred D. 1962. *Strategy and Structure: Chapters in the History of the Industrial Enterprise*. Cambridge, Mass.: M. I. T. Press.

Channon, Derek F. 1973. *The Strategy and Structure of British Enterprise*. London: Macmillan.

Channon, Derek F. 1979. "Strategy, Structure and Financial Performance." *Manchester Business School Review* (Autumn) 4:16-26.

Chaston, Ian. 1982. "Long-Term Strategic Planning Issues in the Aquaculture Industry." *Management Decision* 20(1): 15-21.

Child, John. 1972. "Organizational Structure, Environment, and Performance: The Role of Strategic Choice." *Sociology* (January) 6: 1-22.

Child, John. 1974. "Managerial and Organizational Factors Associated with Company Performance-Part 1." *Journal of Management Studies* (October) 11: 175-189.

Child, John. 1975. "Managerial and Organizational Factors Associated with Company Performance – Part 2." *Journal of Management Studies*. (February) 12: 12-27.

Christensen, H. Kurt and Cynthia A. Montgomery. 1981. "Corporate Economic Performance: Diversification Strategy Versus Market Structure." *Strategic Management Journal* (October-December) 2: 327-343.

Csath, M. 1983. "Strategic Planning – A New Arrival in Hungarian Industry." *Long Range Planning* (April) 16: 85-94.

Cummings, L. L. and Chris J. Berger. 1976. "Organization Structure: How Does It Influence Attitudes and Performance?" *Organizational Dynamics* (Autumn) 5: 34-49.

Cyert, Richard M. and James G. March. 1963. *A Behavioral Theory of the Firm.* Englewood Cliffs, N.J.: Prentice-Hall.

Cymbala, Robert J. 1984. "How Good Information Can Feed the Strategic Planning Process." *International Management* (April) 39: 62-64.

Dalton, Dan R., William D. Todor, Michael J. Spendolini, Gordon J. Fielding, and Lyman W. Porter. 1980. "Organization Structure and Performance: A Critical Review." *Academy of Management Review* (January) 5: 49-54.

Dalton, James A. and David W. Penn. 1976. "The Concentration-Profitability Relationship: Is There a Critical Concentration Ratio?" *The Journal of Industrial Economics* (December) 25: 133-142.

Darden, William R. and James M. Sinkula. 1982. "Grocery Product Marketers 'Creatively' Apply Scanner Data to Strategic Planning Research." *Marketing News* (Sept. 17) 16: 16.

Das, Ranjan and Brajaraj Mohanty. 1981. "Choosing a Diversification Project in a Regulated Economy." *Long Range Planning* (April) 14: 78-86.

Davis, Stanley and Paul R. Lawrence. 1977. *Matrix.* Reading, Mass.: Addison-Wesley.

Day, George S. 1977. "Diagnosing the Product Portfolio." *Journal of Marketing* (April), pp. 29-38.

Deal, Terrence E. and Allen A. Kennedy. 1982. *Corporate Cultures: The Rites and Rituals of Corporate Life.* Reading, Mass.: Addison-Wesley.

DeNoya, Louis E. 1979. "A Simple Approach to the Planning Process." *Planning Review* (January) 7: 7-10.

Denning, B. W. and M. E. Lehr. 1971. "The Extent and Nature of Corporate Long Range Planning in the United Kingdom – I." *The Journal of Management Studies* (May) 8: 145-161.

Denning, B. W. and M. E. Lehr. 1972. "The Extent and Nature of Corporate Long Range Planning in the United Kingdom – II." *The Journal of Management Studies* (February) 9: 1-18.

Devanna, Mary Anne, Charles Fombrun, Noel Tichy, and Lynn Warren. "Strategic Planning and Human Resource Management." 1982. *Human Resource Management* (Spring) 21: 11-17.

Dewar, Robert and James Werbel. 1979. "Universalistic and Contingency Predictions of Employee Satisfactions and Conflict." *Administrative Science Quarterly* (September) 24: 426-448.

Dickson, J.W. 1981. "Participation as a Means of Organizational Control." *Journal of Management Studies* 18: 159-176.

Diffenbach, John. 1983. "Corporate Environmental Analysis in Large U.S. Corporations." *Long Range Planning* (June) 16: 107-116.

Dill, William R. 1958. "Environment as an Influence on Managerial Autonomy." *Administrative Science Quarterly* (March) 2: 409-443.

Downey, H. Kirk and John W. Slocum. 1975. "Uncertainty: Measures, Research and Sources of Variation." *Academy of Management Journal* (September) 18: 562-578.

Drazin, Robert and Andrew M. Van de Ven. 1985. "Alternative Forms of Fit in Contingency Theory." *Administrative Science Quarterly* (December) 30:514-539.

Duncan, Robert B. 1972. "Characteristics of Organizational Environments and Perceived Environmental Uncertainty." *Administrative Science Quarterly* (September) 17: 313-327.

Dundas, Kenneth, N.M. and Peter R. Richardson. 1982. "Implementing the Unrelated Product Strategy." *Strategic Management Journal* (October-December) 3: 287-301.

Dyson, R. G. and M. J. Foster. 1982. "The Relationship of Participation and Effectiveness in Strategic Planning." *Strategic Management Journal* (January-March) 3: 77-88.

Dyson, R. G. and M. J. Foster. 1983. "Effectiveness in Strategic Planning Revisited." *European Journal of Operational Research* (February) 12: 146-158.

Eadle, Douglas C., Nolen M. Ellison, and Grace C. Brown. 1982. "Incremental Strategic Planning: A Creative Adaptation." *Planning Review* (May) 10: 10-15.

Eastlack, Joseph O., Jr. and Philip R. McDonald. 1970. "CEO's Role in Corporate Growth." *Harvard Business Review* (May-June) 48: 150-163.

Egelhoff, William G. 1982. "Strategy and Structure in Multinational Corporations: An Information-Processing Approach." *Administrative Science Quarterly* (September) 27: 435-458.

Emery, J. C. 1969. *Organizational Planning and Control Systems.* Toronto, Canada: Macmillan.

Emery, F. E. and E. L. Trist. 1965. "The Causal Texture of Organizational Environments." *Human Relations* (February) 18: 21-32.

Engi, Dennis. 1984. "Goal Setting and Strategic Planning for a Shale Oil Recovery R&D Program." *Energy Systems and Policy* 8 (1): 29-66.

Eppink, D. Jan. 1978. "Planning for Strategic Flexibility." *Long Range Planning* (August) 11:9-15.

Eppink, D. Jan, Doede Keuning, and Klaas De Jong. 1976. "Corporate Planning in the Netherlands." *Long Range Planning* (October) 9:30-41.

Farley, John U., Donald R. Lehmann, and Michael J. Ryan. 1982. "Patterns in Parameters of Buyer Behavior Models: Generalizing from Sparse Replication." *Marketing Science* (Spring) 1:181-204.

Fayol, Henri. 1949. *General and Industrial Management,* translated by Constance Stours. London: Pitman.

Figenbaum, A. and H. Thomas. 1986. "Dynamic and Risk Measurement Perspectives on Bowman's Risk-Return Paradox for Strategic Management: An Empirical Study." *Strategic Management Journal* (September-October) 7: 395-407.

Finizza, Anthony J. 1980. "Forecasting the Business Environment in an OPEC World: A Limited Box Score." *Chicago MBA* (Spring) 4:5-24.

Ford, Jeffrey D. 1979. "Institutional Versus Questionnaire Measures of Organizational Structure: A Reexamination." *Academy of Management Journal* 22:601-610.

Ford, Jeffrey D. and John W. Slocum, Jr. 1977. "Size, Technology, Environment and the Structure of Organizations." *Academy of Management Review* (October) 2:561-575.

Ford, T. Mitchell. 1981. "Strategic Planning – Myth or Reality? A Chief Executive's View." *Long Range Planning* (December) 14:9-11.

Forehand, Gartie A. and B. von Haller Gilmer. 1964. "Environmental Variation in Studies of Organizational Behavior." *Psychological Bulletin* (December) 62:361-382.

Foster, M. J. 1986. "the Value of Formal Planning for Strategic Decisions: A Comment." *Strategic Management Journal* (March-April) 7:179-182.

Fox, Joesph M. 1975. "Strategic Planning: A Case Study." *Managerial Planning* (May-June) 23:32-38.

Franko, Lawrence G. 1974. "The Move Toward a Multidivisional Structure in European Organizations." *Administrative Science Quarterly* (December) 19:493-506.

Franko, Lawrence G. 1976. *The European Multinationals.* Stamford, Ct.: Greylock.

Frederick, Glenn D. 1983. "The State of Private Sector Strategic Planning in Canada." *Long Range Planning* (June) 16:40-46.

Fredrickson, James W. 1983. "Strategic Process Research: Questions and Recommendations." *Academy of Management Review* (October) 8: 565-575.

Fredrickson, James W. 1984. "The Comprehensiveness of Strategic Decision Processes: Extension, Observations, Future Directions." *Academy of Management Journal* (September) 27:445-466.

Fredrickson, James W. and Terence R. Mitchell. 1984. "Strategic Decision Processes: Comprehensive and Performance in an Industry with an Unstable Environment." *Academy of Management Journal* (June) 27: 399-423.

Fruhan, William E. Jr. 1972. *The Fight for Competitive Advantage: A Study of the United States Domestic Trunk Air Carriers,* Division of Research, Harvard University.

Fruhan, William E. Jr. 1979. *Financial Strategies: Studies in the Creation, Transfer and Destruction of Shareholder Value.* Homewood, Ill.: Irwin.

Fulmer, Robert M. and Leslie W. Rue. 1974. "The Practice and Profitability of Long-Range Planning." *Managerial Planning* (May-June) 22:1-7.

Gabel, H. 1979. "A Simultaneous Equation Analysis of the Structure and Performance of the United States Petroleum Refining Industry." *Journal of Industrial Economics* 28:89-104.

Galbraith, J. 1973. *Designing Complex Organizations.* Reading, Mass.: Addison-Wesley.

Galbraith, Jay R. and Nathanson, Daniel A. 1978. *Strategy Implemenation: The Role of Structure and Process.* St. Paul, Minn.: West.

Galbraith, Jay R. and Nathanson, D. A. 1979. "The Role of Organizational Structure and Process in Strategy Implementation." In Dan E. Schendel and Charles W. Hofer, eds. *Strategic Management* pp. 249-284. Boston: Little, Brown.

Gale, Bradley T. 1972. "Market Share and Rate of Return." *The Review of Economics and Statistics* (November) 54:412-423.

Galer, Graham and Wolfgang Kasper. 1982. "Scenario Planning for Australia." *Long Range Planning* (August) 15:50-55.

Gattis, Daniel R. 1983. "Strategic Planning No Substitute for a Good CEO." *National Underwriter* (September 3) 87:3, 25.

Gelb, Betsy D., H. Kurt Christensen, Arnold C. Cooper, and Cornelius A. DeKluyver. 1982. "Strategic Planning for the Under-Dog/The Dog Business: A Re-examination." *Business Horizons* (November-December) 25:8-18.

Gershefski, George W. and Allan Harvey. 1970. "Corporate Models – The State of the Art." *Management Science* (February) 16:B303-B321.

Ghosh, B. C. and A. Y. C. Nee. 1983a. "Strategic Planning – A Contingency Approach – Part 1: The Strategic Analysis." *Long Range Planning* (August) 16:93-103.

Ghosh, B. C. and A. Y. C. Nee. 1983b. "Strategic Planning – A Contingency Approach – Part 2: The Plan." *Long Range Planning* (December) 16:46-58.

Ginsberg, Ari and N. Venkatraman. 1985. Contingency Perspectives of Organizational Strategy: A Critical Review of the Empirical Research." *Academy of Management Review,* 10:421-434.

Glueck, William F. 1976. *Business Policy: Strategy Formation and Management Action,* 2nd ed., New York: McGraw-Hill.

Glueck, William F. and Lawrence R. Jauch. 1984. *Business Policy and Strategic Management.* New York: McGraw-Hill.

Glueck, William F., S. P. Kaufman, and A. S. Welleck. 1980. "Strategic Management for Competitive Advantage." *Harvard Business Review* 58: 154-161.

Godiwalla, Yezdi Minoo, Wayne A. Meinhart, and William D. Warde. 1979. *Corporate Strategy and Functional Management.* New York: Praeger.

Gort, Michael. 1962. *Diversification and Integration in American Industry.* Princeton, NJ: Princeton University Press.

Gotcher, J. William. 1977. "Strategic Planning in European Multinationals." *Long Range Planning* (October) 10:7-13.

Gray, Daniel H. 1986. "Uses and Misuses of Strategic Planning." *Harvard Business Review* (January-February) 64:89-97.

Greenley, Gordon E. 1986. "Does Strategic Planning Improve Company Performance." *Long Range Planning* 19:101-109.

Grinyer, Peter H., Shawki Al-Bazzaz, and Masoud Yasai-Ardekani. 1986. "Towards a Contingency Theory of Corporate Planning: Findings in 48 U.K. Companies." *Strategic Management Journal* 7:3-28.

Grinyer, Peter H. and David Norburn. 1974. "Strategic Planning in 21 U.K. Companies." *Long Range Planning* (August) 7:80-88.

Grinyer, Peter H. and David Norburn. 1975. "Planning for Existing Markets: Perceptions of Executives and Financial Performance." *The Journal of the Royal Statistical Society.* Series A. 138:70-97.

Grinyer, Peter H., Masoud Yasai-Ardekani, and Shawki Al-Bazzaz. 1980. "Strategy, Structure, the Environment and Financial Performance in 48 United Kingdom Companies." *Academy of Management Journal* (June) 23: 193-220.

Grinyer, Peter H. and Masoud Yasai-Ardekani. 1981. "Strategy, Structure, Size and Bureaucracy." *Academy of Management Journal* (September) 24: 471-486.

Hage, Jerald and Michael Aiken. 1967. "Relationship of Centralization to Other Structural Properties." *Administrative Science Quarterly* (June) 12:72-92.

Hall, David J. and Maurice A. Saias. 1980. "Strategy Follows Structure!" *Strategic Management Journal* (April-June) 1:149-163.

Hall, Marshall and Leonard Weiss. 1967. "Firm Size and Profitability." *The Review of Economics and Statistics* (August) 49:319-331.

Hall, William K. 1974. "The Uncertainty of Uncertainty in Business Planning." *Managerial Planning* (September-October) 23:7-12.

Halpern, Richard S. 1984. "Advice to Researchers: Strategic Planning for the Future!" *European Research* (April) 12:60-67.

Halpin, A. and D. Croft. 1963. *The Organizational Climate of Schools.* Chicago, Ill.: University of Chicago Press.

Hambrick, Donald C. 1983a. "An Empirical Typology of Mature Industrial-Product Environments." *Academy of Management Journal* (June) 26: 213-220.

Hambrick, Donald C. 1983b. "Some Tests of the Effectiveness and Functional Attributes of Miles and Snow's Strategic Types." *Academy of Management Journal* (March) 26:5-26.

Hambrick, Donald C., Ian C. MacMillan, and Diana L. Day. 1982. "Strategic Attributes and Performance in the BCG Matrix – A PIMS-Based Analysis of Industrial Product Business." *Academy of Management Journal* (September) 25:510-531.

Hambrick, Donald C. and David Lei. 1985. "Toward an Empirical Prioritization of Contingency Variables for Business Strategy." *Academy of Management Journal* (December) 28:763-788.

Hampton, Colin C. 1984. "Views of the Role of Strategic Planning." *National Underwriter* 88 (28):11, 16.

Harju, Paavo. 1981. *Attitude of Strategic Managers Toward Formalized Corporate Planning.* Turku, Finland: School of Economics.

Hart, N. Berne. 1984. "Strategic Planning: Responsibility of the CEO." *Magazine of Bank Administration* (March) 60:74-78.

Harvey, E. 1968. "Technology and the Structure of Organizations." *American Sociological Review* 33:247-259.

Haspeslagh, Philippe. 1982. "Portfolio Planning: Uses and Limits." *Harvard Business Review* (January-February) 82:58-73.

Hatten, K. J. and Dan Schendel. 1977. "Heterogeneity Within an Industry: Firm Conduct in the U.S. Brewing Industry, 1952-1971." *Journal of Industrial Economics* (December) 26:97-113.

Hax, Arnoldo C. and Nicolas S. Majluf. 1983a. "The Use of the Growth-Share Matrix in Strategic Planning." *Interfaces* (February) 13:44-60.

Hax, Arnoldo C. and Nicolas S. Majluf. 1983b. "The Use of the Industry Attractiveness–Business Strength Matrix in Strategic Planning." *Interfaces* (April) 13:54-71.

Hax, Arnoldo C. and Nicolas S. Majluf. 1984. "The Corporate Strategic Planning Process." *Interfaces* (January-February) 14:47-60.

Hayes, Samuel L. III, A. Michael Spence, and David Van Praag Marks. 1983. *Competition in the Investment Banking Industry.* Cambridge, Mass.: Harvard University Press.

Hedley, Barry D. 1977. "Strategy and the 'Business Portfolio'." *Long Range Planning* (February) 10:9-15.

Hellriegel, Don and John W. Slocum, Jr. 1974. "Organization Climate: Measures, Research and Contingencies." *Academy of Management Journal* (June) 17:255-280.

Henderson, Bruce D. 1979. *Henderson on Corporate Strategy.* Cambridge, Mass.: Abt. Books.

Henry, Harold W. 1967. *Long Range Planning Practices in 45 Industrial Companies.* Englewood Cliffs, N.J.: Prentice-Hall.

Henry, Harold W. 1981. "Then and Now: A Look at Strategic Planning Systems." *Journal of Business Strategy* (Winter) 1:64-69.

Henry, Harold W. 1982. "A Look at the Strategic Planning Consulting Firms." *Journal of Business Strategy* (Fall) 3:83-86.

Herold, David M. 1972. "Long-Range Planning and Organizational Performance: A Cross-Validation Study." *Academy of Management Journal* (March) 15:91-102.

Higgins, J. C. and R. Finn. 1977. "The Organization and Practice of Corporate Planning in the U.K." *Long Range Planning* (August) 10:88-92.

Higgins, R. B. 1981. "Creating a Climate Conducive to Planning." *Long Range Planning* (February) 14:49-54.

Hirsch, P. 1985. "Organizational Effectiveness and Institutional Environment." *Administrative Science Quarterly* 20:327-344.

Hirschman, Albert O. 1964. "The Paternity of an Index." *American Economic Review* (September) 54:761-762.

Hofer, Charles W. 1975. "Toward a Contingency Theory of Business Strategy." *Academy of Management Journal* (December) 18:784-810.

Hofer, Charles W. 1976. "Research and Strategic Planning: A Survey of Past Studies and Suggestions for Future Efforts." *Journal of Economics and Business* (Spring-Summer) 28:261-286.

Hofer, Charles W. and Dan E. Schendel. 1978. *Strategy Formulation: Analytical Concepts.* St. Paul, Minn.: West.

Holland, Robert C. 1983. "Strategic Planning: Some New Directions." *Journal of Accountancy* (September) 156:130-134.

Holloway, Clark and William R. King. 1979. "Evaluating Alternative Approaches to Strategic Planning." *Long Range Planning* (August) 12: 74-78.

Holloway, Clark and John A. Pearce II. 1982. "Computer Assisted Strategic Planning." *Long Range Planning* (August) 15:56-63.

Holmberg, Stevan R. and H. Kent Baker. 1982. "The CEO's Role in Strategic Planning." *Journal of Bank Research* (Winter) 12:218-227.

Holmes, Geoffrey. 1983. "Planmaster for Strategic Planning." *Accountancy* (January) 94:90-93.

Holzmann, Oscar J., Ronald M. Copeland, and Jack Hayya. 1975. "Income Measures of Conglomerate Performance." *Quarterly Review of Economics and Business* (Autumn) 15:67-78.

Horovitz, J. H. 1979. "Strategic Control: A New Task for Top Management." *Long Range Planning* (June) 12:2-7.

Horovitz, J. H. and R. A. Thietart. 1982. "Strategy, Management Design and Firm Performance." *Strategic Management Journal* (January-March) 3: 67-76.

Huber, G. P., M. J. O'Connell, and L. J. Cummings. 1975. "Perceived Environmental Uncertainty: Effects of Information and Structure." *Academy of Management Journal* 18:725-740.

Hulbert, James M. and William K. Brandt. 1980. *Managing the Multinational Subsidiary.* New York: Holt, Rinehart and Winston.

Hulbert, James M., William K. Brandt, and Raimar Richers. 1980. "Marketing Planning in the Multinational Subsidiary: Practices and Problems." *Journal of Marketing* (Summer) 44:7-15.

Hussey, D. E. 1972. "Strategic Planning for International Business." *Long Range Planning* (June) 5:16-20.

Hussey, D. E. 1978. "Portfolio Analysis: Practical Experience with the Directional Policy Matrix." *Long Range Planning* (August) 11:2-8.

Jacobson, Robert and David A. Aaker. 1985. "Is Market Share All That It's Cracked Up To Be?" *Journal of Marketing* (Fall 1985) 49:11-22.

Jacquemin, Alexis P. and Charles H. Berry. 1979. "Entropy Measure of Diversification and Corporate Growth." *The Journal of Industrial Economics* (June) 27:359-369.

Jaedicke, Carl F. 1981. "Strategic Planning: A View from the Bottom Up." *Public Utilities Fortnightly* (December 3) 108:52-55.

Jagpal, Harsharanjett S. and Ivan E. Brick. 1982. "The Marketing Mix Decision Under Uncertainty." *Marketing Science* 1:79-92.

Jagpal, Harsharanjett S. and J. U. Farley. 1984. "Marketing Policies Under Uncertainty in a Multi-Division Firm." *Mathematical Modeling* 5:129-137.

Jain, Subash. 1984. "Environmental Scanning in U.S. Corporations." *Long Range Planning* (April) 17:117-128.

James, Lawrence R. and Allan P. Jones. 1974. "Organizational Climate: A Review of Theory and Research." *Psychological Bulletin* (December) 81:1096-1112.

Jauch, Lawrence R., Richard N. Osborn, and William F. Glueck. 1980. "Short Term Financial Success in Large Business Organizations; The Environment-Strategy Connection." *Strategic Management Journal* (January-March) 1:49-63.

Joaquim, Manuel E. 1979. "Planning in an International Division." *Managerial Planning* (January-February) 27:7-12.

Johannesson, Russell E. 1973. "Some Problems in the Measurement of Organizational Climate." *Organizational Behavior and Human Performance* 10:118-144.

Jones, David C. 1981. "Darrow: Strategic Planning Important to Career Goals." *National Underwriter* (November 16) 85:32-33.

Jonsson, Sverker and Ingvar Petzaell. 1982. "Forecasting Political Decisions and Their Impact on Business." *Long Range Planning* (August) 15:98-104.

Kallman, Ernest A. and H. Jack Shapiro. 1978. "The Motor Freight Industry – A Case Against Planning." *Long Range Planning* (February) 11:81-86.

Karger, Delmar W. and Zafar A. Malik. 1975. "Long-Range Planning and Organizational Performance." *Long Range Planning* (December) 8:60-64.

Katz, Abraham. 1978. "Planning in the IBM Corporation." *Long Range Planning* (June) 11:2-7.

Katz, Gerald, Leslie Zavodnik, Elaine Markezin. 1983. "Strategic Planning in a Restrictive and Competitive Environment." *Health Care Management Review* (Fall) 8:7-12.

Keegan, Warren J. 1980. *Multinational Marketing Management*, 2nd ed., Englewood Cliffs, N.J.: Prentice-Hall.

Kennedy, Miles H. and Sitikantha Mahapatra. 1975. "Information Analysis for Effective Planning and Control." *Sloan Management Review* (Winter) 16:71-83.

Keown, A. J. and B. W. Taylor. 1978. "Integer Goal Programming Model for the Implementation of Multiple Corporate Objectives." *Journal of Business Research* 6:221-235.

Keppler, Werner, Ingolf Bamberger, and Eduard Gabele. 1979. "Organization for Long Range Planning – A Survey of German Companies." *Long Range Planning* (October) 12:69-90.

Khandwalla, Pradip N. 1972. "Environment and Its Impact on the Organization." *International Studies of Management and Organization* 2:297-313.

Khandwalla, Pradip N. 1973. "Viable and Effective Organizational Designs of Firms." *Academy of Management Journal* (September) 16:481-495.

Khandwalla, Pradip N. 1976. "The Techno-Economic Ecology of Corporate Strategy." *Journal of Management Studies* (February) 13:62-75.

Kiechel III, Walter. 1979. "Playing by the Rules of the Corporate Strategy Game." *Fortune* (September 24), pp. 110-118.

Kiechel III, Walter. 1982. "Corporate Strategists Under Fire." *Fortune* (December 27), pp. 34-39.

Kimberly, John R. 1976. "Organizational Size and the Structuralist Perspective: A Review, Critique, and Proposal." *Administrative Science Quarterly* (December) 21:571-597.

Kimmerly, William C. 1983. "R&D Strategic Planning in Turbulent Environments." *Managerial Planning* (March-April) 31:8-13.

King, William R. 1983. "Evaluating Strategic Planning Systems." *Strategic Management Journal* (July-September) 4:263-277.

King, William R. and J. I. Rodriguez. 1978. "Evaluating Management Information Systems." *MIS Quarterly* (September) 3:43-51.

Kono, Toyohiro. 1984. "Long Range Planning of U.K. and Japanese Corporations – A Comparative Study." *Long Range Planning* 17:58-76.

Koontz, Harold and Cyril O'Donnell. 1972. *Principles of Management: An Analysis of Managerial Functions.* New York: McGraw-Hill.

Kover, Arthur J. 1982. "Strategic Planning: Who Is Beneficiary." *Advertising Age* (January 25) 53:50.

Kriekebaum, Harmut and Ulrich Grimm. 1982. "Planning in a Free Market Economy." *Long Range Planning* (June) 15:103-115.

Kudla, Ronald J. 1976. "Elements of Effective Corporate Planning." *Long Range Planning* (August) 9:82-93.

Kudla, Ronald J. 1978. "The Components of Strategic Planning." *Long Range Planning* (December) 11:48-52.

Kudla, Ronald J. 1980. "The Effects of Strategic Planning on Common Stock Returns." *Academy of Management Journal* (March) 23:5-20.

Kudla, Ronald J. 1981. "Strategic Planning and Risk." *Review of Business and Economic Research* (Fall) 17:1-14.

Kudla, Ronald J. 1982. "The Current Practice of Bank Long Range Planning." *Long Range Planning* (June) 15:132-138.

Larreche, Jean-Claude and V. Srinivasan. 1981. "STRATPORT: A Decision Support System for Strategic Planning," *Journal of Marketing* (Fall) 45:39-52.

Lawrence, Paul R. and Jay W. Lorsch. 1967. *Organizations and Environment.* Cambridge, Mass.: Harvard University Press.

Lawrence, Paul R. 1981. "The Harvard Organization and Environment Research Program." In A. H. Van de Ven and W. F. Joyce, eds., *Perspectives on Organization Design and Behavior,* pp. 331-337. New York: John

Wiley.

Leavitt, Harold. 1962. "Unhuman Organizations." *Harvard Business Review* (July-August) 40:90-98.

Leavitt, Harold. 1965. "Applied Organization Change in Industry." In James March, ed. *The Handbook of Organizations.* Chicago: Rand-McNally.

Leff, Nathaniel H. 1984. "Strategic Planning in an Uncertain World." *Journal of Business Strategy* (Spring) 4:78-80.

Lehmann, Donald R. and Donald G. Morrison. 1979. "A Random Splitting Criterion for Determining the Number of Factors." Working Paper, Columbia University.

Lei, David, Noel Capon, John U. Farley, and James M. Hulbert. 1986. "Corporate Planning Systems in Matrix and Non-Matrix Multinational Firms." Working Paper, Columbia University.

Lenz, R. T. 1980. "Environment, Strategy, Organization Structure and Performance: Patterns in One Industry." *Strategic Management Journal* 1:209-226.

Lenz, R. T. 1981. "'Determinants' of Organizational Performance: An Interdisciplinary Review." *Strategic Management Journal* (April-June) 2:131-154.

Lenz, R. T. and Marjorie A. Lyles. 1981. "Tackling the Human Problems in Planning." *Long Range Planning* (April) 14:72-77.

Leontiades, Milton and Ahmet Tezel. 1980. "Planning Perceptions and Planning Results." *Strategic Management Journal* (January-March) 1:65-75.

Lieberson, S. and J. O'Connor. 1972. "Leadership and Organizational Performance: A Study of Large Corporations." *American Sociological Review* 37:117-130.

Likert, Rensis. 1967. *The Human Organization: Its Management and Value.* New York: McGraw-Hill.

Lindbloom, Charles E. 1959. "The Science of 'Muddling Through.'" *Public Administration Review* (Spring) 19:79-88.

Lindbloom, Charles E. 1979. "Still Muddling, Not Yet Through." *Public Administration Review* (November-December) 39:517-526.

Lindsay, William M. and Leslie W. Rue. 1980. "Impact of the Organization Environment on the Long Range Planning Process: A Contingency View." *Academy of Management Journal* (September) 23:385-404.

Link, Max E. 1983. "Strategic Planning in a Dynamic Environment." *Chief Executive* (Summer) 11:44-45.

Linneman, Robert E. and Harold E. Kline. 1983. "The Use of Multiple Scenarios by U.S. Industrial Companies: A Comparison Study, 1977-1981." *Long Range Planning* (December) 16:94-101.

Litschert, Robert J. 1968. "Some Characteristics of Long-Range Planning: An Industry Study. *Academy of Management Journal* (September) 11:315-328.

Litschert, Robert J. 1971. "The Structure of Long Range Planning Groups." *Academy of Management Journal* (March) 14:33-43.

Litschert, Robert J. and Edward A. Nicholson, Jr. 1974. "Corporate Long-Range Planning Groups – Some Different Approaches." *Long Range Planning* (August) 7:62-66.

Litschert, Robert J. and T. W. Bonham. 1978. "A Conceptual Model of Strategy Formation." *Academy of Management Review* (April) 3:211-219.

Lopez, Felix M. 1981. "Toward a Better System of Human Resource Planning." *Advanced Management Journal* (Spring) 46:4-14.

Lorange, Peter. 1976. "A Framework for Strategic Planning in Multinational Corporations." *Long Range Planning* (June) 9:30-37.

Lorange, Peter. 1979. "Formal Planning Systems: Their Role in Strategy Formulation and Implementation." In Dan E. Schendel and Charles W. Hofer, eds. *Strategic Management.* Cambridge, Mass.: Little, Brown.

Lorange, Peter. 1980. *Corporate Planning: An Executive Viewpoint.* Englewood Cliffs, N.J.: Prentice-Hall.

Lorange, Peter and Richard F. Vancil. 1976. "How To Design a Strategic Planning System." *Harvard Business Review* (September-October) 54:75-81.

Lorsch, Jay and Stephen Allen. 1976. *Managing Diversity and Interdependence.* Boston: Division of Research, Harvard Business School.

Lorsch, Jay and John Morse. 1974. *Organizations and Their Members: A Contingency Approach.* New York: Harper & Row.

McGuire, T. W., R. L. Lucas, J. U. Farley, and L. W. Ring. 1968. "Estimation and Inference When Subsets of a Dependent Variable Are Constrained." *The Journal of the American Statistical Association* (December) 63:1201-1214.

McKelvey, Bill. 1975. "Guidelines for the Empirical Classification of Organizations." *Administrative Science Quarterly* (December) 20:509-525.

McKelvey, Bill. 1978. "Organizational Systematics: Taxonomic Lessons from Biology." *Management Science* (September) 24:1428-1440.

McRorie, John S. 1982. "Strategic Planning: It Can Work at Your Bank." *Savings Bank Journal* (August) 63:17-19.

MacMillan, Ian C., Donald C. Hambrick, and Diana L. Day. 1982. "The Product Portfolio and Profitability – A PIMS-Based Analysis of Industrial Product Businesses." *Academy of Management Journal* (December) 25:733-755.

Malecki, Donald S. 1983. "Four Company Chiefs View Strategic Planning." *National Underwriter* (September) 87:72.

Malik, Zafar A. and Delmar W. Karger. 1975. "Does Long-Range Planning Improve Company Performance?" *Management Review* (September) 64:27-31.

Marakon Associates. 1980. "The Role of Finance in Strategic Planning." *Business Week* Conference.

March, James G. and Herbert A. Simon. 1958. *Organization.* New York: John Wiley.

Meadows, Edward. 1981. "New Targeting for Executive Pay." *Fortune* (May 4) 103:176-177, 180, 184.

Melicher, Ronald W. and David F. Rush. 1973. "The Performance of Conglomerate Firms: Recent Risk and Return Experience." *Journal of Finance* (May) 28:381-388.

Merrill, H. M. and F. C. Schweppe. 1984. "Strategic Planning for Electric Utilities: Problems and Analytic Methods." *Interfaces* (January-February) 14:72-83.

Metz, Edmund J. 1984. "The Missing 'H' in Strategic Planning." *Managerial Planning* (May-June) 32:19-23, 29.

Metzger, Robert O. 1981. "Strategic Planning Can Sharpen Management's Focus on the Future." *Savings and Loan News* (November) 102:58-65.

Michael, Stephen R. 1980. "Tailor-made Planning: Making Planning Fit the Firm." *Long Range Planning* (December) 13:74-79.

Miesing, Paul. 1983. "Limitations of Matrix Models as a Strategic Planning Tool." *Managerial Planning* (May-June) 31:42-45.

Miles, Raymond E. and Charles C. Snow. 1978. *Organizational Strategy, Structure and Process*. New York: McGraw-Hill.

Miller, Danny and Peter H. Friesen. 1977. "Strategy-Making in Context: Ten Empirical Archetypes." *Journal of Management Studies* (October) 14:253-280.

Miller, Danny and Peter H. Friesen. 1978. "Archetypes of Strategy Formulation." *Management Science* (May) 24:921-933.

Miller, Danny and Peter H. Friesen. 1983. "Strategy-Making and Environment: The Third Link." *Strategic Management Journal* (July-September) 4:221-235.

Mills, Chester R. 1984. "Strategic Planning Generates Potent Power for Information Centers." *Data Management* (February) 22:23-25.

Miner, J. 1979. "Commentary." In Dan E. Schendel and Charles W. Hofer, eds. *Strategic Management*. Boston: Little, Brown.

Mintzberg, Henry. 1973. "Strategy-Making in Three Modes." *California Management Review* (Winter) 16:44-53.

Mintzberg, Henry. 1978. "Patterns in Strategy Formulation." *Management Science* (May) 24:934-948.

Mintzberg, Henry, D. Raisinghani, and A. Theoret. 1979. "The Structure of Unstructured Decision Processes." *Administrative Science Quarterly* 21:246-275.

Mohr, L. B. 1971. "Organizational Technology and Organizational Structure." *Administrative Science Quarterly* 16:444-459.

Montebello, Michael and Pierre Bulgues. 1982. "How French Industry Plans." *Long Range Planning* (June) 15:116-121.

Montgomery, Cynthia A. 1982. "The Measurement of Firm Diversification: Some New Empirical Evidence." *Academy of Management Journal* (June) 25:299-307.

Montgomery, David B. and Charles B. Weinberg. 1979. "Toward Strategic Intelligence Systems." *Journal of Marketing* (Fall) 43:41-52.

Mooney, James D. 1947. *Principles of Organization*. New York: Harper.

Mulligan, Robert J. 1981. "Strategic Planning." *Retail Control* (November) 50: 2-8.

Naisbitt, John. 1982. *Megatrends*. New York: Warner.

Nauert, Roger C. 1983. "Jumping the Hurdles to Strategic Planning." *Health Care Financial Management* (August) 37:26-30.

Naylor, Thomas H. 1979. "Organizing for Strategic Planning." *Managerial Planning* (July-August) 28:3-9.

Naylor, Thomas H. 1982. "Effective Use of Strategic Planning, Forecasting, and Modelling in the Executive Suite." *Managerial Planning* (January-February) 30:4-11.

Naylor, Thomas H. 1983. "Strategic Planning and Forecasting." *Journal of Forecasting* (April-June) 2:109-118.

Naylor, Thomas H. and Francis Tapon. 1982. "The Capital Asset Pricing Model: An Evaluation of Its Potential as a Strategic Planning Tool." *Management Science* (October) 28:1166-1173.

Neidell, Lester A. 1983. "Don't Forget the Product Life Cycle for Strategic Planning." *Business* (April-May-June) 33:30-35.

Neubert, Ralph L. 1980. "Strategic Management the Monsanto Way." *Planning Review* (January) 8:3-6, 44-48.

New York Times. 1980. "New Strategies Spur Corporate Divesting." (July 16), pp. D11, D16.

Nielsen, Richard P. 1983a. "Training Programs: Pulling Them into Sync with Your Company's Strategic Planning." *Personnel* (May-June) 60:19-25.

Nielsen, Richard P. 1983b. "Strategic Planning and Consensus Building for External Relations – Five Cases." *Long Range Planning* (December) 16:74-81.

Oliver, Alex R. and Joseph R. Garber. 1983. "Implementing Strategic Planning: Ten Sure-Fire Ways to Do It Wrong." *Business Horizons* (March-April) 26:49-51.

Ouchi, William G. 1981. *Theory Z.* Reading, Mass.: Addison-Wesley.

Paine, Frank T. and Carl R. Anderson. 1977. "Contingencies Affecting Strategy Formulation and Effectiveness: An Empirical Study." *Journal of Management Studies* (May) 14:147-158.

Parker, Lee D. 1980. "The Potential of Long Range Planning." *Accountancy* (January) 91:109-111.

Pascale, Richard T. and Anthony G. Athos. 1981. *The Art of Japanese Management.* New York: Simon and Schuster.

Patel, Peter and Michael Younger. 1978. "A Frame of Reference for Strategy Development." *Long Range Planning* (April) 11:6-12.

Pavan, Robert. 1972. "Strategy and Structure in Italian Enterprise." Unpublished Doctoral Dissertation, Graduate School of Business Administration, Harvard University.

Payne, R. L. and D. C. Pheysey. 1971. "G. G. Stern's Organizational Climate Index: A Reconceptualization and Application to Business Organizations." *Organizational Behavior and Human Performance* 6:77-98.

Payne, R. L. and D. S. Pugh. 1976. "Organizational Structure and Climate." In M. D. Dunnette, ed. *Handbook of Industrial and Organizational Psychology,* 1125-1173. Chicago, Ill.: Rand McNally.

Pennings, Johannes M. 1975. "The Relevance of the Structural-Contingency Model for Organizational Effectiveness." *Administrative Science Quarterly* (September) 20:393-410.

Penrose, Edith. 1955. "Research on the Business Firm: Limits to the Growth and Size of Firms." *American Economic Review* (May) 45:531-543.

Peters, Thomas J. and Robert H. Waterman. 1982. *In Search of Excellence.* New York: Harper and Row.

Pfeffer, Jeffrey and Gerald R. Salancik. 1978. *The External Control of Organizations.* New York: Harper and Row.

Phillips, A. 1976. "A Critique of Empirical Studies of Relations Between Market Structure and Profitability." *Journal of Industrial Economics* 24:241-249.

Phillips, Lynn W. 1981. "Assessing Measurement Error in Key Informant Reports: A Methodological Note on Organizational Analysis in Marketing." *Journal of Marketing Research* (November) 18:395-415.

Pitts, Robert A. 1976. "Diversification Strategies and Organizational Policies of Large Diversified Firms." *Journal of Economics and Business* (Spring-Summer) 28:181-188.

Pitts, Robert A. 1980. "Toward a Contingency Theory of Multibusiness Organization Design." *Academy of Management Review* (April) 5:203-210.

Pitts, Robert A. and H. Donald Hopkins. 1982. "Firm Diversity: Conceptualization and Measurement. *Academy of Management Review* (October) 7:620-629.

Poensgen, Otto. 1974. "Organizational Structure, Context and Performance." Working Paper No. 74-49, European Institute for Advanced Studies.

Pooley-Dyas, Gareth. 1972. "Strategy and Structure of French Enterprise." Unpublished Doctoral Dissertation, Graduate School of Business Administration, Harvard University.

Porter, M. E. 1979. "The Structure within Industries and Companies' Performance." *The Review of Economics and Statistics* (May) 61:214-227.

Porter, M. E. 1980. *Competitive Strategy.* New York: Free Press.

Probert, David E. 1981. "The Development of a Long-Range Planning Model for the British Telecommunications Business: 'From Initiation to Implementation.' " *Journal of the Operational Research Society* (August) 32:695-719.

Pugh, D. S., D. J. Hickson, and C. Turner. 1968. "Dimensions of Organization Structure." *Administrative Science Quarterly* 13:65-105.

Quinn, James Brian. 1980. *Strategies for Change—Logical Incrementalism.* Homewood, Ill.: Irwin.

Raimond, Paul. 1983. "Corporate Planning Can Work for Your Practice, Too." *Accountancy* (August) 94:94-95.

Ramunujam, Vasudevan and N. Venkatraman. 1984. "An Inventory and Critique of Strategy Research Using the PIMS Database." *Academy of Management Review* 9:138-151.

Randall, Robert M. 1984. "Sniping at Strategic Planning." *Planning Review*

(May) 12:8-11.

Rappaport, Alfred. 1981. "Selecting Strategies that Create Shareholder Value." *Harvard Business Review* (May-June) 59:139-149.

Rector, Robert L. 1983. "Decision Support Systems – Strategic Planning Tool." *Managerial Planning* (May-June) 31:36-40.

Reid, Samuel R. 1968. *Mergers, Managers and the Economy.* New York: McGraw-Hill.

Reinhardt, W. A. 1984. "An Early Warning System for Strategic Planning." *Long Range Planning* (Spring) 17:25-34.

Rhoades, Stephen A. 1973. "The Effect of Diversification on Industry Profit Performance in 241 Manufacturing Industries: 1963." *The Review of Economics and Statistics* (May) 55:146-155.

Rhoades, Stephen A. 1974. "A Further Evaluation of the Effect of Diversification on Industry Profit Performance." *The Review of Economics and Statistics* (November) 56:557-558.

Rhyne, Lawrence C. 1985. "The Relationship of Information Usage Characteristics to Planning System Sophistication: An Empirical Examination." *Strategic Management Journal* 6:319-337.

Rhyne, Lawrence C. 1986. "The Relationship of Strategic Planning to Financial Performance." *Strategic Management Journal* (September-October) 7:423-436.

Ringbakk, Kjell A. 1969. "Organized Planning in Major U.S. Companies." *Long Range Planning* (December) 2:46-57.

Ringbakk, Kjell A. 1971. "Why Planning Fails." *European Business* (Spring), pp. 15-27.

Ringbakk, Kjell A. 1972. "The Corporate Planning Life Cycle – An International Point of View." *Long Range Planning* (September) 5:10-20.

Robinson, Richard B., Jr. and John A. Pearce II. 1983. "The Impact of Formalized Strategic Planning on Financial Performance in Small Organizations." *Strategic Management Journal* (July-September) 4:197-207.

Robinson, S. J. Q., R. E. Hichens, and D. P. Wade. 1978. "The Directional Policy Matrix – Tool for Strategic Planning." *Long Range Planning* (June) 11:8-15.

Robinson, William T. and Claes Fornell. 1985. "Sources of Market Pioneer Advantages in Consumer Goods Industries." *Journal of Marketing Research* (August) 22:305-317.

Roney, C. W. 1977. "The Two Purposes of Business Planning." *Managerial Planning,* (November-December) 25:1-6.

Rose, Peter S. 1982. "Planning Elements: Steps and Strategies, Part 1." *Canadian Banker and ICB Review* (June) 89:50-55.

Rothschild, William E. 1976. *Putting It All Together.* New York: AMACOM.

Rothschild, William E. 1979. *Strategic Alternatives: Selection, Development and Implementation.* New York: AMACOM.

Rue, Leslie W. and Robert M. Fulmer. 1973. "Is Long-Range Planning Profitable?" *Proceedings.* Academy of Management, pp. 66-72.

Rumelt, Richard P. 1974. *Strategy, Structure, and Economic Performance.*

Boston, Mass. Division of Research, Graduate School of Business Administration, Harvard University.

Rumelt, Richard P. 1982. "Diversification Strategy and Profitability." *Strategic Management Journal* (October-December) 3:359-369.

Russell, Lloyd J. 1983. "Strategic Planning—What's Wrong with Retailer Strategies?" *Retail Control* (February) 51:2-8.

Salter, Malcolm and Wolf A. Weinhold. 1979. *Diversification Through Acquisition: Strategies for Creating Economic Value.* New York: Free Press.

Saunders, Charles B. and Francis D. Tuggle. 1977. "Why Planners Don't." *Long Range Planning* (June) 10:19-24.

Sayles, Leonard (n.d.). "The Role of Planners: A Critical Staff Function." Working Notes, Columbia University.

Schaffir, Walter B. and Thomas J. Lobe. 1984. "Strategic Planning: The Impact at Five Companies." *Planning Review* (March) 12:39-41.

Schendel, Dan and G. Richard Patton. 1978. "A Simultaneous Equation Model of Corporate Strategy." *Management Science* (November) 24:1611-1621.

Schneider, Benjamin and C. J. Bartlett. 1968. "Individual Differences and Organizational Climate I: The Research Plan and Questionnaire Development." *Personnel Psychology* 21:323-333.

Schneider, Benjamin and C. J. Bartlett. 1970. "Individual Differences and Organizational Climate II: Measurement of Organizational Climate by the Multi-Trait, Multi-Rater Matrix." *Personnel Psychology* 23:493-512.

Schoeffler, Sidney, Robert D. Buzzell, and Donald E. Heany. 1974. "Impact of Strategic Planning on Profit Performance." *Harvard Business Review* (March-April) 52:137-146.

Schoeffler, Sidney. 1977. "Cross-sectional Study of Strategy, Structure, and Performance: Aspects of the PIMS Program." In Hans B. Thorelli, ed. *Strategy and Structure Performance,* pp. 108-121. Bloomington, Ind.: Indiana University Press.

Schofield, Douglas F. 1983. "Strategic Planning at La Roche College: A Case Study." *Planning Review* (September) 11:24-28, 41.

Schollhammer, Hans. 1970. "Corporate Planning in France." *The Journal of Management Studies* (February) 7:60-77.

Scholz, Christian. 1984. "Planning Procedures in German Companies—Findings and Consequences." *Long Range Planning* (Winter) 17:94-103.

Schumpeter, Joseph A. 1942. *Capitalism, Socialism and Democracy.* New York: Harper and Brothers.

Scott, Bruce, R. 1973. "The Industrial State: Old Myths and New Realities." *Harvard Business Review* (March-April) 51:133-148.

Sekiguchi, Harold S. and Stanford I. Storey. 1984. "Strategic Planning Practices of Investor-Owned Electric Utilities." *Managerial Planning* (May-June) 32:45-51.

Shant, J. K., E. G. Niblack, and W. T. Sandalls. 1973. "Balance 'Creativity' and 'Practicality' in Formal Planning." *Harvard Business Review* 51:87-95.

Shapiro, H. Jack, and Ernest A. Kallman. 1978. "Long Range Planning Is Not for Everyone." *Planning Review* (September) 6:27-29, 34.

Shepherd, William G. 1972. "The Elements of Market Structure." *The Review of Economics and Statistics* (February) 54:25-37.

Shuman, Jack N. 1982. "Strategic Planning and Information Systems." *Bulletin of ASIS* (June) 8:23-27.

Sloan, Michael P. 1984. "Strategic Planning by Multiple Political Futures Techniques." *Management International Review* 24:4-17.

Smart, Carolyne and Ilan Vertinsky. 1984. "Strategy and the Environment: A Study of Corporate Responses to Crises." *Strategic Management Journal* (July-September) 5:199-213.

Snow, Charles C. and Donald C. Hambrick. 1980. "Measuring Organizational Strategies: Some Theoretical and Methodological Problems." *Academy of Management Review* (October) 5:527-538.

Snow, Charles C. and Lawrence G. Hrebiniak. 1980. "Strategy, Distinctive Competence, and Organizational Performance." *Administrative Science Quarterly* (June) 25:317-336.

So, Frank S. 1984. "Strategic Planning: Reinventing the Wheel?" *Planning* (February) 50:16-21.

Steer, Peter, and John Cable 1978. "Internal Organization and Profit: An Empirical Analysis of Large U.K. Companies." *Journal of Industrial Economics* (September) 27:13-30.

Steiner, George A. 1963. *Managerial Long-Range Planning.* New York: McGraw-Hill.

Steiner, George A. 1970. "Rise of the Corporate Planner." *Harvard Business Review* (September-October) 48:133-139.

Steiner, George A. 1974. "How To Improve Your Long Range Planning." *Managerial Planning* (September-October) 23:13-17.

Steiner, George A. 1979. *Strategic Planning: What Every Manager Must Know.* New York: Free Press.

Steiner, George A. 1983. "Formal Strategic Planning in the United States Today." *Long Range Planning* (June) 16:12-17.

Steiner, George A. and Hans Schollhammer. 1975. "Pitfalls in Multinational Long-Range Planning." *Long Range Planning* (April) 8:2-12.

Stopford, John M. 1968. "Growth and Organizational Change in the Multinational Field." Unpublished Doctoral Dissertation, Graduate School of Business Administration, Harvard University.

Stopford, John M. and Louis T. Wells, Jr. 1972. *Managing the Multinational Enterprise.* New York: Basic Books.

Strategic Planning Associates Inc. 1981. *Strategy and Shareholder Value: The Value Curve.* Washington, D.C.: Strategic Planning Associates.

Strigel, W. H. 1970. "Planning in West German Industry." *Long Range Planning* (September) 3:9-15.

Tagiuri, Renato and George H. Litwin, eds. 1968. *Organization Climate: Explorations of a Concept.* Boston, Mass.: Harvard University.

Tannenbaum, A. S. 1968. *Control in Organizations.* New York: McGraw-Hill.

Taylor, Bernard. 1984. "Strategic Planning—Which Style Do You Need?" *Long Range Planning* (June) 17:51-62.

Taylor, Frederick W. 1911. *The Principles of Scientific Management.* New York: Harper and Brothers.

Terpstra, David E. 1981. "Relationship Between Methodological Rigor and Reported Outcomes in Organization Development Evaluation Research." *Journal of Applied Psychology* 66:541-543.

Terreberry, Shirley. 1968. "The Evolution of Organizational Environments." *Administrative Science Quarterly* (March) 12:590-613.

Thanheiser, Heinz. 1972. "Strategy and Structure of German Firms." Unpublished Doctoral Dissertation, Graduate School of Business Administration, Harvard University.

Thomas, Philip S. 1980. "Environmental Scanning – The State of the Art." *Long Range Planning* (February) 13:20-28.

Thompson, James D. 1967. *Organizations in Action.* New York: McGraw-Hill.

Thune, Stanley S. and Robert J. House. 1970. "Where Long-Range Planning Pays Off." *Business Horizons* (August) 13:81-87.

Tomlinson, Rolfe C. and Robert G. Dyson. 1983. "Some Systems Aspects of Strategic Planning." *Journal of the Operational Research Society* 34:765-778.

Turk, Herman. 1970. "Interorganizational Networks in Urban Society: Initial Perspectives and Comparative Research." *American Sociological Review* (February) 35:1-18.

Tushman, M. and D. Nadler. 1978. "Information Processing as an Integrating Concept in Organization Design." *Academy of Management Review* 3:613-624.

U.S. Office of Management and Budget. 1972. *Standard Industrial Classification Manual.* Washington, D.C.: U.S. Government Printing Office.

Unger, Laszlo. 1983. "Strategic Planning for Commodities and Specialities." *Long Range Planning* (August) 16:12-20.

Urwick, Lyndall F. 1944. *The Elements of Administration.* New York: Harper and Brothers.

Value Line. 1977–1981. *The Value Line Investment Survey.* New York: A. Bernhard and Company.

Vancil, Richard F., Francis J. Aguilar, and Robert A. Howell, eds. 1968. *Formal Planning Systems–1968.* Cambridge, Mass.: Division of Case Distribution, Harvard Business School.

Vancil, Richard F. and Peter Lorrange. 1975. "Strategic Planning in Diversified Companies." *Harvard Business Review* (January-February) 53:81-90.

Vancil, Richard F. 1979. *Decentralization: Managerial Ambiguity by Design.* Homewood, Ill.: Dow Jones Irwin.

Van de Ven, Andrew H. and Robert Drazin. 1985. "The Concept of Fit in Contingency Theory." In B. Straw and L. L. Cummings, eds. *Research in Organizational Behavior,* Greenwich, CT.: JAI Press, 7:333-365.

Van de Ven, A., A. Delbecq, and R. Koenig. 1976. "Determinants of Coordination Modes Within Organizations." *American Sociological Review* (April) 41:322-338.

Vernon, J. 1972. *Market Structure and Industrial Performance: A Review of*

Statistical Findings. Boston, Mass.: Allyn and Bacon.

Von Lanzenaur, Christoph H. and Michael R. Sprung. 1982. "Developing Inflation Scenarios." *Long Range Planning* (August) 15:37-44.

Wack, Pierre. 1985. "Scenarios: Uncharted Waters Ahead." *Harvard Business Review* (September-October) 63:73-89.

Walker, Arthur and Jay W. Lorsch. 1970. "Organizational Choice: Product Versus Function." In Jay W. Lorsch, ed. *Studies in Organization Design.* Homewood, Ill.: Irwin.

Wallace, Robert E. 1984. "The MIS Strategic Planning Process." *Journal of Information Systems Management* (Winter) 1:93-96.

Ward, Lane D. 1982. "Eight Steps to Strategic Planning for Training Managers." *Training* (November) 19:22-25, 28-29.

Warren, E. Kirby. 1966. *Long Range Planning: The Executive Viewpoint,* Englewood Cliffs, N.J.: Prentice-Hall.

Weber, Max. 1947. *The Theory of Social and Economic Organization,* translated by A. M. Henderson and Talcott Parsons, Glencoe, Ill.: Free Press.

Weele, Ray V. 1980. "The Expanded Role of Controllership in Strategic Planning." *Managerial Planning* (September-October) 29:16-18, 22, 38.

Weick, Karl E. 1969. *The Social Psychology of Organizing.* Reading, Mass.: Addison-Wesley.

Weick, Karl. 1979. *The Social Psychology of Organizing,* 2nd ed. Reading, Mass.: Addison-Wesley.

Weiss, L. 1971. "Quantitative Studies of Industrial Organization." In M. Intriligator, ed. *Frontiers of Quantitative Economics.* London: North Holland.

Welch, Jonathan B. 1984. "Strategic Planning Could Improve Your Share Price." *Long Range Planning* (April) 17:144-147.

Wensley, Robin. 1982. "PIMS and BCG: New Horizons or False Dawn?" *Strategic Management Journal* 3:147-158.

Weston, J. Fred and Surendra K. Mansinghka. 1971. "Tests of the Efficiency Performance of Conglomerate Firms." *Journal of Finance* 26:919-936.

Wheelwright, Steven C. 1984. "Strategy, Management, and Strategic Planning Approaches." *Interfaces* (January-February) 14:19-33.

Williamson, Oliver E. 1975. *Markets and Hierarchies, Analysis and Antitrust Implications.* New York: The Free Press.

Wilson, Ian H., William R. George, and Paul J. Solomon. 1978. "Strategic Planning for Marketeers." *Business Horizons* (December) 21:65-73.

Wind, Yoram. 1982. *Product Policy: Concepts, Methods and Strategy.* Reading, Mass.: Addison-Wesley.

Wind, Yoram and Vijay Mahajan. 1981. "Designing Product and Business Portfolios." *Harvard Business Review* (January-February), 59:155-165.

Windsor, Duane and George Greanias. 1983. "Long-Range Planning in a Politicized Environment." *Long Range Planning* (June) 16:82-91.

Winn, Daryl N. 1975. *Industrial Market Structure and Performance,*

1966-1968. Ann Arbor, Mich.: University of Michigan.

Wold, Herman. 1975a. *Modeling in Complex Situations with Soft Information.* Gothenburg, Sweden: University of Gothenburg.

Wold, Herman. 1975b. Group Report: Modeling in Complex Situations with Soft Information. Third Congress of Econometrics Aug. 21-26, Toronto. *Research Report* 75:4. Uppsala: University of Uppsala, Institute of Statistics.

Wold, Herman. 1977. Open Path Models with Latent Variables. In: H. Albach, E. Helmstedter, and R. Henn, eds. *Kwantitative Wirtschafts-forschung: Wilhelm Krelle zum 60,* pp. 729-754. Geburtstag: Mohr, Tubinger.

Wold, Herman, 1978. Ways and Means of Interdisciplinary Studies. In: *Transactions of the Sixth International Conference on the Unity of the Sciences,* 1977, pp. 1071-1095. New York: International Cultural Foundation.

Wold, Herman. 1980. "Model Construction and Evaluation When Theoretical Knowledge Is Scarce." In Jan Kmenta and James B. Ramsey, eds. *Evaluation of Econometric Models,* pp. 47-74. New York: Academic Press.

Woo, Carolyn Y. 1984. "An Empirical Test of Value-Based Planning Models and Implications." *Management Science* (September) 30:1031-1050.

Wood, D. Robley, Jr. 1980. "Long Range Planning in Large United States Banks." *Long Range Planning* (June) 13:91-98.

Wood, D. Robley, Jr. and R. Lawrence LaForge. 1979. "The Impact of Comprehensive Planning on Financial Performance." *Academy of Management Journal* (September) 22:516-526.

Wood, D. Robley, Jr. and R. Lawrence LaForge. 1981. "Toward the Development of a Planning Scale: An Example from the Banking Industry." *Strategic Management Journal* (April-June) 2:209-216.

Woodburn, Trevor L. 1984. "Corporate Planning in South African Companies." *Long Range Planning* (February) 17:84-99.

Woodman, Richard W. and Donald C. King. 1978. "Organizational Climate: Science or Folklore." *Academy of Management Review* (October) 3:816-826.

Woodward, Joan. 1965. *Industrial Organization.* London: Oxford University Press.

Wright, David. 1982. "New Zealand – A Newcomer to Planning." *Long Range Planning* (June) 15:122-131.

Wright, Peter, David Townsend, Jerry Kinard, and Joe Iverstine. 1982. "The Developing World to 1990: Trends and Implications for Multinational Business." *Long Range Planning* (August) 15:116-125.

Wright, Robert V. L. 1974. *A System for Managing Diversity.* Cambridge, Mass.: Arthur D. Little.

Wright, Sara, Noel Capon, John U. Farley, and James M. Hulbert. 1985. "Organizational Processes and Economic Performance: A Contingency Approach." Working paper, Columbia University.

Wrigley, Leonard. 1970. "Divisional Autonomy and Diversification." Unpublished Doctoral Dissertation, Graduate School of Business Administration, Harvard University.

Author Index

Aaker, David A., 173
Abell, Derek F., 173
Abernathy, William J., 173
Abou-Zeid, R., 165
Ackerman, Robert W., 41
Ackoff, R.L., 144, 155
Adamson, Joel, 5
Aguilar, Francis J., 2, 37, 369
Aiken, Michael, 147
Al-Bazzaz, Shawki, 5, 42, 160, 204
Aldrich, Howard, 146
Allen, Stephen A., 41
Anderson, Carl R., 7, 148, 149
Andrews, K.R., 162
Ang, James S., 4, 290
Ansoff, H. Igor, 2, 69, 163, 164, 165,
    166, 167, 282, 289, 290, 369
Argyris, C., 153
Armstrong, J. Scott, 4, 282, 290, 292
Athos, Anthony G., 201
Athreya, M., 41, 42
Austin, Douglas V., 4
Avner, Jay, 282, 289, 290

Baker, H. Kent, 4, 42
Ball, Leslie D., 42
Bamberger, Imgolf, 5
Bandeen, Robert A., 43
Banks, Robert L., 39
Barber, John M., 4
Bartlett, C.J., 202, 369
Bass, Frank M., 152, 171
Beard, Donald W., 163, 172, 174
Beattie, D.L., 171
Berg, Norman A., 199
Berger, Chris J., 203

Bernhard, Arnold, 9, 293
Berry, Charles H., 171
Bettis, Richard A., 171, 172
Bhatty, Egbert F., 5
Bonham, T.W., 151
Boston Consulting Group, 2, 173
Bouamrene, M. A., 4
Boulton, William R., 146
Bourgeois, L.J., III, 150, 155, 163
Bower, Joseph L., 369
Brandenburg, Richard G., 282, 289, 290
Brandt, W.K., 38, 41, 169, 290, 369
Brick, Ivan E., 293
Brown, Alvin, 150
Brown, Arnold, 43
Brown, Grace C., 42
Brown, James R., 9
Bulgues, Pierre, 5
Burns, Tom, 147, 349
Business Week, 3, 69, 164, 170, 172
Buzzell, Robert D., 4, 69, 173, 281,
    292, 350, 369

Cable, John, 204
Camillus, John C., 31, 42, 43
Campbell, John P., 201
Capon, Noel, 1, 5, 12, 53, 63, 65, 97,
    144, 151, 155, 162, 168, 172, 204,
    219, 220, 267, 271, 281, 324
Carlson, Thomas S., 27, 28, 29
Carter, John R., 170, 171
Cattin, Philippe, 152
Caves, Richard E., 171, 198
Chandler, Alfred D., 3, 163, 195, 348,
    349, 369
Channon, Derek F., 167, 196, 204, 349

Chaston, Ian, 4
Child, John, 153, 324, 369
Christensen, C.P., 162
Christensen, H. Kurt, 39, 171, 172, 350
Christodoulou, Chris, 97, 219, 220
Chua, Jess H., 4, 290
Cooper, Arnold C., 39
Copeland, Ronald M., 171
Croft, D., 203
Csath, M., 5
Cummings, L.J., 145
Cummings, L.L., 203
Cyert, Richard M., 151, 369
Cymbala, Robert J., 37

Dalton, Dan R., 203, 350
Dalton, James A., 173
Darden, William R., 37
Das, Ranjan, 5
Davis, Stanley, 197
Day, George S., 2, 39, 69, 369
Day, Diana L., 174
De Jong, Klaas, 4
Deal, Terrence E., 201
DeKluyver, Cornelius A., 39
Delbecq, A., 199
Denning, B.W., 282, 289, 290
DeNoya, Louis E., 28
Dess, Gregory G., 163, 172, 174
Devanna, Mary Anne, 5, 39
Dickson, J.W., 41
Diffenbach, John, 37
Dill, William R., 144
Downey, H. Kirk, 145
Drazin, Robert, 327
Duncan, Robert B., 145, 148
Dundas, Kenneth N.M., 172
Dunnette, Marvin D., 201
Dyson, R.G., 5, 39, 42

Eadle, Douglas C., 42
Eastlack, Joseph O., Jr., 282
Egelhoff, William G., 169, 198, 206, 369
Ellison, Nolen, M., 42
Emery, F.E., 144
Emery, J.C., 199
Engi, Dennis, 4
Eppink, D. Jan, 4, 29

Farley, John U., 1, 5, 12, 53, 63, 97,
    151, 168, 172, 204, 219, 220, 267,
    271, 273, 281, 293, 324, 346
Fayol, Henri, 150, 350
Fielding, Gordon J., 203, 350
Finn, R., 4, 28
Finniza, Anthony J., 39
Flavell, R., 4
Fombrun, Charles, 5, 39
Ford, Jeffrey D., 200
Ford, T. Mitchell, 43
Forehand, Gartie A., 201
Foster, M.J., 5, 42
Fox, Joseph M., 27
Franklin, Stephen G., 146
Franko, Lawrence G., 197
Frederick, Glenn D., 5
Fredrickson, James W., 7, 30, 281, 325
Friesen, Peter H., 7, 38, 146, 148,
    154, 176, 257
Fruhan, William E., Jr., 39, 152
Fulmer, Robert M., 289, 292, 325

Gabel, H., 152
Gabele, Eduard, 5
Galbraith, Jay R., 31, 41, 147, 162,
    164, 197, 198, 203, 206
Gale, Bradley T., 4, 69, 173, 281, 292,
    350, 369
Galer, Graham, 5
Garber, Joseph R., 42
Gattis, Daniel R., 42
Gelb, Betsy D., 39
George, William R., 37
Gershefski, George W., 282, 289, 291
Ghosh, B.C., 5, 38
Gilmer, B. von Haller, 201
Ginsberg, Ari, 176
Glueck, William F., 52, 144, 149, 165
Godiwalla, Yezdi Minoo, 37
Gort, Michael, 171
Gotcher, J. William, 28
Gray, Daniel H., 363
Greanias, George, 37, 38
Greenley, Gordon E., 282
Grimm, Ulrich, 5
Grinyer, Peter H., 5, 42, 160, 204,
    282, 289, 290
Guth, W.D., 162

Hage, Jerald, 147
Hall, David J., 31
Hall, Marshall, 173
Hall, William K., 27, 29
Halpern, Richard S., 5
Halpin, A., 203
Hambrick, Donald C., 146, 174, 175, 176, 257, 324, 348
Hammond, John S., 173
Hampton, Colin C., 4
Harju, Paavo, 289
Hart, N. Berne, 4, 42
Harvey, Allan, 282, 289, 291
Harvey, E., 148
Haspeslagh, Philippe, 2, 39
Hatten, K.J., 152, 173
Hax, Arnoldo C., 1, 2, 3, 39, 69
Hayes, Samuel L., III, 152
Hedley, Barry D., 2
Hellriegel, Don, 201
Henderson, Bruce D., 3, 369
Henry, Harold W., 5, 31, 148
Herold, David M., 282, 292
Hichens, R.E., 29
Hickson, D.J., 195, 200, 369
Higgins, J.C., 4, 28
Higgins, R.B., 42
Hirsch, P., 152
Hirschman, Albert O., 170
Hofer, Charles W., 1, 2, 26, 146, 162, 163, 164, 369
Holland, Robert C., 4
Holloway, Clark, 27, 39
Holmberg, Stevan R. 4, 42
Holmes, Geoffrey, 39
Holzmann, Oscar J., 171
Hopkins, H. Donald, 170
Horovitz, J.H., 42, 43
House, Robert J., 282, 289, 291, 292, 325
Howell, Robert A., 2, 369
Hrebiniak, Lawrence G., 175
Huber, G.P., 145
Hulbert, James M., 1, 5, 12, 38, 41, 53, 63, 65, 97, 144, 151, 155, 162, 168, 169, 172, 204, 219, 220, 267, 281, 290, 324, 369
Hussey, D.E., 3, 28, 69, 369

Iverstine, Joe, 37

Jacobson, Robert, 173
Jacquemin, Alexis P., 171
Jaedicke, Carl F., 4, 43
Jagpal, Harsharanjett S., 293
Jain, Subash, 37, 39
James, Lawrence R., 201
Jauch, Lawrence R. 149, 165
Joaquim, Manuel E., 27
Johannesson, Russell E., 202, 369
Jones, Allan P., 201
Jones, David C., 4, 37
Jonsson, Sverker, 5, 37

Kallman, Ernest A., 282
Karger, Delmar W., 282, 289, 290
Kasper, Wolfgang, 5
Katz, Abraham, 42
Katz, Gerald, 37
Kaufman, S.P., 52
Keegan, Warren, 369
Kelley, Richard, M., 4
Kennedy, Allen A., 201
Kennedy, Miles H., 44
Keown, A.J., 165
Keppler, Werner, 5
Keuning, Doede, 4
Khandwalla, Pradip N., 42, 148, 163, 164, 369
Kiechel III, Walter, 2, 3
Kimberly, John R., 169, 170
Kimmerly, William C., 5
King, Donald C., 202, 369
King, William R., 27, 290, 291
Kinnard, Jerry, 37
Klein, Harold E., 38
Koenig, Harold F., 9
Koenig, R., 199
Koontz, Harold, 203
Kono, Toyohiro, 5
Kover, Arthur J., 4
Kriekebaum, Harmut, 5
Kroeten, Terrence T., 9
Kudla, Ronald J., 4, 28, 282, 289, 290

La Forge, R. Lawrence, 4, 289, 325
Larreche, Jean-Claude, 39
Lawler, Edward E. III, 201
Lawrence, Paul R., 40, 147, 153, 197, 324

Leavitt, Harold, 194
Leff, Nathaniel H., 42
Lehmann, Donald R., 104, 151, 220, 271, 346
Lehr, M.E., 282, 289, 290
Lei, David, 204, 220, 267, 324
Lenz, R.T., 43, 152
Lieberson, S., 172
Likert, Rensis, 203
Lindbloom, Charles E., 30
Lindsay, William M., 43, 146, 148
Link, Max E., 42
Linneman, Robert E., 38
Litschert, Robert J., 26, 148, 151
Litwin, George H., 201
Lobe, Thomas J., 43
Lopez, Felix M., 39
Lorange, Peter, 26, 27, 29, 41, 42, 43, 369
Lorsch, Jay, 40, 41, 147, 153, 197, 324
Lucas, R.L., 273
Lusch, Robert F., 9
Lyles, Marjorie A., 43

McDonald, Philip R., 282
McGuire, T.W., 273
McKelvey, Bill, 257
MacMillan, Ian C., 174
McRorie, John S., 4
Mahajan, Vijay, 39
Mahapatra, Sitikantha, 44
Majluf, Nicolas S., 1, 2, 3, 39, 69
Malecki, Donald S., 4
Malik, Zafar A., 282, 289, 290
Masinghka, Surendra K., 171
Marakon Associates, 39
March, James G., 146, 151, 369
Marks, David Van Praag, 152
Markezin, Elaine, 37
Martin, Elizabeth, 168, 172, 220
Meadows, Edwards, 43
Meinhart, Wayne A., 37
Melicher, Ronald W., 171
Merrill, H.M., 38
Metz, Edmund J., 39, 43
Metzger, Robert O., 4
Michael, Stephen R., 38, 43
Miesing, Paul, 39
Miles, Raymond E., 175, 198, 350

Miller, Danny, 7, 38, 146, 148, 154, 176, 257
Mills, Chester R., 4
Miner, J., 153
Minoo, Yendi, 37
Mintzberg, Henry, 30, 38, 42, 162, 369
Mitchell, Terence R., 7, 281, 325
Mohanty, Brajaraj, 5
Morh, L. B., 199
Montebello, Michael, 5
Montgomery, Cynthia A., 167, 171, 172, 350
Montgomery, David B., 38
Mooney, James D., 150
Morrison, Donald G., 104
Mulligan, Robert J., 4

Nadler, D., 199
Naisbitt, John, 1
Nathanson, D.A., 31, 162, 164, 197, 198, 203, 206
Nauert, Roger C., 43
Naylor, Thomas H., 26, 37, 39
Nee, A.Y.C., 5, 38
Neidell, Lester A., 39
New York Times, 1
Niblack, E.G., 41
Nicholson, Edward A. Jr., 26
Neilsen, Richard P., 42, 43
Norburn, David, 5, 282, 289, 290

O'Connell, M.J., 145
O'Connor, J., 172
O'Donnell, Cyril, 203
Oliver, Alex R., 42
Osborn, Richard N., 149
Ouchi, William G., 201

Paine, Frank T., 7, 148, 149
Parker, Lee D., 4
Pascale, Richard T., 201
Patel, Peter, 3, 69
Patton, G. Richard, 4
Pavan, Robert, 167, 196, 349
Payne, R.L., 201, 202, 369
Pearce, John A., 11, 39, 282, 289, 325
Penn, David W., 173
Pennings, Johannes M., 153, 281, 324
Penrose, Edith, 169

Peters, Thomas J., 1, 151, 201, 205, 210, 329, 350
Petzaell, Ingvar, 5, 37
Pfeffer, Jeffrey, 150, 155
Pharr, Steven W., 9
Pheysey, D.C., 202, 369
Phillips, A., 152
Phillips, Lynn W., 9
Pitts, Robert A., 170, 199
Poensgen, Otto, 204
Pooley-Dyas, Gareth, 167, 196, 349
Porter, Lyman, 203, 350
Porter, M.E., 38, 66, 70, 152, 171
Portner, Fred E., 282, 289, 290
Probert, David E., 4
Pugh, D.S., 195, 200, 201, 369

Quinn, James Brian, 30

Radosevich, Raymond, 282, 289, 290
Raimond, Paul, 5
Randall, Robert M., 39
Rappaport, Alfred, 39
Rector, Robert L., 39
Reid, Samuel R., 171
Reinhardt, W.A., 37
Rhoades, Stephen A., 170, 171
Rhyne, Lawrence C., 37, 282
Richardson, Peter R., 172
Richers, Raimar, 38
Ring, L.W., 273
Ringbakk, Kjell A., 2, 369
Robinson, Richard B., Jr., 282, 289, 325
Robinson, S.J.Q., 29
Roney, C.W., 28
Rose, Peter S., 5
Rothschild, William E., 1
Rue, Leslie W., 146, 289, 292, 325
Rumelt, Richard P., 3, 13, 151, 164, 167, 168, 169, 171, 172, 173, 196, 200, 204, 205, 291, 348, 350, 369
Rush, David F., 171
Ryan, Michael J., 346
Russell, Lloyd J., 4

Saias, Maurice A., 31
Salancik, Gerald R., 150, 155
Salomon, Paul J., 37
Salter, Malcolm, 169

Sandalls, W.T., 41
Saunders, Charles B., 26, 28
Sayles, Leonard, 42
Scampini, Thomas J., 4
Schaffir, Walter B., 43
Schendel, Dan, 1, 4, 152, 162, 163, 173, 369
Schneider, Benjamin, 202, 369
Schoeffler, Sidney, 4, 69, 173, 281, 292, 350, 369
Schofield, Douglas F., 37
Schollhammer, Hans, 5, 43
Scholz, Christian, 5
Schumpeter, Joseph A., 33
Schweppe, F.C., 38
Scott, Bruce R., 167
Sekiguchi, Harold S., 4
Shant, J.K., 41
Shapiro, H. Jack, 282
Shepherd, William G., 173
Shuman, Jack N., 4
Simon, Herbert A., 146
Sinkula, James M., 37
Sloan, Michael P., 38
Slocum, John W. Jr., 145, 200, 201
Smart, Carolyne, 149
Snow, Charles C., 175, 176, 198, 350
So, Frank S., 4
Spence, A. Michael, 152, 171
Spendolini, Michael, 203, 350
Sprung, Michael R., 5
Srinivasan, V., 39
Stalker, G.M., 147, 349
Steer, Peter, 204
Steiner, George A., 1, 2, 28, 43, 369
Stewart, John M., 166
Stopford, John M., 169, 369
Storey, Stanford I., 4
Strategic Planning Associates, 39
Strigel, W.H., 5
Sultan, Ralph G.M., 4, 69, 173, 281, 292, 350, 369

Tagiuri, Renato, 201
Tannenbaum, A.S., 42
Tapon, Francis, 39
Taylor, Bernard, 42, 43, 165
Taylor, Frederick W., 150, 350
Terpstra, David E., 292

Terreberry, Shirley, 144, 145
Thanheiser, Heinz, 167, 196, 350
Thietart, R.A., 42
Thomas, Phillip S., 37
Thompson, James D., 144, 145, 147, 162, 199
Thune, Stanley S., 282, 289, 291, 292, 325
Tichy, Noel, 5, 39
Todor, William D., 203, 350
Tomlinson, Rolfe C., 39
Townsend, David, 37
Trist, E.L., 144
Tuggle, Francis D., 26, 28
Turner, C., 195, 200, 369
Tushman, M., 199

Unger, Laszlo, 4
U.S. Office of Management and Budget, 171
Urwick, Lyndall, 150

Vancil, Richard F., 2, 26, 27, 43, 163, 369
Van de Ven, A., 199, 327
Venkatraman, N., 176
Vernon, J., 152
Vertinsky, Ilan, 149
Von Lanzenaur, Christoph H., 5

Wack, Pierre, 37
Wade, D.P., 29
Warde, William D., 37
Walker, Arthur, 41
Wallace, Robert E., 4
Ward, Lane D., 5
Warren, E. Kirby, 2

Warren, Lynn, 5, 39
Waterman, Robert H., 1, 151, 201, 205, 210, 329, 350
Wayne, Kenneth, 173
Weber, Max, 150, 350
Weele, Ray V., 5
Weick, Karl E. Jr., 145, 150, 157, 201
Weinberg, Charles B., 38
Weinhold, Wolff A., 169
Weiss, L., 152, 173
Welch, Jonathan B., 289
Welleck, A.S., 52
Wells, Louis T., 169, 369
Weston, J. Fred, 171
Wheelwright, Steven C., 30, 39
Williamson, Oliver E., 33, 196, 369
Wilson, Ian H., 37
Wind, Yoram, 39
Windsor, Duane, 37, 38
Winn, Daryl N., 173
Wittinck, Dick, 152, 171
Wold, Herman, 103
Woo, Carolyn Y., 39
Wood, D. Robley, Jr., 4, 289, 325
Woodburn, Trevor, L., 5, 41, 42
Woodman, Richard W., 202, 369
Woodward, Joan, 349
Wright, David, 5
Wright, Peter, 37
Wright, Robert V.L., 3
Wright, Sara, 220, 281, 324,
Wrigley, Leonard, 3, 166, 196, 348

Yasai-Ardekani, Masoud, 5, 160, 204
Younger, Michael, 3, 69

Zavodnik, Leslie, 37

Subject Index

Acquisition strategy, 17, 67, 98, 335, 338; and consultants, 84–85; and Corporate Financial Planners, 189; and Division Strategic Planners, 189; and environment, 155; and growth, 171; and sales, 189–190; scales, 113, 237, 240–241; and strategy, 169, 170, 189–190, 192, 242

Adaptive dimension of planning, 23, 36–40, 50–51, 64–76, 98–99, 336; and classification of planning, 48; and planning practice, 62; scales, 111–115, 121, 230

Administrative intensity, 201, 205, 216

Advertising–to–sales ratio, 152

Alternatives, generation of, 38, 40, 56, 61

Alternatives to strategic planning, 30–32

Analytic devices, 69–70, 98

Analyzer corporate strategy, 175

Ansoff, Igor, 69

Arthur D. Little Co., 69

Atmosphere, 35, *See also* Organizational climate

Australian companies, 12, 63, 97, 219–220, 334

Beer industry, 152

Beta measure, 290

Board of directors, 227; and environment, 236; frequency of meetings, 206; influence on planning, 81–83, 99, 116, 236, 240, 324

Booz Allen and Hamilton, 69

Boston Consulting Group, 69, 174

Bottom-up planning, 41–42, 336, 360; and goals, 116, 240, 246

Bounded rationality, 34

Budgets for planning, 63, 97

Budgeting models, 71, 98

Business count methods, 170–171

Business-level strategy, 163, 173-174

Business Week, 362

CAB, 152

Capital asset pricing models, 39

Capital goods, 10

Capital intensity, 181, 355; and profits, 173–174; and size of company, 173

Capital spending per share, 290

Cash flow, 49; discounted, 74; and portfolio models, 70; and resource allocation, 74, 75, 114; and sales, 294, 302

Cash management plans, 25

Categories of planning systems, 47–51, 61, 333, 342–344; and adaptive scales, 114–115; classification and prediction, 58–60; and environment, 52–53, 56, 57, 61; factor analysis, 52–57, 58, 61; and integrative scales, 118–121; and self-report of firms, 51–52; *see also* Corporate Financial Planners; Corporate Strategic Planners; Division Strategic Planners; Division Financial Planners; Non-Planners

Centralization of organization, 201, 205–206, 216; and Corporate Strategic Planners, 216; and Non-Planners, 205, 333, *see also* Decentralization

CEOs and planning, 41–42, 81, 83,

CEOs and planning *(Continued)*
99, 116, 227, 230, 246, 259, 360; and
Corporate Strategic Planners, 83, 85,
336; and goals, 81, 85, 99, 106, 117,
236, 334; and performance, 303, 319
Change, 27, 28–29, 337; and Corporate
Strategic Planners, 236; scales, 234,
236; *see also* Uncertainty
Ciba-Geigy, 37
Cluster analysis, 257–266, 271
Communication. *See* Information flow
Companies participating in study, 7–8;
and data collection, 8–9; financial
performance, 9–10; international
operations, 12–13; and product life
cycles, 11–12; sales revenues, 10, 12;
types of business, 10–11
Compensation, 95–96, 101, 335; *see also*
Reward system
Competitive analysis, 66, 98, 145, 157,
227, 259, 334, 336, 337; and
performance, 319; and pressure for
planning, 151; scales, 113, 248; and
uncertainty, 235
Complexity of organization, 200–201
Comprehensiveness of planning, 114,
121
Conflict resolution, 41, 89–93, 99
Consultants: and acquisition strategy,
84–85; and environment, 148;
influence on planning, 84–85, 99;
and portfolio models, 53
Contentment with organization, 226, 227
264, 339; and Corporate Strategic
Planners, 231
Context of plans, 76, 98, 99
Contextual environment, 144
Contingency planning, 38; and
Corporate Strategic Planners, 335;
and environment, 147–149,
150–151; lack of, 67, 68, 98; and
performance, 323–328
Contingent/occurrence perspective on
research, 349–350
Contingent/performance perspective on
research, 350-351
Control and information systems, 206,
217; *see also* Information flow
Conventional wisdom on planning
implementation, 333–336
Cooperation, 215

Corporate culture. *See* Organizational
climate
Corporate Financial Planners: and
acquisition and divestiture, 189;
categorization, 49, 51, 58, 333;
individual measurements, 57; and integrative scales, 120; and organizational climate, 270; and organization structure, 247, 271; and performance, 298–299; and planning
personnel, 63, 231; and revenue
growth, 190; and strategy, 269; and
time horizons of planning, 78
Corporate headquarters and divisions,
199–200
Corporate planning vs. strategic planning, 26, 28, 29
Corporate Strategic Planners: and acquisition and divestiture, 189, 192, 242,
338; and adaptive planning, 98,
114–115, 124, 336; and analytic
devices, 69; categorization, 49, 51,
333; and centralization, 216; and
CEO influence, 83, 85, 336; and conflict resolution, 89–93; and content
of plans, 76; and contentment with
organization, 231; and contingency
planning, 335; and decentralization,
205–206, 216, 270; and diversification, 185, 192, 338; and entrepreneurial behavior, 215, 231, 339; and
environment, 76, 157–158, 159, 236,
269, 336, 337; follow-up studies,
353–354; and forecasting, 65–66,
159, 160, 335; and formal planning,
51; and global planning, 57, 58, 68,
98, 235, 336; and goals, 76, 85, 96,
178, 179, 191, 337; and information
flow, 57, 336; and integration of
planning, 78, 87, 99, 118–120, 124,
336; and internal innovation, 242;
and international diversification,
187–188, 192, 242, 338; and line
managers and planning 85–86, 215,
335–336; and market dominance,
158, 160, 337; and market growth,
182, 242, 337; and mission, 76, 191;
and models, 71, 336; and new products, 182–183, 191–192, 242,
337–338; and organizational climate,
211–217, 231, 270; and organization

structure, 205, 208, 215–216, 246–247, 270, 338–339; over-staffing, 215; and performance, 94, 95, 96, 100, 298, 300, 301, 302, 307–308, 336, 340–341; and planning departments, 63, 64, 87, 88, 89, 99–100, 265, 335; and portfolio models, 69; and product life cycles, 186, 192, 338; and research and development, 184, 191–192, 337; and resource allocation, 73–74–75, 98, 335, 336; and revenues, 190; and scientific personnel recruitment, 208; and second-level planning, 83, 205–206, 333; and size of companies, 192, 242; and strategy, 242, 269; and time horizon of planning, 67, 78–79, 98, 114, 335; and transfer pricing, 209; and uncertainty, 159, 236, 335

Creativity and planning, 28

Data base system usage, 71
Data collection methods of study, 8–9
Debt/equity ratios, 290
Debt leverage and profit, 174
Decentralization, 31, 243, 246; and Corporate Strategic Planners, 205–206, 216, 270; groups, 263–267; and performance, 203, 210–211, 357
Decision making, 27; and centralization, 205–206; and decentralization, 32; models, 71; participative, 41, 226, 227, 264–265, 267, 277, 339
Decline stage of life cycle, 12
Defender corporate strategy, 175
Demand: as environmental factor, 157, 337; forecasting, 64, 65, 98, 158, 159, 334; impact, 145
Depth of planning, 56, 58, 117–118, 121
Deregulation, 352
Differentiation, 40, 147, 181
Directional Policy Matrix, 3
Distribution of corporate plans, 94
Disturbed-reactive environment, 145
Diversification strategy, 3, 13–14, 67, 151, 166–168, 184–187; and Corporate Strategic Planners, 185, 192, 338; and Division Financial Planners, 189; and divisionalization, 196–197; internal, 200; and Non-Planners, 181; and organizational

structure, 199–200; and performance, 170–172, 300; and sales, 13–14
Divestiture, 17, 98, 335; and consultants, 84–85; and Corporate Strategic Planners, 189, 242; and environment, 155; number of, 189; scales, 113, 237, 240–241; and strategy, 169, 189–190, 192
Dividend maintenance as goal, 178
Dividends/net income as performance measure, 290
Division-level planners, 43–44, 47–48
Division Financial Planners, 277; and acquisition and divestiture, 189; and adaptive planning scales, 115; categorization, 49, 51, 58, 333; and diversification, 189; individual measurements, 57; and integrative scales, 120; and organizational climate, 251, 270; and organization structure, 247, 270; and performance, 299, 301, 302; and strategy, 242, 269
Division Strategic Planners: and acquisition and divestiture, 189; categorization, 49, 51, 52, 58, 333; and environment, 236; individual measurements, 57; and models, 71; and organizational climate, 231, 270; and organization structure, 270; and performance, 95, 298; and planning groups, 265; and portfolio changes, 114; and scientific personnel recruitment, 208; and strategy, 242, 269
Domestic strategy groups, 262–263, 266, 273, 356
Dominant business firms, 113–114, 166–168, 171–172, 184–185
DuPont, 163

Earnings per share, 49, 75, 114
Econometric models, 71
Economic factors and planning, 29, 64, 334
Economic threory and planning, 33–36
Effectiveness of strategic planning, 358
Employees, number of, 237
Entrepreneurial behavior, 210–211, 215, 267; and Corporate Strategic Planners, 215, 231, 339; and incentives,

Entrepreneurial behavior *(Continued)* 216, 242, 246, 263, 264; scales, 226, 230

Entropy index, 171

Entry strategy. *See* Market entry

Environment, 6, 17, 143–160, 336–337, 339, 361; and acquisition, 155; analysis of, 37–38, 40, 66, 148, 243; attributes of, 145–147, 153, 155; and board of directors, 236; and categorizations of planners, 52–53, 56, 57, 61; and change, 27, 28, 29; and consultants, 148; and contingency planning, 147–149, 150–151; and Corporate Strategic Planners, 76, 157–158, 159, 236, 269, 336, 337; and Division Strategic Planners, 236; elements of, 144–145, 153, 154; forecasting, 29, 64–66, 113; goals, 148; groups, 259–260, 273; historic and future, 155–157, 159–160; and information flow, 148, 236; and managerial choice, 149–150, 162–163; measurement of, 154–155; and Non-Planners, 236; and organization structure, 153; and performance, 148, 151–153, 303, 304, 325, 355; scales, 112–113, 231–236, 249, 345; and slack resources, 151–153; and strategy, 28–29, 149, 150, 357–358; and uncertainty, 145–147, 148, 154, 234, 235–236; and universalistic perspective, 150–151

Exit, 181

Experience curve, 2, 173

Extensive planners, 266, 269, 270, 273, 357

Financial integration, 43–44

Financial performance as planning determinant, 151

Financial planning, 40, 48–49, 77; *see also* Corporate Financial Planners; Division Financial Planners

Follow-the-leader market strategy, 166

Follow-up studies, 353–354

Forecasting, 31–34, 334, 360; and categorization of planners, 33; confidence in ability, 158, 160; and Corporate Financial Planners, 65–66, 159, 160, 335; and demand, 64, 65, 98, 158, 159, 334; economic, 63, 334; models, 71, scales, 113; sociocultural, 64, 65, 98, 158, 334; technological, 65, 98, 334; transmission of, 79, 99, 106, 116

Formal written plans, 52, 53–54, 57, 336.

Formalization of organization, 201

Formalization of planning, 94, 117–118, 122

Fortune 500 companies, 5–6, 168, 169, 331 and organization structure, 196, 197; and performance, 282; and sample design, 6–8, 9–10

Fully integrated planners, 258–259, 265, 266, 270, 273; and performance, 303–306, 357

Functional organization, 196, 197, 204

Functional perspective on planning, 23, 36–44, 45, 60–61, 335; adaptive dimension, 23, 36–40, 60–61; integrative dimension, 23, 36, 40–44, 61, 230; and performance, 311–314

Functional-with-subsidiaries organization, 196

Future research needs, 351–357

General Electric, 3, 69; and environment, 37

General Motors, 163

Geographic diversification, 164

Geographic divisions, 196, 197, 198, 206

Gestalt analysis, 17, 176, 257–277

Globalness of planning, 38, 40, 68, 98, 227, 248, 335; and categorization of planners, 56, 57, 58, 61; and Corporate Strategic Planners, 57, 58, 68, 98, 335, 336; and organization structure, 243; and performance, 304, 355; and strategy, 241; and uncertainty, 235

Goals, 17, 85, 249, 259; and assets, return on, 177, 178; and bottom-up formulation, 116, 240, 246; and CEOs, 81, 85, 99, 106, 117, 236, 334; changes in, 179; clarity of, 100; and Corporate Strategic Planners, 76, 85,

96, 178, 179, 191, 337; and environment, 148; and line management, 42; and performance, 95, 96, 303, 304, 319; and planners, 106, 339; qualitative, 178-179, 191, 337; quantitative, 177-178, 191, 337; and sales, 177, 178; scales 118, 230; second- level, 179-180, 191, 334; and strategic planning concept, 26, 28
Growth stage of life cycle, 12

Harvard Business School, Business Policy group, 161-162
Hewlett-Packard, 30
Hierarchies and planning, 33-35
Hirschman index, 170-171
Holding Companies, 196, 197, 199, 204
Hostile environment, 148, 234, 236, 355

Image as goal, 178
Implementation of planning, 43, 81
Individual freedom and responsibility, 215
Industrial goods strategy, 237, 240, 355
Influence sources: board of directors, 81-83, 99, 116, 236, 240, 324; CEOs, 41-42, 81, 83, 99, 116, 227, 230, 246, 259, 360; consultants, 84-85, 99; external, 84-85, 99; internal, 81-84, 99, 116, 227, 240, 243, 246, 267; line management, 81, 85-86, 99, 106, 115, 117, 227, 243, 246, 334
Information flow, 227, 241, 360; and environment, 148, 236; and hierarchies, 35; and integration of planning, 41, 79-81; internal, 79, 99, 116; and line management 79-80, 259; and organization structure, 243; and performance, 309, 321; and planners, 42, 99; and process model, 106; scales, 115, 116, 248; and task forces, 246; and top management, 79, 99, 116
Innovation, 34, 148; groups, 261; and organization structure, 200, 208; and performance, 356; scales, 237; and time horizon, 38; see also internal innovation
Inputs of planning, 44-46, 61, 100
Inside influence. See Influence, internal
Integration of plans, 77-79, 87, 99, 106,

243, 361; and Corporate Strategic Planners, 78, 87, 99, 118-120, 124, 336; and information flow, 41, 79-81; scales, 116-122, 227, 230-231, 249
Integrative dimension of planning, 77-85, 99, 336; and classification of planning systems, 47-48; and planners, 86, 94
Intended strategy, 162, 191
Interdependence of business divisions 198-199, 208-210, 243, 246, 263; and performance, 356
Interdivisional communication, 243
Internal innovation, 192, 237, 240 242, 337, 355
Internal procurement, 209, 216, 243
International operations, 4, 5, 12-13, 17, 38, 187-188, 335; and Corporate Strategic Planners, 187-188, 192, 242, 338; and marketing, 188, 237, 241, 242; and organization structure, 197-198, 206-208, 216; and performance, 361; and sales, 12-13, 188, 338; scales, 237, 241
Introductory stage of life cycle, 12
Investment banking, strategic groups, 152
Investment criteria and planning, 39 40, 114, 334

Life cycle. See Product life cycle
Line management, 42, 63, 359; attitude toward planning, 99, 117, 215, 217, 222, 236, 240-241, 246, 249, 259, 334, 336, 360; compensation criteria, 100; and Corporate Strategic Planners, 85-86, 215, 335-336; influence on planning, 81, 85-86, 99, 106, 115, 117, 227, 243, 246, 334; and information flow, 79-80, 259; interaction, 229-230; scales, 117, 226
Logical incrementalism, 30, 32
Long-run average cost curve, 2
Long-term planning, 26-27, 29, 334-335, 340-342

M-form of organization, 196, 200
Management information system, 4-5

Managerial implications of planning, 357–362

Manufacturing companies, 11; and Corporate Strategic Planners, 186; international operations, 13

Marginal planners, 259, 266, 273, 304

Market development, 74, 166

Market dominance, 157, 158, 160, 337

Market entry strategy, 165–166, 180–184, 337–338; international, 169

Market environment, 144, 152, 155

Market growth, 3, 48–49; and Corporate Strategic Planners, 182, 242, 337; as environmental factor, 155; and resource allocation, 74, 75, 76, 99, 114, 334; scales, 114, 237; and strategy, 181, 182, 237, 240, 241, 261, 357

Market segments, 237, 261–262, 270, 371

Market Share, 3, 69; and performance, 316; and profits, 173; and resource allocation, 75, 334; scale, 114, 237; and strategy, 181, 237, 246, 261

Marketing strategy, 17, 180–184; international, 188, 237, 241, 242

Matrices, 39, 338

Matrix organizational form, 198, 206–208, 216

McKinsey & Company, 3, 69

Mergers, 170, 352

Me-too market strategy, 166

Mission, 17, 67; changes, 180; formalized statement, 180, 191; second-level, 334; and strategy, 165

Models, 15, 23, 70–72, 98, 259, 303; and computers, 39, 71–72, 98, 316, 334; and Corporate Strategic Planners, 71, 336; and decision making, 71; and Division Strategic Planners, 71; and environment, 148; and performance, 71, 316; scale, 113; and second-level management, 71

Multidivision structure, 35

Multiproduct businesses, 10–11

Necessity for strategic planning, 358

Net operating profits forecast, 49, 74, 114

New process research, 184

New product development, 27, 148, 166, 261; budgeting, 183–184, and Corporate Strategic Planning, 182–183, 191–192, 242, 337–338; and organization structure, 208, 216; scales, 237, 241

Non-Planners: and adaptive planning, 114; categorization, 49, 51, 58; and centralization, 205, 333; and diversification, 185; and environment, 236; follow-up studies, 353; and goals, 85, 179; individual measurements, 57; and integrative scales, 120; and organizational climate, 231; and organization structure, 247, 270; and performance, 299, 300, 301, 306–308, 340–341; and planning groups, 265; and research and development, 183; and revenue growth, 190; and strategy, 242

Not-at-all planners, 259, 266, 273, 304

Occurrence research, 348

Operating plans, 25, 67, 98

Opportunism, 35

Organic organization structure group 263, 267, 270, 357

Organizational climate, 6, 14, 17, 106 210–216, 339; and Corporate Financial Planners, 211–217, 231, 270; and Corporate Strategic Planners, 270; defined, 201–202; and Division Financial Planners, 251, 270; and Division Strategic Planners, 231, 270; groups, 264–265, 267, 273; and hierarchy, 35; measurement, 202–203; and Non-Planners, 231; and performance, 204–205, 309, 356; scales, 223–231, 248, 249, 345

Organizational fluidity, 226, 230, 231

Organization structure, 3, 6, 14, 17, 63–64, 215–217, 338–339, 361; and Corporate Financial Planners, 247, 271; and Corporate Strategic Planners, 205, 208, 215–217, 246–247, 270; dimensions, 200–201; and diversification, 199–200; and Division Financial Planners, 247, 270; and Division Strategic Planners, 270; and environment, 153; formal, 194–195,

205-210, 216; and globalness of planning, 243; groups, 263-264, 266-267, 270, 273; and information flow, 243; and innovation, 200, 208; and interdependence of units, 198-199; and international operations, 197-198, 206-208, 216; and macrostructure, 195-197, 205-206; and microstructure, 198-200; and new product development, 208, 216; and Non-Planners, 247, 270; and performance, 203-204, 329, 357; and resource allocation, 243; and resource sharing, 200, 216, 242, 246; scales, 242-247, 248, 345; and size of company, 170; and specialization, 199, 200, 216, 243, 338, 356

Outputs of planning, 44-46, 61, 106, 309, 322

Patent protection, 182, 337
Performance, 4, 32, 41, 281-329, 335; analytical methods of measuring, 16, 282, 290-294, 347-348; atmosphere at review, 95, 99, 230, 240, 241, 246, 361; bias in measurement, 291-292; and CEOs, 303, 319; and compensation, 95-96, 101, 235; and competitive analysis, 319; and conceptualization of planning, 282, 289-290; and contingency planning, 323-328; and Corporate Financial Planners, 298-299; and Corporate Strategic Planners, 94, 95, 96, 100, 298, 300, 301, 302, 307-308, 336; criteria, 118, 248; and decentralization, 203, 210-211, 357; and diversification, 170-172, 300; and Division Financial Planners, 299, 301, 302; and Division Strategic Planners, 95, 298; and environment, 148, 151-153, 303, 304, 325, 355; frequency of review, 94-95, 100, 304; and fully integrated planners, 258-259, 265, 266, 269, 270, 273; and functional perspective, 311-314; and goals, 95, 96, 303, 304, 319; and information flow, 309, 321; and innovation, 356; and international operations, 361; and long-term planning, 340-341;

and market share, 316; and market structure, 152; models, 71, 316; and Non-Planners, 299, 300, 301, 306-308, 340, 341; and organizational climate, 204-205, 309, 356; and organization structure, 203-204, 329, 357; and planners, 309, 316-319; and portfolio planning, 316, 328-329; previous studies of, 282-289; and process approach to planning, 308-310; and product life cycle, 301, 319; and return on capital, 292-294, 305, 314-315, 328; reviews, 46, 94-96, 116, 118; scales, 113, 118, 226, 230; and second-level management, 95; and size of company, 172-173, 300, 325; and specialization, 172, 356; and strategic planning tools, 309, 316; and strategy, 170-173, 355, 356; universalistic studies of, 281, 350

Personnel and planning, 63-64
Pharmaceutical industry, 152-153
Phonographic record industry, 152-153
Pioneer market strategy, 166
Placid-clustered environment, 145
Placid-randomized environment, 145
Planners: background, 63-64, 97, 227, 246, 334; budget, 63, 340; and Corporate Financial Planners, 63, 231; and Corporate Strategic Planners, 63, 64, 87, 88, 89, 99-100, 335; and Division Financial Planners, 63, 265; and Division Strategic Planners, 265; and goals, 106, 334; and information flow, 42, 99; integrative function, 86-88, 115, 117, 241; and performance, 309, 316-319; reporting relationships, 89, 100, 117, 259, 334; and resource allocation, 195; status and authority, 43, 88-89, 99-100, 115, 117, 240, 259, 303, 304; training, 63-64

Policy matrices, 3, 69, 113
Political analysis, 37
Portfolio approach to planning, 2-3, 38-39, 50, 69-70, 98, 259, 263, 303; and categorization of planners, 53, 56; and consultants, 53; and Corporate Strategic Planners, 69, 335;

Portfolio approach to planning *(Cont.)* criticism of, 362; and performance, 316, 328–329; scales, 113; and uncertainty, 35, 235

Process approach to planning, 23, 44–46, 61; components, relationship among, 108, 111, 335; and functional perspective, 46; and performance, 308–310; synthesis, 103–111, 124

Product categories, 185–186, 192

Product differentiation, 182

Product diversification, 164, 337; *see also* Diversification

Product/division organization, 196, 197, 198, 206, 208, 338

Product life cycle: and acquisition and divestiture, 189–190; assessment, 163; and Corporate Strategic Planners, 186, 192, 338; and market entry, 183; and performance, 301, 319; and revenues, 12; stages of, 12; and strategy, 175, 186–187, 192

Product/market fit analysis, 69

Product portfolio, 2–3, 69–70

Profit Impact of Market Strategy (PIMS), 4, 69, 281; and companies in study, 10–11; and environmental factors, 146–147; and market share/profits, 173; model usage, 71; and performance, 281, 292

Prospector corporate strategy, 175–176

Quality leadership as goal, 178

Raw materials, 10, 157, 186, 338

Reactor corporate strategy, 175

Realized strategy, 162, 191

Regulated industries, 152, 157, 158

Regulatory analysis, 37

Related business firms, 13–14, 166–168, 171–172, 184

Research and development, 166, 176, 183–184, 191–192, 337; budgets, 183–184; and Corporate Strategic Planners, 184, 191–192, 337; and investment decisions, 74; and Non-Planners, 183; returns on, and relatedness of business, 172; sharing of, 208–209

Resource allocation, 29, 30, 39, 40, 72–76, 98–99, 106, 259, 334, 360; and cash flow, 74, 75, 114; and Corporate Strategic Planners, 73, 74–75, 98, 335, 336; criteria, 114; and international strategy, 241; and market growth, 74, 75, 76, 99, 114, 334; and market share, 75, 334; and organization structure, 243; and planners, 195; and portfolio models, 70; and sales, 74, 75, 114; scales, 227, 230, 248

Resource sharing and organization structure, 200, 216, 242, 246

Responsibility, delegation of, 226, 227, 230, 231

Return on assets, 172, 177, 178

Return on capital, 281, 292–294, 304, 340, 347, 353, 354, 358

Return on equity, 171, 172, 177, 178

Return on investment: forecast, 49; as goal, 177, 178; as performance measure, 281; and resource allocation, 74, 75, 114

Return on net worth, 244

Reward system, 41, 43, 211, 215; and entrepreneurial behavior, 216, 242, 246, 263, 264; scales, 226

Risk taking, effects of planning on, 73, 98, 148, 293, 334

Royal Dutch Shell, 37, 69

Sales revenues, 237; and acquisition and divestiture, 189–190; and advertising, 152; and cash flow, 294, 302; and companies participating in study, 10, 12; and diversification, 13–14; and goals, 177, 178; and growth forecasts, 49, 74, 75, 114; and international operations, 12–13, 188, 338; as performance measure, 294; and resource allocation, 74, 75, 114; return on, 294, 302

Sample design of research, 6–8

Savings and loan industry, 253

Scales of planning, 15, 17, 23, 124–126, 221–256; and acquisition strategy, 113, 237, 240–241; adaptive, 111–115, 121, 230; and change, 29, 337; and competitive analysis, 113,

248; and comprehensiveness of planning, 114, 121; construction and analysis, 221–223; and divestiture, 113, 237, 240–241; and entrepreneurial behavior, 226, 230; and environment, 112–113, 231–236, 249, 345; factor analysis, 121–124, 223; forecasting, 113; and globalness of planning, 113, 230; and goals, 115, 116; and information flow, 115, 116 248; and innovation, 237; integrative, 116–122; and international operations, 237, 241; and line management, 117, 226; and market growth, 114, 237; and market share, 114, 237; and new product development, 237, 241; and organizational climate, 223–231, 248, 249, 345; and organization structure, 242–247, 248, 249, 345; and performance, 113, 118, 226–230; and portfolio planning, 113; and resource allocation, 113–114, 227, 230; and size of company, 237; and strategy, 237–242, 248; and uncertainty, 234–236

Scenario development, 27, 38
Scientific personnel, recruitment of, 208
Sears Roebuck, 163
Second-level planning, 56, 335; content of plans, 76; and Corporate Strategic Planners, 63, 205–206, 333; and formalization of planning, 117; and goals, 179–180, 191, 334; and interrelationships of units, 208–210; and linkage with corporate planning, 72; and mission, 334; and models, 71; and performance review, 95; and top management, 81, 83, 85, 88, 99, 116, 205–206

Seat-of-pants planning, 259, 266, 270, 273, 303
Segmented market strategy, 166, 356
Service industry, 352
Service leadership as goal, 178
Service revenues, 10
Simple/complex dimension of environment, 145, 146
Single-business firms, 13–14, 166–167, 184, 192; and organization structure, 196

Size of companies, 17, 28; and capital intensity, 173; and Corporate Strategic Planning, 192, 242; and organization structure, 170; and performance, 172–173, 300, 325; scale, 237; and strategy, 169–170, 190, 192
Slack resources, 151
Small numbers bargaining, 35
Sociocultural forecasting, 64, 65, 98, 158, 334
Soft modeling, 103–111, 124, 223
South Africa, 42
Specialization, 185; and organization structure, 199, 200, 216, 243, 338, 356; and performance, 172, 356; and second-level units, 209–210
Standard Oil, 163
Static/dynamic element of environment, 145, 146
Stock market values, 177, 178
Stock price as performance measure, 290
Strategic groups, 152
Strategic management, 171–172
Strategic planning, concept defined, 25–29, 357–358
Strategic Planning Institute, 4
Strategic planning tools, 53, 58, 61, 106, 335, 360; and categorization of planners, 59–72; and participative decision making, 227; and performance, 309, 316; scale, 113
Strategy, 163–170, 337–338; and acquisition, 169, 170, 189–190, 192, 242; and Corporate Financial Planners, 269; and Corporate Strategic Planners, 176–177; definition, 161–163; and Division Financial Planners, 242, 269; and Division Strategic Planners, 242, 269; and globalness of planning, 241; and goals, 164–165, 177–180; and innovation, 175, 192, 270, 273; and market growth, 181, 182, 237, 240, 241, 261, 357; and market share, 181, 237, 241, 261; and organization structure, 164; and performance, 170–173, 355, 356; and product life cycle, 175, 186–187, 192; scales, 237–242, 248; and size of companies, 169–170, 190, 192; and time horizon of planning, 241

Strategy Center concept, 3, 69
Support personnel, 201
Synergy, 164, 167, 171, 356
Synoptic formalism, 30, 31

Takeover, 157
Task environment, 144, 146
Task forces, 242, 246, 264, 267, 270, 357
Teams and committees, 41
Technology: changes, 157, 337; forecasting, 65, 98, 334; interdependence, 243; leadership as goal, 178, 179; scale, 234
Texas Instruments, 30
Time horizon of planning, 27, 38, 40, 41, 67, 335; and Corporate Financial Planners, 78; and environment, 148; and Corporate Strategic Planners, 67, 78–79, 98, 114, 335; and innovation, 38; and integration of planning, 78–79, 98; scales, 113, 116; and strategy, 241; and task forces, 246
Top management, 41–42; changes and planning, 28; and information flow, 79, 99, 116; interest in planning department, 87
Transaction costs, 35
Transactional environment, 144, 153

Transfer pricing, 209, 216, 243
Turbulent environment, 147

U-form of organization, 196
Uncertainty, 28–29, 73, 98, 334; and competitive analysis, 235; and Corporate Strategic Planners, 159, 236, 335; as environmental factor, 145–147, 148, 154, 234, 235–236; and globalness of planning, 235; and hierarchy, 33–34; scales, 234–236
United Kingdom, 204
Universalistic/occurrence perspective on planning, 348–349
Universalistic/performance perspective on planning, 350–351
Unrelated business firms, 14, 168, 171–172, 184, 192
Updating of corporate plans, 94, 100

Value added by planning, 86–87, 100, 246; scale, 117
Value-based planning, 30, 39
Vertical integration, 164, 173–174, 181, 185
Volume expansion, 164

Welch, Jack, 358

DATE DUE

		FEB 1 9 1998	
		CIRC MAR 1 3 1998	